PEARSON   ALWAYS LEARNING

Keith Mulbery • Cynthia Krebs • Lynn Hogan
Eric Cameron • Jason Davidson • Linda K. Lau
Rebecca Lawson • Jerri Williams • Amy Rutledge

Series Editor
Mary Anne Poatsy

Series Created by
Dr. Robert T. Grauer

Exploring Microsoft® Office 2016
Volume 1
Excel

Custom Edition for Camden County College

Taken from:
Exploring Microsoft® Office 2016, Volume 1
by Keith Mulbery, Cynthia Krebs, Lynn Hogan, Eric Cameron,
Jason Davidson, Linda K. Lau, Rebecca Lawson,
Jerri Williams, and Amy Rutledge
Series Editor: Mary Anne Poatsy
Series Created by Dr. Robert T. Grauer

Cover Art: Courtesy of Brand X Pictures.

Taken from:

Exploring Microsoft® Office 2016, Volume 1
by Keith Mulbery, Cynthia Krebs, Lynn Hogan, Eric Cameron, Jason Davidson, Linda K. Lau, Rebecca Lawson,
Jerri Williams, and Amy Rutledge
Series Editor: Mary Anne Poatsy
Series Created by Dr. Robert T. Grauer
Copyright © 2017 by Pearson Education, Inc.
New York, New York 10013

This special edition published in cooperation with Pearson Education, Inc.

All trademarks, service marks, registered trademarks, and registered service marks are the property of their
respective owners and are used herein for identification purposes only.

Pearson Education, Inc., 330 Hudson Street, New York, New York 10013
A Pearson Education Company
www.pearsoned.com

Printed in the United States of America

000200010272044627

JK

ISBN 10: 1-323-50889-9
ISBN 13: 978-1-323-50889-3

15 2020

Dedications

For my husband, Ted, who unselfishly continues to take on more than his share to support me throughout the process; and for my children, Laura, Carolyn, and Teddy, whose encouragement and love have been inspiring.

Mary Anne Poatsy

I dedicate this book in memory to Grandpa Herman Hort, who dedicated his life to his family and to the education field as a teacher and administrator. He inspired a daughter and several grandchildren to become passionate educators and provide quality curriculum to students.

Keith Mulbery

For my children for all of believing in me, encouraging me, and supporting me. Thank you Marshall Krebs, Jaron Krebs, Jenalee Krebs Behle, and Michelle Krebs. To my writing mentor, Dr. Keith Mulbery, for the same reasons.

Cynthia Krebs

I dedicate this work to my wonderful family—my husband, Paul, and my daughters, Jenn and Alli. You have made this adventure possible with your support, encouragement, and love. You inspire me!

Lynn Hogan

I dedicate this book to my wife Anny, for supporting me through the writing process, to my nieces Daniela and Gabriela, who someday will be old enough to think it is cool their names are in a book, and to my students, who make a career in teaching fulfilling. May you all go forward, change the world and inspire others.

Eric Cameron

I dedicate this book in loving memory of my grandfather Laurence L. Leggett. A passionate lifelong educator, gifted musician, and incredible role model. I will never forget our time together. I strive every day to make you proud.

Jason Davidson

I dedicate this book to my only child, Catherine Shen, who taught me that there is another wonderful life outside of my work. My life has been more fulfilling and exciting with her in it. I also dedicate this book to the loving memory of my dog, Harry, who was by my side, through thick and thin, for 16 years. I miss him dearly every day.

Linda K. Lau

This book is dedicated to my children and to my students to inspire them to never give up and to always keep reaching for their dreams.

Rebecca Lawson

I offer thanks to my family and colleagues who have supported me on this journey. I would like to dedicate the work I have performed toward this undertaking to my little grandson, Yonason Meir (known for now as Mei-Mei), who as his name suggests, is the illumination in my life.

Jerri Williams

To my husband Dan, whose encouragement, patience, and love helped make this endeavor possible. Thank you for taking on the many additional tasks at home so that I could focus on writing.

Amy Rutledge

About the Authors

Mary Anne Poatsy, Series Editor, Windows 10 Author

Mary Anne is a senior faculty member at Montgomery County Community College, teaching various computer application and concepts courses in face-to-face and online environments. She holds a B.A. in Psychology and Education from Mount Holyoke College and an M.B.A. in Finance from Northwestern University's Kellogg Graduate School of Management.

Mary Anne has more than 12 years of educational experience. She is currently adjunct faculty at Gwynedd-Mercy College and Montgomery County Community College. She has also taught at Bucks County Community College and Muhlenberg College, as well as conducted personal training. Before teaching, she was Vice President at Shearson Lehman in the Municipal Bond Investment Banking Department.

Dr. Keith Mulbery, Excel Author

Dr. Keith Mulbery is the Department Chair and a Professor in the Information Systems and Technology Department at Utah Valley University (UVU), where he currently teaches systems analysis and design, and global and ethical issues in information systems and technology. He has also taught computer applications, C# programming, and management information systems. Keith served as Interim Associate Dean, School of Computing, in the College of Technology and Computing at UVU.

Keith received the Utah Valley State College Board of Trustees Award of Excellence in 2001, School of Technology and Computing Scholar Award in 2007, and School of Technology and Computing Teaching Award in 2008. He has authored more than 17 textbooks, served as Series Editor for the Exploring Office 2007 series, and served as developmental editor on two textbooks for the Essentials Office 2000 series. He is frequently asked to give presentations and workshops on Microsoft Office Excel at various education conferences.

Keith received his B.S. and M.Ed. in Business Education from Southwestern Oklahoma State University and earned his Ph.D. in Education with an emphasis in Business Information Systems at Utah State University. His dissertation topic was computer-assisted instruction using Prentice Hall's Train and Assess IT program (the predecessor to MyITLab) to supplement traditional instruction in basic computer proficiency courses.

Cynthia Krebs, PowerPoint Author

Cynthia Krebs is the Program Director of Business and Marketing Education at Utah Valley University. She is a tenured professor in the Information Systems and Technology Department at UVU where she teaches the Methods of Teaching Business, Marketing, and Digital Technology course to future teachers, as well as classes in basic computer applications and business proficiency applications. She holds a B.S and M.S. in Business Education with an emphasis in Economic Education. Cynthia has received numerous awards, and has presented extensively at the local, regional, and national levels as well as consulting with government organizations and businesses.

Cynthia lives by a peaceful creek I in Springville, Utah. When she isn't teaching or writing, she enjoys spending time with her children, spoiling her grandchildren Ava, Bode, Solee, Morgan, and Preslee. She loves traveling and reading.

Lynn Hogan, Word Author

Lynn Hogan teaches at the University of North Alabama, providing instruction in the area of computer applications. With over 30 years of educational experience at the community college and university level, Lynn has taught applications, programming, and concepts courses in both online and classroom environments. She received an M.B.A. from the University of North Alabama and a Ph.D. from the University of Alabama.

Lynn is a co-author of Practical Computing and has served on the authoring team of Your Office as well as the Exploring Office 2010 series. She resides in Alabama with her husband and two daughters.

Eric Cameron, Access Author

Eric Cameron is a tenured Associate Professor at Passaic County Community College, where he has taught in the Computer and Information Sciences department since 2001. He holds an M.S. in Computer Science and a B.S. degree in Computer Science with minors in Mathematics and Physics, both from Montclair State University. He currently co-chairs the College's General Education committee and served as a member of the College's Academic Assessment, College Writing, and Educational Technology committees at various points. Eric has also developed degrees in Graphic Design and Medical Informatics for the College. Eric previously worked as a software engineer both as a full-time employee and contractor, most recently for ITT/Exelis (now part of Harris Corporation).

This is Eric's fourth publication for Pearson, after authoring Web 2.0 and Windows 8 books in the Your Office series and co-authoring the Exploring Access 2013 text.

Jason Davidson, Excel Author

Jason Davidson is a faculty member in the College of Business at Butler University, where he teaches Advanced Web Design, Data Networks, Data Analysis and Business Modeling, and introductory information systems courses. He is the co-author of Exploring Microsoft Excel 2013 Comprehensive, Exploring Microsoft Office 2013 Volume 2, Exploring Microsoft Office 2013 Plus, and Exploring VBA for Microsoft Office 2013.

With a background in media development, prior to joining the faculty at Butler, he worked in the technical publishing industry. Along with teaching, he currently serves as an IT consultant for regional businesses in the Indianapolis area. He holds a B.A. in Telecommunication Arts from Butler University and an M.B.A. from Morehead State University. He lives in Indianapolis, Indiana, and in his free time enjoys road biking, photography, and spending time with his family.

Dr. Linda K. Lau, Word Author

Since 1994, Dr. Linda K. Lau is a Management Information Systems (MIS) faculty at the College of Business and Economics, Longwood University, located in Farmville, Virginia. She received the Outstanding Academic Advisor Award in 2006. Besides teaching and advising, Linda has authored and co-authored numerous journal and conference articles and textbooks, edited two books, and sat on several editorial boards. Her current research interest focuses on cyber security and forensics, and she is the associate editor for the Journal of Digital Forensics, Security and Law (JDFSL). Linda earned her Ph.D. from Rensselaer Polytechnic Institute in 1993, and her MBA and Bachelor of Science from Illinois State University in 1987 and 1986, respectively. In her younger days, Linda worked as a flight attendant for Singapore International Airlines for six years before coming to America to pursue her academic dream. She also worked as a financial consultant with Salomon Smith Barney from 1999–2000 before returning to the academic world. Linda resides in Richmond with her family.

Rebecca Lawson, PowerPoint Author

Rebecca Lawson is a professor in the Computer Information Technologies program at Lansing Community College. She coordinates the curriculum, develops the instructional materials, and teaches for the E-Business curriculum. She also serves as the Online Faculty Coordinator at the Center for Teaching Excellence at LCC. In that role, she develops and facilitates online workshops for faculty learning to teach online. Her major areas of interest include online curriculum quality assurance, the review and development of printed and online instructional materials, the assessment of computer and Internet literacy skill levels to facilitate student retention, and the use of social networking tools to support learning in blended and online learning environments.

Jerri Williams, Access Author

Jerri Williams is a Senior Instructor at Montgomery County Community College in Pennsylvania. Jerri also works as an independent corporate trainer, technical editor, and content developer. She is interested in travel, cooking, movies, and tending to her colonial farmhouse. Jerri is married, and is the mother of two daughters, Holly (an Accounting graduate and full-time mother to an adorable son, Meir) and Gwyneth (a corporate defense attorney). Jerri and Gareth live in the suburbs of Philadelphia. They enjoy their home and garden, and spending time with family and good friends.

Amy Rutledge, Common Features Author

Amy Rutledge is a Special Instructor of Management Information Systems at Oakland University in Rochester, Michigan. She coordinates academic programs in Microsoft Office applications and introductory management information systems courses for the School of Business Administration. Before joining Oakland University as an instructor, Amy spent several years working for a music distribution company and automotive manufacturer in various corporate roles including IT project management. She holds a B.S. in Business Administration specializing in Management Information Systems, and a B.A. in French Modern Language and Literature. She holds an M.B.A from Oakland University. She resides in Michigan with her husband, Dan and daughters Emma and Jane.

Dr. Robert T. Grauer, Creator of the Exploring Series

Bob Grauer is an Associate Professor in the Department of Computer Information Systems at the University of Miami, where he is a multiple winner of the Outstanding Teaching Award in the School of Business, most recently in 2009. He has written numerous COBOL texts and is the vision behind the Exploring Office series, with more than three million books in print. His work has been translated into three foreign languages and is used in all aspects of higher education at both national and international levels. Bob Grauer has consulted for several major corporations including IBM and American Express. He received his Ph.D. in Operations Research in 1972 from the Polytechnic Institute of Brooklyn.

Brief Contents

Excel

CHAPTER 1	Introduction to Excel	402
CHAPTER 2	Formulas and Functions	486
CHAPTER 3	Charts	532
CHAPTER 4	Datasets and Tables	596

Application Capstone Exercises

Excel Application Capstone Exercise	1190
GLOSSARY	1201
INDEX	1213

Contents

Microsoft Office Excel 2016

■ CHAPTER ONE Introduction to Excel: Creating and Formatting a Worksheet 402

CASE STUDY OK OFFICE SYSTEMS	402
INTRODUCTION TO SPREADSHEETS	404
Exploring the Excel Window	404
Entering and Editing Cell Data	407
HANDS-ON EXERCISES 1	
Introduction to Spreadsheets	413
MATHEMATICAL OPERATIONS AND FORMULAS	417
Creating Formulas	417
Displaying Cell Formulas	420
HANDS-ON EXERCISES 2	
Mathematical Operations and Formulas	422
WORKSHEET STRUCTURE AND CLIPBOARD TASKS	427
Managing Columns and Rows	427
Selecting, Moving, Copying, and Pasting Data	432
HANDS-ON EXERCISES 3	
Worksheet Structure and Clipboard Tasks	438

WORKSHEET FORMATTING	444
Applying Cell Styles, Alignment, and Font Options	444
Applying Number Formats	447
HANDS-ON EXERCISES 4	
Worksheet Formatting	450
WORKSHEETS, PAGE SETUP, AND PRINTING	455
Managing Worksheets	455
Selecting Page Setup Options	457
Previewing and Printing a Worksheet	463
HANDS-ON EXERCISES 5	
Worksheets, Page Setup, and Printing	465
CHAPTER OBJECTIVES REVIEW	469
KEY TERMS MATCHING	471
MULTIPLE CHOICE	472
PRACTICE EXERCISES	473
MID-LEVEL EXERCISES	479
BEYOND THE CLASSROOM	482
CAPSTONE EXERCISE	483

■ CHAPTER TWO Formulas and Functions: Performing Quantitative Analysis 486

CASE STUDY TOWNSEND MORTGAGE COMPANY	486
FORMULA BASICS	488
Using Relative, Absolute, and Mixed Cell References in Formulas	488
HANDS-ON EXERCISES 1	
Formula Basics	492
FUNCTION BASICS	495
Inserting a Function	495
Inserting Basic Math and Statistics Functions	497
Using Date Functions	501
HANDS-ON EXERCISES 2	
Function Basics	503

LOGICAL, LOOKUP, AND FINANCIAL FUNCTIONS	508
Determining Results with the IF Function	508
Using Lookup Functions	511
Calculating Payments with the PMT Function	514
HANDS-ON EXERCISES 3	
Logical, Lookup, and Financial Functions	516
CHAPTER OBJECTIVES REVIEW	521
KEY TERMS MATCHING	522
MULTIPLE CHOICE	523
PRACTICE EXERCISES	524
MID-LEVEL EXERCISES	527
BEYOND THE CLASSROOM	530
CAPSTONE EXERCISE	531

■ CHAPTER THREE **Charts:** Depicting Data Visually 532

CASE STUDY COMPUTER JOB OUTLOOK	532
CHART BASICS	534
Selecting the Data Source	534
Choosing a Chart Type	536
Moving, Sizing, and Printing a Chart	548
HANDS-ON EXERCISES 1	
Chart Basics	552
CHART ELEMENTS	558
Adding, Editing, and Formatting Chart Elements	559
HANDS-ON EXERCISES 2	
Chart Elements	569
CHART DESIGN AND SPARKLINES	574
Applying a Chart Style and Colors	574

Modifying the Data Source	575
Creating and Customizing Sparklines	577
HANDS-ON EXERCISES 3	
Chart Design and Sparklines	580
CHAPTER OBJECTIVES REVIEW	583
KEY TERMS MATCHING	585
MULTIPLE CHOICE	586
PRACTICE EXERCISES	587
MID-LEVEL EXERCISES	591
BEYOND THE CLASSROOM	594
CAPSTONE EXERCISE	595

■ CHAPTER FOUR **Datasets and Tables:** Managing Large Volumes of Data 596

CASE STUDY REID FURNITURE STORE	596
LARGE DATASETS	598
Freezing Rows and Columns	599
Printing Large Datasets	600
HANDS-ON EXERCISES 1	
Large Datasets	604
EXCEL TABLES	609
Understanding the Benefits of Data Tables	609
Designing and Creating Tables	609
Applying a Table Style	614
HANDS-ON EXERCISES 2	
Excel Tables	616
TABLE MANIPULATION	621
Creating Structured References in Formulas	621
Sorting Data	622
Filtering Data	624

HANDS-ON EXERCISES 3	
Table Manipulation	629
TABLE AGGREGATION AND CONDITIONAL FORMATTING	636
Adding a Total Row	636
Applying Conditional Formatting	638
Creating a New Rule	643
HANDS-ON EXERCISES 4	
Table Aggregation and Conditional Formatting	646
CHAPTER OBJECTIVES REVIEW	651
KEY TERMS MATCHING	652
MULTIPLE CHOICE	653
PRACTICE EXERCISES	654
MID-LEVEL EXERCISES	658
BEYOND THE CLASSROOM	660
CAPSTONE EXERCISE	661

Application Capstone Exercises

Excel Application Capstone Exercise	1190
GLOSSARY	1201
INDEX	1213

Acknowledgments

The Exploring team would like to acknowledge and thank all the reviewers who helped us throughout the years by providing us with their invaluable comments, suggestions, and constructive criticism.

Adriana Lumpkin
Midland College

Alan S. Abrahams
Virginia Tech

Alexandre C. Probst
Colorado Christian University

Ali Berrached
University of Houston–Downtown

Allen Alexander
Delaware Technical & Community College

Andrea Marchese
Maritime College, State University of New York

Andrew Blitz
Broward College; Edison State College

Angel Norman
University of Tennessee, Knoxville

Angela Clark
University of South Alabama

Ann Rovetto
Horry-Georgetown Technical College

Astrid Todd
Guilford Technical Community College

Audrey Gillant
Maritime College, State University of New York

Barbara Stover
Marion Technical College

Barbara Tollinger
Sinclair Community College

Ben Brahim Taha
Auburn University

Beverly Amer
Northern Arizona University

Beverly Fite
Amarillo College

Biswadip Ghosh
Metropolitan State University of Denver

Bonita Volker
Tidewater Community College

Bonnie Homan
San Francisco State University

Brad West
Sinclair Community College

Brian Powell
West Virginia University

Carol Buser
Owens Community College

Carol Roberts
University of Maine

Carolyn Barren
Macomb Community College

Carolyn Borne
Louisiana State University

Cathy Poyner
Truman State University

Charles Hodgson
Delgado Community College

Chen Zhang
Bryant University

Cheri Higgins
Illinois State University

Cheryl Brown
Delgado Community College

Cheryl Hinds
Norfolk State University

Cheryl Sypniewski
Macomb Community College

Chris Robinson
Northwest State Community College

Cindy Herbert
Metropolitan Community College–Longview

Craig J. Peterson
American InterContinental University

Dana Hooper
University of Alabama

Dana Johnson
North Dakota State University

Daniela Marghitu
Auburn University

David Noel
University of Central Oklahoma

David Pulis
Maritime College, State University of New York

David Thornton
Jacksonville State University

Dawn Medlin
Appalachian State University

Debby Keen
University of Kentucky

Debra Chapman
University of South Alabama

Debra Hoffman
Southeast Missouri State University

Derrick Huang
Florida Atlantic University

Diana Baran
Henry Ford Community College

Diane Cassidy
The University of North Carolina at Charlotte

Diane L. Smith
Henry Ford Community College

Dick Hewer
Ferris State College

Don Danner
San Francisco State University

Don Hoggan
Solano College

Don Riggs
SUNY Schenectady County Community College

Doncho Petkov
Eastern Connecticut State University

Donna Ehrhart
State University of New York at Brockport

Elaine Crable
Xavier University

Elizabeth Duett
Delgado Community College

Erhan Uskup
Houston Community College–Northwest

Eric Martin
University of Tennessee

Erika Nadas
Wilbur Wright College

Floyd Winters
Manatee Community College

Frank Lucente
Westmoreland County Community College

G. Jan Wilms
Union University

Gail Cope
Sinclair Community College

Gary DeLorenzo
California University of Pennsylvania

Gary Garrison
Belmont University

Gary McFall
Purdue University

George Cassidy
Sussex County Community College

Gerald Braun
Xavier University

Gerald Burgess
Western New Mexico University

Gladys Swindler
Fort Hays State University

Hector Frausto
California State University
Los Angeles

Heith Hennel
Valencia Community College

Henry Rudzinski
Central Connecticut State University

Irene Joos
La Roche College

Iwona Rusin
Baker College; Davenport University

J. Roberto Guzman
San Diego Mesa College

Jacqueline D. Lawson
Henry Ford Community College

Jakie Brown Jr.
Stevenson University

James Brown
Central Washington University

James Powers
University of Southern Indiana

Jane Stam
Onondaga Community College

Janet Bringhurst
Utah State University

Jean Welsh
Lansing Community College

Jeanette Dix
Ivy Tech Community College

Jennifer Day
Sinclair Community College

Jill Canine
Ivy Tech Community College

Jill Young
Southeast Missouri State University

Jim Chaffee
The University of Iowa Tippie College of
Business

Joanne Lazirko
University of Wisconsin–Milwaukee

Jodi Milliner
Kansas State University

John Hollenbeck
Blue Ridge Community College

John Seydel
Arkansas State University

Judith A. Scheeren
Westmoreland County Community College

Judith Brown
The University of Memphis

Juliana Cypert
Tarrant County College

Kamaljeet Sanghera
George Mason University

Karen Priestly
Northern Virginia Community College

Karen Ravan
Spartanburg Community College

Karen Tracey
Central Connecticut State University

Kathleen Brenan
Ashland University

Ken Busbee
Houston Community College

Kent Foster
Winthrop University

Kevin Anderson
Solano Community College

Kim Wright
The University of Alabama

Kristen Hockman
University of Missouri–Columbia

Kristi Smith
Allegany College of Maryland

Laura Marcoulides
Fullerton College

Laura McManamon
University of Dayton

Laurence Boxer
Niagara University

Leanne Chun
Leeward Community College

Lee McClain
Western Washington University

Linda D. Collins
Mesa Community College

Linda Johnsonius
Murray State University

Linda Lau
Longwood University

Linda Theus
Jackson State Community College

Linda Williams
Marion Technical College

Lisa Miller
University of Central Oklahoma

Lister Horn
Pensacola Junior College

Lixin Tao
Pace University

Loraine Miller
Cayuga Community College

Lori Kielty
Central Florida Community College

Lorna Wells
Salt Lake Community College

Lorraine Sauchin
Duquesne University

Lucy Parakhovnik
California State University, Northridge

Lynn Keane
University of South Carolina

Lynn Mancini
Delaware Technical Community College

Mackinzee Escamilla
South Plains College

Marcia Welch
Highline Community College

Margaret McManus
Northwest Florida State College

Margaret Warrick
Allan Hancock College

Marilyn Hibbert
Salt Lake Community College

Mark Choman
Luzerne County Community College

Maryann Clark
University of New Hampshire

Mary Beth Tarver
Northwestern State University

Mary Duncan
University of Missouri–St. Louis

Melissa Nemeth
Indiana University-Purdue University
Indianapolis

Melody Alexander
Ball State University

Michael Douglas
University of Arkansas at Little Rock

Michael Dunklebarger
Alamance Community College

Michael G. Skaff
College of the Sequoias

Michele Budnovitch
Pennsylvania College of Technology

Mike Jochen
East Stroudsburg University

Mike Michaelson
Palomar College

Mike Scroggins
Missouri State University

Mimi Spain
Southern Maine Community College

Muhammed Badamas
Morgan State University

NaLisa Brown
University of the Ozarks

Nancy Grant
Community College of Allegheny County–
South Campus

Nanette Lareau
University of Arkansas Community
College–Morrilton

Nikia Robinson
Indian River State University

Pam Brune
Chattanooga State Community College

Pam Uhlenkamp
Iowa Central Community College

Patrick Smith
Marshall Community and Technical College

Paul Addison
Ivy Tech Community College

Paula Ruby
Arkansas State University

Peggy Burrus
Red Rocks Community College

Peter Ross
SUNY Albany

Philip H. Nielson
Salt Lake Community College

Philip Valvalides
Guilford Technical Community College

Ralph Hooper
University of Alabama

Ranette Halverson
Midwestern State University

Richard Blamer
John Carroll University

Richard Cacace
Pensacola Junior College

Richard Hewer
Ferris State University

Richard Sellers
Hill College

Rob Murray
Ivy Tech Community College

Robert Banta
Macomb Community College

Robert Dušek
Northern Virginia Community College

Robert G. Phipps Jr.
West Virginia University

Robert Sindt
Johnson County Community College

Robert Warren
Delgado Community College

Rocky Belcher
Sinclair Community College

Roger Pick
University of Missouri at Kansas City

Ronnie Creel
Troy University

Rosalie Westerberg
Clover Park Technical College

Ruth Neal
Navarro College

Sandra Thomas
Troy University

Sheila Gionfriddo
Luzerne County Community College

Sherrie Geitgey
Northwest State Community College

Sherry Lenhart
Terra Community College

Sophia Wilberscheid
Indian River State College

Sophie Lee
California State University,
Long Beach

Stacy Johnson
Iowa Central Community College

Stephanie Kramer
Northwest State Community College

Stephen Z. Jourdan
Auburn University at Montgomery

Steven Schwarz
Raritan Valley Community College

Sue A. McCrory
Missouri State University

Sumathy Chandrashekar
Salisbury University

Susan Fuschetto
Cerritos College

Susan Medlin
UNC Charlotte

Susan N. Dozier
Tidewater Community College

Suzan Spitzberg
Oakton Community College

Suzanne M. Jeska
County College of Morris

Sven Aelterman
Troy University

Sy Hirsch
Sacred Heart University

Sylvia Brown
Midland College

Tanya Patrick
Clackamas Community College

Terri Holly
Indian River State College

Terry Ray Rigsby
Hill College

Thomas Rienzo
Western Michigan University

Tina Johnson
Midwestern State University

Tommy Lu
Delaware Technical Community College

Troy S. Cash
Northwest Arkansas Community College

Vicki Robertson
Southwest Tennessee Community

Vickie Pickett
Midland College

Weifeng Chen
California University of Pennsylvania

Wes Anthony
Houston Community College

William Ayen
University of Colorado at Colorado Springs

Wilma Andrews
Virginia Commonwealth University

Yvonne Galusha
University of Iowa

Special thanks to our content development and technical team:

Barbara Stover	Patti Hammerle	Linda Pogue
Julie Boyles	Jean Insigna	Steven Rubin
Lisa Bucki	Elizabeth Lockley	Mara Zebest
Lori Damanti	Joyce Nielsen	
Sallie Dodson	Janet Pickard	

Preface

The Exploring Series and You

Exploring is Pearson's Office Application series that requires students like you to think "beyond the point and click." In this edition, we have worked to restructure the Exploring experience around the way you, today's modern student, actually use your resources.

The goal of Exploring is, as it has always been, to go farther than teaching just the steps to accomplish a task—the series provides the theoretical foundation for you to understand when and why to apply a skill. As a result, you achieve a deeper understanding of each application and can apply this critical thinking beyond Office and the classroom.

The How & Why of This Revision

Outcomes matter. Whether it's getting a good grade in this course, learning how to use Excel so students can be successful in other courses, or learning a specific skill that will make learners successful in a future job, everyone has an outcome in mind. And outcomes matter. That is why we revised our chapter opener to focus on the outcomes students will achieve by working through each Exploring chapter. These are coupled with objectives and skills, providing a map students can follow to get everything they need from each chapter.

Critical Thinking and Collaboration are essential 21st century skills. Students want and need to be successful in their future careers—so we used motivating case studies to show relevance of these skills to future careers and incorporated Soft Skills, Collaboration, and Analysis Cases with Critical Thinking steps in this edition to set students up for success in the future.

Students today read, prepare, and study differently than students used to. Students use textbooks like a tool—they want to easily identify what they need to know and learn it efficiently. We have added key features such as Tasks Lists (in purple), Step Icons, Hands-On Exercise Videos, and tracked everything via page numbers that allow efficient navigation, creating a map students can easily follow.

Students are exposed to technology. The new edition of Exploring moves beyond the basics of the software at a faster pace, without sacrificing coverage of the fundamental skills that students need to know.

Students are diverse. Students can be any age, any gender, any race, with any level of ability or learning style. With this in mind, we broadened our definition of "student resources" to include physical Student Reference cards, Hands-On Exercise videos to provide a secondary lecture-like option of review; and MyITLab, the most powerful and most ADA-compliant online homework and assessment tool around with a direct 1:1 content match with the Exploring Series. Exploring will be accessible to all students, regardless of learning style.

Providing You with a Map to Success to Move Beyond the Point and Click

All of these changes and additions will provide students an easy and efficient path to follow to be successful in this course, regardless of where they start at the beginning of this course. Our goal is to keep students engaged in both the hands-on and conceptual sides, helping achieve a higher level of understanding that will guarantee success in this course and in a future career.

In addition to the vision and experience of the series creator, Robert T. Grauer, we have assembled a tremendously talented team of Office Applications authors who have devoted themselves to teaching the ins and outs of Microsoft Word, Excel, Access, and PowerPoint. Led in this edition by series editor Mary Anne Poatsy, the whole team is dedicated to the Exploring mission of moving students **beyond the point and click**.

Key Features

The **How/Why Approach** helps students move beyond the point and click to a true understanding of how to apply Microsoft Office skills.

- **White Pages/Yellow Pages** clearly distinguish the theory (white pages) from the skills covered in the Hands-On Exercises (yellow pages) so students always know what they are supposed to be doing and why.

- **Case Study** presents a scenario for the chapter, creating a story that ties the Hands-On Exercises together.

- **Hands-On Exercise Videos** are tied to each Hands-On Exercise and walk students through the steps of the exercise while weaving in conceptual information related to the Case Study and the objectives as a whole.

The **Outcomes focus** allows students and instructors to know the higher-level learning goals and how those are achieved through discreet objectives and skills.

- **Outcomes** presented at the beginning of each chapter identify the learning goals for students and instructors.

- **Enhanced Objective Mapping** enables students to follow a directed path through each chapter, from the objectives list at the chapter opener through the exercises at the end of the chapter.
    - **Objectives List:** This provides a simple list of key objectives covered in the chapter. This includes page numbers so students can skip between objectives where they feel they need the most help.
    - **Step Icons:** These icons appear in the white pages and reference the step numbers in the Hands-On Exercises, providing a correlation between the two so students can easily find conceptual help when they are working hands-on and need a refresher.
    - **Quick Concepts Check:** A series of questions that appear briefly at the end of each white page section. These questions cover the most essential concepts in the white pages required for students to be successful in working the Hands-On Exercises. Page numbers are included for easy reference to help students locate the answers.
    - **Chapter Objectives Review:** Appears toward the end of the chapter and reviews all important concepts throughout the chapter. Newly designed in an easy-to-read bulleted format.

Watch the Video for this Hands-On Exercise!

- **MOS Certification Guide** for instructors and students to direct anyone interested in prepping for the MOS exam to the specific locations to find all content required for the test.

End-of-Chapter Exercises offer instructors several options for assessment. Each chapter has approximately 11–12 exercises ranging from multiple choice questions to open-ended projects.

ANALYSIS CASE

CREATIVE CASE

- **Multiple Choice, Key Terms Matching, Practice Exercises, Mid-Level Exercises, Beyond the Classroom Exercises, and Capstone Exercises** appear at the end of all chapters.
    - **Enhanced Mid-Level Exercises** include a **Creative Case** (for PowerPoint and Word), which allows students some flexibility and creativity, not being bound by a definitive solution, and an **Analysis Case** (for Excel and Access), which requires students to interpret the data they are using to answer an analytic question, as well as **Discover Steps**, which encourage students to use Help or to problem-solve to accomplish a task.

- **Application Capstone** exercises are included in the book to allow instructors to test students on the entire contents of a single application.

MyITLab® HOE1 Training   MyITLab® Grader

Resources

Instructor Resources

The Instructor's Resource Center, available at **www.pearsonhighered.com**, includes the following:

- **Instructor Manual** provides one-stop-shop for instructors, including an overview of all available resources, teaching tips, as well as student data and solution files for every exercise.

- **Solution Files with Scorecards** assist with grading the Hands-On Exercises and end-of-chapter exercises.

- **Prepared Exams** allow instructors to assess all skills covered in a chapter with a single project.

- **Rubrics** for Mid-Level Creative Cases and Beyond the Classroom Cases in Microsoft Word format enable instructors to customize the assignments for their classes.

- **PowerPoint Presentations** with notes for each chapter are included for out-of-class study or review.

- **Multiple Choice, Key Term Matching, and Quick Concepts Check Answer Keys**

- **Test Bank** provides objective-based questions for every chapter.

- **Scripted Lectures** offer an in-class lecture guide for instructors to mirror the Hands-On Exercises.

- **Syllabus Templates**
  - Outcomes, Objectives, and Skills List
  - Assignment Sheet
  - File Guide

Student Resources

Student Data Files

Access your student data files needed to complete the exercises in this textbook at **www.pearsonhighered.com/exploring**.

Available in MyITLab

- **Hands-On Exercise Videos** allow students to review and study the concepts taught in the Hands-On Exercises.
- **Audio PowerPoints** provide a lecture review of the chapter content, and include narration.
- **Multiple Choice quizzes** enable you to test concepts you have learned by answering auto-graded questions.
- **Book-specific 1:1 Simulations** allow students to practice in the simulated Microsoft Office 2016 environment using hi-fidelity, HTML5 simulations that directly match the content in the Hands-On Exercises.
- **eText** available in some MyITLab courses and includes links to videos, student data files, and other learning aids.
- **Book-specific 1:1 Grader Projects** allow students to complete end of chapter Capstone Exercises live in Microsoft Office 2016 and receive immediate feedback on their performance through various reports.

Introduction to Excel

LEARNING OUTCOME You will create and format a basic Excel worksheet.

OBJECTIVES & SKILLS: After you read this chapter, you will be able to:

Introduction to Spreadsheets

OBJECTIVE 1: EXPLORE THE EXCEL WINDOW   404
Identify Excel Window Elements; Identify Columns, Rows, and Cells; Navigate in and Among Worksheets

OBJECTIVE 2: ENTER AND EDIT CELL DATA   407
Enter Text, Use Auto Fill to Complete a Sequence, Enter Values, Enter a Date, Clear Cell Contents

HANDS-ON EXERCISE 1:
Introduction to Spreadsheets   413

Mathematical Operations and Formulas

OBJECTIVE 3: CREATE FORMULAS   417
Use Cell References in Formulas, Apply the Order of Operations, Use Semi-Selection to Create a Formula, Copy Formulas

OBJECTIVE 4: DISPLAY CELL FORMULAS   420
Display Cell Formulas

HANDS-ON EXERCISE 2:
Mathematics and Formulas   422

Worksheet Structure and Clipboard Tasks

OBJECTIVE 5: MANAGE COLUMNS AND ROWS   427
Insert Cells, Columns, and Rows; Delete Cells, Columns, and Rows; Hide a Column or Row; Adjust Column Width; Adjust Row Height

OBJECTIVE 6: SELECT, MOVE, COPY, AND PASTE DATA   432

Select a Range, Move a Range, Copy and Paste a Range, Use Paste Options and Paste Special

HANDS-ON EXERCISE 3:
Worksheet Structure and Clipboard Tasks   438

Worksheet Formatting

OBJECTIVE 7: APPLY CELL STYLES, ALIGNMENT, AND FONT OPTIONS   444
Apply a Cell Style, Merge and Center Data, Change Cell Alignment, Wrap Text, Increase Indent, Apply a Border, Apply Fill Color

OBJECTIVE 8: APPLY NUMBER FORMATS   447
Apply Number Formats, Increase and Decrease Decimal Places

HANDS-ON EXERCISE 4:
Worksheet Formatting   450

Worksheets, Page Setup, and Printing

OBJECTIVE 9: MANAGE WORKSHEETS   455
Insert a Worksheet, Delete a Worksheet, Copy or Move a Worksheet, Rename a Worksheet, Group Worksheets

OBJECTIVE 10: SELECT PAGE SETUP OPTIONS   457
Set Page Orientation, Select Scaling Options, Set Margin Options, Create a Header or Footer, Select Sheet Options

OBJECTIVE 11: PREVIEW AND PRINT A WORKSHEET   463
View in Print Preview, Set Print Options, Print a Worksheet

HANDS-ON EXERCISE 5:
Worksheets, Page Setup, and Printing   465

CASE STUDY | OK Office Systems

Alesha Bennett, the general manager at OK Office Systems (OKOS), asked you to calculate the retail price, sale price, and profit analysis for selected items on sale this month. Using markup rates provided by Alesha, you will calculate the retail price, the amount OKOS charges its customers for the products. You will calculate sale prices based on discount rates between 10% and 30%. Finally, you will calculate the profit margin to determine the percentage of the final sale price over the cost.

After you create the initial pricing spreadsheet, you will be able to change values and see that the formulas update the results automatically. In addition, you will insert data for additional sale items or delete an item based on the manager's decision. After inserting formulas, you will format the data in the worksheet to have a professional appearance.

Creating and Formatting a Worksheet

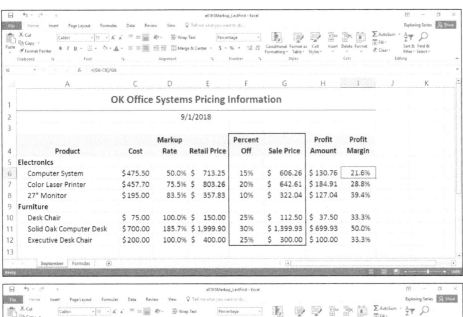

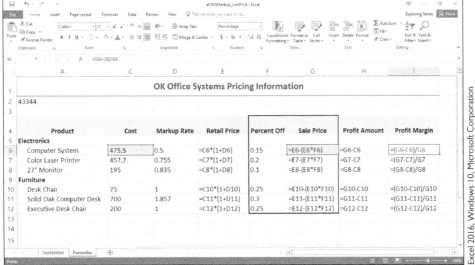

FIGURE 1.1 Completed OKOS Worksheet

CASE STUDY | OK Office Systems

Starting File	File to be Submitted
e01h1Markup	e01h5Markup_LastFirst

Introduction to Spreadsheets

Organizing, calculating, and evaluating quantitative data are important skills needed today for personal and managerial decision making. You track expenses for your household budget, maintain a savings plan, and determine what amount you can afford for a house or car payment. Retail managers create and analyze their organizations' annual budgets, sales projections, and inventory records. Charitable organizations track the donations they receive, the distribution of those donations, and overhead expenditures.

You should use a spreadsheet to maintain data and perform calculations. A ***spreadsheet*** is an electronic file that contains a grid of columns and rows used to organize related data and to display results of calculations, enabling interpretation of quantitative data for decision making.

Performing calculations using a calculator and entering the results into a ledger can lead to inaccurate values. If an input value is incorrect or needs to be updated, you have to recalculate the results manually, which is time-consuming and can lead to inaccuracies. A spreadsheet makes data entry changes easy. If the formulas are correctly constructed, the results recalculate automatically and accurately, saving time and reducing room for error.

In this section, you will learn how to design spreadsheets. In addition, you will explore the Excel window and learn the name of each window element. Then, you will enter text, values, and dates in a spreadsheet.

Exploring the Excel Window

In Excel, a ***worksheet*** is a single spreadsheet that typically contains descriptive labels, numeric values, formulas, functions, and graphical representations of data. A ***workbook*** is a collection of one or more related worksheets contained within a single file. By default, new workbooks contain one worksheet. Storing multiple worksheets within one workbook helps organize related data together in one file and enables you to perform calculations among the worksheets within the workbook. For example, you might want to create a budget workbook of 13 worksheets, one for each month to store your personal income and expenses and a final worksheet to calculate totals across the entire year.

Identify Excel Window Elements

Like other Microsoft Office programs, the Excel window contains the Quick Access Toolbar, the title bar, sizing buttons, and the Ribbon. In addition, Excel contains unique elements. Figure 1.2 identifies elements specific to the Excel window, and Table 1.1 lists and describes the Excel window elements.

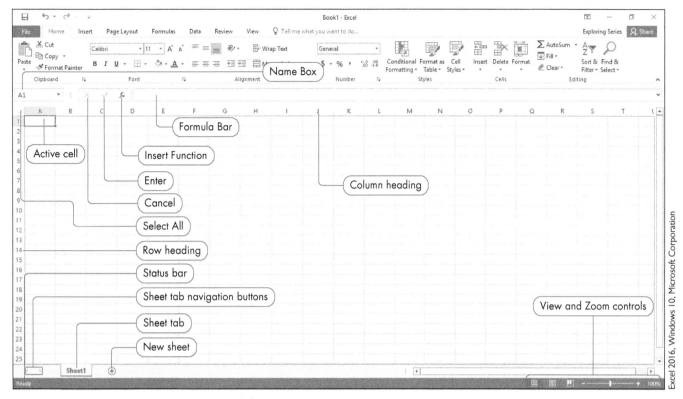

FIGURE 1.2 Excel Window

Excel 2016, Windows 10, Microsoft Corporation

TABLE 1.1	Excel Elements
Element	**Description**
Name Box	An element located below the Ribbon and displays the address of the active cell. Use the Name Box to go to a cell, assign a name to one or more cells, or select a function.
Cancel ☒	When you enter or edit data, click Cancel to cancel the data entry or edit, and revert back to the previous data in the cell, if any. Cancel changes from gray to red when you position the pointer over it.
Enter ☑	When you enter or edit data, click Enter to accept data typed in the active cell and keep the current cell active. Enter changes from gray to blue when you position the pointer over it.
Insert Function *fx*	Click to display the Insert Function dialog box to search for and select a function to insert into the active cell. The Insert Function icon changes from gray to green when you position the pointer over it.
Formula Bar	An element located below the Ribbon and to the right of the Insert Function command. Shows the contents of the active cell. You enter or edit cell contents here or directly in the active cell. Drag the bottom border of the Formula Bar down to increase the height of the Formula Bar to display large amounts of data or a long formula contained in the active cell.
Select All ☐	The triangle at the intersection of the row and column headings in the top-left corner of the worksheet. Click it to select everything contained in the active worksheet.
Column headings	The letters above the columns. For example, B is the letter above the second column.
Row headings	The numbers to the left of the rows, such as 1, 2, 3, and so on. For example, 3 is the row heading for the third row.
Active cell	The current cell, which is indicated by a dark green border.
Sheet tab	A visual label that looks like a file folder tab. A sheet tab shows the name of a worksheet contained in the workbook. When you create a new Excel workbook, the default worksheet is named Sheet1.
New sheet ⊕	Click to insert a new worksheet to the right of the current worksheet.
Sheet tab navigation	If your workbook contains several worksheets, Excel may not show all the sheet tabs at the same time. Use the buttons to display the first, previous, next, or last worksheet.
Status bar	The row at the bottom of the Excel window. It displays information about a selected command or operation in progress. For example, it displays *Select destination and press ENTER or choose Paste* after you use the Copy command.
View controls	Icons on the right side of the status bar that control how the worksheet is displayed. Click a view control to display the worksheet in Normal, Page Layout, or Page Break Preview. **Normal view** displays the worksheet without showing margins, headers, footers, and page breaks. **Page Layout view** shows the margins, header and footer area, and a ruler. **Page Break Preview** indicates where the worksheet will be divided into pages.
Zoom control	Drag the zoom control to increase the size of the worksheet onscreen to see more or less of the worksheet data.

Pearson Education, Inc.

Identify Columns, Rows, and Cells

A worksheet contains columns and rows, with each column and row assigned a heading. Columns are assigned alphabetical headings from columns A to Z, continuing from AA to AZ, and then from BA to BZ until XFD, which is the last of the possible 16,384 columns. Rows have numeric headings ranging from 1 to 1,048,576. Depending on your screen resolution, you may see more or fewer columns and rows than what are shown in the figures in this book.

The intersection of a column and a row is a *cell*; a total of more than 17 billion cells are available in a worksheet. Each cell has a unique *cell address*, identified by first its column letter and then its row number. For example, the cell at the intersection of column C and row 6 is cell C6 (see Figure 1.3). The active cell is the current cell. Excel displays a dark green border around the active cell in the worksheet, and the Name Box shows the location of the active cell, which is C6 in Figure 1.3. The contents of the active cell, or the formula used to calculate the results of the active cell, appear in the Formula Bar. Cell references are useful when referencing data in formulas, or in navigation.

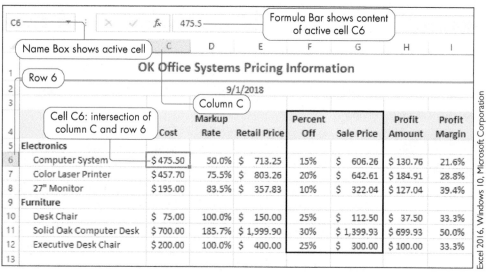

FIGURE 1.3 Columns, Rows, and Cells

Navigate in and Among Worksheets

To navigate to a new cell, click it or use the arrow keys on the keyboard. When you press Enter, the next cell down in the same column becomes the active cell. If you work in a large worksheet, use the vertical and horizontal scroll bars to display another area of the worksheet and click in the desired cell to make it the active cell. The keyboard contains several keys that can be used in isolation or in combination with other keys to navigate in a worksheet. Table 1.2 lists the keyboard navigation methods. The Go To command is helpful for navigating to a cell that is not visible onscreen.

TABLE 1.2   Keystrokes and Actions

Keystroke	Used to
↑	Move up one cell in the same column.
↓	Move down one cell in the same column.
←	Move left one cell in the same row.
→	Move right one cell in the same row.
Tab	Move right one cell in the same row.
Page Up	Move the active cell up one screen.
Page Down	Move the active cell down one screen.
Home	Move the active cell to column A of the current row.
Ctrl+Home	Make cell A1 the active cell.
Ctrl+End	Make the rightmost, lowermost active corner of the worksheet—the intersection of the last column and row that contains data—the active cell. Does not move to cell XFD1048576 unless that cell contains data.
F5 or Ctrl+G	Display the Go To dialog box to enter any cell address.

Pearson Education, Inc.

To display the contents of another worksheet within the workbook, click the sheet tab at the bottom of the workbook window, above the status bar. After you click a sheet tab, you can then navigate within that worksheet.

Entering and Editing Cell Data

You should plan the structure of a worksheet before you start entering data. Using the OKOS case presented at the beginning of the chapter as an example, use the following steps to plan the worksheet design, enter and format data, and complete the workbook. Refer to Figure 1.1 for the completed workbook.

Plan the Worksheet Design

1. **State the purpose of the worksheet.** The purpose of the OKOS worksheet is to store data about products on sale and to calculate important details, such as the retail price based on markup, the sales price based on a discount rate, and the profit margin.

2. **Decide what outputs are needed to achieve the purpose of the worksheet.** Outputs are the results you need to calculate. For the OKOS worksheet, the outputs include columns to calculate the retail price (i.e., the selling price to your customers), the sale price, and the profit margin. In some worksheets, you might want to create an *output area*, the region in the worksheet to contain formulas dependent on the values in the input area.

3. **Decide what input values are needed to achieve the desired output.** Input values are the initial values, such as variables and assumptions. You may change these values to see what type of effects different values have on the end results. For the OKOS worksheet, the input values include the costs OKOS pays the manufacturers, the markup rates, and the proposed discount rates for the sale. In some worksheets, you should create an *input area*, a specific region in the worksheet to store and change the variables used in calculations. For example, if you applied the same Markup Rate and same Percent Off for all products, it would be easier to create an input area at the top of the worksheet to change the values in one location rather than in several locations.

Enter and Format the Data

4. **Enter the labels, values, and formulas in Excel.** Use the design plan (steps 2–3) as you enter labels, input values, and formulas to calculate the output. In the OKOS worksheet, descriptive labels (the product names) appear in the first column to indicate that the values on a specific row pertain to a specific product. Descriptive labels appear at the top of each column, such as Cost and Retail Price, to describe the values in the respective column. Change the input values to test that your formulas produce correct results. If necessary, correct any errors in the formulas to produce correct results. For the OKOS worksheet, change some of the original costs and markup rates to ensure the calculated retail price, selling price, and profit margin percentage results update correctly.

5. **Format the numerical values in the worksheet.** Align decimal points in columns of numbers and add number formats and styles. In the OKOS worksheet, you will use Accounting Number Format and the Percent Style to format the numerical data. Adjust the number of decimal places as needed.

6. **Format the descriptive titles and labels.** Add bold and color to headings so that they stand out and are attractive. Apply other formatting to headings and descriptive labels. In the OKOS worksheet, you will center the main title over all the columns, bold and center column labels over the columns, and apply other formatting to the headings.

Complete the Workbook

7. **Document the workbook as thoroughly as possible.** Include the current date, your name as the workbook author, assumptions, and purpose of the workbook. Some people provide this documentation in a separate worksheet within the workbook. You can also add some documentation in the Properties section when you click the File tab.

8. **Save and share the completed workbook.** Preview and prepare printouts for distribution in meetings, send an electronic copy of the workbook to those who need it, or upload the workbook on a shared network drive or in the cloud.

Enter Text

STEP 1 ⟩⟩ **Text** is any combination of letters, numbers, symbols, and spaces not used in calculations. Excel treats phone numbers, such as 555-1234, and Social Security numbers, such as 123-45-6789, as text entries. You enter text for a worksheet title to describe the contents of the worksheet, as row and column labels to describe data, and as cell data. In Figure 1.4, the cells in column A contain text, such as Class. Text aligns at the left cell margin by default.

To enter text in a cell, complete the following steps:

1. Make sure the cell is active where you want to enter text.
2. Type the text. If you want to enter a numeric value as text, such as a class section number, type an apostrophe and the number, such as '002.
3. Make another cell the active cell after entering data by completing one of the following steps:
   - Press Enter on the keyboard.
   - Press an arrow key on the keyboard.
   - Press Tab on the keyboard.

   Keep the current cell active after entering data by completing one of the following steps:
   - Press Ctrl+Enter on the keyboard.
   - Click Enter (the check mark between the Name Box and the Formula Bar).

As soon as you begin typing a label into a cell, the **AutoComplete** feature searches for and automatically displays any other label in the same column that matches the letters you type. The top half of Figure 1.4 shows Spreadsheet Apps is typed in cell A3. When you start to type *Sp* in cell A4, AutoComplete displays Spreadsheet Apps because a text entry in the same column already starts with *Sp*. Press Enter to accept the repeated label, or continue typing to enter a different label, such as Spanish II. The bottom half of Figure 1.4 shows that '002 was entered in cell B4 to start the text with a 0. Otherwise, Excel would have eliminated the zeros in the class section number. Ignore the error message that displays when you intentionally use an apostrophe to enter a number which is not actually a value.

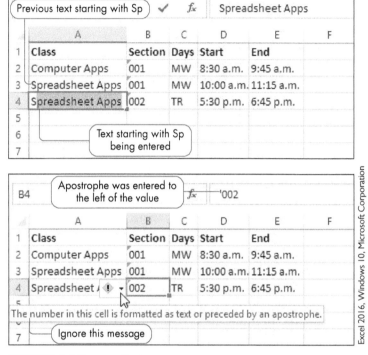

FIGURE 1.4 Entering Text

Use Auto Fill to Complete a Sequence

STEP 2 ›› While AutoComplete helps to complete a label that is identical to another label in the same column, **Auto Fill** is a feature that helps you complete a sequence of words or values. For example, if you enter January in a cell, use Auto Fill to fill in the rest of the months in adjacent cells so that you do not have to type the rest of the month names. Auto Fill can help you complete other sequences, such as quarters (Qtr 1, etc.), weekdays, and weekday abbreviations after you type the first item in the sequence. Figure 1.5 shows the results of filling in months, abbreviated months, quarters, weekdays, abbreviated weekdays, and increments of 5.

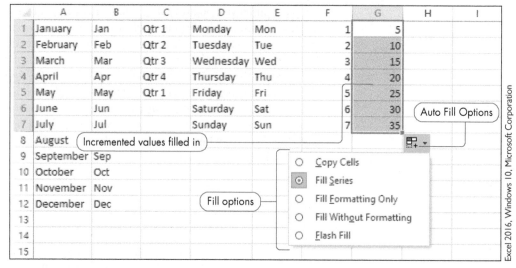

FIGURE 1.5 Auto Fill Examples

To use Auto Fill to complete a series of text (such as month names), complete the following steps:

1. Type the first label (e.g., January) in the starting cell (e.g., cell A1) and press Ctrl+Enter to keep that cell the active cell.
2. Point to the **fill handle** (a small green square in the bottom-right corner of the active cell) until the pointer changes to a thin black plus sign.
3. Drag the fill handle to repeat the content in other cells (e.g., through cell A12).

Immediately after you use Auto Fill, Excel displays Auto Fill Options in the bottom-right corner of the filled data (refer to Figure 1.5). Click Auto Fill Options to display several fill options: Copy Cells, Fill Series, Fill Formatting Only, Fill Without Formatting, or Flash Fill. The menu will also include other options, depending on the cell content: Fill Months for completing months; Fill Weekdays for completing weekdays; and Fill Days, Fill Weekdays, Fill Months, Fill Years to complete dates. Select Fill Formatting Only when you want to copy the formats but not complete a sequence. Select Fill Without Formatting when you want to complete the sequence but do not want to format the rest of the sequence.

To use Auto Fill to fill a sequence of consecutive numbers (such as 1, 2, 3, etc.), complete the following steps:

1. Type the first number in the starting cell (e.g., cell F1) and press Ctrl+Enter to keep that cell the active cell.
2. Drag the fill handle to fill the content in other cells. Excel will copy the same number for the rest of the cells.
3. Click Auto Fill Options and select Fill Series. Excel will change the numbers to be in sequential order, starting with the original value you typed.

For non-consecutive numeric sequences, you must specify the first two values in sequence. For example, if you want to fill in 5, 10, 15, and so on, you must enter 5 and 10 in two adjacent cells before using Auto Fill so that Excel knows to increment by 5.

To use Auto Fill to fill a sequence of number patterns (such as 5, 10, 15, 20 shown in the range G1:G7 in Figure 1.5), complete the following steps:

1. Type the first two numbers of the sequence in adjoining cells.
2. Select those two cells containing the starting two values.
3. Drag the fill handle to fill in the rest of the sequence.

> **TIP: FLASH FILL**
>
> Flash Fill is a similar feature to Auto Fill in that it can quickly fill in data for you; however, *Flash Fill* uses data in previous columns as you type in a new label in an adjoining column to determine what to fill in. For example, assume that column A contains a list of first and last names (such as Penny Sumpter in cell A5), but you want to have a column of just first names. To do this, type Penny's name in cell B5, click Fill in the Editing group on the Home tab and select Flash Fill to fill in the rest of column B with people's first names based on the data entered in column A.

Enter Values

STEP 3 » *Values* are numbers that represent a quantity or a measurable amount. Excel usually distinguishes between text and value data based on what you enter. The primary difference between text and value entries is that value entries can be the basis of calculations, whereas text cannot. In Figure 1.3, the data below the Cost, Markup Rates, and Percent Off labels are values. Values align at the right cell margin by default. After entering values, align decimal places and apply formatting by adding characters, such as $ or %. Entering values is the same process as entering text: Type the value in a cell and click Enter or press Enter.

> **TIP: ENTERING VALUES WITH TRAILING ZEROS OR PERCENTAGES**
>
> You do not need to type the last 0 in 475.50 shown in cell C6 in Figure 1.3. Excel will remove or add the trailing 0 depending on the decimal place formatting. Similarly, you do not have to type the leading 0 in a percentage before the decimal point. Type a percent in the decimal format, such as .5 for 50%. You will later format the value.

Enter Dates and Times

STEP 4 » You can enter dates and times in a variety of formats. You should enter a static date to document when you create or modify a workbook or to document the specific point in time when the data were accurate, such as on a balance sheet or income statement. Later, you will learn how to use formulas to enter dates that update to the current date. In Figure 1.6, the data in column A contains the date 9/1/2018 but in different formats. Dates are values, so they align at the right side of a cell. The data in column C contains the time 2:30 PM but in different formats.

	A	B	C	D
1	9/1/2018		2:30:00 PM	
2	Saturday, September 1, 2018		14:30	
3	9/1		2:30 PM	
4	9/1/18		14:30:00	
5	09/01/18		2:30:00 PM	
6	1-Sep			
7	1-Sep-18			
8	September 1, 2018			
9				

Excel 2016, Windows 10, Microsoft Corporation

FIGURE 1.6 Date and Time Examples

Excel displays dates differently from the way it stores dates. For example, the displayed date 9/1/2018 represents the first day in September in the year 2018. Excel stores dates as serial numbers starting at 1 with January 1, 1900, so that you can create formulas, such as to calculate how many days exist between two dates. For example, 9/1/2018 is stored as 43344.

Edit and Clear Cell Contents

After entering data in a cell, you may need to change it. For example, you may want to edit a label to make it more descriptive, such as changing a label from OKC Office Systems Information to OKC Office Systems Pricing Information. Furthermore, you might realize a digit is missing from a value and need to change 500 to 5000.

To edit the contents of a cell, compete the following steps:

1. Click the cell.
2. Click in the Formula Bar or press F2 to put the cell in edit mode. The insertion point displays on the right side of the data in the cell when you press F2.
3. Make the changes to the content in the cell.
4. Click or press Enter.

You may want to clear or delete the contents in a cell if you no longer need data in a cell.

To clear the contents of a cell, complete the following steps:

1. Click the cell.
2. Press Delete or click the cell, click Clear in the Editing group on the Home tab, and select the desired option (see Figure 1.7).

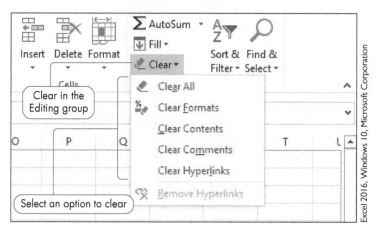

FIGURE 1.7 Clear Options

Quick Concepts

1. What are two major advantages of using an electronic spreadsheet instead of a paper-based ledger? *p. 404*

2. What are the visual indicators that a cell is the active cell? *p. 406*

3. What steps should you perform before entering data into a worksheet? *pp. 407-408*

4. What three types of content can you can enter into a cell? Give an example (different from those in the book) for each type. *pp. 408-411*

Hands-On Exercises

Watch the Video for this Hands-On Exercise!

MyITLab®
HOE1 Training

Skills covered: Enter Text • Use Auto Fill to Complete a Sequence • Enter Values • Enter a Date • Clear Cell Contents

1 Introduction to Spreadsheets

As the assistant manager of OKOS, you will create a worksheet that shows the cost (the amount OKOS pays its suppliers), the markup percentage (the amount by which the cost is increased), and the retail selling price. You also will list the discount percentage (such as 25% off) for each product, the sale price, and the profit margin percentage.

STEP 1 》 ENTER TEXT

Now that you have planned the OKOS worksheet, you are ready to enter labels for the title, column labels, and row labels. You will type a title in cell A1, product labels in the first column, and row labels in the fourth row. Refer to Figure 1.8 as you complete Step 1.

	A	B	C	D	E	F	G	H	I
1	OK Office Sys	Step b: Enter text for first product	nation						
2				Steps b and c: Labels extend into empty column B					
3									
4	Product	Code	Cost	Markup Ra	Retail Pric	Percent O	Sale Price	Profit Margin	
5	Computer System					0.15			
6	Color Laser Printer					0.2			
7	Filing Cabinet					0.1			
8	Desk Chair			Step c: Name of products		0.25			
9	Solid Oak Computer Desk					0.3			
10	27" Monitor					0.1			
11									
12									

Excel 2016, Windows 10, Microsoft Corporation

FIGURE 1.8 Text Entered in Cells

a. Open *e01h1Markup* and save it as **e01h1Markup_LastFirst**.

> When you save files, use your last and first names. For example, as the Excel author, I would save my workbook as *e01h1Markup_MulberyKeith*.

> **TROUBLESHOOTING:** If you make any major mistakes in this exercise, you can close the file, open *e01h1Markup* again, and then start this exercise over.

b. Click **cell A5**, type **Computer System**, and then press **Enter**.

> When you press Enter, the next cell down—cell A6 in this case—becomes the active cell. The text does not completely fit in cell A5, and some of the text appears in cell B5. If you make cell B5 the active cell, the Formula Bar is empty, indicating that nothing is stored in that cell.

c. Type **Color Laser Printer** in **cell A6** and press **Enter**.

> When you start typing C in cell A6, AutoComplete displays a ScreenTip suggesting a previous text entry starting with C—Computer System—but keep typing to enter Color Laser Printer instead.

d. Continue typing the rest of the text in **cells A7** through **A10** as shown in Figure 1.8. Text in column A appears to flow into column B.

> You just entered the product labels to describe the data in each row.

> **TROUBLESHOOTING:** If you make an error, click in the cell containing the error and retype the label, or press F2 to edit the cell contents, move the insertion point using the arrow keys, press Backspace or Delete to delete the incorrect characters, type the correct characters, and press Enter. If you type a label in an incorrect cell, click the cell and press Delete.

   e. Click **Save** on the Quick Access Toolbar to save the changes you made to the workbook.

You should develop a habit of saving periodically. That way if your system unexpectedly shuts down, you will not lose everything you worked on.

STEP 2 ›› **USE AUTO FILL TO COMPLETE A SEQUENCE**

You want to assign a product code for each product on sale. You will assign consecutive numbers 101 to 106. After typing the first code number, you will use Auto Fill to complete the rest of the series. Refer to Figures 1.9 and 1.10 as you complete Step 2.

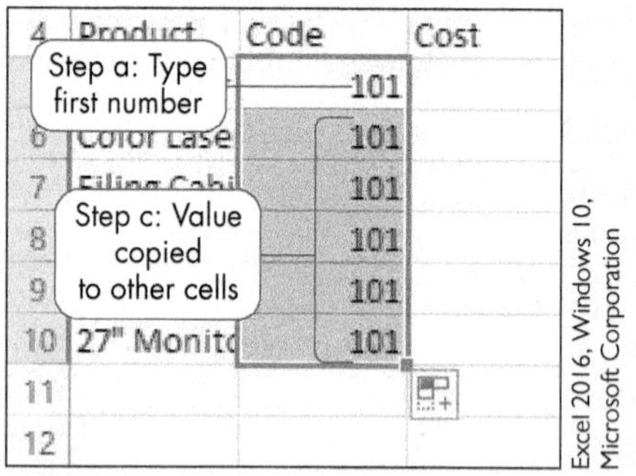

FIGURE 1.9 Auto Fill Copied Original Value

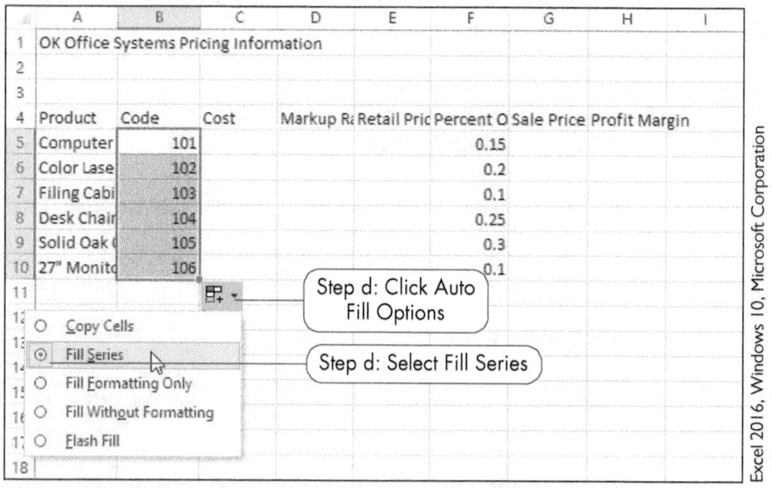

FIGURE 1.10 Auto Fill Sequence

   a. Click **cell B5**, type **101**, and then press **Ctrl+Enter**.

The product name Computer System no longer overlaps into column B after you enter data into cell B5. The data in cell A5 is not deleted; the rest of the label is hidden until you increase the column width later.

   b. Position the pointer on the fill handle in the bottom-right corner of **cell B5**.

The pointer looks like a black plus sign when you point to a fill handle.

c. Double-click the **cell B6 fill handle**.

Excel copies 101 as the item number for the rest of the products. Excel stops inserting item numbers in column B when it detects the last label in cell A10 (refer to Figure 1.9).

d. Click **Auto Fill Options** and select **Fill Series**. Save the workbook.

Excel changes the duplicate values to continue sequentially in a series of numbers.

STEP 3 ⟩⟩ ENTER VALUES

Now that you have entered the descriptive labels and item numbers, you will enter the cost and markup rate for each product. Refer to Figure 1.11 as you complete Step 3.

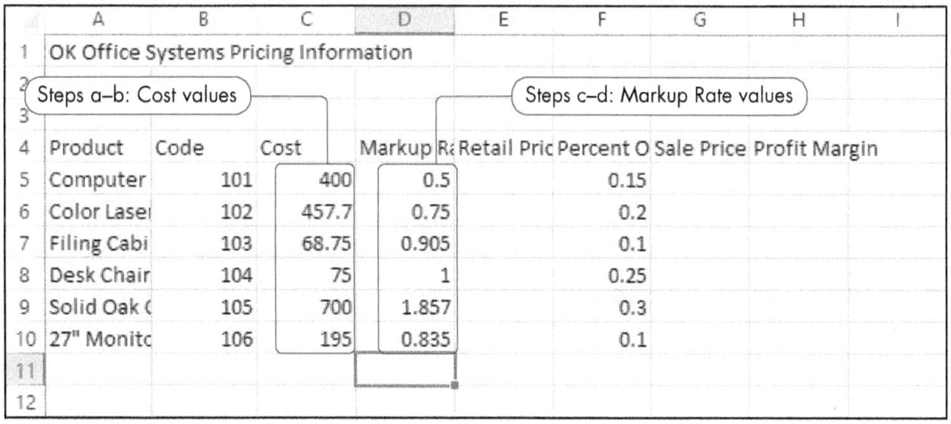

	A	B	C	D	E	F	G	H	I
1	OK Office Systems Pricing Information								
2	Steps a–b: Cost values				Steps c–d: Markup Rate values				
3									
4	Product	Code	Cost	Markup R:	Retail Pric	Percent O	Sale Price	Profit Margin	
5	Computer	101	400	0.5		0.15			
6	Color Lase	102	457.7	0.75		0.2			
7	Filing Cabi	103	68.75	0.905		0.1			
8	Desk Chair	104	75	1		0.25			
9	Solid Oak (	105	700	1.857		0.3			
10	27" Monitc	106	195	0.835		0.1			
11									
12									

FIGURE 1.11 Values Entered in Cells

Excel 2016, Windows 10, Microsoft Corporation

a. Click **cell C5**, type **400**, and then press **Enter**.

b. Type the remaining costs in **cells C6** through **C10** shown in Figure 1.11.

To improve your productivity, use the number keypad (if available) on the right side of your keyboard. It is much faster to type values and press Enter on the number keypad rather than to use the numbers on the keyboard. Make sure Num Lock is active before using the number keypad to enter values.

c. Click **cell D5**, type **0.5**, and then press **Enter**.

You entered the markup rate as a decimal instead of a percentage. You will apply Percent Style later, but now you will concentrate on data entry.

d. Type the remaining values in **cells D6** through **D10** as shown in Figure 1.11. Save the workbook.

STEP 4 ›› ENTER A DATE AND CLEAR CELL CONTENTS

As you review the worksheet, you realize you need to provide a date to indicate when the sale starts. Refer to Figure 1.12 as you complete Step 4.

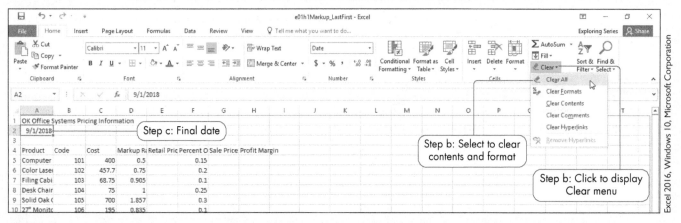

FIGURE 1.12 Date Entered in a Cell

a. Click **cell A2**, type **9/1**, and then press **Enter**.

The date aligns on the right cell margin by default. Excel displays 1-Sep instead of 9/1.

b. Click **cell A2**, click **Clear** in the Editing group on the Home tab, and then select **Clear All**.

The Clear All command clears both cell contents and formatting in the selected cell(s).

c. Type **9/1/2018** in **cell A2** and press **Ctrl+Enter**.

> **TROUBLESHOOTING:** If you did not use Clear All and typed 9/1/2018 in cell A2, Excel would have retained the previous date format and displayed 1-Sep again.

When you type the month, day, and year such as 9/1/2018, Excel enters the date in that format (unless it has a different date format applied).

d. Save the workbook. Keep the workbook open if you plan to continue with the next Hands-On Exercise. If not, close the workbook, and exit Excel.

Mathematical Operations and Formulas

A *formula* combines cell references, arithmetic operations, values, and/or functions used in a calculation. Formulas transform static numbers into meaningful results that update as values change. For example, a payroll manager can build formulas to calculate the gross pay, deductions, and net pay for an organization's employees, or a doctoral student can create formulas to perform various statistical calculations to interpret his or her research data.

In this section, you will learn how to use mathematical operations in Excel formulas. You will refresh your memory of the mathematical order of operations and learn how to construct formulas using cell addresses so that when the value of an input cell changes, the result of the formula changes without you having to modify the formula.

Creating Formulas

Use formulas to help you analyze how results will change as the input data changes. You can change the value of your assumptions or inputs and explore the results quickly and accurately. For example, if your rent increases, how does that affect your personal budget? Analyzing different input values in Excel is easy after you build formulas. Simply change an input value and observe the change in the formula results. In the OKOS product sales worksheet, the results for the Retail Price, Sale Price, and Profit Margin labels were calculated by using formulas (refer to Figure 1.1).

Use Cell References in Formulas

STEP 1 ⟩⟩ You should use cell references instead of values in formulas where possible. You may include values in an input area—such as dates, salary, or costs—that you will need to reference in formulas. Referencing these cells in your formulas, instead of typing the value of the cell to which you are referring, keeps your formulas accurate if you change values to perform a what-if analysis.

Figure 1.13 shows a worksheet containing input values and results of formulas. The figure also displays the actual formulas used to generate the calculated results. For example, cell E2 contains the formula =B2+B3. Excel uses the value stored in cell B2 (10) and adds it to the value stored in cell B3 (2). The result (12) appears in cell E2 instead of the actual formula. The Formula Bar displays the formula entered into the active cell.

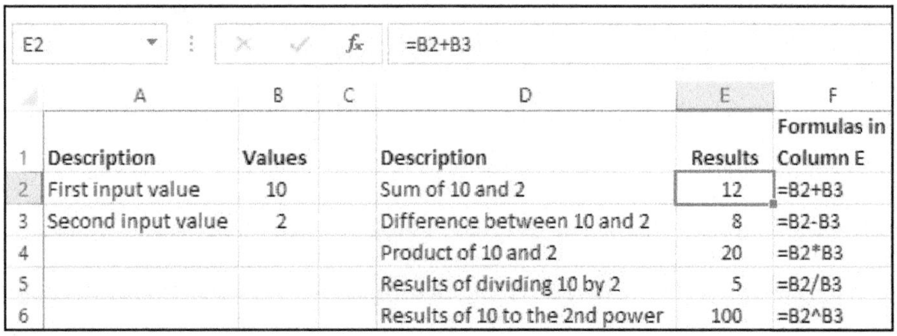

E2	▼	⋮	✕	✓	*fx*	=B2+B3		
	A	B	C		D		E	F
	Description	Values		Description			Results	Formulas in Column E
1								
2	First input value	10		Sum of 10 and 2			12	=B2+B3
3	Second input value	2		Difference between 10 and 2			8	=B2-B3
4				Product of 10 and 2			20	=B2*B3
5				Results of dividing 10 by 2			5	=B2/B3
6				Results of 10 to the 2nd power			100	=B2^B3

FIGURE 1.13 Formula Results

To enter a formula, complete the following steps:

1. Click the cell.
2. Type an equal sign (=), followed by the arithmetic expression, using cell references instead of values. Do not include any spaces in the formula.
3. Click Enter or press Enter.

TIP: EQUAL SIGN NEEDED

If you type B2+B3 without the equal sign, Excel does not recognize that you entered a formula and stores the "formula" as text.

TIP: UPPER OR LOWERCASE

When you create a formula, type the cell references in uppercase, such as =B2+B3, or lowercase, such as =b2+b3. Excel changes cell references to uppercase automatically.

In Figure 1.13, cell B2 contains 10, and cell B3 contains 2. Cell E2 contains =B2+B3 but shows the result 12. If you change the value of cell B3 to 5, cell E2 displays the new result, which is 15. However, if you had typed actual values in the formula, =10+2, you would have to edit the formula to =10+5, even though the value in cell B3 was changed to 5. Using values in formulas can cause problems as you might forget to edit the formula or you might have a typographical error if you edit the formula. Always design worksheets in such a way as to be able to place those values that might need to change as input values. Referencing cells with input values in formulas instead of using the values themselves will avoid having to modify your formulas if an input value changes later.

TIP: WHEN TO USE A VALUE IN A FORMULA

Use cell references instead of actual values in formulas, unless the value will never change. For example, if you want to calculate how many total months are in a specified number of years, enter a formula such as =B5*12, where B5 contains the number of years. You might want to change the number of years, so you type that value in cell B5. However, every year always has 12 months, so you can use the value 12 in the formula.

Apply the Order of Operations

The **order of operations** (also called order of precedence) are rules that controls the sequence in which arithmetic operations are performed, which affects the result of the calculation. Excel performs mathematical calculations left to right in this order: **P**arentheses, **E**xponentiation, **M**ultiplication or **D**ivision, and finally **A**ddition or **S**ubtraction. Some people remember the order of operations with the phrase *Please Excuse My Dear Aunt Sally*.

Table 1.3 lists the primary order of operations. Use Help to learn about the complete order of precedence.

TABLE 1.3	Order of Operations	
Order	**Description**	**Symbols**
1	Parentheses	( )
2	Exponentiation	^
3	Multiplication and Division	* and / (respectively)
4	Addition and Subtraction	+ and − (respectively)

Pearson Education, Inc.

Figure 1.14 shows formulas, the sequence in which calculations occur, calculations, the description, and the results of each order of operations. The highlighted results are the final formula results. This figure illustrates the importance of symbols and use of parentheses.

	A	B	C	D	E	F
1	Input		Formula	Sequence	Description	Result
2	2		=A2+A3*A4+A5	1	3 (cell A3) * 4 (cell A4)	12
3	3			2	2 (cell A2) + 12 (order 1)	14
4	4			3	14 (order 2) + 5 (cell A5)	19
5	5					
6			=(A2+A3)*(A4+A5)	1	2 (cell A2) + 3 (cell A3)	5
7				2	4 (cell A4) + 5 (cell A5)	9
8				3	5 (order 1) * 9 (order 2)	45
9						
10			=A2/A3+A4*A5	1	2 (cell A2) / 3 (cell A3)	0.666667
11				2	4 (cell A4) * 5 (cell A5)	20
12				3	0.666667 (order 1) + 20 (order 2)	20.66667
13						
14			=A2/(A3+A4)*A5	1	3 (cell A3) + 4 (cell A4)	7
15				2	2 (cell A2) / 7 (order 1)	0.285714
16				3	0.285714 (order 2) * 5 (cell A5)	1.428571
17						
18			=A2^2+A3*A4%	1	4 (cell A4) is converted to percentage	0.04
19				2	2 (cell A2) to the power of 2	4
20				3	3 (cell A3) * 0.04 (order 1)	0.12
21				4	4 (order 2) + 0.12 (order 3)	4.12

Excel 2016, Windows 10, Microsoft Corporation

FIGURE 1.14 Formula Results Based on Order of Operations

Use Semi-Selection to Create a Formula

STEP 2 ⟩⟩ To decrease typing time and ensure accuracy, use **semi-selection**, a process of selecting a cell or range of cells for entering cell references as you create formulas. Semi-selection is often called **pointing** because you use the pointer to select cells as you build the formula. Some people prefer using the semi-selection method instead of typing a formula so that they can make sure they use the correct cell references as they build the formula.

To use the semi-selection technique to create a formula, complete the following steps:

1. Click the cell where you want to create the formula.
2. Type an equal sign (=) to start a formula.
3. Click the cell that contains the value to use in the formula. A moving marquee appears around the cell or range you select, and Excel displays the cell or range reference in the formula.
4. Type a mathematical operator.
5. Continue clicking cells, selecting ranges, and typing operators to finish the formula. Use the scroll bars if the cell is in a remote location in the worksheet, or click a worksheet tab to see a cell in another worksheet.
6. Press Enter to complete the formula.

Copy Formulas

STEP 3 ⟩⟩ After you enter a formula in a cell, you duplicate the formula without retyping the formula for other cells that need a similar formula. Previously, you learned about the Auto Fill feature that enables you to use the fill handle to fill in a series of values, months, quarters, and weekdays. You can also use the fill handle to copy the formula in the active cell to adjacent cells down a column or across a row, depending on how the data are organized. Cell references in copied formulas adjust based on their relative locations to the original formula.

> **To copy a formula to other cells using the fill handle, complete the following steps:**
>
> 1. Click the cell with the content you want to copy to make it the active cell.
> 2. Point to the fill handle in the bottom-right corner of the cell until the pointer changes to the fill pointer (a thin black plus sign).
> 3. Drag the fill handle to copy the formula.

Displaying Cell Formulas

STEP 4 ⟩⟩ Excel shows the result of the formula in the cell (see the top half of Figure 1.15); however, you might want to display the formulas instead of the calculated results in the cells (see the bottom half of Figure 1.15). Displaying the cell formulas may help you double-check all your formulas at one time or troubleshoot a problem with a formula instead of clicking in each cell containing a formula and looking at just the Formula Bar.

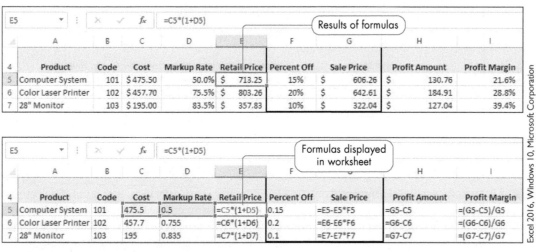

FIGURE 1.15 Formulas and Formula Results

> **To display cell formulas in the worksheet, complete one of the following steps:**
>
> - Press Ctrl and the grave accent (`) key, sometimes referred to as the tilde key, in the top-left corner of the keyboard, below the Esc key.
> - Click Show Formulas in the Formula Auditing group on the Formulas tab.

To hide the formulas and display the formula results again, repeat the preceding process.

Quick Concepts

5. What is the order of operations? Provide and explain two examples that use four different operators: one with parentheses and one without. *p. 418*

6. Why should you use cell references instead of typing values in formulas? *p. 418*

7. When would it be useful to display formulas instead of formula results in a worksheet? *p. 420*

Hands-On Exercises

Watch the Video for this Hands-On Exercise!

MyITLab®
HOE2 Training

Skills covered: Use Cell References in Formulas • Apply the Order of Operations • Use Semi-Selection to Create a Formula • Copy Formulas • Display Cell Formulas

2 Mathematical Operations and Formulas

In Hands-On Exercise 1, you created the basic worksheet for OKOS by entering text, values, and a date for items on sale. Now you will insert formulas to calculate the missing results—specifically, the retail (before sale) price, sale price, and profit margin. You will use cell addresses in your formulas, so when you change a referenced value, the formula results will update automatically.

STEP 1 ›› USE CELL REFERENCES IN A FORMULA AND APPLY THE ORDER OF OPERATIONS

The first formula you create will calculate the retail price. The retail price is the price you originally charge. It is based on a percentage of the original cost so that you earn a profit. Refer to Figure 1.16 as you complete Step 1.

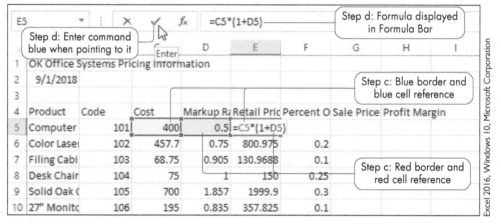

FIGURE 1.16 Retail Price Formula

a. Open *e01h1Markup_LastFirst* if you closed it at the end of Hands-On Exercise 1 and save it as **e01h2Markup_LastFirst**, changing h1 to h2.

b. Click **cell E5**.

Cell E5 is the cell where you will enter the formula to calculate the retail selling price of the first item.

c. Type **=C5*(1+D5)** and view the formula and the colored cells and borders on the screen.

As you build or edit a formula, each cell address in the formula displays in a specific color, and while you type or edit the formula, the cells referenced in the formula have a temporary colored border. For example, in the formula =C5*(1+D5), C5 appears in blue, and D5 appears in red. Cell C5 has a temporarily blue border and light blue shading, and cell D5 has a temporarily red border with light red shading to help you identify cells as you construct your formulas (refer to Figure 1.16).

You enclosed 1+D5 in parentheses to control the order of operations so that 1 is added to the value in cell D5 (0.5). The result is 1.5, which represents 150% of the cost. That result is then multiplied by the value in C5 (400). If you did not use the parentheses, Excel would multiply the value in C5 by 1 (which would be 400) and add that result to the value in D5 (0.5) for a final result of 400.5, which would have given you incorrect results.

An alternative formula also calculates the correct retail price: =C5*D5+C5 or =C5+C5*D5. In this formula, 400 (cell C5) is multiplied by 0.5 (cell D5); that result (200) represents the dollar value of the markup. Excel adds the value 200 to the original cost of 400 to obtain 600, the retail price. You were instructed to enter =C5*(1+D5) to demonstrate the order of operations.

d. Click **Enter** ☑ (between the Name Box and the Formula Bar) and view the formula in the Formula Bar to check it for accuracy.

The result of the formula, 600, appears in cell E5, and the formula displays in the Formula Bar. This formula first adds 1 (the decimal equivalent of 100%) to 0.5 (the value stored in cell D5). Excel multiplies that sum of 1.5 by 400 (the value stored in cell C5). This calculation reflects a retail price is 150% of the original cost.

> **TROUBLESHOOTING:** If the result is not correct, click the cell and look at the formula in the Formula Bar. Click in the Formula Bar, edit the formula to match the formula shown in Step c, and click Enter (the check mark between the Name Box and the Formula Bar). Make sure you start the formula with an equal sign.

e. Position the pointer on the **cell E5 fill handle**. When the pointer changes from a white plus sign to a thin black plus sign, double-click the **fill handle**.

Excel copies the retail price formula for the remaining products in your worksheet. Excel detects when to stop copying the formula when it detects the last label in the dataset.

f. Click **cell E6**, the cell containing the first copied retail price formula, look at the Formula Bar, and then save the workbook.

The formula in cell E6 is =C6*(1+D6). It was copied from the formula in cell E5, which is =C5*(1+D5). Excel adjusts the row references in this formula as you copied the formula down a column so that the results are based on each row's data.

> **TROUBLESHOOTING:** The result in cell E7 may show more decimal places than shown in Figure 1.16. Do not worry about this slight difference.

STEP 2 ›› USE SEMI-SELECTION AND APPLY THE ORDER OF OPERATIONS TO CREATE A FORMULA

Now that you have calculated the retail price, you will calculate a sale price. This week, the computer is on sale for 15% off the retail price. Refer to Figure 1.17 as you complete Step 2.

G6			fx	=E6-(E6*F6)				
	A	B	C	D	E	F	G	H	I
1	OK Office Systems Pricing Information								
2	9/1/2018			Step e: Formula for second product			Steps b-c: Type original formula in cell G5		
3									
4	Product	Code	Cost	Markup Ra	Retail Pric	Percent O	Sale Price	Profit Margin	
5	Computer	101	400	0.5	600	0.15	510		
6	Color Laser	102	457.7	0.75	800.975	0.2	640.78		
7	Filing Cabi	103	68.75	0.905	130.9688	0.1	117.8719	Step d: Results of copied formula	
8	Desk Chair	104	75	1	150	0.25	112.5		
9	Solid Oak (	105	700	1.857	1999.9	0.3	1399.93		
10	27" Monito	106	195	0.835	357.825	0.1	322.0425		

FIGURE 1.17 Sale Price Formula

Excel 2016, Windows 10, Microsoft Corporation

a. Click **cell G5**, the cell where you will enter the formula to calculate the sale price.

b. Type **=**, click **cell E5**, type **-**, click **cell E5**, type *****, and then click **cell F5**. Notice the color-coding in the cell addresses. Press **Ctrl+Enter** to keep the current cell the active cell.

You used the semi-selection method to enter a formula. The result is 510. Looking at the formula, you might think E5–E5 equals zero; remember that because of the order of operations, multiplication is calculated before subtraction. The product of 600 (cell E5) and 0.15 (cell F5) equals 90, which is then subtracted from 600 (cell E5), so the sale price is 510.

> **TROUBLESHOOTING:** You should check the result for logic. Use a calculator to spot-check the accuracy of formulas. If you mark down merchandise by 15% of its regular price, you are charging 85% of the regular price. You should spot-check your formula to ensure that 85% of 600 is 510 by multiplying 600 by 0.85.

c. Click **cell G5**, type **=E5-(E5*F5)**, and then click **Enter**.

Although the parentheses are not needed because the multiplication occurs before the subtraction, it may be helpful to add parentheses to make the formula easier to interpret.

d. Double-click the **cell G5 fill handle** to copy the formula down column G.

e. Click **cell G6**, the cell containing the first copied sale price formula, view the Formula Bar, and save the workbook.

The original formula was =E5-(E5*F5). The copied formula in cell G6 is adjusted to =E6-(E6*F6) so that it calculates the sales price based on the data in row 6.

STEP 3 ›› USE CELL REFERENCES IN A FORMULA AND APPLY THE ORDER OF OPERATIONS

After calculating the sale price, you want to know the profit margin OKOS will earn. OKOS paid $400 for the computer and will sell it for $510. The profit of $110 is then divided by the $400 cost, which gives OKOS a profit margin of 0.215686, which will be formatted later as a percent 21.6%. Refer to Figure 1.18 as you complete Step 3.

	A	B	C	D	E	F			I
H5			f_x	=(G5-C5)/G5			Step b: Formula in Formula Bar		
1	OK Office Systems Pricing Information								
2	9/1/2018							Step c: Results after copying the formula	
3									
4	Product	Code	Cost	Markup Ra	Retail Pric	Percent O	Sale Price	Profit Margin	
5	Computer	101	400	0.5	600	0.15	510	0.215686	
6	Color Laser	102	457.7	0.75	800.975	0.2	640.78	0.285714	
7	Filing Cabi	103	68.75	0.905	130.9688	0.1	117.8719	0.41674	
8	Desk Chair	104	75	1	150	0.25	112.5	0.333333	
9	Solid Oak (	105	700	1.857	1999.9	0.3	1399.93	0.499975	
10	27" Monitc	106	195	0.835	357.825	0.1	322.0425	0.39449	
11									
12									

FIGURE 1.18 Profit Margin Formula

Excel 2016, Windows 10, Microsoft Corporation

a. Click **cell H5**, the cell where you will enter the formula to calculate the profit margin.

The profit margin is the profit (difference in sales price and cost) percentage of the sale price.

b. Type **=(G5-C5)/G5** and notice the color-coding in the cell addresses. Press **Ctrl+Enter**.

The formula must first calculate the profit, which is the difference between the sale price (510) and the original cost (400). The difference (110) is then divided by the sale price (510) to determine the profit margin of 0.215686, or 21.6%.

c. Double-click the **cell H5 fill handle** to copy the formula down the column.

d. Click **cell H6**, the cell containing the first copied profit margin formula, look at the Formula Bar, and then save the workbook.

The original formula was =(G5-C5)/G5, and the copied formula in cell H6 is =(G6-C6)/G6.

STEP 4 ⟫ **DISPLAY CELL FORMULAS**

You want to see how the prices and profit margins are affected when you change some of the original cost values. For example, the supplier might notify you that the cost to you will increase. In addition, you want to see the formulas displayed in the cells temporarily. Refer to Figures 1.19 and 1.20 as you complete Step 4.

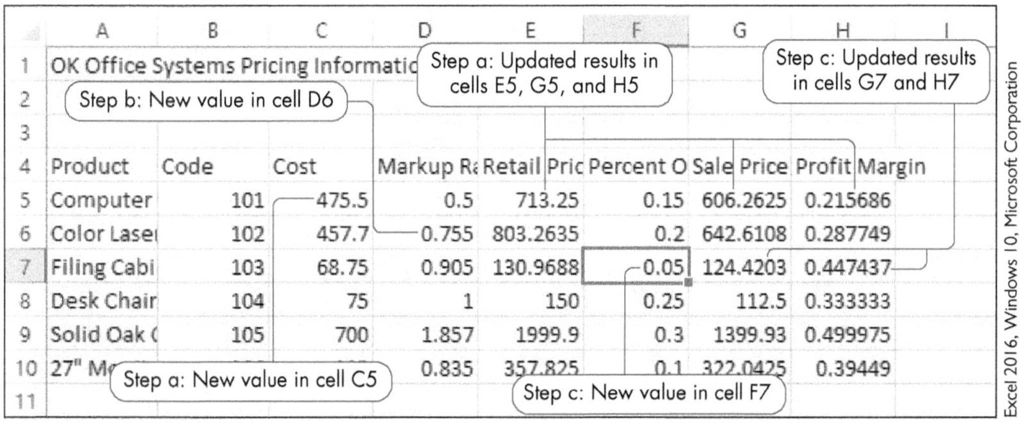

FIGURE 1.19 Results of Changed Values

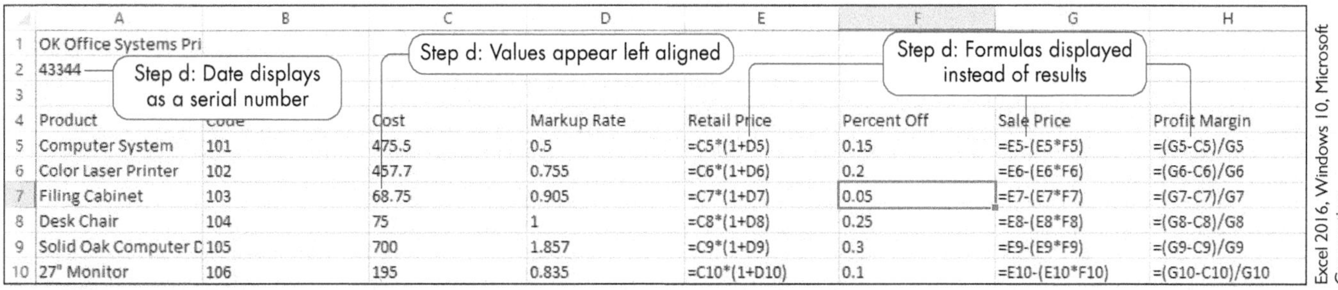

FIGURE 1.20 Formulas Displayed in the Worksheet

a. Click **cell C5**, type **475.5**, and then press **Enter**.

The results of the retail price, sale price, and profit margin formulas change based on the new cost.

b. Click **cell D6**, type **0.755**, and then press **Enter**.

The results of the retail price, sale price, and profit margin formulas change based on the new markup rate.

c. Click **cell F7**, type **0.05**, and then press **Ctrl+Enter**.

The results of the sale price and profit margin formulas change based on the new markdown rate. Note that the retail price did not change because that formula is not based on the markup rate.

d. Press **Ctrl+`** (the grave accent mark).

The workbook now displays the formulas rather than the formula results (refer to Figure 1.20). This is helpful when you want to review several formulas at one time. Numbers are left-aligned, and the date displays as a serial number when you display formulas.

e. Press **Ctrl+`** (the grave accent mark).

The workbook now displays the formula results in the cells again.

f. Save the workbook. Keep the workbook open if you plan to continue with the next Hands-On Exercise. If not, close the workbook, and exit Excel.

Worksheet Structure and Clipboard Tasks

Although you plan worksheets before entering data, you might need to insert a new row to accommodate new data, delete a column that you no longer need, hide a column of confidential data before printing worksheets for distribution, or adjust the size of columns and rows so that the data fit better. Furthermore, you may decide to move data to a different location in the same worksheet or even to a different worksheet. Instead of deleting the original data and typing it in the new location, select and move data from one cell to another. In some instances, you might want to create a copy of data entered so that you can explore different values and compare the results of the original data set and the copied and edited data set.

In this section, you will learn how to make changes to columns and rows. Furthermore, you will also learn how to select ranges, move data to another location, copy data to another range, and use the Paste Special feature.

Managing Columns and Rows

As you enter and edit worksheet data, you might need to adjust the row and column structure to accommodate new data or remove unnecessary data. You can add rows and columns to add new data and delete data, columns, and rows that you no longer need. Adjusting the height and width of rows and columns, respectively, can often present the data better.

Insert Cells, Columns, and Rows

STEP I ▶▶ After you construct a worksheet, you might need to insert cells, columns, or rows to accommodate new data. For example, you might want to insert a new column to perform calculations or insert a new row to list a new product.

> **To insert a new column or row, complete the following set of steps:**
>
> 1. Click in the column or row.
> 2. Click the Insert arrow in the Cells group on the Home tab (see Figure 1.21).
> 3. Select Insert Sheet Columns or Insert Sheet Rows.

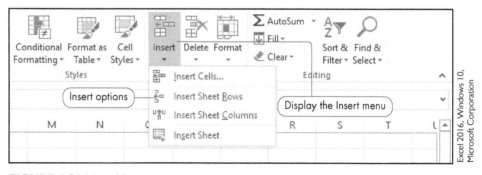

FIGURE 1.21 Insert Menu

Alternatively, you can use a shortcut menu. Right-click the column (letter) or row (number) heading. Then select Insert from the shortcut menu

Excel inserts new columns to the left of the current column and new rows above the active row. If the current column is column C and you insert a new column, the new column becomes column C, and the original column C data are now in column D. Likewise, if the current row is 5 and you insert a new row, the new row is row 5, and the original row 5 data are now in row 6. When you insert cells, rows, and columns, cell addresses in formulas adjust automatically.

Inserting a cell is helpful when you realize that you left out an entry after you have entered all of the data. Instead of inserting a new row or column, you just want to move the existing content down or over to enter the missing value. You can insert a single cell in a particular row or column.

To insert one or more cells, complete the following steps:

1. Click in the cell where you want the new cell.
2. Click the Insert arrow in the Cells group on the Home tab.
3. Select Insert Cells.
4. Select an option from the Insert dialog box (see Figure 1.22) to position the new cell and click OK.

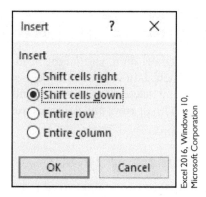

FIGURE 1.22 Insert Dialog Box

Alternatively, click Insert in the Cells group. The default action of clicking Insert is to insert a cell at the current location, which moves existing data down in that column only.

Delete Cells, Columns, and Rows

STEP 2 ⟫ If you no longer need a cell, column, or row, you should delete it. For example, you might want to delete a row containing a product you no longer carry. In these situations, you are deleting the entire cell, column, or row, not just the contents of the cell to leave empty cells. As with inserting new cells, columns, or rows, any affected formulas adjust the cell references automatically.

To delete a column or row, complete the following sets of steps:

1. Click the column or row heading for the column or row you want to delete.
2. Click Delete in the Cells group on the Home tab.

Alternatively, click in any cell within the column or row you want to delete, click the Delete arrow in the Cells group on the Home tab (see Figure 1.23), and then select Select Delete Sheet Columns or Delete Sheet Rows. Another alternative is to right-click the column letter or row number for the column or row you want to delete and then select Delete from the shortcut menu.

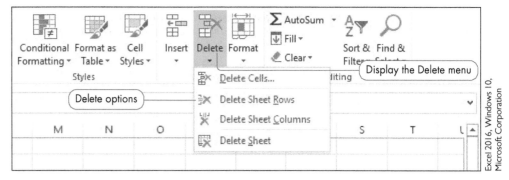

FIGURE 1.23 Delete Menu

To delete a cell or cells, complete the following steps:

1. Select the cell(s).
2. Click the Delete arrow in the Cells group.
3. Select Delete Cells to display the Delete dialog box (see Figure 1.24).
4. Click the appropriate option to shift cells left or up and click OK.

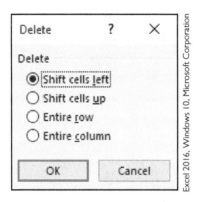

FIGURE 1.24 Delete Dialog Box

Alternatively, click Delete in the Cells group. The default action of clicking Delete is to delete the active cell, which moves existing data up in that column only.

Hide and Unhide Columns and Rows

If your worksheet contains information you do not want to display, hide some columns and/or rows before you print a copy for public distribution. However, the column or row is not deleted. If you hide column B, you will see columns A and C side by side. If you hide row 3, you will see rows 2 and 4 together. Figure 1.25 shows that column B and row 3 are hidden. Excel displays a double line between column headings (such as between A and C), indicating one or more columns are hidden, and a double line between row headings (such as between 2 and 4), indicating one or more rows are hidden.

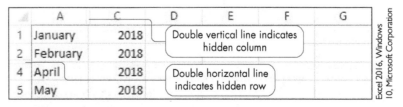

FIGURE 1.25 Hidden Columns and Rows

To hide a column or row, complete one of the following sets of steps:

1. Select a cell or cells in the column or row you want to hide.
2. Click Format in the Cells group on the Home tab (refer to Figure 1.26),
3. Point to Hide & Unhide.
4. Select Hide Columns or Hide Rows, depending on what you want to hide.

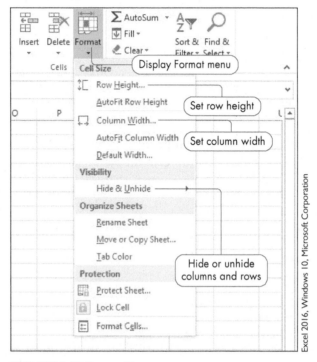

FIGURE 1.26 Format Menu

Alternatively, you can right-click the color or row heading(s) you want to hide. Then select Hide.

You can hide multiple columns and rows at the same time. To select adjacent columns (such as columns B through E) or adjacent rows (such as rows 2 through 4), drag across the adjacent column or row headings and use the Hide command.

To hide nonadjacent columns or rows, complete the following steps:

1. Press and hold Ctrl while you click the desired column or row headings.
2. Use any acceptable method to hide the selected columns or rows.

To unhide a column or row, complete the following steps:

1. Select the columns or rows on both sides of the hidden column or row. For example, if column B is hidden, drag across column letters A and C.
2. Click Format in the Cells group on the Home tab (refer to Figure 1.26), point to Hide & Unhide, and select Unhide Columns or Unhide Rows, depending on what you want to display again.

> **TIP: UNHIDING COLUMN A, ROW 1, AND ALL HIDDEN ROWS/COLUMNS**
> Unhiding column A or row 1 is different because you cannot select the row or column on either side. To unhide column A or row 1, type A1 in the Name Box and press Enter. Click Format in the Cells group on the Home tab, point to Hide & Unhide, and select Unhide Columns or Unhide Rows to display column A or row 1, respectively. If you want to unhide all columns and rows, click Select All (the triangle above the row 1 heading and to the left of the column A heading) and use the Hide & Unhide submenu.

Adjust Column Width

STEP 3 ▶▶ After you enter data in a column, you often need to adjust the ***column width***—the horizontal measurement of a column in a table or a worksheet. In Excel, column width is measured by the number of characters or pixels. For example, in the worksheet you created in Hands-On Exercises 1 and 2, the labels in column A displayed into column B when those adjacent cells were empty. However, after you typed values in column B, the labels in column A appeared cut off. You will need to widen column A to show the full name of all of your products.

TIP: POUND SIGNS DISPLAYED

Numbers and dates appear as a series of pound signs (######) when the cell is too narrow to display the complete value, and text appears to be truncated.

To widen a column to accommodate the longest label or value in a column, complete one of the following sets of steps:

- Point to the right vertical border of the column heading. When the pointer displays as a two-headed arrow, double-click the border. For example, if column B is too narrow to display the content in that column, double-click the right vertical border of the column B heading.
- Click Format in the Cells group on the Home tab (refer to Figure 1.26) and select AutoFit Column Width.

To adjust the width of a column to an exact width, complete the following sets of steps:

- Drag the vertical border to the left to decrease the column width or to the right to increase the column width. As you drag the vertical border, Excel displays a ScreenTip specifying the width (see Figure 1.27) from 0 to 255 characters and in pixels.
- Click Format in the Cells group on the Home tab (refer to Figure 1.26), select Column Width, type a value that represents the maximum number of characters to display in the Column width box in the Column Width dialog box, and then click OK.

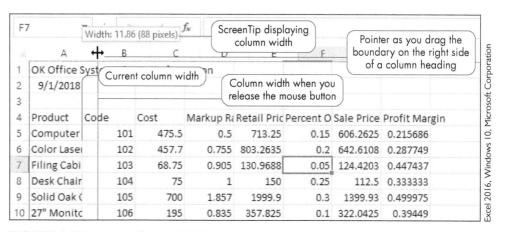

FIGURE 1.27 Increasing Column Width

Adjust Row Height

You can adjust the ***row height***—the vertical measurement of the row—in a way similar to how you change column width by double-clicking the border between row numbers or by selecting Row Height or AutoFit Row Height from the Format menu (refer to Figure 1.26). In Excel, row height is a value between 0 and 409 based on point size (abbreviated as pt) and pixels. Whether you are measuring font sizes or row heights, one point size is equal to 1/72 of an inch. Your row height should be taller than your font size. For example, with an 11-pt font size, the default row height is 15.

TIP: MULTIPLE COLUMN WIDTHS AND ROW HEIGHTS

You can set the size for more than one column or row at a time to make the selected columns or rows the same size. Drag across the column or row headings for the area you want to format, and set the size using any method.

Selecting, Moving, Copying, and Pasting Data

You may already know the basics of selecting, cutting, copying, and pasting data in other programs, such as Microsoft Word. These tasks are somewhat different when working in Excel.

Select a Range

STEP 4 ▶▶ A ***range*** refers to a group of adjacent or contiguous cells in a worksheet. A range may be as small as a single cell or as large as the entire worksheet. It may consist of a row or part of a row, a column or part of a column, or multiple rows or columns, but will always be a rectangular shape, as you must select the same number of cells in each row or column for the entire range. A range is specified by indicating the top-left and bottom-right cells in the selection. For example, in Figure 1.28, the date is a single-cell range in cell A2, the Color Laser Printer data are stored in the range A6:H6, the cost values are stored in the range C5:C10, and the sales prices and profit margins are stored in range G5:H10. A ***nonadjacent range*** contains multiple ranges, such as D5:D10 and F5:F10. At times, you will select nonadjacent ranges so that you can apply the same formatting at the same time, such as formatting the nonadjacent range D5:D10 and F5:F10 with Percent Style.

	A	B	C	D	E	F	G	H	I
1	OK Office Systems Pricing Information								
2	9/1/2018								
3									
4	Product	Code	Cost	Markup R	Retail Pric	Percent O	Sale Price	Profit Margin	
5	Computer System	101	475.5	0.5	713.25	0.15	606.2625	0.215686	
6	Color Laser Printer	102	457.7	0.755	803.2635	0.2	642.6108	0.287749	
7	Filing Cabinet	103	68.75	0.905	130.9688	0.05	124.4203	0.447437	
8	Desk Chair	104	75	1	150	0.25	112.5	0.333333	
9	Solid Oak Computer Desk	105	700	1.857	1999.9	0.3	1399.93	0.499975	
10	27" Monitor	106	195	0.835	357.825	0.1	322.0425	0.39449	
11									

Labels in figure: Rectangular range of cells; Range in a row; Single-cell range; Range in a column

FIGURE 1.28 Sample Ranges

Table 1.4 lists methods to select ranges, including nonadjacent ranges.

TABLE 1.4	Selecting Ranges
To Select:	**Do This:**
A range	Drag until you select the entire range. Alternatively, click the first cell in the range, press and hold Shift, and click the last cell in the range.
An entire column	Click the column heading.
An entire row	Click the row heading.
Current range containing data, including headings	Click in the range of data and press Ctrl+A.
All cells in a worksheet	Click Select All or press Ctrl+A twice.
Nonadjacent range	Select the first range, press and hold Ctrl, and select additional range(s).

A green border appears around a selected range. Any command you execute will affect the entire range. The range remains selected until you select another range or click in any cell in the worksheet.

> **TIP: NAME BOX**
> Use the Name Box to select a range by clicking in the Name Box, typing a range address such as B15:D25, and pressing Enter.

Move a Range

You can move cell contents from one range to another. For example, you might want to move an input area from the right side of the worksheet to above the output range. When you move a range containing text and values, the text and values do not change. However, any formulas that refer to cells in that range will update to reflect the new cell addresses.

To move a range, complete the following steps:

1. Select the range.
2. Click Cut in the Clipboard group to copy the range to the Clipboard (see Figure 1.29). Unlike cutting data in other Microsoft Office applications, the data you cut in Excel remain in their locations until you paste them elsewhere. A moving dashed green border surrounds the selected range and the status bar displays *Select destination and press ENTER or choose Paste.*
3. Ensure the destination range—the range where you want to move the data—is the same size or greater than the size of the cut range.
4. Click in the top-left corner of the destination range, and use the Paste command (see Figure 1.29). If any cells within the destination range contain data, Excel overwrites that data when you use the Paste command.

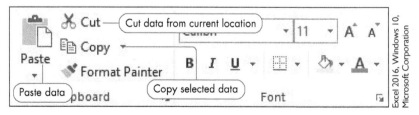

FIGURE 1.29 Cut, Copy, Paste

Copy and Paste a Range

STEP 5 >> You may want to copy cell contents from one range to another. When you copy a range, the original data remain in their original locations. For example, you might copy your January budget to another worksheet to use as a model for creating your February budget. Cell references in copied formulas adjust based on their relative locations to the original data. Furthermore, you want to copy formulas from one range to another range. In this situation where you cannot use the fill handle, you will use the Copy and Paste functions to copy the formula.

To copy a range, complete the following steps:

1. Select the range.
2. Click Copy in the Clipboard group (refer to Figure 1.29) to copy the contents of the selected range to the Clipboard. A moving dashed green border surrounds the selected range and the status bar displays *Select destination and press ENTER or choose Paste*.
3. Ensure the destination range—the range where you want to copy the data—is the same size or greater than the size of the copied range.
4. Click in the top-left corner of the destination range where you want the duplicate data, and click Paste (refer to Figure 1.29). If any cells within the destination range contain data, Excel overwrites that data when you use the Paste command. The original range still has the moving dashed green border, and the pasted copied range is selected with a solid green border. Figure 1.30 shows a selected range (A4:H10) and a copy of the range (J4:Q10). Immediately after you click Paste, the *Paste Options button* displays in the bottom-right corner of the pasted data. Click the arrow to select a different result for the pasted data.
5. Press Esc to turn off the moving dashed border around the originally selected range.

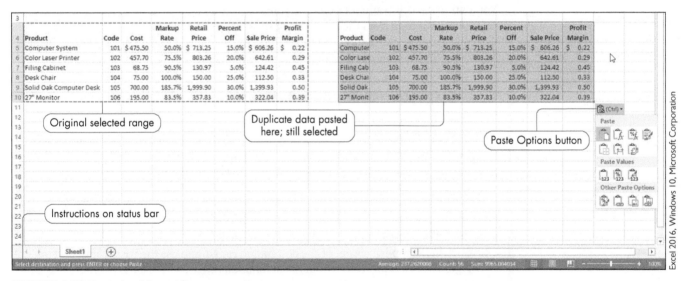

FIGURE 1.30 Copied and Pasted Range

TIP: COPY AS PICTURE
Instead of clicking Copy, if you click the Copy arrow in the Clipboard group, you can select Copy (the default option) or Copy as Picture. When you select Copy as Picture, you copy an image of the selected data. Then paste the image elsewhere in the workbook or in a Word document or PowerPoint presentation. However, when you copy the data as an image, you cannot edit individual cell data after you paste the image.

Use Paste Options and Paste Special

 STEP 6 ⟩⟩ Sometimes you might want to paste data in a different format than they are in the Clipboard. For example, you might want to preserve the results of calculations before changing the original data. To do this, you can paste the data as values. If you want to copy data from Excel and paste them into a Word document, you can paste the Excel data as a worksheet object, as unformatted text, or in another format.

> **To paste data from the Clipboard into a different format, complete the following steps:**
>
> 1. Click the Paste arrow in the Clipboard group (see Figure 1.31).
> 2. Point to command to see a ScreenTip and a preview of how the pasted data will look.
> 3. Click the option you want to apply.

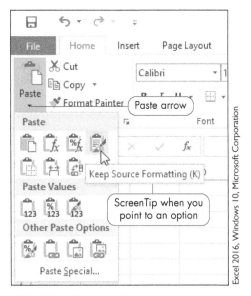

FIGURE 1.31 Paste Options

Table 1.5 lists and describes some of the options in the Paste gallery that opens when you click the Paste arrow in the Clipboard or the Paste Options button that displays immediately after you use Paste. Paste options enable you to paste content or attributes, such as a formula or format.

TABLE 1.5   Paste Options

Icon	Option Name	Paste Description
	Paste	Cell contents and all formatting from copied cells
	Formulas	Formulas, but no formatting, from copied cells
	Formulas & Number Formatting	Formulas and number formatting, such as Currency, but no font formatting, such as font color, fill color, or borders
	Keep Source Formatting	Cell contents and formatting from copied cells
	No Borders	Cell contents, number formatting, and text formatting except borders
	Keep Source Column Widths	Cell contents, number and text formatting, and the column width of the source data when pasting in another column
	Transpose	Transposes data from rows to columns and columns to rows
	Values	Unformatted values that are the results of formulas, not the actual formulas
	Values & Number Formatting	Values that are the results of formulas, not the actual formulas; preserves number formatting but not text formatting
	Values & Source Formatting	Values that are the results of formulas, not the actual formulas; preserves number and text formatting
	Formatting	Number and text formatting only from the copied cells; no cell contents
	Paste Link	Creates a reference to the source cells (such as =$G$15), not the cell contents; preserves number formatting but not text formatting
	Picture	Creates a picture image of the copied data; pasted data is not editable
	Linked Picture	Creates a picture with a reference to the copied cells; if the original cell content changes, so does the picture
	Paste Special	Opens the Paste Special dialog box (see Figure 1.32)

Pearson Education, Inc.

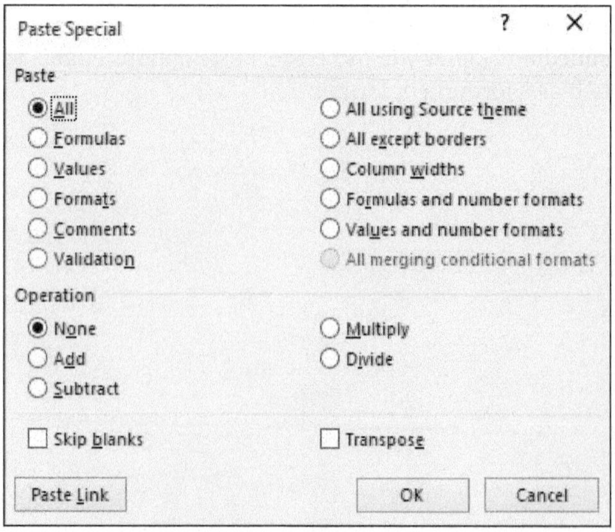

FIGURE 1.32 Paste Special Dialog Box

TIP: TRANSPOSING COLUMNS AND ROWS

After entering data into a worksheet, you might want to transpose the columns and rows so that the data in the first column appear as column labels across the first row, or the column labels in the first row appear in the first column. Figure 1.33 shows the original data with the months in column A and the utility costs in columns B, C, and D. In the transposed data, the months are shown in the first row, and each row contains utility information. The original formats (bold and right-aligned) are copied in the transposed data.

	A	B	C	D	E	F	G	H	I	J
1	**Month**	**Gas**	**Electric**	**Water**		**Month**	January	February	March	
2	January	$275	$120	$35		**Gas**	$275	$265	$200	
3	February	$265	$114	$35		**Electric**	$120	$114	$118	
4	March	$200	$118	$35		**Water**	$35	$35	$35	
5										(Ctrl)
6										

Excel 2016, Windows 10, Microsoft Corporation

FIGURE 1.33 Transposed Data

Copy Excel Data to Other Programs

You can copy Excel data and use it in other applications, such as in a Word document or in a PowerPoint slide show. For example, you might perform statistical analyses in Excel and copy the data into a research paper in Word. Or, you might want to create a budget in Excel and copy the data into a PowerPoint slide show for a meeting.

After selecting and copying a range in Excel, you must decide how you want the data to appear in the destination application. Click the Paste arrow in the destination application to see a gallery of options or to select the Paste Special option.

Quick Concepts

8. Give an example of when you would delete a column versus when you would hide a column. ***pp. 428-429***
9. When should you adjust column widths instead of using the default width? ***p. 431***
10. Why would you use the Paste Special options in Excel? ***p. 435***

Hands-On Exercises

Skills covered: Insert Columns
and Rows • Delete a Row • Hide a
Column • Adjust Column Width •
Adjust Row Height • Select a Range
• Move a Range • Copy and Paste a
Range • Use Paste Special

3 Worksheet Structure and Clipboard Tasks

You want to insert a column to calculate the amount of markup and delete a row containing data you no longer need. You also want to adjust column widths to display the labels in the columns. In addition, your supervisor asked you to enter data for a new product. Because it is almost identical to an existing product, you will copy the original data and edit the copied data to save time. You also want to experiment with the Paste Special option to see the results of using it in the OKOS workbook.

STEP 1 ›› INSERT A COLUMN AND ROWS

You decide to add a column to display the amount of profit. Because profit is a dollar amount, you want to keep the profit column close to another column of dollar amounts. Therefore, you will insert the profit column before the profit margin (percentage) column. You will insert new rows for product information and category names. Refer to Figure 1.34 as you complete Step 1.

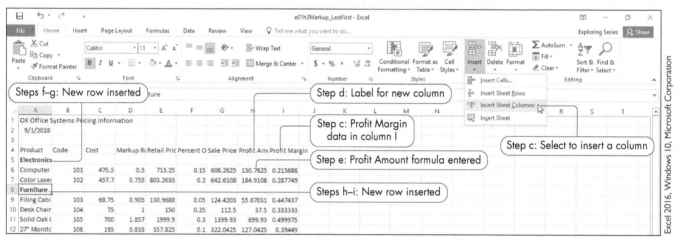

FIGURE 1.34 Column and Rows Inserted

a. Open *e01h2Markup_LastFirst* if you closed it at the end of Hands-On Exercise 2 and save it as **e01h3Markup_LastFirst**, changing h2 to h3.

b. Click **cell H5** (or any cell in column H).

You want to insert a column between the Sale Price and Profit Margin columns so that you can calculate the profit amount in dollars.

c. Click the **Insert arrow** in the Cells group and select **Insert Sheet Columns**.

You inserted a new blank column H. The data in the original column H are now in column I.

d. Click **cell H4**, type **Profit Amount**, and then press **Enter**.

e. Ensure the active cell is **cell H5**. Type **=G5-C5** and click **Enter**. Double-click the **cell H5 fill handle**.

You calculated the profit amount by subtracting the original cost from the sale price and then copied the formula down the column.

f. Right-click the **row 5 heading** and select **Insert** from the shortcut menu.

You inserted a new blank row 5, which is selected. The original rows of data move down a row each.

g. Click **cell A5**. Type **Electronics** and press **Ctrl+Enter**. Click **Bold** in the Font group on the Home tab.

You typed and applied bold formatting to the category name Electronics above the list of electronic products.

h. Right-click the **row 8 heading** and select **Insert** from the shortcut menu.

You inserted a new blank row 8. The data that was originally on row 8 is now on row 9.

i. Click **cell A8**. Type **Furniture** and press **Ctrl+Enter**. Click **Bold** in the Font group on the Home tab and save the workbook.

You typed and applied bold formatting to the category name Furniture above the list of furniture products.

STEP 2 ❯❯ DELETE A ROW AND HIDE A COLUMN

You just realized that you do not have enough filing cabinets in stock to offer on sale, so you need to delete the Filing Cabinet row. The item numbers are meaningful to you, but the numbers are not necessary for the other employees. Before distributing the worksheet to the employees, you want to hide column B. Because you might need to see that data later, you will hide it rather than delete it. Refer to Figure 1.35 as you complete Step 2.

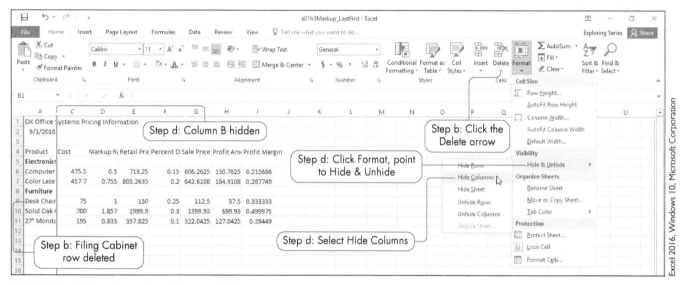

FIGURE 1.35 Row Deleted and Column Hidden

a. Click **cell A9** (or any cell on row 9), the row that contains the Filing Cabinet data.

b. Click the **Delete arrow** in the Cells group and select **Delete Sheet Rows**.

The Filing Cabinet row is deleted, and the remaining rows move up one row.

> **TROUBLESHOOTING:** If you accidentally delete the wrong row or accidentally selected Delete Sheet Columns instead of Delete Sheet Rows, click Undo on the Quick Access Toolbar to restore the deleted row or column.

c. Click the **column B heading**.

d. Click **Format** in the Cells group, point to **Hide & Unhide**, and then select **Hide Columns**.

Excel hides column B. You see a gap in column heading letters A and C, indicating column B is hidden instead of deleted.

e. Save the workbook.

As you review your worksheet, you notice that the labels in column A appear cut off. You will increase the width of that column to display the entire product names. In addition, you want to make row 1 taller. Refer to Figure 1.36 as you complete Step 3.

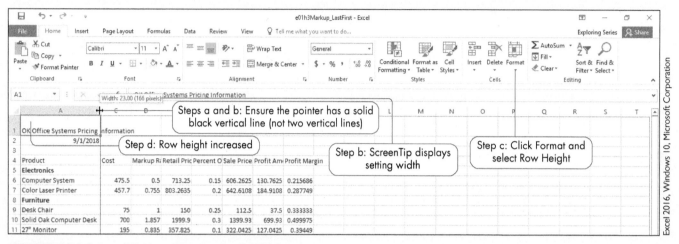

FIGURE 1.36 Column Width and Row Height Changed

a. Point to the right border of column A. When the pointer looks like a double-headed arrow with a solid black vertical line, double-click the border.

When you double-click the border between two columns, Excel adjusts the width of the column on the left side of the border to fit the contents of that column. Excel increased the width of column A based on the cell containing the longest content (the title in cell A1). You decide to adjust the column width to the longest product name instead.

b. Point to the right border of column A until the double-headed arrow appears. Drag the border to the left until the ScreenTip displays **Width: 23.00 (166 pixels)**. Release the mouse button.

You decreased the column width to 23 for column A. The longest product name is visible. You will not adjust the other column widths until after you apply formats to the column headings in Hands-On Exercise 4.

c. Click **cell A1**. Click **Format** in the Cells group and select **Row Height**.

The Row Height dialog box opens so that you can adjust the height of the current row.

d. Type **30** in the **Row height box** and click **OK**. Save the workbook.

You increased the height of the row that contains the worksheet title so that it is more prominent.

You want to move the 27" Monitor product to be immediately after the Color Laser Printer product. Before moving the 27" Monitor row, you will insert a blank row between the Color Laser Printer and Furniture rows. Refer to Figure 1.37 as you complete Step 4.

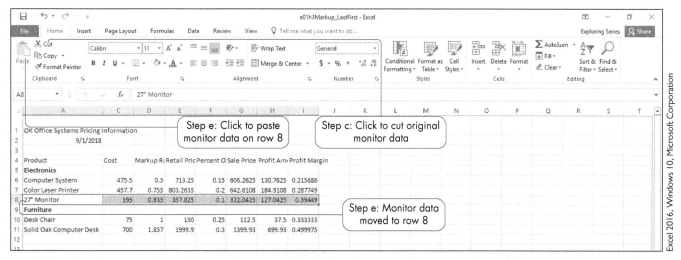

FIGURE 1.37 Row Moved to New Location

a. Right-click the **row 8 heading** and select **Insert** from the menu.

   You will insert a blank row so that you can move the 27" Computer Monitor data to be between the Color Laser Printer and Furniture rows.

b. Select the **range A12:I12**.

   You selected the range of cells containing the 27" Monitor data.

c. Click **Cut** in the Clipboard group.

   A moving dashed green border outlines the selected range. The status bar displays the message *Select destination and press ENTER or choose Paste*.

d. Click **cell A8**.

   This is the first cell in the destination range. If you cut and paste a row without inserting a new row first, Excel will overwrite the original row of data, which is why you inserted a new row in step a.

e. Click **Paste** in the Clipboard group and save the workbook.

   The 27" Monitor product data is now located on row 8.

STEP 5 ►► COPY AND PASTE A RANGE

Alesha told you that a new chair is on its way. She asked you to enter the data for the Executive Desk Chair. Because most of the data is the same as the Desk Chair data, you will copy the original Desk Chair data, edit the product name, and change the cost to reflect the cost of the second chair. Refer to Figure 1.38 as you complete Step 5.

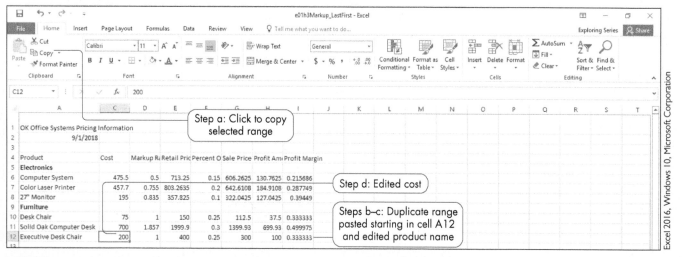

FIGURE 1.38 Data Copied and Edited

a. Select the **range A10:I10** and click **Copy** in the Clipboard group.

You copied the row containing the Desk Chair product data to the Clipboard.

b. Click **cell A12**, click **Paste** in the Clipboard group, and then press **Esc**.

The pasted range is selected in row 12.

c. Click **cell A12**, press **F2** to activate Edit Mode, press **Home**, type **Executive**, press **Spacebar**, and then press **Enter**.

You edited the product name to display Executive Desk Chair.

d. Change the value in **cell C12** to **200**. Save the workbook.

The formulas calculate the results based on the new cost of 200 for the Executive Desk Chair.

STEP 6 ►► USE PASTE SPECIAL

During your lunch break, you want to experiment with some of the Paste Special options. Particularly, you are interested in pasting Formulas and Value & Source Formatting. First, you will apply bold and a font color to the title to help you test these Paste Special options. Refer to Figure 1.39 as you complete Step 6.

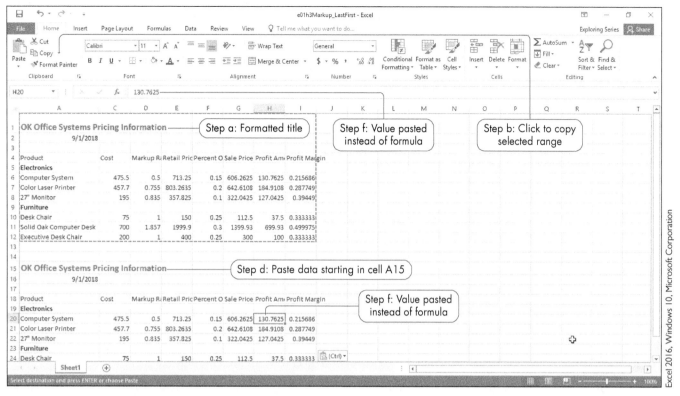

FIGURE 1.39 Paste Special Results

a. Click **cell A1**. Change the font size to **14**, click **Bold**, click the **Font Color arrow** in the Font group and then select **Gold, Accent 4, Darker 50%**.

You will format text to see the effects of using different Paste Special options.

b. Select the **range A1:I12** and click **Copy** in the Clipboard group.

c. Click **cell A15**, the top-left corner of the destination range.

d. Click the **Paste arrow** in the Clipboard group and point to **Formulas**, the second icon from the left in the Paste group.

Without clicking the command, Excel shows you a preview of what that option would do. The pasted copy would not contain the font formatting you applied to the title or the bold on the two category names. In addition, the pasted date would appear as a serial number. The formulas would be maintained.

e. Position the pointer over **Values & Source Formatting**, the first icon from the right in the Paste Values group.

This option would preserve the formatting, but it would convert the formulas into the current value results.

f. Click **Values & Source Formatting**, click **cell H6** to see a formula, and then click **cell H20**. Press **Esc** to turn off the border.

Cell H6 contains a formula, but in the pasted version, the equivalent cell H20 has converted the formula result into an actual value. If you were to change the original cost on row 20, the contents of cell H20 would not change. In a working environment, this is useful only if you want to capture the exact value in a point in time before making changes to the original data.

g. Save the workbook. Keep the workbook open if you plan to continue with the next Hands-On Exercise. If not, close the workbook and exit Excel.

Worksheet Formatting

After entering data and formulas, you should format the worksheet. A professionally formatted worksheet—through adding appropriate symbols, aligning decimals, and using fonts and colors to make data stand out—makes finding and analyzing data easy. You apply different formats to accentuate meaningful details or to draw attention to specific ranges in a worksheet.

In this section, you will learn to apply a cell style, different alignment options, including horizontal and vertical alignment, text wrapping, and indent options. In addition, you will learn how to format different types of values.

Applying Cell Styles, Alignment, and Font Options

STEP 1 ▶▶ Different areas of a worksheet should have different formatting. For example, the title may be centered in 16-pt size; column labels may be bold, centered, and Dark Blue font; and input cells may be formatted differently from output cells. You can apply different formats individually, or you can apply a group of formats by selecting a cell style. A ***cell style*** is a collection of format settings to provide a consistent appearance within a worksheet and among similar workbooks. A cell style controls the following formats: font, font color and font size, borders and fill colors, alignment, and number formatting.

> **To apply a cell style to a cell or a range of cells, complete the following steps:**
>
> 1. Click Cell Styles in the Styles group on the Home tab to display the Cell Styles gallery (see Figure 1.40).
> 2. Position the pointer over a style name to see a Live Preview of how the style will affect the selected cell or range. The gallery provides a variety of built-in styles to apply to your worksheet data.
> 3. Click a style to apply it to the selected cell or range.

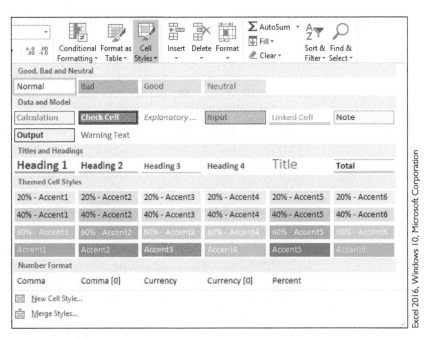

FIGURE 1.40 Cell Styles

Alignment refers to how data are positioned in the boundaries of a cell. Each type of data has a default alignment. Text aligns at the left cell margin, and dates and values align at the right cell margin. You should change the alignment of cell contents to improve the appearance of data within the cells. The Alignment group (see Figure 1.41) on the Home tab contains several commands to help you align and format data.

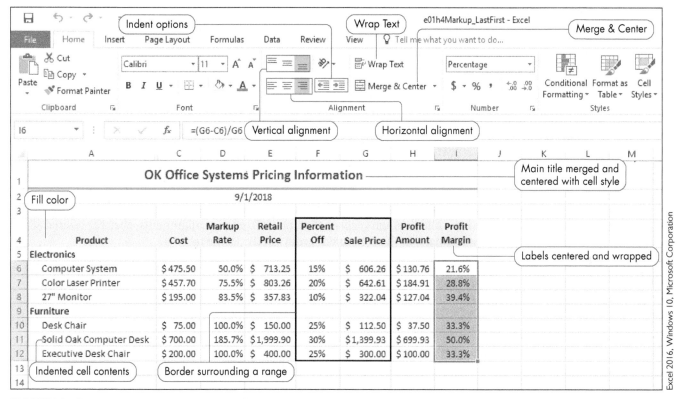

FIGURE 1.41 Alignment and Font Settings Applied

TIP: ALIGNMENT OPTIONS

The Format Cells dialog box contains additional alignment options. To open the Format Cells dialog box, click the Dialog Box Launcher in the Alignment group on the Home tab. The Alignment tab in the dialog box contains the options for aligning data.

Merge and Center Labels

STEP 1 ▶▶ You may want to place a title at the top of a worksheet and center it over the columns of data in the worksheet. You can center main titles over all columns in the worksheet, and you can center category titles over groups of related columns. You can also merge cells on adjacent rows.

To merge and center cells, complete the following steps:

1. Enter the text in the top left cell of the range.
2. Select the range of cells across which you want to center the label.
3. Click Merge & Center in the Alignment group on the Home tab.

Only data in the far left cell (or top-right cell) are merged. Any other data in the merged cells are deleted. Excel merges the selected cells together into one cell, and the merged cell address is that of the original cell on the left. The data are centered within the merged cell.

If you want to split a merged cell into multiple cells, click the merged cell and click Merge & Center. Unmerging places the data in the top-left cell.

For additional options, click the Merge & Center arrow. Table 1.6 lists the four merge options.

TABLE 1.6 Merge Options	
Option	**Results**
Merge & Center	Merges selected cells and centers data into one cell.
Merge Across	Merges the selected cells but keeps text left aligned or values right aligned.
Merge Cells	Merges a range of cells on multiple rows as well as in multiple columns.
Unmerge Cells	Separates a merged cell into multiple cells again.

Pearson Education, Inc.

Change Horizontal and Vertical Cell Alignment

STEP 2 ⟫ *Horizontal alignment* specifies the position of data between the left and right cell margins, and *vertical alignment* specifies the position of data between the top and bottom cell margins. Bottom Align is the default vertical alignment (as indicated by the light green background on the Ribbon), and Align Left is the default horizontal alignment for text. In Figure 1.41, the labels on row 4 have Center horizontal alignment and the title in row 1 has Middle Align vertical alignment. To change alignments, click the desired alignment setting(s) in the Alignment group on the Home tab.

> **TIP: ROTATE CELL DATA**
> People sometimes rotate headings in cells. To rotate data in a cell, click Orientation in the Alignment group and select an option, such as Angle Clockwise.

Wrap Text

Sometimes you have to maintain specific column widths, but the data do not fit entirely. Use *wrap text* to make data appear on multiple lines by adjusting the row height to fit the cell contents within the column width. Excel wraps the text on two or more lines within the cell. In Figure 1.41, the Markup Rate and Percent Off labels on row 4 are examples of wrapped text.

To wrap text within a cell, complete the following steps:

1. Click the cells or select the range of cells that contain labels that need to be wrapped.
2. Click Wrap Text in the Alignment group.

> **TIP: LINE BREAK IN A CELL**
> If a long text label does not fit well in a cell even after you have applied wrap text, you might want to insert a line break to display the text label on multiple lines within the cell. To insert a line break while you are typing a label, press Alt+Enter where you want to start the next line of text within the cell.

Increase and Decrease Indent

STEP 3 ⟫ Cell content is left-aligned or right-aligned based on the default data type. However, you can *indent* the cell contents to offset the data from its current alignment. For example, text is left-aligned, but you can indent it to offset it from the left side. Indenting helps others see the hierarchical structure of data. Accountants often indent the word Totals in financial statements so that it stands out from a list of items above the total row. Values are right-aligned by default, but you can indent a value to offset it from the right side of the cell. In Figure 1.41, Computer System and Desk Chair are indented.

To increase or decrease the indent of data in a cell, complete the following steps:

1. Click the cell that contains data.
2. Click Increase Indent or Decrease Indent in the Alignment group.

TIP: INDENTING VALUES

Values are right aligned by default. You should align the decimal places in a column of values. If the column label is wide, the values below it appear too far on the right. To preserve the values aligning at the decimal places, use the Align Right horizontal alignment and click Increase Indent to shift the values over to the left a little for better placement.

Apply Borders and Fill Color

STEP 4 ⟩⟩ You can apply a border or fill color to accentuate data in a worksheet. A **border** is a line that surrounds a cell or a range of cells. Use borders to offset some data from the rest of the worksheet data. To apply a border, select the cell or range that you want to have a border, click the Borders arrow in the Font group, and select the desired border type. In Figure 1.41, a border surrounds the range F4:G12. To remove a border, select No Border from the Borders menu.

Add some color to your worksheets to emphasize data or headers by applying a fill color. **Fill color** is a background color that displays behind the data in a cell so that the data stand out. You should choose a fill color that contrasts with the font color. For example, if the font color is Black, Text 1, you might choose Yellow fill color. If the font color is White, Background 1, you might apply Blue or Dark Blue fill color. The color palette contains two sections: Theme Colors and Standard Colors. The Theme Colors section displays variations of colors that match the current theme applied in the worksheet. For example, it contains shades of blue, such as Blue, Accent 5, Lighter 80%. The Standard Colors section contains basic colors, such as Dark Red and Red.

To apply a fill color, complete the following steps:

1. Select the cell or range that you want to have a fill color.
2. Click the Fill Color arrow on the Home tab to display the color palette.
3. Select the color choice from the Fill Color palette. In Figure 1.41, the column labels in row 4 contain the Blue, Accent 1, Lighter 80% fill color. If you want to remove a fill color, select No Fill from the bottom of the palette. Select More Colors to open the Colors dialog box, click the Standard tab or Custom tab, and then click a color.

For additional border and fill color options, complete the following steps:

1. Click the Dialog Box Launcher in the Font group to display the Format Cells dialog box.
2. Click the Border tab to select border options, including the border line style and color.
3. Click the Fill tab to set the background color, fill effects, and patterns.

Applying Number Formats

Values have no special formatting when you enter data. However, you should apply **number formats**, settings that control how a value is displayed in a cell. For example, you might want to apply either the Accounting or Currency number format to monetary values. Changing the number format changes the way the number displays in a cell, but the format does not change the stored value. If, for example, you enter 123.456 into a cell and format the cell with the Currency number type, the value shows as $123.46 onscreen, but the actual value 123.456 is used for calculations. When you apply a number format, specify the number of decimal places to display onscreen.

Apply a Number Format

STEP 5 »» The default number format is General, which displays values as you originally enter them. General number format does not align decimal points in a column or include symbols, such as dollar signs, percent signs, or commas. Table 1.7 lists and describes the primary number formats in Excel.

TABLE 1.7   Number Formats

Format Style	Display
General	A number as it was originally entered. Numbers are shown as integers (e.g., 12345), decimal fractions (e.g., 1234.5), or in scientific notation (e.g., 1.23E+10) if the number exceeds 11 digits.
Number	A number with or without the 1,000 separator (e.g., a comma) and with any number of decimal places. Negative numbers can be displayed with parentheses and/or red.
Currency	A number with the 1,000 separator and an optional dollar sign (which is placed immediately to the left of the number). Negative values are preceded by a minus sign or are displayed with parentheses or in red. Two decimal places display by default.
Accounting Number Format	A number that contains the $ on the left side of the cell and formats the value with a comma for every three digits on the left side of the decimal point and displays two digits to the right of the decimal point. Negative values display in parentheses, and zero values display as hyphens.
Comma Style	A number is formatted with a comma for every three digits on the left side of the decimal point and displays two digits to the right of the decimal point. Used in conjunction with Accounting Number Format to align commas and decimal places.
Date	The date in different ways, such as Long Date (March 14, 2016) or Short Date (3/14/16 or 14-Mar-16).
Time	The time in different formats, such as 10:50 PM or 22:50 (military time).
Percent Style	The value as it would be multiplied by 100 (for display purpose), with the percent symbol. The default number of decimal places is zero if you click Percent Style in the Number group or two decimal places if you use the Format Cells dialog box. However, you should typically increase the number of decimal points to show greater accuracy.
Fraction	A number as a fraction; use when no exact decimal equivalent exists. A fraction is entered into a cell as a formula such as =1/3. If the cell is not formatted as a fraction, the formula results display.
Scientific	A number as a decimal fraction followed by a whole number exponent of 10; for example, the number 12345 would appear as 1.23E+04. The exponent, +04 in the example, is the number of places the decimal point is moved to the left (or right if the exponent is negative). Very small numbers have negative exponents.
Text	The data left aligned; is useful for numerical values that have leading zeros and should be treated as text, such as postal codes or phone numbers. Apply Text format before typing a leading zero so that the zero displays in the cell.
Special	A number with editing characters, such as hyphens in a Social Security number.
Custom	Predefined customized number formats or special symbols to create your own customized number format.

The Number group on the Home tab contains commands for applying *Accounting Number Format*, *Percent Style*, and *Comma Style* numbering formats. You can click the Accounting Number Format arrow and select other denominations, such as English pounds or euros. For other number formats, click the Number Format arrow and select the numbering format you want to use. For more specific numbering formats than those provided, select More Number Formats from the Number Format menu or click the Number Dialog Box Launcher to open the Format Cells dialog box with the Number tab options readily available. Figure 1.42 shows different number formats applied to values.

	A	B
1	General	1234.567
2	Number	1234.57
3	Currency	$1,234.57
4	Accounting	$ 1,234.57
5	Comma	1,234.57
6	Percent	12%
7	Short Date	3/1/2018
8	Long Date	Thursday, March 1, 2018

Excel 2016, Windows 10, Microsoft Corporation

FIGURE 1.42 Number Formats

Increase and Decrease Decimal Places

STEP 5 ›› After applying a number format, you may need to adjust the number of decimal places that display. For example, if you have an entire column of monetary values formatted in Accounting Number Format, Excel displays two decimal places by default. If the entire column of values contains whole dollar values and no cents, displaying *.00* down the column looks cluttered. Decrease the number of decimal places to show whole numbers only.

> **To change the number of decimal places displayed, complete the following steps:**
>
> 1. Click the cell or select a range of cells containing values that need to have fewer or more decimal places.
> 2. Click Increase Decimal in the Number group on the Home tab to display more decimal places for greater precision or Decrease Decimal to display fewer or no decimal places.

Quick Concepts

11. What is the importance of formatting a worksheet? *p. 444*

12. Describe five alignment and font formatting techniques used to format labels that are discussed in this section. *p. 444*

13. What are the main differences between Accounting Number Format and Currency format? Which format has its own command on the Ribbon? *p. 448*

Hands-On Exercises

Watch the Video for this Hands-On Exercise!

MyITLab®
HOE4 Training

4 Worksheet Formatting

In the first three Hands-On Exercises, you entered data about products on sale, created formulas to calculate markup and profit, and inserted new rows and columns to accommodate the labels Electronics and Furniture to identify the specific products. You are ready to format the worksheet. Specifically, you will center the title, align text, format values, and apply other formatting to enhance the readability of the worksheet.

STEP 1 ▶▶ APPLY A CELL STYLE AND MERGE AND CENTER THE TITLE

To make the title stand out, you want to apply a cell style and center it over all the data columns. You will use the Merge & Center command to merge cells and center the title at the same time. Refer to Figure 1.43 as you complete Step 1.

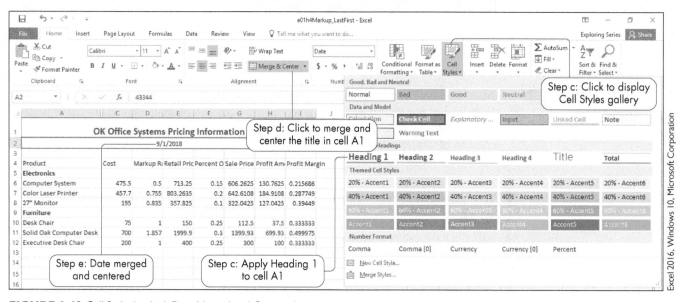

FIGURE 1.43 Cell Style Applied; Data Merged and Centered

a. Open *e01h3Markup_LastFirst* if you closed it at the end of Hands-On Exercise 3 and save it as **e01h4Markup_LastFirst**, changing h3 to h4.

b. Select the **range A15:I26** and press **Delete**.

You maintained a copy of your Paste Special results in the *e01h3Markup_LastFirst* workbook, but you do not need it to continue.

c. Select the **range A1:I1**, click **Cell Styles** in the Styles group on the Home tab, and then click **Heading 1**.

You applied the Heading 1 style to the range A1:I1. This style formats the contents with 15-pt font size, Blue-Gray, Text 2 font color, and a thick blue bottom border.

d. Click **Merge & Center** in the Alignment group.

Excel merges cells in the range A1:I1 into one cell and centers the title horizontally within the merged cell, which is cell A1.

> **TROUBLESHOOTING:** If you merge too many or not enough cells, unmerge the cells and start again. To unmerge cells, click in the merged cell. The Merge & Center command is shaded in green when the active cell is merged. Click Merge & Center to unmerge the cell. Then select the correct range to merge and use Merge & Center again.

e. Select the **range A2:I2**. Click **Merge & Center** in the Alignment group. Save the workbook.

> **TROUBLESHOOTING:** If you try to merge and center data in the range A1:I2, Excel will keep the top-left data only and delete the date. To merge separate data on separate rows, you must merge and center data separately.

STEP 2 » CHANGE CELL ALIGNMENT

You will wrap the text in the column headings to avoid columns that are too wide for the data, but which will display the entire text of the column labels. In addition, you will horizontally center column labels between the left and right cell margins. Refer to Figure 1.44 as you complete Step 2.

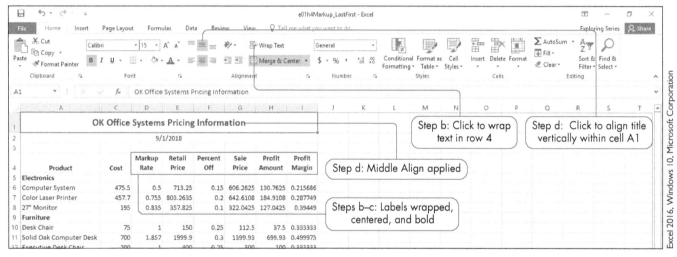

FIGURE 1.44 Formatted Column Labels

a. Select the **range A4:I4** to select the column labels.

b. Click **Wrap Text** in the Alignment group.

The multiple-word column headings are now visible on two lines within each cell.

c. Click **Center** in the Alignment group and click **Bold** in the Font group to format the selected column headings.

The column headings are centered horizontally between the left and right edges of each cell.

d. Click **cell A1**, which contains the title, click **Middle Align** in the Alignment group, and then save the workbook.

Middle Align vertically centers data between the top and bottom edges of the cell.

STEP 3 ➤➤ INCREASE INDENT

As you review the first column, you notice that the category names, Electronics and Furniture, do not stand out. You decide to indent the labels within each category to better display which products are in each category. Refer to Figure 1.45 as you complete Step 3.

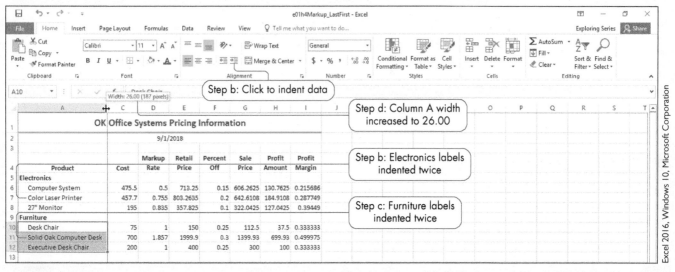

FIGURE 1.45 Indented Cell Contents

a. Select the **range A6:A8**, the cells containing Electronic products labels.

b. Click **Increase Indent** in the Alignment group twice.

The three selected product names are indented below the Electronics heading.

c. Select the **range A10:A12**, the cells containing furniture products, and click **Increase Indent** twice.

The three selected product names are indented below the Furniture heading. Notice that the one product name appears cut off.

d. Increase the column A width to **26.00**. Save the workbook.

STEP 4 ➤➤ APPLY A BORDER AND FILL COLOR

You want to apply a light blue fill color to highlight the column headings. In addition, you want to emphasize the percent off and sale prices. You will do this by applying a border around that range. Refer to Figure 1.46 as you complete Step 4.

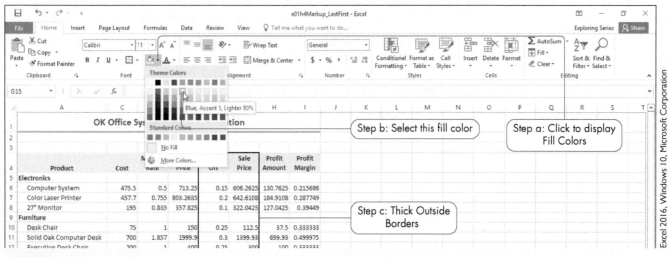

FIGURE 1.46 Border and Fill Color Applied

a. Select the **range A4:I4** and click the **Fill Color arrow** in the Font group.

b. Click **Blue, Accent 1, Lighter 80%** in the Theme Colors section (second row, fifth column).

You applied a fill color to the selected cells to draw attention to these cells.

c. Select the **range F4:G12**, click the **Border arrow** in the Font group, and then select **Thick Outside Borders**.

You applied a border around the selected cells.

d. Click in an empty cell below the columns of data to deselect the cells. Save the workbook.

STEP 5 ▶️ **APPLY NUMBER FORMATS AND INCREASE AND DECREASE DECIMAL PLACES**

You need to format the values to increase readability and look more professional. You will apply number formats and adjust the number of decimal points displayed. Refer to Figure 1.47 as you complete Step 5.

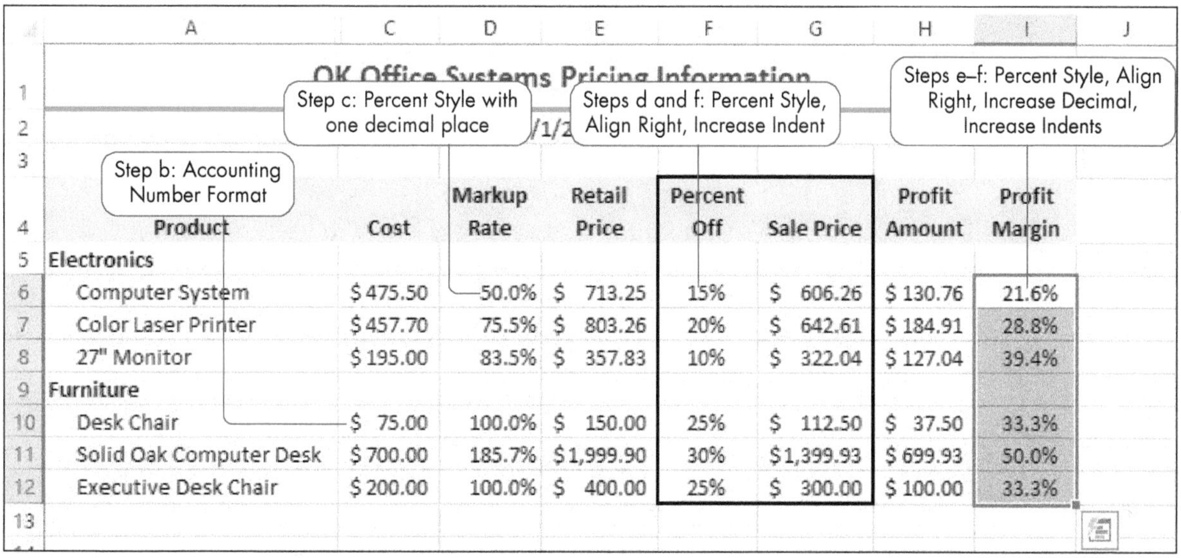

FIGURE 1.47 Number Formats and Decimal Places

a. Select the **range C6:C12.** Press and hold **Ctrl** as you select the **ranges E6:E12** and **G6:H12**.

Because you want to apply the same format to nonadjacent ranges, you hold down Ctrl while selecting each range.

b. Click **Accounting Number Format** in the Number group. If some cells display pound signs, increase the column widths as needed.

You formatted the selected nonadjacent ranges with the Accounting Number Format. The dollar signs align on the left cell margins and the decimals align.

c. Select the **range D6:D12**, click **Percent Style** in the Number group, and then click **Increase Decimal** in the Number group.

You formatted the values in the selected range with Percent Style and increased the decimal to show one decimal place to avoid misleading your readers by displaying the values as whole percentages.

d. Apply **Percent Style** to the **range F6:F12**.

e. Select the **range I6:I12**, apply **Percent Style**, and then click **Increase Decimal**.

f. Select the **range F6:F12**, click **Align Right**, and then click **Increase Indent** twice. Select the **range I6:I12**, click **Align Right**, and then click **Increase Indent**.

With values, you want to keep the decimal points aligned, but you can then use Increase Indent to adjust the indent so that the values appear more centered below the column labels.

g. Save the workbook. Keep the workbook open if you plan to continue with the next Hands-On Exercise. If not, close the workbook and exit Excel.

Worksheets, Page Setup, and Printing

When you start a new blank workbook in Excel, the workbook contains one worksheet named Sheet1. However, you can add additional worksheets. The text, values, dates, and formulas you enter into the individual worksheets are saved under one workbook file name. Having multiple worksheets in one workbook is helpful to keep related items together.

Although you might distribute workbooks electronically as email attachments or you might upload workbooks to a corporate server, you should prepare the worksheets in case you need to print them or in case others who receive an electronic copy of your workbook want to print the worksheets.

In this section, you will copy, move, and rename worksheets. You will also select options on the Page Layout tab. Specifically, you will use the Page Setup, Scale to Fit, and Sheet Options groups. After selecting page setup options, you will learn how to print your worksheet.

Managing Worksheets

Creating a multiple-worksheet workbook takes some planning and maintenance. Worksheet tab names should reflect the contents of the respective worksheets. In addition, you can insert, copy, move, and delete worksheets within the workbook. You can even apply background color to the worksheet tabs so that they stand out onscreen. Figure 1.48 shows a workbook in which the sheet tabs have been renamed, colors have been applied to worksheet tabs, and a worksheet tab has been right-clicked so that the shortcut menu appears.

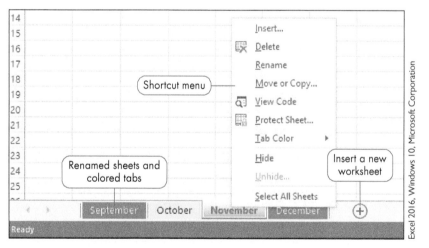

FIGURE 1.48 Worksheet Tabs

The active sheet tab has a green horizontal bar below the sheet name, and the sheet name is bold and green. If a color (such as Red) has been applied to the sheet tab, the tab shows in the full color when it is not active. When that sheet is active, the sheet tab color is a gradient of the selected color.

Insert and Delete a Worksheet

Sometimes you need more than one worksheet in the workbook. For example, you might want one worksheet for each month to track your monthly income and expenses for one year. When tax time comes around, you have all your data stored in one workbook file. You can insert additional, rename, copy, and move worksheets. Adding worksheets within one workbook enables to you save related sheets of data together.

To insert a new worksheet, complete one of the following sets of steps:

- Click New sheet to the right of the last worksheet tab.
- Click the Insert arrow (either to the right or below Insert) in the Cells group on the Home tab and select Insert Sheet.
- Right-click any sheet tab, select Insert from the shortcut menu (refer to Figure 1.48), click Worksheet in the Insert dialog box, and click OK.
- Press Shift+F11.

If you no longer need the data in a worksheet, delete the worksheet. Doing so will eliminate extra data in a file and reduce file size.

To delete a worksheet in a workbook, complete one of the following sets of steps:

- Click the Delete arrow (either to the right or below Delete) in the Cells group on the Home tab and select Delete Sheet.
- Right-click any sheet tab and select Delete from the shortcut menu (refer to Figure 1.48).

If the sheet you are trying to delete contains data, Excel will display a warning: *Microsoft Excel will permanently delete this sheet. Do you want to continue?* Click Delete to delete the worksheet, or click Cancel to keep the worksheet. If you try to delete a blank worksheet, Excel will not display a warning; it will immediately delete the sheet.

Copy or Move a Worksheet

STEP 1 ›› After creating a worksheet, you may want to copy it to use as a template or starting point for similar data. For example, if you create a worksheet for your September budget, you might want to copy the worksheet and easily edit the data on the copied worksheet to enter data for your October budget. Copying the entire worksheet saves you a lot of valuable time in entering and formatting the new worksheet, and it preserves the column widths and row heights. The process for copying a worksheet is similar to moving a sheet.

To copy a worksheet, complete one of the following sets of steps:

- Press and hold Ctrl as you drag the worksheet tab.
- Right-click the sheet tab, select Move or Copy to display the Move or Copy dialog box, select the *To book* and *Before sheet* options (refer to Figure 1.49), click the *Create a copy* check box, and then click OK.

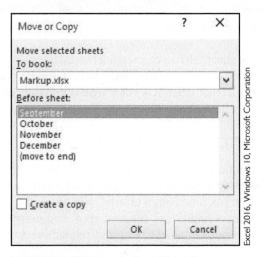

FIGURE 1.49 Move or Copy Dialog Box

You can arrange the worksheet tabs in a different sequence. For example, if the December worksheet is to the left of the October and November worksheets, move the December worksheet to be in chronological order.

To move a worksheet, complete one of the following sets of steps:

- Drag a worksheet tab to the desired location. As you drag a sheet tab, the pointer resembles a piece of paper. A down-pointing triangle appears between sheet tabs to indicate where the sheet will be placed when you release the mouse button.
- Click Format in the Cells group on the Home tab (refer to Figure 1.35) and select Move or Copy Sheet.
- Right-click the sheet tab you want to move and select Move or Copy to display the Move or Copy dialog box. You can move the worksheet within the current workbook or to a different workbook. In the *Before sheet* list, select the worksheet you want to come after the moved worksheet and click OK.

Rename a Worksheet

The default worksheet name Sheet1 does not describe the contents of the worksheet. You should rename worksheet tabs to reflect the sheet contents. For example, if your budget workbook contains monthly worksheets, name the worksheets September, October, etc. Although you can have spaces in worksheet names, keep worksheet names relatively short. The longer the worksheet names, the fewer sheet tabs you will see at the bottom of the workbook window without scrolling.

To rename a worksheet, complete one of the following sets of steps:

- Double-click a sheet tab, type the new name, and then press Enter.
- Click the sheet tab for the sheet you want to rename, click Format in the Cells group on the Home tab (refer to Figure 1.35), select Rename Sheet, type the new sheet name, and then press Enter.
- Right-click the sheet tab, select Rename from the shortcut menu (refer to Figure 1.48), type the new sheet name, and then press Enter.

> **TIP: CHANGE TAB COLOR**
> You can change the color of each worksheet tab to emphasize the difference among the sheets. For example, you might apply red to the September tab and yellow to the October tab. Right-click a sheet tab, select Tab Color, and select a color from the color palette.

Selecting Page Setup Options

The Page Setup group on the Page Layout tab contains options to set the margins, select orientation, specify page size, select the print area, and apply other options (see Figure 1.50). The Scale to Fit group contains options for adjusting the scaling of the spreadsheet on the printed page. When possible, use the commands in these groups to apply page settings. Table 1.8 lists and describes the commands in the Page Setup group.

FIGURE 1.50 Page Layout Tab

TABLE 1.8   Page Setup Commands

Command	Description
Margins	Displays a menu to select predefined margin settings. The default margins are 0.75" top and bottom and 0.7" left and right. You will often change these margin settings to balance the worksheet data better on the printed page. If you need different margins, select Custom Margins.
Orientation	Displays orientation options. The default page orientation is portrait, which is appropriate for worksheets that contain more rows than columns. Select landscape orientation when worksheets contain more columns than can fit in portrait orientation. For example, the OKOS worksheet might appear better balanced in landscape orientation because it has eight columns.
Size	Displays a list of standard paper sizes. The default size is 8 ½" by 11". If you have a different paper size, such as legal paper, select it from the list.
Print Area	Displays a list to set or clear the print area. When you have very large worksheets, you might want to print only a portion of that worksheet. To do so, select the range you want to print, click Print Area in the Page Setup group, and select Set Print Area. When you use the Print commands, only the range you specified will be printed. To clear the print area, click Print Area and select Clear Print Area.
Breaks	Displays a menu to insert or remove page breaks.
Background	Enables you to select an image to appear as the background behind the worksheet data when viewed onscreen (backgrounds do not appear when the worksheet is printed).
Print Titles	Enables you to select column headings and row labels to repeat on multiple-page printouts.

Pearson Education, Inc.

TIP: APPLYING PAGE SETUP OPTIONS TO MULTIPLE WORKSHEETS

When you apply Page Setup Options, those settings apply to the current worksheet only. However, you can apply page setup options, such as margins or a header, to multiple worksheets at the same time. To select adjacent sheets, click the first sheet tab, press and hold Shift, and click the last sheet tab. To select nonadjacent sheets, press and hold Ctrl as you click each sheet tab. Then choose the Page Setup options to apply to the selected sheets. When you are done, right-click a sheet tab and select Ungroup Sheets.

Specify Page Options

STEP 2 »» To apply several page setup options at once or to access options not found on the Ribbon, click the Page Setup Dialog Box Launcher. The Page Setup dialog box organizes options into four tabs: Page, Margins, Header/Footer, and Sheet. All tabs contain Print and Print Preview buttons. Figure 1.51 shows the Page tab.

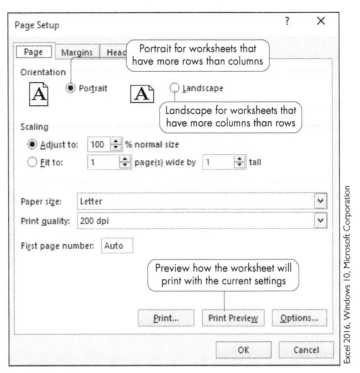

FIGURE 1.51 Page Setup Dialog Box: Page Tab

The Page tab contains options to select the orientation and paper size. In addition, it contains scaling options that are similar to the options in the Scale to Fit group on the Page Layout tab. You use scaling options to increase or decrease the size of characters on a printed page, similar to using a zoom setting on a photocopy machine. You might want to use the *Fit to* option to force the data to print on a specified number of pages.

Set Margin Options

The Margins tab (see Figure 1.52) contains options for setting the specific margins. In addition, it contains options to center the worksheet data horizontally or vertically on the page, which are used to balance worksheet data equally between the left and right margins or top and bottom margins, respectively.

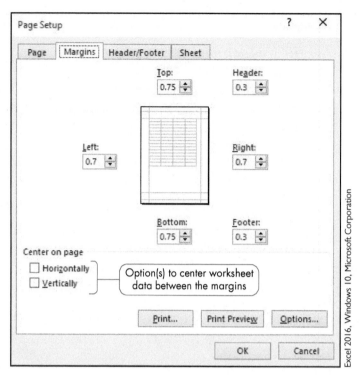

FIGURE 1.52 Page Setup Dialog Box: Margins Tab

Excel 2016, Windows 10, Microsoft Corporation

Create Headers and Footers

STEP 3)) The Header/Footer tab (see Figure 1.53) lets you create a header and/or footer that appears at the top and/or bottom of every printed page. Click the arrows to choose from several preformatted entries, or alternatively, click Custom Header or Custom Footer, insert text and other objects, and click the appropriate formatting button to customize the headers and footers. Use headers and footers to provide additional information about the worksheet. You can include your name, the date the worksheet was prepared, and page numbers, for example.

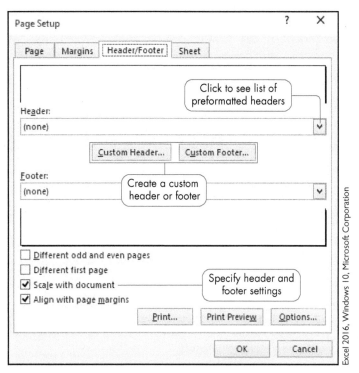

FIGURE 1.53 Page Setup Dialog Box: Header/Footer Tab

You can create different headers or footers on different pages, such as one header with the file name on odd-numbered pages and a header containing the date on even-numbered pages. Click the *Different odd and even pages* check box to select it in the Page Setup dialog box (see Figure 1.53).

You might want the first page to have a different header or footer from the rest of the printed pages, or you might not want a header or footer to show up on the first page but want the header or footer to display on the remaining pages. Click the *Different first page* check box to select it in the Page Setup dialog box to specify a different first page header or footer.

Instead of creating headers and footers using the Page Setup dialog box, you can click the Insert tab and click Header & Footer in the Text group. Excel displays the worksheet in Page Layout view with the insertion point in the center area of the header. Click inside the left, center, or right section of a header or footer. When you click inside a section within the header or footer, Excel displays the Header & Footer Tools Design contextual tab (see Figure 1.54). Enter text or insert data from the Header & Footer Elements group on the tab. Table 1.9 lists and describes the options in the Header & Footer Elements group. To get back to Normal view, click any cell in the worksheet and click Normal in the Workbook Views group on the View tab.

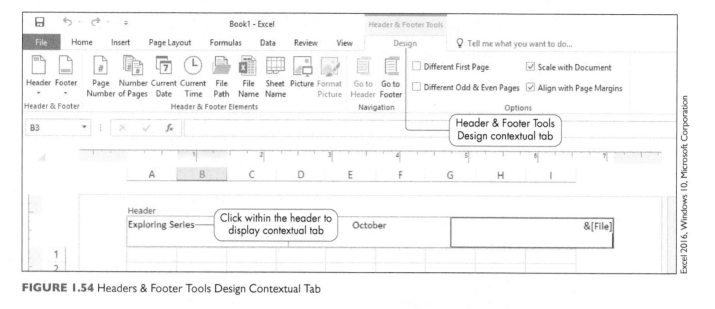

FIGURE 1.54 Headers & Footer Tools Design Contextual Tab

TABLE 1.9	Header & Footer Elements Options
Option Name	**Result**
Page Number	Inserts the code &[Page] to display the current page number.
Number of Pages	Inserts the code &[Pages] to display the total number of pages that will print.
Current Date	Inserts the code &[Date] to display the current date, such as 5/19/2018. The date is updated to the current date when you open or print the worksheet.
Current Time	Inserts the code &[Time] to display the current time, such as 5:15 PM. The time is updated to the current time when you open or print the worksheet.
File Path	Inserts the code &[Path]&[File] to display the path and file name, such as C:\Users\Keith\Documents\e01h4Markup. This information changes if you save the workbook with a different name or in a different location.
File Name	Inserts the code &[File] to display the file name, such as e01h4Markup. This information changes if you save the workbook with a different name.
Sheet Name	Inserts the code &[Tab] to display the worksheet name, such as September. This information changes if you rename the worksheet.
Picture	Inserts the code &[Picture] to display and print an image as a background behind the data, not just the worksheet.
Format Picture	Enables you to adjust the brightness, contrast, and size of an image after you use the Picture option.

TIP: VIEW TAB

If you click the View tab and click Page Layout, Excel displays an area *Click to add header* at the top of the worksheet.

Select Sheet Options

The Sheet tab (see Figure 1.55) contains options for setting the print area, print titles, print options, and page order. Some of these options are also located in the Sheet Options group on the Page Layout tab.

By default, Excel displays gridlines onscreen to show you each cell's margins, but the gridlines do not print unless you specifically select the Gridlines check box in the Page Setup dialog box or the Print Gridlines check box in the Sheet Options group on the Page Layout tab. In addition, Excel displays row (1, 2, 3, etc.) and column (A, B, C, etc.) headings onscreen. However, these headings do not print unless you click the *Row and column headings* check box in the Page Setup dialog box or click the Print Headings check box in the Sheet Options group on the Page Layout tab. For most worksheets, you do not need to print gridlines and row/column headings. However, when you want to display and print cell formulas instead of formula results, you might want to print the gridlines and row/column headings. Doing so will help you analyze your formulas. The gridlines help you see the cell boundaries, and the headings help you identify what data are in each cell. At times, you might want to display gridlines to separate data on a regular printout to increase readability.

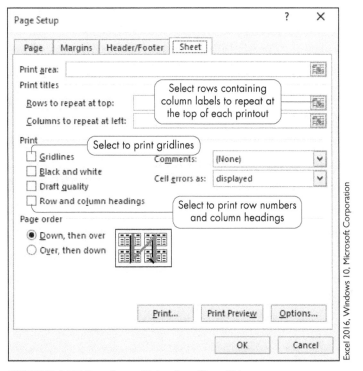

FIGURE 1.55 Page Setup Dialog Box: Sheet Tab

TIP: REPEATING ROWS AND COLUMNS

If you have spreadsheet data that would take more than one printed page, open the Page Setup dialog box, click the Sheet tab, click in the *Rows to repeat at top* box, and then select the row(s) containing column labels. That way, when the pages print, the rows containing the descriptive column labels will repeat at the top of each printed page so that you can easily know what data is in each column. Likewise, if the spreadsheet has too many columns to print on one page, you can click in the *Columns to repeat at left* box on the Sheet tab within the Page Setup dialog box and select the column(s) so that the row labels will display on the left side of each printed page.

Previewing and Printing a Worksheet

STEP 4 ❯❯ Microsoft Office Backstage view displays print options and displays the worksheet in print preview mode. Print preview helps you see before printing if the data are balanced on the page or if data will print on multiple pages.

You can specify the number of copies to print and which printer to use to print the worksheet. The first option in the Settings area specifies what to print. The default option is Print Active Sheets. You might want to choose other options, such as Print Entire Workbook or Print Selection, or specify which pages to print. If you are connected to a printer capable of duplex printing, you can print on only one side or print on both sides. You can also collate, change the orientation, specify the paper size, adjust the margins, and adjust the scaling.

The bottom of the Print window indicates how many pages will print. If you do not like how the worksheet will print, click Page Setup at the bottom of the print settings to open the Page Setup dialog box so that you can adjust margins, scaling, column widths, and so on until the worksheet data appear the way you want them to print.

TIP: PRINTING MULTIPLE WORKSHEETS

To print more than one worksheet at a time, select the sheets you want to print. To select adjacent sheets, click the first sheet tab, press and hold Shift, and click the last sheet tab. To select nonadjacent sheets, press and hold Ctrl as you click each sheet tab. When you display the Print options in Microsoft Office Backstage view, Print Active Sheets is one of the default settings. If you want to print all of the worksheets within the workbook, change the setting to Print Entire Workbook.

Quick Concepts

14. Why would you insert several worksheets of data in one workbook instead of creating a separate workbook for each worksheet? *p. 455*

15. Why would you select a *Center on page* option in the Margins tab within the Page Setup dialog box if you have already set the margins? *p. 459*

16. List at least five elements you can insert in a header or footer. *p. 462*

17. Why would you want to print gridlines and row and column headings? *p. 463*

Hands-On Exercises

Watch the Video
for this Hands-On
Exercise!

MyITLab®
HOE5 Training

Skills covered: Copy or Move a Worksheet • Rename a Worksheet • Group Worksheets • Set Page Orientation • Select Scaling Options • Set Margin Options • Create a Header or Footer • View in Print Preview • Print a Worksheet

5 Worksheets, Page Setup, and Printing

You are ready to complete the OKOS worksheet. You want to copy the existing worksheet so that you display the results on the original sheet and display formulas on the duplicate sheet. Before printing the worksheet for your supervisor, you want to make sure the data will appear professional when printed. You will adjust some page setup options to put the finishing touches on the worksheet.

STEP 1 ›› COPY, MOVE, AND RENAME A WORKSHEET

You want to copy the worksheet, move it to the right side of the original worksheet, and rename the duplicate worksheet so that you can show formulas on the duplicate sheet. Refer to Figure 1.56 as you complete Step 1.

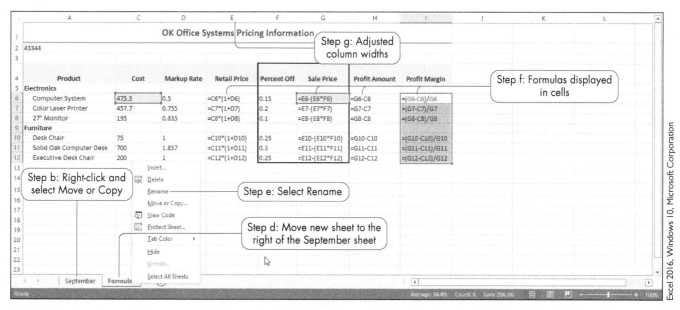

FIGURE 1.56 Worksheets

a. Open *e01h4Markup_LastFirst* if you closed it at the end of Hands-On Exercise 4 and save it as **e01h5Markup_LastFirst**, changing h4 to h5.

b. Right-click the **Sheet1 tab** at the bottom of the worksheet and select **Move or Copy**.

The Move or Copy dialog box opens so that you can move the existing worksheet or make a copy of it.

c. Click the **Create a copy check box** to select it and click **OK**.

The duplicate worksheet is named Sheet1 (2) and is placed to the left of the original worksheet.

d. Drag the **Sheet1 (2) worksheet tab** to the right of the Sheet1 worksheet tab.

The duplicate worksheet is now on the right side of the original worksheet.

e. Right-click the **Sheet1 sheet tab**, select **Rename**, type **September**, and then press **Enter**. Rename Sheet1 (2) as **Formulas**.

You renamed the original worksheet as September to reflect the September sales data, and you renamed the duplicate worksheet as Formulas to indicate that you will keep the formulas displayed on that sheet.

f. Press **Ctrl+`** to display the formulas in the Formulas worksheet.

g. Change these column widths in the Formulas sheet:

- Column A **(13.00)**
- Columns C and D **(6.00)**
- Columns E, G, H, and I **(7.00)**
- Column F **(5.00)**

You reduced the column widths so that the data will fit on a printout better.

h. Save the workbook.

STEP 2 ►► **SET PAGE ORIENTATION, SCALING, AND MARGIN OPTIONS**

Because the worksheet has several columns, you decide to print it in landscape orientation. You want to set a 1" top margin and center the data between the left and right margins. Furthermore, you want to make sure the data fits on one page on each sheet. Currently, if you were to print the Formulas worksheet, the data would print on two pages. Refer to Figure 1.57 as you complete Step 2.

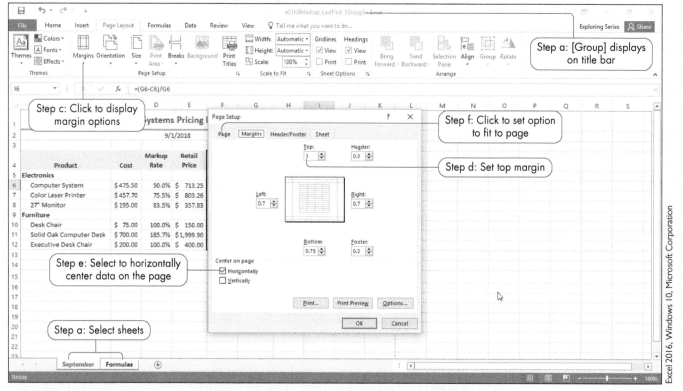

FIGURE 1.57 Page Setup Options Applied

a. Click the **September sheet tab**, press and hold down **Ctrl**, and then click the **Formulas sheet tab**.

Both worksheets are grouped together as indicated by [Group] after the file name on the title bar. Anything you do on one sheet affects both sheets.

b. Click the **Page Layout tab**, click **Orientation** in the Page Setup group, and then select **Landscape** from the list.

Because both worksheets are grouped, both worksheets are formatted in landscape orientation.

c. Click **Margins** in the Page Setup group on the Page Layout tab and select **Custom Margins**.

The Page Setup dialog box opens with the Margins tab options displayed.

d. Click the **Top spin arrow** to display **1**.

Because both worksheets are grouped, the 1" top margin is set for both worksheets.

e. Click the **Horizontally check box** to select it in the Center on page section.

Because both worksheets are grouped, the data on each worksheet are centered between the left and right margins.

f. Click the **Page tab** within the Page Setup dialog box, click **Fit to** in the Scaling section, and then click **OK**. Save the workbook.

The Fit to option ensures that each sheet fits on one page.

STEP 3 ›› CREATE A HEADER

To document the grouped worksheets, you want to include your name, the sheet name, and the file name in a header. Refer to Figure 1.58 as you complete Step 3.

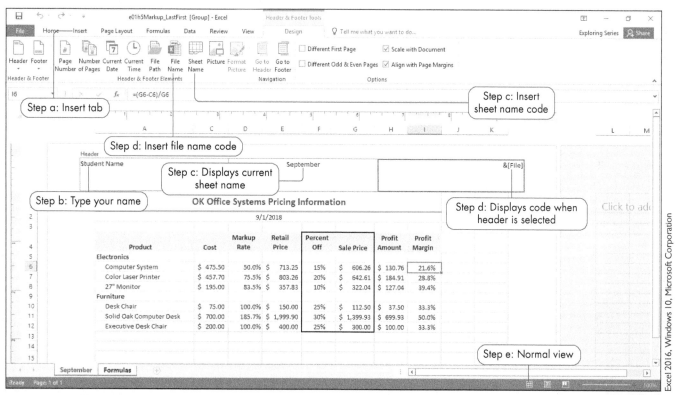

FIGURE 1.58 Header

a. Ensure the worksheets are still grouped, click the **Insert tab**, and then click **Header & Footer** in the Text group.

Excel displays the Header & Footer Tools Design contextual tab and the worksheet displays in Page Layout view, which displays the header area, margin space, and ruler. The insertion point blinks inside the center section of the header.

b. Click in the left section of the header and type your name.

c. Click in the center section of the header and click **Sheet Name** in the Header & Footer Elements group on the Design tab.

Excel inserts the code &[Tab]. This code displays the name of the worksheet. If you change the worksheet tab name, the header will reflect the new sheet name.

d. Click in the right section of the header and click **File Name** in the Header & Footer Elements group on the Design tab.

Excel inserts the code &[File]. This code displays the name of the file. Because the worksheets were grouped when you created the header, a header will appear on both worksheets. The file name will be the same; however, the sheet names will be different.

e. Click in any cell in the worksheet, click **Normal** on the status bar, and then save the workbook.

Normal view displays the worksheet, but does not display the header or margins.

f. Click the **Review tab** and click **Spelling** in the Proofing group. Correct all errors, if any, and click **OK** when prompted with the message, *Spell check complete. You're good to go!* Save the workbook.

You should always spell-check a workbook before publishing it.

STEP 4 》》 **VIEW IN PRINT PREVIEW AND PRINT**

Before printing the worksheets, you should preview it. Doing so helps you detect margin problems and other issues, such as a single row or column of data flowing onto a new page. Refer to Figure 1.59 as you complete Step 4.

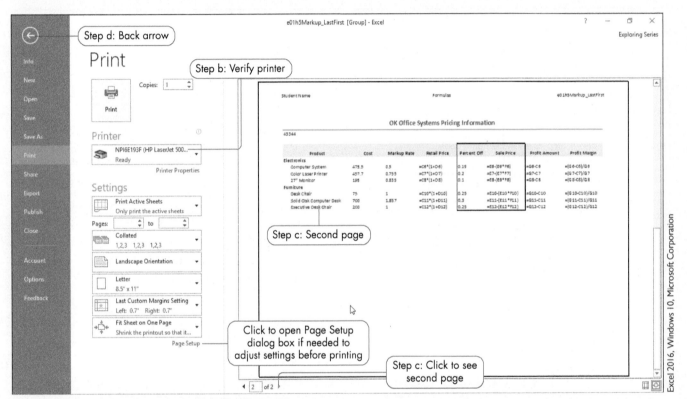

FIGURE 1.59 Worksheet in Print Preview

a. Click the **File tab** and click **Print**.

The Microsoft Office Backstage view displays print options and a preview of the worksheet.

b. Verify the Printer box displays the printer that you want to use to print your worksheet, and verify the last Settings option displays Fit Sheet on One Page.

The bottom of Backstage shows 1 of 2, indicating two pages will print.

c. Click **Next Page** to see the second page, which is the data on the Formulas worksheet, and verify the last Settings option displays Fit Sheet on One Page.

Check the Print Preview window to make sure the data are formatted correctly and would print correctly.

d. Click the **Back arrow** and save the workbook.

Although you did not print the worksheets, all the print options are saved.

e. Save and close the file. Based on your instructor's directions, submit e01h5Markup_LastFirst. Once the file is closed, the Formulas sheet may not display the formulas when you open the workbook again. If that happens, press **Ctrl+`** again.

Chapter Objectives Review

After reading this chapter, you have accomplished the following objectives:

1. Explore the Excel window.

- A worksheet is a single spreadsheet containing data. A workbook is a collection of one or more related worksheets contained in a single file.
- Identify Excel window elements: The Name Box displays the name of the current cell. The Formula Bar displays the contents of the current cell. The active cell is the current cell. A sheet tab shows the name of the worksheet.
- Identify columns, rows, and cells: Columns have alphabetical headings, such as A, B, C. Rows have numbers, such as 1, 2, 3. A cell is the intersection of a column and row and is indicated with a column letter and a row number.
- Navigate in and among worksheets: Use the arrow keys to navigate within a sheet, or use the Go To command to go to a specific cell. Click a sheet tab to display the contents on another worksheet.

2. Enter and edit cell data.

- You should plan the worksheet design by stating the purpose, deciding what output you need, and then identifying what input values are needed. Next, you enter and format data in a worksheet. Finally, you document, save, and then share a workbook.
- Enter text: Text may contain letters, numbers, symbols, and spaces. Text aligns at the left side of a cell.
- Use Auto Fill to complete a sequence. Auto Fill can automatically fill in sequences, such as month names or values, after you enter the first label or value. Double-click the fill handle to fill in the sequence.
- Enter values: Values are numbers that represent a quantity. Values align at the right side of a cell by default.
- Enter dates and times: Excel stores dates and times as serial numbers so that you can calculate the number of days between dates or times.
- Edit and clear contents: You might want to edit the contents of a cell to correct errors or to make labels more descriptive. Use the Clear option to clear the cell contents and/or formats.

3. Create formulas.

- A formula is used to perform a calculation. The formula results display in the cell.
- Use cell references in formulas: Use references, such as =B5+B6, instead of values within formulas.
- Apply the order of operations: The most commonly used operators are performed in this sequence: Parentheses, exponentiation, multiplication, division, addition, and subtraction.

- Use semi-selection to create a formula: When building a formula, click a cell containing a value to enter that cell reference in the formula.
- Copy formulas with the fill handle: Double-click the fill handle to copy a formula down a column.

4. Display cell formulas.

- By default, the results of formulas appear in cells.
- Display formulas by pressing Ctrl+`.

5. Manage columns and rows.

- Insert cells, columns, and rows: Insert a cell to move the remaining cells down or to the right. Insert a new column or row for data.
- Delete cells, columns, and rows: You should delete cells, columns, and rows you no longer need.
- Hide and unhide columns and rows: Hiding rows and columns protects confidential data from being displayed.
- Adjust column width: Double-click between the column headings to widen a column based on the longest item in that column, or drag the border between column headings to increase or decrease a column width.
- Adjust row height: Drag the border between row headings to increase or decrease the height of a row.

6. Select, move, copy, and paste data.

- Select a range: A range may be a single cell or a rectangular block of cells.
- Move a range to another location: After selecting a range, cut it from its location. Then select the top-left corner of the destination range to make it the active cell and paste the range there.
- Copy and paste a range: After selecting a range, click Copy, click the top-left corner of the destination range, and then click Paste to make a copy of the original range.
- Use Paste Options and Paste Special: The Paste Special option enables you to specify how the data are pasted into the worksheet.
- Copy Excel data to other programs: You can copy Excel data and paste it in other programs, such as in Word or PowerPoint.

7. Apply cell styles, alignment, and font options.

- Cell styles contain a collection of formatting, such as font, font color, font size, fill, and borders. You can apply an Excel cell style to save formatting time.
- Merge and center labels: Type a label in the left cell, select a range including the data you typed, and then click Merge & Center to merge cells and center the label within the newly merged cell.

- Change horizontal and vertical cell alignment: The default horizontal alignment depends on the data entered, and the default vertical alignment is Bottom Align.
- Wrap text: Use the Wrap Text option to present text on multiple lines in order to avoid having extra-wide columns.
- Increase and decrease indent: To indicate hierarchy of data or to offset a label, increase or decrease how much the data are indented in a cell.
- Apply borders and fill colors: Borders and fill colors help improve readability of worksheets.

8. Apply number formats.

- Apply a number format: The default number format is General, which does not apply any particular format to values. Apply appropriate formats to values to present the data with the correct symbols and decimal alignment. For example, Accounting Number Format is a common number format for monetary values.
- Increase and decrease decimal places: After applying a number format, you might want to increase or decrease the number of decimal places displayed.

9. Manage worksheets.

- Insert and delete a worksheet: You can insert new worksheets to include related data within one workbook, or you can delete extra worksheets you do not need.

- Copy or move a worksheet: Drag a sheet tab to rearrange the worksheets. You can copy a worksheet within a workbook or to another workbook.
- Rename a worksheet: The default worksheet tab name is Sheet1, but you should change the name to describe the contents of the worksheet.

10. Select page setup options.

- The Page Layout tab on the Ribbon contains options for setting margins, selecting orientation, specifying page size, selecting the print area, and applying other settings.
- Specify page options: Page options include orientation, paper size, and scaling.
- Set margin options: You can set the left, right, top, and bottom margins. In addition, you can center worksheet data horizontally and vertically on a page.
- Create headers and footers: Insert a header or footer to display documentation, such as your name, date, time, and worksheet tab name.
- Select sheet options: Sheet options control the print area, print titles, print options, and page order.

11. Preview and print a worksheet.

- Before printing a worksheet, you should display a preview to ensure the data will print correctly. The Print Preview helps you see if margins are correct or if isolated rows or columns will print on separate pages.
- After making appropriate adjustments, you can print the worksheet.

Key Terms Matching

Match the key terms with their definitions. Write the key term letter by the appropriate numbered definition.

a. Alignment
b. Auto Fill
c. Cell
d. Column width
e. Fill color
f. Fill handle
g. Formula
h. Formula Bar
i. Input area
j. Name Box

k. Order of operations
l. Output area
m. Range
n. Row height
o. Sheet tab
p. Text
q. Value
r. Workbook
s. Worksheet
t. Wrap text

1. _____ A spreadsheet that contains formulas, functions, values, text, and visual aids. **p. 404**

2. _____ A file containing related worksheets. **p. 404**

3. _____ A range of cells containing values for variables used in formulas. **p. 407**

4. _____ A range of cells containing results based on manipulating the variables. **p. 407**

5. _____ Identifies the address of the current cell. **p. 405**

6. _____ Displays the content (text, value, date, or formula) in the active cell. **p. 405**

7. _____ Displays the name of a worksheet within a workbook. **p. 405**

8. _____ The intersection of a column and row. **p. 406**

9. _____ Includes letters, numbers, symbols, and spaces. **p. 408**

10. _____ A number that represents a quantity or an amount. **p. 411**

11. _____ Rules that control the sequence in which Excel performs arithmetic operations. **p. 418**

12. _____ Enables you to copy the contents of a cell or cell range or to continue a sequence by dragging the fill handle over an adjacent cell or range of cells. **p. 409**

13. _____ A small green square at the bottom-right corner of a cell. **p. 410**

14. _____ The horizontal measurement of a column. **p. 431**

15. _____ The vertical measurement of a row. **p. 432**

16. _____ A rectangular group of cells. **p. 432**

17. _____ The position of data between the cell margins. **p. 445**

18. _____ Formatting that enables a label to appear on multiple lines within the current cell. **p. 446**

19. _____ The background color appearing behind data in a cell. **p. 447**

20. _____ A combination of cell references, operators, values, and/or functions used to perform a calculation. **p. 417**

Multiple Choice

I. Which step is *not* part of planning a worksheet design?

(a) Decide what input values are needed.

(b) State the purpose of the worksheet.

(c) Decide what outputs are needed to achieve the purpose.

(d) Enter labels, values, and formulas.

2. You just copied a range of data containing formulas. However, you want to preserve the formula results and the original number and text formatting in the pasted range. Which paste option would you select?

(a) Formulas

(b) Keep Source Formatting

(c) Values & Source Formatting

(d) Values & Number Formatting

3. Given the formula =B1*B2+B3/B4^2, what operation is calculated first?

(a) B1*B2

(b) B2+B3

(c) B3/B4

(d) B4^2

4. How can you display formulas within the cells instead of the cell results?

(a) Press Ctrl+G.

(b) Press Ctrl+`.

(c) Click Cell References on the Home tab.

(d) Press Ctrl+C.

5. What is a fast way to apply several formats at one time?

(a) Click each one individually.

(b) Apply a cell style.

(c) Use Auto Fill.

(d) Use Copy and Paste options.

6. Which of the following is *not* an alignment option?

(a) Increase Indent

(b) Merge & Center

(c) Fill Color

(d) Wrap Text

7. Which of the following characteristics is *not* applicable to the Accounting Number Format?

(a) Dollar sign immediately on the left side of the value

(b) Commas to separate thousands

(c) Two decimal places

(d) Zero values displayed as hyphens

8. You selected and copied worksheet data containing formulas. However, you want the pasted copy to contain the current formula results rather than formulas. What do you do?

(a) Click Paste in the Clipboard group on the Home tab.

(b) Click the Paste arrow in the Clipboard group and select Formulas.

(c) Click the Paste arrow in the Clipboard group and select Values & Source Formatting.

(d) Display the Paste Special dialog box and select Formulas & Number Formatting.

9. Assume that the data on a worksheet consume a whole printed page and a couple of columns on a second page. You can do all of the following *except* what to force the data to print all on one page?

(a) Decrease the Scale value.

(b) Increase the left and right margins.

(c) Decrease column widths if possible.

(d) Select a smaller range as the print area.

10. What should you do if you see pound signs (###) instead of values or results of formulas?

(a) Increase the zoom percentage.

(b) Delete the column.

(c) Adjust the row height.

(d) Increase the column width.

Practice Exercises

Mathematics Review

You want to brush up on your math skills to test your logic by creating formulas in Excel. You realize that you should avoid values in formulas most of the time. Therefore, you created an input area that contains values you will use in your formulas. To test your knowledge of formulas, you will create an output area that will contain a variety of formulas using cell references from the input area. You will include a formatted title, the date prepared, and your name. After creating and verifying formula results, you will change input values and observe changes in the formula results. You want to display cell formulas, so you will create a picture copy of the formulas view. Refer to Figure 1.60 as you complete this exercise.

	A	B	C	D	E
1				Excel Formulas and Order of Precedence	
2	Date Created:	42614		Student Name	
3					
4	Input Area:			Output Area:	
5	First Value	2		Sum of 1st and 2nd values	=B5+B6
6	Second Value	4		Difference between 4th and 1st values	=B8-B5
7	Third Value	6		Product of 2nd and 3rd values	=B6*B7
8	Fourth Value	8		Quotient of 3rd and 1st values	=B7/B5
9				2nd value to the power of 3rd value	=B6^B7
10				1st value added to product of 2nd and 4th values and difference between sum and 3rd value	=B5+B6*B8-B7
11				Product of sum of 1st and 2nd and difference between 4th and 3rd values	=(B5+B6)*(B8-B7)
12				Product of 1st and 2nd added to product of 3rd and 4th values	=(B5*B6)+(B7*B8)

FIGURE 1.60 Formula Practice

a. Open *e01p1Math* and save it as **e01p1Math_LastFirst**.

b. Type the current date in **cell B2** in this format: 9/1/2018. Type your first and last names in **cell D2**.

c. Adjust the column widths by doing the following:
   - Click in any cell in column A and click **Format** in the Cells group.
   - Select **Column Width**, type **12.57** in the Column width box, and then click **OK**.
   - Click in any cell in column B and set the width to **11**.
   - Click in any cell in column D and set the width to **35.57**.

d. Select the **range A1:E1**, click **Merge & Center** in the Alignment group, click **Bold** in the Font group, and then change the font size to **14**.

e. Select the **range B5:B8** and click **Center** in the Alignment group.

f. Select the **range D10:D12** and click **Wrap Text** in the Alignment group.

g. Enter the following formulas in column E:
   - Click **cell E5**. Type **=B5+B6** and press **Enter**. Excel adds the value stored in cell B5 (1) to the value stored in cell B6 (2). The result (3) appears in cell E5, as described in cell D5.
   - Enter appropriate formulas in **cells E6:E8**, pressing **Enter** after entering each formula. Subtract to calculate a difference, multiply to calculate a product, and divide to calculate a quotient.
   - Type **=B6^B7** in **cell E9** and press **Enter**. Calculate the answer: 2*2*2 = 8.
   - Enter **=B5+B6*B8-B7** in **cell E10** and press **Enter**. Calculate the answer: 2*4 = 8; 1+8 = 9; 9-3 = 6. Multiplication occurs first, followed by addition, and finally subtraction.
   - Enter **=(B5+B6)*(B8-B7)** in **cell E11** and press **Enter**. Calculate the answer: 1+2 = 3; 4-3 = 1; 3*1 = 3. This formula is almost identical to the previous formula; however, calculations in parentheses occur before the multiplication.
   - Enter **=B5*B6+B7*B8** in **cell E12** and press **Enter**. Calculate the answer: 1*2 = 2; 3*4 = 12; 2+12 = 14.

Excel 2016, Windows 10, Microsoft Corporation

h. Edit a formula and the input values:

- Click **cell E12** and click in the Formula Bar to edit the formula. Add parentheses as shown: **=(B5*B6)+(B7*B8)** and click **Enter** to the left side of the Formula Bar. The answer is still 14. The parentheses do not affect order of operations because multiplication occurred before the addition. The parentheses help improve the readability of the formula.
- Type **2** in **cell B5**, **4** in **cell B6**, **6** in **cell B7**, and **8** in **cell B8**.
- Double-check the results of the formulas using a calculator or your head. The new results in cells E5:E12 should be 6, 6, 24, 3, 4096, 28, 12, and 56, respectively.

i. Double-click the **Sheet1 tab**, type **Results**, and then press **Enter**. Right-click the **Results sheet tab**, select **Move or Copy**, click **(move to end)** in the *Before sheet* section, click the **Create a copy check box** to select it, and click **OK**. Double-click the **Results (2) sheet tab**, type **Formulas**, and then press **Enter**.

j. Ensure that the Formulas sheet tab is active, click the **Formulas sheet tab** and click **Show Formulas** in the Formula Auditing group. Double-click between the column A and column B headings to adjust the column A width. Double-click between the column B and column C headings to adjust the column B width. Set **24.00 width** for column D.

k. Ensure that the Formulas worksheet is active, click the **Page Layout tab**, and do the following:

- Click the **Gridlines Print check box** to select it in the Sheet Options group.
- Click the **Headings Print check box** to select it in the Sheet Options group.

l. Click the **Results sheet tab**, press and hold **Ctrl**, and click the **Formulas sheet tab** to select both worksheets. Do the following:

- Click **Orientation** in the Page Setup group and select **Landscape**.
- Click the **Insert tab**, click **Header & Footer** in the Text group. Click **Go to Footer** in the Navigation group.
- Type your name on the left side of the footer.
- Click in the center section of the footer and click **Sheet Name** in the Header & Footer Elements group.
- Click in the right section of the footer and click **File Name** in the Header & Footer elements group.

m. Click in the worksheet, press **Ctrl+Home**, and click **Normal View** on the status bar.

n. Click the **File tab** and click **Print**. Verify that each worksheet will print on one page. Press **Esc** to close the Print Preview, and right-click the worksheet tab and click **Ungroup Sheets**.

o. Save and close the file. Based on your instructor's directions, submit e01p1Math_LastFirst.

2 Calendar Formatting

FROM SCRATCH

You want to create a calendar for July 2018. The calendar will enable you to practice alignment settings, including center, merge and center, and indents. In addition, you will need to adjust column widths and increase row height to create cells large enough to enter important information, such as birthdays, in your calendar. You will create a formula and use Auto Fill to complete the days of the week and the days within each week. To improve the appearance of the calendar, you will add fill colors, font colors, and borders to create a red, white, and blue effect to celebrate Independence Day. Refer to Figure 1.61 as you complete this exercise.

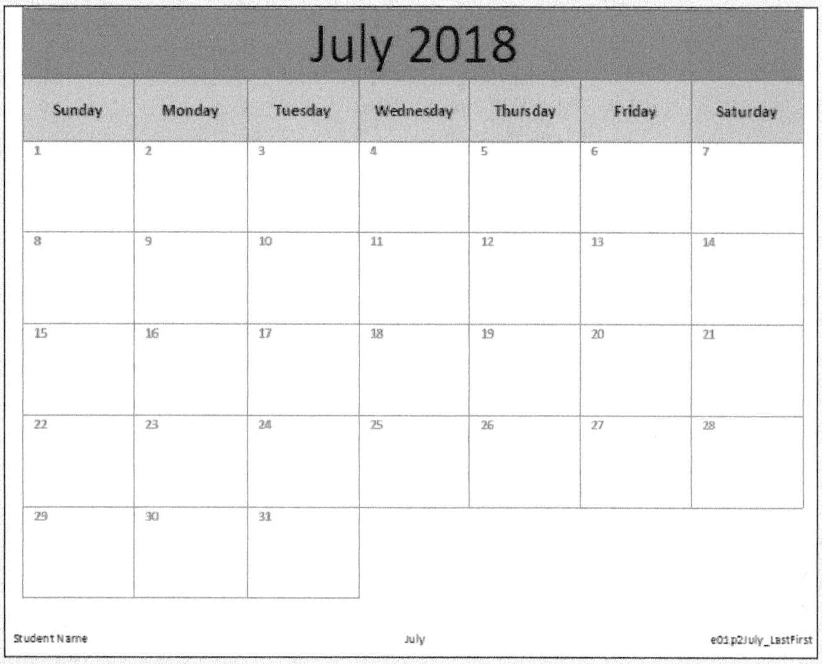

July 2018

Sunday	Monday	Tuesday	Wednesday	Thursday	Friday	Saturday
1	2	3	4	5	6	7
8	9	10	11	12	13	14
15	16	17	18	19	20	21
22	23	24	25	26	27	28
29	30	31				

Student Name   July   e01p2July_LastFirst

Excel 2016, Windows 10, Microsoft Corporation

FIGURE 1.61 Calendar

a. Click the **File tab**, select **New**, and click **Blank workbook**. Save the workbook as **e01p2July_LastFirst**.

b. Type **'July 2018** in **cell A1** and click **Enter** on the left side of the Formula Bar.

> **TROUBLESHOOTING:** If you do not type the apostrophe before July 2018, the cell will display July-18 instead of July 2018.

c. Format the title:
   - Select the **range A1:G1** and click **Merge & Center** in the Alignment group.
   - Change the font size to **48**.
   - Click the **Fill Color arrow** and click **Blue** in the Standard Colors section of the color palette.
   - Click **Middle Align** in the Alignment group.

d. Complete the days of the week:
   - Type **Sunday** in **cell A2** and click **Enter** to the left side of the Formula Bar.
   - Drag the **cell A2 fill handle** across the row through **cell G2** to use Auto Fill to complete the rest of the weekdays.
   - Ensure that the **range A2:G2** is selected. Click the **Fill Color arrow** and select **Blue, Accent 1, Lighter 40%** in the Theme Colors section of the color palette.
   - Apply bold and change the font size to **14 size** to the selected range.
   - Click **Middle Align** and click **Center** in the Alignment group to format the selected range.

e. Complete the days of the month:
   - Type **1** in **cell A3** and press **Ctrl+Enter**. Drag the **cell A3 fill handle** across the row through **cell G3**.
   - Click **Auto Fill Options** in the bottom-right corner of the copied data and select **Fill Series** to change the numbers to 1 through 7.
   - Type **=A3+7** in **cell A4** and press **Ctrl+Enter**. Usually you avoid numbers in formulas, but the number of days in a week is always 7. Drag the **cell A4 fill handle** down through **cell A7** to get the date for each Sunday in July.

- Keep the **range A4:A7** selected and drag the fill handle across through **cell G7**. This action copies the formulas to fill in the days in the month.
- Select the **range D7:G7** and press **Delete** to delete the extra days 32 through 35 because July has only 31 days.

f. Format the columns and rows:
- Select **columns A:G**. Click **Format** in the Cells group, select **Column Width**, type **16** in the Column width box, and then click **OK**.
- Select **row 2**. Click **Format** in the Cells group, select **Row Height**, type **54**, and then click **OK**.
- Select **rows 3:7**. Set the row height to **80**.

g. Apply borders around the cells:
- Select the **range A1:G7**. Click the **Borders arrow** in the Font group and select **More Borders** to display the Format Cells dialog box with the Border tab selected.
- Click the **Color arrow** and select **Red**.
- Click **Outline** and **Inside** in the Presets section. Click **OK**. This action applies a red border inside and outside the selected range.

h. Clear the border formatting around cells that do not have days:
- Select the **range D7:G7**.
- Click **Clear** in the Editing group and select **Clear All**. This action removes the red borders around the cells after the last day of the month.

i. Format the days in the month:
- Select the **range A3:G7**. Click **Top Align** and **Align Left** in the Alignment group.
- Click **Increase Indent** in the Alignment group to offset the days from the border.
- Click **Bold** in the Font group, click the **Font Color arrow** and select **Blue**, and click the **Font Size arrow**, and then select **12**.

j. Double-click the **Sheet1 tab**, type **July**, and then press **Enter**.

k. Deselect the range and click the **Page Layout tab** and do the following:
- Click **Orientation** in the Page Setup group and select **Landscape**.
- Click **Margins** in the Page Setup group and select **Custom Margins**. Click the **Horizontally check box** to select it in the *Center on page* section and click **OK**.

l. Click the **Insert tab** and click **Header & Footer** in the Text group and do the following:
- Click **Go to Footer** in the Navigation group.
- Click in the left side of the footer and type your name.
- Click in the center of the footer and click **Sheet Name** in the Header & Footer Elements group on the Design tab.
- Click in the right side of the footer and click **File Name** in the Header & Footer Elements group on the Design tab.
- Click in any cell in the workbook, press **Ctrl+Home**, and then click **Normal** on the status bar.

m. Save and close the file. Based on your instructor's directions, submit e01p2July_LastFirst.

3 Downtown Theatre

You are the assistant manager at Downtown Theatre, where touring Broadway plays and musicals are performed. You will analyze ticket sales by completing a worksheet that focuses on seating charts for each performance. The spreadsheet will identify the seating sections, total seats in each section, and the number of seats sold for a performance. You will then calculate the percentage of seats sold and unsold. Refer to Figure 1.62 as you complete this exercise.

	A	B	C	D	E	F
1			**Downtown Theatre**			
2			Ticket Sales by Seating Section			
3			3/31/2018			
4						
5	Section	Available Seats	Seats Sold	Percentage Sold	Percentage Unsold	
6	Box Seats	25	12	48.0%	52.0%	
7	Front Floor	120	114	95.0%	5.0%	
8	Back Floor	132	108	81.8%	18.2%	
9	Tier 1	40	40	100.0%	0.0%	
10	Mezzanine	144	138	95.8%	4.2%	
11	Balcony	106	84	79.2%	20.8%	

FIGURE 1.62 Theatre Seating Data

a. Open *e01p3TicketSales* and save it as **e01p3TicketSales_LastFirst**.
b. Double-click the **Sheet1 sheet tab**, type **Seating**, and press **Enter**.
c. Type **3/31/2018** in **cell A3** and press **Enter**.
d. Format the title:
   - Select the **range A1:E1** and click **Merge & Center** in the Alignment group.
   - Click **Cell Styles** in the Styles group and select **Title** in the Titles and Headings section.
   - Click **Bold** in the Font group.
e. Format the subtitle and date:
   - Use the Merge & Center command to merge the **range A2:E2** and center the subtitle.
   - Use the Merge & Center command to merge the **range A3:E3** and center the date.
f. Select the **range A5:E5**, click **Wrap Text**, click **Center**, and click **Bold** to format the column labels.
g. Right-click the **row 9 heading** and select **Insert** from the shortcut menu to insert a new row. Type the following data in the new row: **Back Floor, 132, 108**.
h. Move the Balcony row to be the last row by doing the following:
   - Click the **row 6 heading** and click **Cut** in the Clipboard group on the Home tab.
   - Right-click the **row 12 heading** and select **Insert Cut Cells** from the menu.
i. Adjust column widths by doing the following:
   - Double-click between the column A and column B headings.
   - Select **columns B** and **C headings** to select the columns, click **Format** in the Cells group, select **Column Width**, type **9** in the **Column width box**, and then click **OK**. Because columns B and C contain similar data, you set the same width for these columns.
   - Set the width of columns D and E to **12**.
j. Select the **range B6:C11**, click **Align Right** in the Alignment group, and then click **Increase Indent** twice in the Alignment group.

k. Click **cell D6** and use semi-selection to calculate and format the percentage of sold and unsold seats by doing the following:

- Type **=**, click **cell C6**, type **/**, and then click **cell B6** to enter =C6/B6.
- Press **Tab** to enter the formula and make cell E6 the active cell. This formula divides the number of seats sold by the total number of Box Seats.
- Type **=(B6-C6)/B6** and click **Enter** on the left side of the Formula Bar to enter the formula and keep cell E6 the active cell. This formula must first subtract the number of sold seats from the available seats to calculate the number of unsold seats. The difference is divided by the total number of available seats to determine the percentage of unsold seats.
- Select the **range D6:E6**, click **Percent Style** in the Number group, and then click **Increase Decimal** in the Number group. Keep the range selected.
- Double-click the **cell E6 fill handle** to copy the selected formulas down their respective columns. Keep the range selected.
- Click **Align Right** in the Alignment group and click **Increase Indent** twice in the Alignment group. These actions will help center the data below the column labels. Do not click Center; doing so will center each value and cause the decimal points not to align. Deselect the range.

l. Display and preserve a screenshot of the formulas by doing the following:

- Click **New sheet**, double-click the **Sheet1 sheet tab**, type **Formulas**, and then press **Enter**.
- Click the **View tab** and click **Gridlines** in the Show group to hide the gridlines on the Formulas worksheet. This action will prevent the cell gridlines from bleeding through the screenshot you are about to embed.
- Click the **Seating sheet tab**, click the **Formulas tab** on the Ribbon, and then click **Show Formulas** in the Formula Auditing group to display cell formulas.
- Click **cell A1** and drag down to **cell E11** to select the range of data.
- Click the **Home tab**, click **Copy arrow** in the Clipboard group, select **Copy as Picture**, and then click **OK** in the Copy Picture dialog box.
- Click the **Formulas sheet tab**, click **cell A1**, and then click **Paste**.
- Click the **Page Layout tab**, click **Orientation** in the Page Setup group, and then select **Landscape** to change the orientation for the Formulas sheet.
- Click the **Seating sheet tab**, click the **Formulas tab**, and then click **Show Formulas** in the Formula Auditing group to hide the cell formulas.

m. Click the **Seating sheet tab**, press **Ctrl** and click the **Formulas sheet tab** to group the two sheets. Click the **Page Layout tab**, click **Margins** in the Page Setup group, and then select **Custom Margins**. Click the **Horizontally check box** to select it and click **Print Preview**. Excel centers the data horizontally based on the widest item in each worksheet. Verify that the worksheets each print on one page. If not, go back into the Page Setup dialog box for each worksheet and reapply settings if needed. Press **Esc** to leave the Print Preview mode.

n. Click the **Page Setup Dialog Box Launcher**, click the **Header/Footer tab** in the Page Setup dialog box, click **Custom Footer**, click in the left section of the header and type your name, click in the center section of the header, click **Insert Sheet Name**, click in the **right section of the header**, click **Insert File Name**, and then click **OK** to close the Footer dialog box. Click **OK** to close the Page Setup dialog box.

o. Right-click the **Seating sheet tab** and select **Ungroup Sheets**.

p. Save and close the file. Based on your instructor's directions, submit e01p3TicketSales_LastFirst.

Mid-Level Exercises

1 Guest House Rental Rates

ANALYSIS
CASE

You manage a beach guest house in Ft. Lauderdale containing three types of rental units. Prices are based on peak and off-peak times of the year. You want to calculate the maximum daily revenue for each rental type, assuming all units are rented. In addition, you will calculate the discount rate for off-peak rental times. Finally, you will improve the appearance of the worksheet by applying font, alignment, and number formats.

a. Open *e01m1Rentals* and save it as **e01m1Rentals_LastFirst**.

b. Apply the **Heading 1** cell style to the **range A1:G1** and the **20% - Accent1** cell style to the **range A2:G2**.

c. Merge and center Peak Rentals in the **range C4:D4**, over the two columns of peak rental data. Apply **Dark Red fill color** and **White, Background 1 font color**.

d. Merge and center Off-Peak Rentals in the **range E4:G4** over the three columns of off-peak rental data. Apply **Blue fill color** and **White, Background 1 font color**.

e. Center and wrap the headings on row 5. Adjust the width of columns D and F, if needed. Center the data in the **range B6:B8**.

f. Create and copy the following formulas:
- Calculate the Peak Rentals Maximum Revenue by multiplying the number of units by the peak rental price per day.
- Calculate the Off-Peak Rentals Maximum Revenue by multiplying the number of units by the off-peak rental price per day.
- Calculate the Discount rate for the Off-Peak rental price per day. For example, using the peak and off-peak per day values, the studio apartment rents for 75% of its peak rental rate. However, you need to calculate and display the off-peak discount rate, which is .20 for the Studio Apartment. To calculate the discount rate, divide the off-peak per day rate by the peak per day rate. Subtract that result from 1, which represents 100%.

g. Format the monetary values with **Accounting Number Format**. Format the Discount Rate formula results in **Percent Style** with one decimal place. Adjust column widths if necessary to display the data.

DISCOVER

h. Apply **Blue, Accent 1, Lighter 80% fill color** to the **range E5:G8**.

i. Select the **range C5:D8** and apply a custom color with **Red 242**, **Green 220**, and **Blue 219**.

★ **j.** Answer the four questions below the worksheet data. If you change any values to answer the questions, change the values back to the original values.

k. Create a copy of the Rental Rates worksheet, place the new sheet to the right side of the original worksheet, and rename the new sheet **Formulas**. Display cell formulas on the Formulas sheet.

l. Group the worksheets and do the following:
- Select landscape orientation.
- Set **1"** top, bottom, left, and right margins. Center the data horizontally on the page.
- Insert a footer with your name on the left side, the sheet name code in the center, and the file name code on the right side.
- Apply the setting to fit to one page.

m. Click the **Formulas sheet tab** and set options to print gridlines and headings. Adjust column widths.

n. Save and close the file. Based on your instructor's directions, submit e01m1Rentals_LastFirst.

2 Real Estate Sales Report

You are a small real estate agent in Indianapolis. You track the real estate properties you list for clients. You want to analyze sales for selected properties. Yesterday, you prepared a workbook with a worksheet for recent sales data and another worksheet listing several properties you listed. You want to calculate the number of days that the houses were on the market and their sales percentage of the list price. In one situation, the house was involved in a bidding war between two families that really wanted the house. Therefore, the sale price exceeded the list price.

a. Open *e01m2Sales* and save it as **e01m2Sales_LastFirst**.

b. Delete the row that has incomplete sales data. The owners took their house off the market.

c. Type **2018-001** in **cell A5** and use Auto Fill to complete the series to assign a property ID to each property.

d. Calculate the number of days each house was on the market in column C. Copy the formula down that column.

e. Format list prices and sold prices with **Accounting Number Format** with zero decimal places.

f. Calculate the sales price percentage of the list price in cell H5. The second house was listed for $500,250, but it sold for only $400,125. Therefore, the sale percentage of the list price is 79.99%. Format the percentages with two decimal places.

g. Wrap the headings on row 4.

h. Insert a new column between the Date Sold and List Price columns. Do the following:
   - Move the Days on Market range C4:C13 to the new column.
   - Delete the empty column C.

i. Edit the list date of the 41 Chestnut Circle house to be **4/22/2018**. Edit the list price of the house on Amsterdam Drive to be **$355,000**.

j. Select the property rows and set a **25 row height** and apply **Middle Align**.

k. Apply the **All Borders** border style to the **range A4:H12**. Adjust column widths as necessary.

l. Apply **Align Right** and indent twice the values in the **range E5:E12**.

m. Apply **120% scaling**.

n. Delete the Properties worksheet.

o. Insert a new worksheet and name it **Formulas**.

p. Use the Select All feature to select all data on the Houses Sold worksheet and copy it to the Formulas worksheet.

q. Complete the following steps on the Formulas worksheet:
   - Hide the Date Listed and Date Sold columns.
   - Display cell formulas.
   - Set options to print gridlines and row and column headings.
   - Adjust column widths.

r. Group the worksheets and do the following:
   - Set landscape orientation.
   - Center the page horizontally and vertically between the margins.
   - Insert a footer with your name on the left side, the sheet tab code in the center, and the file name code on the right side.

s. Save and close the file. Based on your instructor's directions, submit e01m2Sales_LastFirst.

3 Problem Solving with Classmates

Your instructor wants all students in the class to practice their problem-solving skills. Pair up with a classmate so that you can create errors in a workbook and then see how many errors your classmate can find in your worksheet and how many errors you can find in your classmate's worksheet.

a. Create a folder named **Exploring** on your OneDrive and give access to that drive to a classmate and your instructor.

b. Open *e01h5Markup_LastFirst*, which you created in the Hands-On Exercises, and save it as **e01m3Markup_LastFirst**, changing h5 to m3.

c. Edit each main formula to have a deliberate error (such as a value or incorrect cell reference) in it and then copy the formulas down the columns.

d. Save the workbook to your shared folder on your OneDrive.

e. Open the workbook your classmate saved on his or her OneDrive and save the workbook with your name after theirs, such as *e01m3Markup_MulberyKeith_KrebsCynthia*.

f. Find the errors in your classmate's workbook, insert comments to describe the errors, and then correct the errors.

g. Save the workbook back to your classmate's OneDrive and close the file. Based on your instructor's directions, submit e01m3Markup_LastFirst_LastFirst.

Beyond the Classroom

Tip Distribution

You are a server at a restaurant in Portland. You must tip the bartender 13% of each customer's drink sales and the server assistant 1.75% of the food sales plus 2% of the drink sales. You want to complete a worksheet that shows the sales, tips, and your net tip. Open *e01b1Server* and save it as **e01b1Server_LastFirst**.

Insert a column between the Drinks and Tip Left columns. Type the label **Subtotal** in cell D6. Calculate the food and drinks subtotal for the first customer and copy the formula down the column. In column F, enter a formula to calculate the amount of the tip as a percentage of the subtotal for the first customer's sales. Format the results with Percent Style with one decimal place. Type **13%** in cell G7, type **1.75%** in cell H7, and type **2%** in cell I7. Copy these percentage values down these three columns. Horizontally center the data in the three percentage columns.

In cell J7, calculate the bartender's tip for the first customer, using the rule specified in the first paragraph. In cell K7, calculate the assistant's tip for the first customer, using the rule specified in the first paragraph. In cell L7, calculate your net tip after giving the bartender and server their share of the tips. Copy the formulas from the range J7:L7 down their respective columns. Merge and center **Customer Subtotal and Tip** in the range B5:E5, **Tip Rates** in the range F5:I5, and **Tip Amounts** in the range J5:L5. Apply Currency format to the monetary values. Apply borders around the Tip Rates and Tip Amounts sections similar to the existing border around the Customer Subtotal and Tip section. For the range A6:L6, apply **Orange, Accent 2, Lighter 40%** fill color, center horizontal alignment, and wrap text. Apply **Orange, Accent 2, Lighter 80%** fill color to the values in the Tip Left column and the My Net Tip column.

Set 0.2" left and right margins, select Landscape orientation, and set the scaling to fit to one page. Include a footer with your name on the left footer, the sheet name code in the center, and file name code on the right side. Copy the worksheet and place the copied worksheet on the right side of the original worksheet. Rename the copied worksheet as **Tip Formulas**. On the Tip Formulas worksheet, display cell formulas, print gridlines, print headings, and adjust the column widths. Change the Tips sheet tab color to **Orange, Accent 2**, and change the Tip Formulas sheet tab color to **Orange, Accent 2, Darker 25%**. Save and close the file. Based on your instructor's directions, submit e01b1Server_LastFirst.

Net Proceeds from House Sale

Daryl Patterson is a real estate agent. He wants his clients to have a realistic expectation of how much money they will receive when they sell their houses. Sellers know they have to pay a commission to the agent and pay off their existing mortgages; however, many sellers forget to consider they might have to pay some of the buyer's closing costs, title insurance, and prorated property taxes. The realtor commission and estimated closing costs are based on the selling price and the respective rates. The estimated property taxes are prorated based on the annual property taxes and percentage of the year. For example, if a house sells three months into the year, the seller pays 25% of the property taxes. Daryl created a worksheet to enter values in an input area to calculate the estimated deductions at closing and calculate the estimated net proceeds the seller will receive. However, the worksheet contains errors. Open *e01b2Proceeds* and save it as **e01b2Proceeds_LastFirst**. Review the font formatting and alignment for consistency.

Use Help to learn how to insert comments into cells. As you identify the errors, insert comments in the respective cells to explain the errors. Correct the errors, including formatting errors. Apply Landscape orientation, 115% scaling, 1.5" top margin, and center horizontally. Insert your name on the left side of the header, the sheet name code in the center, and the file name code on the right side. Save and close the file. Based on your instructor's directions, submit e01b2Proceeds_LastFirst.

Capstone Exercise

You are a division manager for a regional hearing-aid company in Cheyenne, Wyoming. Your sales managers travel frequently to some of the offices in the western region. You need to create a travel expense report for your managers to use to record their budgeted and actual expenses for their travel reports. The draft report contains a title, input areas, and a detailed expense area.

Format the Title and Complete the Input Areas

Your first tasks are to format the title and complete the input area. The input area contains two sections: Standard Inputs that are identical for all travelers and Traveler Inputs that the traveler enters based on his or her trip.

a. Open *e01c1Travel* and save it as **e01c1Travel_LastFirst**.

b. Merge and center the title over the **range A1:E1** and set the row height for the first row to **40**.

c. Apply the **Input cell style** to the **ranges B3:B6, E3:E4**, and **E6:E7**, and then apply the **Calculation cell style** to **cell E5**. Part of the borders are removed when you apply these styles.

d. Select the **ranges A3:B6** and **D3:E7**. Apply **Thick Outside Borders**.

e. Enter **6/1/2018** in **cell E3** for the departure date, **6/5/2018** in **cell E4** for the return date, **149** in **cell E6** for the hotel rate per night, and **18%** in **cell E7** for the hotel tax rate.

f. Enter a formula in **cell E5** to calculate the number of days between the return date and the departure date.

Insert Formulas

The Detailed Expenses section contains the amount budgeted for the trip, the actual expenses reported by the traveler, percentage of the budget spent on each item, and the amount the actual expense went over or under budget. You will insert formulas for this section. Some budgeted amounts are calculated based on the inputs. Other budgeted amounts, such as airfare, are estimates.

a. Enter the amount budgeted for Mileage to/from Airport in **cell B12**. The amount is based on the mileage rate and roundtrip to the airport from the Standard Inputs section.

b. Enter the amount budgeted for Airport Parking in **cell B13**. This amount is based on the airport parking daily rate and the number of total days traveling (the number of nights + 1) to include both the departure and return dates. For example, if a person departs on June 1 and returns on June 5, the total number of nights at a hotel is 4, but the total number of days the vehicle is parked at the airport is 5.

c. Enter the amount budgeted for Hotel Accommodations in **cell B16**. This amount is based on the number of nights, the hotel rate, and the hotel tax rate.

d. Enter the amount budgeted for Meals in **cell B17**. This amount is based on the daily meal allowance and the total travel days (# of hotel nights + 1).

e. Enter the % of Budget in **cell D12**. This percentage indicates the percentage of actual expenses to budgeted expenses. Copy the formula to the **range D13:D18**.

f. Enter the difference between the actual and budgeted expenses in **cell E12**. Copy the formula to the **range E13:E18**. If the actual expenses exceeded the budgeted expenses, the result should be positive. If the actual expenses were less than the budgeted expense, the result should be negative, indicating under budget.

Add Rows, Indent Labels, and Move Data

The Detailed Expenses section includes a heading Travel to/from Destination. You want to include two more headings to organize the expenses. Then you will indent the items within each category. Furthermore, you want the monetary columns together, so you will insert cells and move the Over or Under column to the right of the Actual column.

a. Insert a new row 15. Type **Destination Expenses** in **cell A15**. Bold the label.

b. Insert a new row 19. Type **Other** in **cell A19**. Bold the label.

c. Indent twice the labels in the **ranges A12:A14, A16:A18**, and **A20**.

d. Select the **range D10:D21** and insert cells to shift the selected cells to the right.

e. Cut the **range F10:F21** and paste it in the **range D10:D21** to move the Over or Under data in the new cells you inserted.

Format the Detailed Expenses Section

You are ready to format the values to improve readability. You will apply Accounting Number Format to the monetary values on the first and total rows, Comma Style to the monetary values in the middle rows, and Percent Style for the percentages.

a. Apply **Accounting Number Format** to the **ranges B12:D12** and **B21:D21**.

b. Apply **Comma Style** to the **range B13:D20**.

c. Apply **Percent Style** with one decimal place to the **range E12:E20**.

d. Underline the **range: B20:D20**. Do not use the border feature.

e. Apply the cell style **Bad** to **cell D21** because the traveler went over budget.

f. Select the **range A10:E21** and apply **Thick Outside Borders**.

g. Select the **range A10:E10**, apply **Blue-Gray, Text 2, Lighter 80% fill color**, apply **Center** alignment, and apply **Wrap Text**.

Manage the Workbook

You will apply page setup options, insert a footer, and, then duplicate the Expenses statement worksheet.

a. Spell-check the workbook and make appropriate corrections.

b. Set a **1.5"** top margin and select the margin setting to center the data horizontally on the page.

c. Insert a footer with your name on the left side, the sheet name code in the center, and the file name code on the right side.

d. Copy the Expenses worksheet, move the new worksheet to the end, and rename it **Formulas**.

e. Display the cell formulas on the Formulas worksheet, change to landscape orientation, and adjust column widths. Use the Page Setup dialog box or the Page Layout tab to print gridlines and row and column headings.

f. Save and close the file. Based on your instructor's directions, submit e01c1Travel_LastFirst.

Formulas and Functions

LEARNING OUTCOME   You will apply formulas and functions to calculate and analyze data.

OBJECTIVES & SKILLS: After you read this chapter, you will be able to:

Formula Basics

OBJECTIVE 1: USE RELATIVE, ABSOLUTE, AND MIXED CELL REFERENCES IN FORMULAS   488
Use a Relative Cell Reference, Use an Absolute Cell Reference, Use a Mixed Cell Reference

HANDS-ON EXERCISE 1:
Formula Basics   492

Function Basics

OBJECTIVE 2: INSERT A FUNCTION   495
Insert a Function, Insert a Function Using Formula AutoComplete, Use the Insert Function Dialog Box

OBJECTIVE 3: INSERT BASIC MATH AND STATISTICS FUNCTIONS   497
Use the SUM Function, Use the AVERAGE and MEDIAN Functions, Use the MIN and MAX Functions, Use the COUNT Functions, Perform Calculations with Quick Analysis Tools

OBJECTIVE 4: USE DATE FUNCTIONS   501
Use the TODAY Function, Use the NOW Function

HANDS-ON EXERCISE 2:
Function Basics   503

Logical, Lookup, and Financial Functions

OBJECTIVE 5: DETERMINE RESULTS WITH THE IF FUNCTION   508
Use the IF Function

OBJECTIVE 6: USE LOOKUP FUNCTIONS   511
Use the VLOOKUP Function, Create the Lookup Table, Use the HLOOKUP Function

OBJECTIVE 7: CALCULATE PAYMENTS WITH THE PMT FUNCTION   514
Use the PMT Function

HANDS-ON EXERCISE 3:
Logical, Lookup, and Financial Functions   516

CASE STUDY | Townsend Mortgage Company

You are an assistant to Erica Matheson, a mortgage broker at the Townsend Mortgage Company. Erica spends her days reviewing mortgage rates and trends, meeting with clients, and preparing paperwork. She relies on your expertise in using Excel to help analyze mortgage data.

Today, Erica provided you with sample mortgage data: loan number, house cost, down payment, mortgage rate, and the length of the loan in years. She asked you to perform some basic calculations so that she can check the output provided by her system to verify if it is calculating results correctly. She wants you to calculate the amount financed, the periodic interest rate, the total number of payment periods, the percent of the house cost that is financed, and the payoff year for each loan. In addition, you will calculate totals, averages, and other basic statistics.

Furthermore, she has asked you to complete another worksheet that uses functions to look up interest rates from a separate table, calculate the monthly payments, and determine how much (if any) the borrower will have to pay for private mortgage insurance (PMI).

Performing Quantitative Analysis

	A	B	C	D	E	F	G	H	I	J	K	L
1	**Townsend Mortgage Company**											
2												
3		**Input Area**										
4	Today's Date:	10/2/2018										
5	Pmts Per Year:	12										
6												
7	Loan #	House Cost	**Down** Payment	**Amount** Financed	**Mortgage** Rate	**Rate Per** Period	Years	**# of Pmt** Periods	**%** Financed	**Date** Financed	**Payoff** Year	
8	452786	$ 400,000	$ 80,000	$ 320,000	3.625%	0.302%	25	300	80.0%	5/1/2016	2041	
9	453000	$ 425,000	$ 60,000	$ 365,000	3.940%	0.328%	30	360	85.9%	11/3/2016	2046	
10	453025	$ 175,500	$ 30,000	$ 145,500	3.550%	0.296%	25	300	82.9%	4/10/2017	2042	
11	452600	$ 265,950	$ 58,000	$ 207,950	2.500%	0.208%	15	180	78.2%	10/14/2017	2032	
12	452638	$ 329,750	$ 65,000	$ 264,750	3.250%	0.271%	30	360	80.3%	2/4/2018	2048	
13												
14		**Summary Statistics**										
15	Statistics	House Cost	**Down** Payment	**Amount** Financed								
16	Total	$ 1,596,200	$ 293,000	$ 1,303,200								
17	Average	$ 319,240	$ 58,600	$ 260,640								
18	Median	$ 329,750	$ 60,000	$ 264,750								
19	Lowest	$ 175,500	$ 30,000	$ 145,500								
20	Highest	$ 425,000	$ 80,000	$ 365,000								
21	# of Mortgages	5	5	5								

Details | Payment Info | (+)

Ready

FIGURE 2.1 Townsend Mortgage Company Worksheet

CASE STUDY | Townsend Mortgage Company

Starting File	File to be Submitted
e02h1Loans	**e02h3Loans_LastFirst**

Formula Basics

When you increase your understanding of formulas, you can build robust workbooks that perform a variety of calculations for quantitative analysis. Your ability to build sophisticated workbooks and to interpret the results increases your value to any organization. By now, you should be able to build simple formulas using cell references and mathematical operators and use the order of operations to control the sequence of calculations in formulas.

In this section, you will create formulas in which cell addresses change or remain fixed when you copy them.

Using Relative, Absolute, and Mixed Cell References in Formulas

When you copy a formula, Excel either adjusts or preserves the cell references in the copied formula based on how the cell references appear in the original formula. Excel uses three different ways to reference a cell in a formula: relative, absolute, and mixed. Relative references change when a formula is copied. For example, if a formula containing the cell A1 is copied down one row in the column, the reference would become A2. In contrast, absolute references remain constant, no matter where they are copied. Mixed references are a combination of both absolute and relative, where part will change and part will remain constant.

When you create a formula that you will copy to other cells, ask yourself the following question: Do the cell references contain constant or variable values? In other words, should the cell references be adjusted or always refer to the same cell location, regardless of where the copied formula is located?

Use a Relative Cell Reference

STEP 1 》》 A *relative cell reference* is the default method of referencing in Excel. It indicates a cell's relative location, such as five rows up and one column to the left, from the original cell containing the formula. When you copy a formula containing a relative cell reference, the cells referenced in the copied formula change relative to the position of the copied formula. Regardless of where you paste the formula, the cell references in the copied formula maintain the same relative distance from the cell containing the copied formula, as the cell references the relative location to the original formula cell.

In Figure 2.2, the formulas in column F contain relative cell references. When you copy the original formula =D2-E2 from cell F2 down one row to cell F3, the copied formula changes to =D3-E3. Because you copy the formula *down* the column to cell F3, the column letters in the formula stay the same, but the row numbers change to reflect the row to which you copied the formula. Using relative referencing is an effective time saving tool. For example, using relative cell addresses to calculate the amount financed ensures that each borrower's down payment is subtracted from his or her respective house cost.

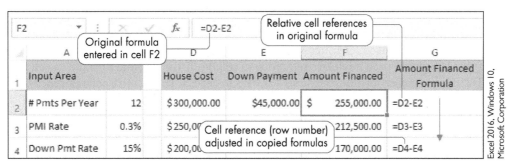

FIGURE 2.2 Relative Cell References

Use an Absolute Cell Reference

STEP 2 In many calculations there are times in which a value should remain constant, such as an interest rate or payoff date. In these situations absolute cell references are utilized. An **absolute cell reference** provides a constant reference to a specific cell. When you copy a formula containing an absolute cell reference, the cell reference in the copied formula does not change, regardless of where you copy the formula. An absolute cell reference appears with a dollar sign before both the column letter and row number, such as $B$4.

In Figure 2.3, the down payment is calculated by multiplying the house cost by the down payment rate (15%). Each down payment calculation uses a different purchase price and constant down payment rate, therefore an absolute reference is required. Cell E2 contains =D2*$B$4 ($300,000*15.0%) to calculate the first borrower's down payment ($45,000). When you copy the formula down to the next row, the copied formula in cell E3 is =D3*$B$4. The relative cell reference D2 changes to D3 (for the next house cost) and the absolute cell reference $B$4 remains the same to refer to the constant 15.0% down payment rate. This formula ensures that the cell reference to the house cost changes for each row but that the house cost is always multiplied by the rate in cell B4.

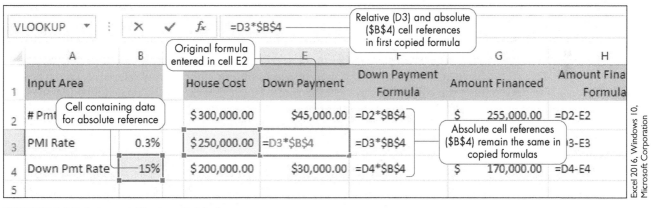

FIGURE 2.3 Relative and Absolute Cell References

TIP: INPUT AREA AND ABSOLUTE CELL REFERENCES

To illustrate the effect of modifying an assumption (e.g., the down payment rate changes from 15% to 20%), it is efficient to enter the new input value in only one cell (e.g., B4) rather than including the same value in a string of formulas. In Figure 2.3, values that can be modified, such as the down payment rate, are put in an input area. Generally, formulas use absolute references to the cells in the input area. For example, B4 is an absolute cell reference in all the down payment calculations. If the value in B4 is modified, Excel recalculates the amount of down payment for all the down payment formulas. By using cell references from an input area, you can perform what-if analyses very easily.

When utilizing the fill option to copy a formula, if an error or unexpected result occurs, a good starting point for troubleshooting is checking input values to determine if an absolute or mixed reference is needed. Figure 2.4 shows what happens if the down payment formula used a relative reference to cell B4. If the original formula in cell E2 is =D2*B4, the copied formula becomes =D3*B5 in cell E3. The relative cell reference to B4 changes to B5 when you copy the formula down. Because cell B5 is empty, the $350,000 house cost in cell D3 is multiplied by 0, giving a $0 down payment, which is not a valid down payment amount.

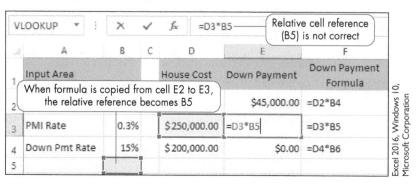

FIGURE 2.4 Error in Formula

Use a Mixed Cell Reference

STEP 3 ⟫ A *mixed cell reference* combines an absolute cell reference with a relative cell reference. When you copy a formula containing a mixed cell reference, either the column letter or the row number that has the absolute reference remains fixed while the other part of the cell reference that is relative changes in the copied formula. $B4 and B$4 are examples of mixed cell references. In the reference $B4, the column B is absolute, and the row number is relative; when you copy the formula, the column letter B does not change, but the row number will change. In the reference B$4, the column letter B changes, but the row number, 4, does not change. To create a mixed reference, type the dollar sign to the left of the part of the cell reference you want to be absolute.

In the down payment formula, you can change the formula in cell E2 to be =D2*B$4. Because you are copying down the same column, only the row reference 4 must be absolute; the column letter stays the same. Figure 2.5 shows the copied formula =D3*B$4 in cell E3. In situations where you can use either absolute or mixed references, consider using mixed references to shorten the length of the formula.

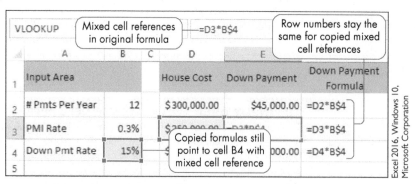

FIGURE 2.5 Relative and Mixed Cell References

Quick Concepts

1. What happens when you copy a formula containing a relative cell reference one column to the right? *p. 488*

2. Why would you use an absolute reference in a formula? *p. 489*

3. What is the benefit of using a mixed reference? *p. 490*

Hands-On Exercises

Skills covered: Use a Relative Cell Reference • Use an Absolute Cell Reference • Use a Mixed Cell Reference

1 Formula Basics

Erica prepared a workbook containing data for five mortgages financed with the Townsend Mortgage Company. The data include house cost, down payment, mortgage rate, number of years to pay off the mortgage, and the financing date for each mortgage.

STEP 1 » USE A RELATIVE CELL REFERENCE

You will calculate the amount financed by each borrower by creating a formula with relative cell references that calculates the difference between the house cost and the down payment. After verifying the results of the amount financed by the first borrower, you will copy the formula down the Amount Financed column to calculate the other borrowers' amounts financed. Refer to Figure 2.6 as you complete Step 1.

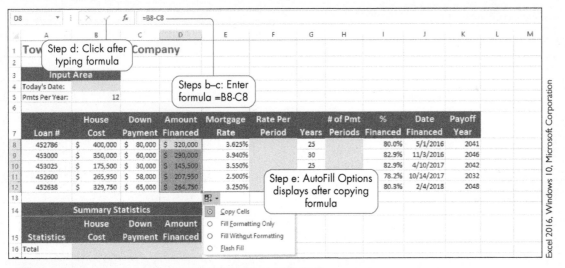

FIGURE 2.6 Formula Containing Relative Cell Reference Copied

a. Open *e02h1Loans* and save it as **e02h1Loans_LastFirst**.

> **TROUBLESHOOTING:** If you make any major mistakes in this exercise, you can close the file, open *e02h1Loans* again, and then start this exercise over.

The workbook contains two worksheets: Details (for Hands-On Exercises 1 and 2) and Payment Info (for Hands-On Exercise 3). You will enter formulas in the shaded cells.

b. Click **cell D8** in the Details sheet. Type = and click **cell B8**, the cell containing the first borrower's house cost.

c. Type - and click **cell C8**, the cell containing the down payment by the first borrower.

d. Click **Enter** ✓ (the check mark between the Name Box and Formula Bar) to complete the formula.

The first borrower financed (i.e., borrowed) $320,000, the difference between the cost ($400,000) and the down payment ($80,000).

e. Double-click the **cell D8 fill handle**.

You copied the formula down the Amount Financed column for each mortgage row.

f. Click **cell D9** and view the formula in the Formula Bar.

The formula in cell D8 is =B8-C8. The formula copied to cell D9 is =B9-C9. Because the original formula contained relative cell references, when you copy the formula down to the next row, the row numbers for the cell references change. Each result represents the amount financed for that particular borrower.

g. Press ⬇ and look at the cell references in the Formula Bar to see how the references change for each formula you copied. Save the workbook with the new formula you created.

STEP 2 ❯❯ **USE AN ABSOLUTE CELL REFERENCE**

Column E contains the mortgage rate for each loan. Because the borrowers will make monthly payments, you will modify the given annual interest rate (APR) to a monthly rate by dividing it by 12 (the number of payments in one year) for each borrower. Refer to Figure 2.7 as you complete Step 2.

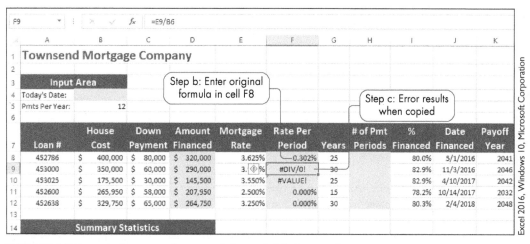

FIGURE 2.7 Formula Containing Incorrect Relative Cell Reference Copied

a. Click **cell F8**.

You will create a formula to calculate the monthly interest rate for the first borrower.

b. Type **=E8/B5** and click **Enter** (the check mark between the Name Box and the Formula Bar).

Typically, you should avoid typing values directly in formulas. Therefore, you use a reference to cell B5, where the number of payments per year is placed in the input area, so that the company can change the payment period to bimonthly (24 payments per year) or quarterly (four payments per year) without adjusting the formula.

c. Double-click the **cell F8 fill handle**, click **cell F9**, and then view the results (see Figure 2.7).

An error icon displays to the left of cell F9, which displays #DIV/0!, and cell F10 displays #VALUE!. The original formula was =E8/B5. Because you copied the formula =E8/B5 down the column, the first copied formula is =E9/B6, and the second copied formula is =E10/B7. Although you want the mortgage rate cell reference (E8) to change (E9, E10, etc.) from row to row, you do not want the divisor (cell B5) to change. You need all formulas to divide by the value stored in cell B5, so you will edit the formula to make B5 an absolute reference.

d. Click **Undo** in the Quick Access Toolbar to undo the AutoFill process. With F8 as the active cell, click to the right of **B5** in the Formula Bar.

e. Press **F4** and click **Enter** (the check mark between the Name Box and the Formula Bar).

Excel changes the cell reference from B5 to $B$5, making it an absolute cell reference.

f. Double-click the fill handle to copy the formula down the Rate Per Period column. Click **cell F9** and view the formula in the Formula Bar.

The formula in cell F9 is =E9/$B$5. The reference to E9 is relative and the reference to B5 is absolute. The results of all the calculations in the Rate Per Period column are now correct.

g. Save the workbook.

STEP 3 >> USE A MIXED CELL REFERENCE

The next formula you create will calculate the total number of payment periods for each loan. Refer to Figure 2.8 as you complete Step 3.

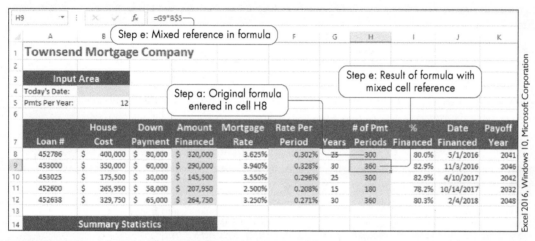

FIGURE 2.8 Formula Containing Mixed Cell Reference Copied

a. Click **cell H8** and type **=G8*B5**.

You will multiply the number of years (25) by the number of payment periods in one year (12) using cell references.

b. Press **F4** to make the B5 cell reference absolute and click **Enter**.

You want B5 to be absolute so that the cell reference remains B5 when you copy the formula. The product of 25 years and 12 months is 300 months or payment periods.

c. Copy the formula down the # of Pmt Periods column.

The first copied formula is =G9*$B$5, and the result is 360. You want to see what happens if you change the absolute reference to a mixed reference and copy the formula again. Because you are copying down a column, the column letter B can be relative because it will not change either way, but the row number 5 must be absolute.

d. Ensure that cell H8 is the active cell and click **Undo** on the Quick Access Toolbar to undo the copied formulas.

e. Click within the **$B$5 cell reference** in the Formula Bar. Press **F4** to change the cell reference to a mixed cell reference: B$5. Press **Ctrl+Enter** and copy the formula down the # of Pmt Periods column. Click **cell H9**.

The first copied formula is =G9*B$5 and the result is still 360. In this situation, using either an absolute reference or a mixed reference provides the same results.

f. Save the workbook. Keep the workbook open if you plan to continue with the next Hands-On Exercise. If not, close the workbook and exit Excel.

Function Basics

An Excel *function* is a predefined computation that simplifies creating a formula that performs a complex calculation. Excel contains more than 400 functions, which are organized into 14 categories. Table 2.1 lists and describes the primary function categories used in this chapter.

TABLE 2.1	Function Categories and Descriptions
Category	**Description**
Date & Time	Provides methods for manipulating date and time values.
Financial	Performs financial calculations, such as payments, rates, present value, and future value.
Logical	Performs logical tests and returns the value of the tests. Includes logical operators for combined tests, such as AND, OR, and NOT.
Lookup & Reference	Looks up values, creates links to cells, or provides references to cells in a worksheet.
Math & Trig	Performs standard math and trigonometry calculations.
Statistical	Performs common statistical calculations, such as averages and standard deviations.

Pearson Education, Inc.

When using functions, you must adhere to correct *syntax*, the rules that dictate the structure and components required to perform the necessary calculations. Start a function with an equal sign, followed by the function name, and then its arguments enclosed in parentheses.

- The function name describes the purpose of the function. For example, the function name SUM indicates that the function sums, or adds, values.

- A function's *arguments* specify the inputs—such as cells, values, or arithmetic expressions—that are required to complete the operation. In some cases, a function requires multiple arguments separated by commas.

In this section, you will learn how to insert common functions using the keyboard and the Insert Function and Function Arguments dialog boxes.

Inserting a Function

To insert a function by typing, first type an equal sign, and then begin typing the function name. *Formula AutoComplete* displays a list of functions and defined names that match letters as you type a formula. For example, if you type =SU, Formula AutoComplete displays a list of functions and names that start with *SU* (see Figure 2.9). You can double-click the function name from the list or continue typing the function name. You can even point to a list item and see the ScreenTip describing the function.

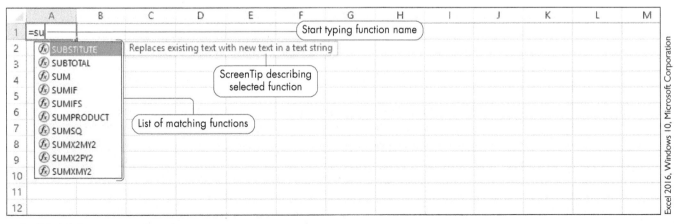

FIGURE 2.9 Formula AutoComplete

After you type the function name and opening parenthesis, Excel displays the *function ScreenTip*, a small pop-up description that displays the function's arguments. The argument you are currently entering is bold in the function ScreenTip (see Figure 2.10). Square brackets indicate optional arguments. For example, the SUM function requires the number1 argument, but the number2 argument is optional. Click the argument name in the function ScreenTip to select the actual argument in the formula you are creating if you want to make changes to the argument.

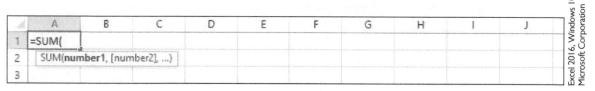

FIGURE 2.10 Function ScreenTip

You can also use the Insert Function dialog box to search for a function, select a function category, and select a function from the list (see Figure 2.11). The dialog box is helpful if you want to browse a list of functions, especially if you are not sure of the function you need and want to see descriptions.

To display the Insert Function dialog box, click Insert Function 𝑓ₓ (located between the Name Box and the Formula Bar) or click Insert Function in the Function Library group on the Formulas tab. From within the dialog box, select a function category, such as Most Recently Used, and select a function to display the syntax and a brief description of that function. Click *Help on this function* to display details about the selected function.

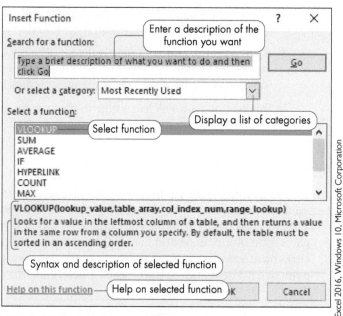

FIGURE 2.11 Insert Function Dialog Box

When you find the function you want, click OK. The Function Arguments dialog box opens so that you can enter the arguments for that specific function (see Figure 2.12). Argument names in bold (such as number1 in the SUM function) are required. Argument names that are not bold (such as number2 in the SUM function) are optional. The function can operate without the optional argument, which is used when you need additional specifications to calculate a result.

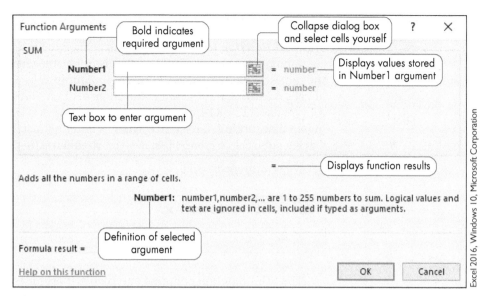

FIGURE 2.12 Function Arguments Dialog Box

Type the cell references in the argument boxes, or click a collapse button to the right side of an argument box to collapse the dialog box and select the cell or range of cells in the worksheet to designate as that argument. If you click the collapse button to select a range, you need to click the expand button to expand the dialog box again. You also have the ability to manually select the cells for the argument without clicking the collapse button. The collapse button is best used if the desired cells for the arguments view is obstructed. The value, or results, of a formula contained in the argument cell displays on the right side of the argument box (such as 5; 10; 15; 20; 25—the values stored in the range A1:A5 used for the number1 argument). If the argument is not valid, Excel displays an error description on the right side of the argument box.

The bottom of the Function Arguments dialog box displays a description of the function and a description of the argument containing the insertion point. As you enter arguments, the bottom of the dialog box also displays the results of the function, such as 75.

TIP: #NAME?
If you enter a function and #NAME? displays in the cell, you might have mistyped the function name. To avoid this problem, select the function name from the Formula AutoComplete list as you type the function name, or use the Insert Function dialog box. You can type a function name in lowercase letters. If you type the name correctly, Excel converts the name to all capital letters when you press Enter, indicating that you spelled the function name correctly.

Inserting Basic Math and Statistics Functions

Excel includes commonly used math and statistical functions that you can use for a variety of calculations. For example, you can insert functions to calculate the total amount you spend on dining out in a month, the average amount you spend per month purchasing music online, your highest electric bill, and your lowest time to run a mile this week. When using these functions, a change in the values within the ranges referenced will change the results of the function.

Use the SUM Function

STEP 1 ▶▶ The **SUM function** totals values in one or more cells and displays the result in the cell containing the function. This function is more efficient to create when you need to add the values contained in three or more contiguous cells. For example, to add the contents of cells A2 through A14, you could enter =A2+A3+A4+A5+A6+A7+A8+A9+A10+ A11+A12+A13+A14, which is time-consuming and increases the probability of entering an inaccurate cell reference, such as entering a cell reference twice or accidentally leaving out a cell reference. Instead, you should use the SUM function, =SUM(A2:A14).

=SUM(number1, [number2],…)

> **TIP: FUNCTION SYNTAX**
> In this book, the function syntax lines are highlighted. Brackets [ ] indicate optional arguments; however, do not actually type the brackets when you enter the argument.

The SUM function contains one required argument (number1) that represents a range of cells to add. The range, such as A2:A14, specifies the first and last of an adjacent group of cells containing values to SUM. Excel will sum all cells within that range. The number2 optional argument is used when you want to sum values stored in nonadjacent cells or ranges, such as =SUM(A2:A14,F2:F14). The ellipsis in the function syntax indicates that you can add as many additional ranges as desired, separated by commas.

> **TIP: AVOIDING FUNCTIONS FOR BASIC FORMULAS**
> Do not use a function for a basic mathematical expression. For example, although =SUM(B4/C4) produces the same result as =B4/C4, the SUM function is not needed to perform the basic arithmetic division. Furthermore, someone taking a quick look at that formula might assume it performs addition instead of division. Use the most appropriate, clear-cut formula, =B4/C4.

> **To insert the SUM function (for example, to sum the values of a range), complete one of the following steps:**
>
> - Type =SUM(type the range), and press Enter.
> - Type =SUM(drag to select the range, then type the closing) and press Enter.
> - Click a cell, click Sum $\boxed{\Sigma \text{ AutoSum } \cdot}$ in the Editing group on the Home tab, press Enter to select the suggested range (or drag to select a range), and then press Enter.
> - Click in a cell, click AutoSum in the Function Library group on the Formulas tab, either press Enter to select the suggested range or type the range, and then press Enter.
> - Click the cell directly underneath the range you would like to SUM and press Alt=.

Figure 2.13 shows the result of using the SUM function in cell D2 to total scores (898).

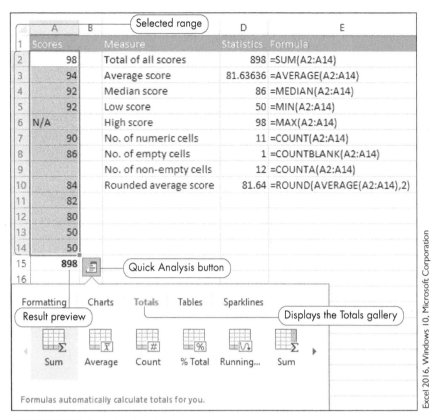

FIGURE 2.13 Function Results

TIP: SUM ARROW

If you click Sum in the Editing group on the Home tab or in the Function Library group on the Formulas tab, Excel inserts the SUM function. However, if you click the Sum arrow, Excel displays a list of basic functions to select: Sum, Average, Count Numbers, Max, and Min. If you want to insert another function, select More Functions from the list.

TIP: NEST FUNCTIONS AS ARGUMENTS

A *nested function* occurs when one function is embedded as an argument within another function. Each function has its own set of arguments that must be included. For example, cell D10 in Figure 2.13 contains =ROUND(AVERAGE(A2:A14),2). The ROUND function requires two arguments: number (the number to be rounded) and num_digits (the number of decimals to which the number is to be rounded).

The AVERAGE function is used to create the number to be rounded, and is nested in the number argument of the ROUND function. AVERAGE(A2:A14) returns 81.63636. That value is then rounded to two decimal places, indicated by 2 in the num_digits argument. The result is 81.64. If you change the second argument from 2 to 0, such as =ROUND(AVERAGE (A2:A14),0), the result would be 82.

Use the AVERAGE and MEDIAN Functions

STEP 2 ❯❯ People often describe data based on central tendency, which means that values tend to cluster around a central value. Excel provides two functions to calculate central tendency: AVERAGE and MEDIAN. The **AVERAGE function** calculates the arithmetic mean, or average, for the values in a range of cells. You can use this function to calculate the class average on a biology test or the average number of points scored per game by a basketball player. In Figure 2.13, =AVERAGE(A2:A14) in cell D3 returns 81.63636 as the average test score. The AVERAGE function ignores empty cells and cells containing N/A or text.

=AVERAGE (number1,[number2],…)

STEP 3 ⟩⟩ The ***MEDIAN function*** finds the midpoint value, which is the value that one half of the data set is above or below. The median is particularly useful because extreme values often influence arithmetic mean calculated by the AVERAGE function. In Figure 2.13, the two extreme test scores of 50 distort the average. The rest of the test scores range from 80 to 98. Cell D4 contains =MEDIAN(A2:A14). The median for test scores is 86, which indicates that half the test scores are above 86 and half the test scores are below 86. This statistic is more reflective of the data set than the average. The MEDIAN function ignores empty cells and cells containing N/A or text.

=MEDIAN(number1,[number2],...)

Use the MIN and MAX Functions

STEP 4 ⟩⟩ The ***MIN function*** analyzes an argument list to determine the lowest value, such as the lowest score on a test. Manually inspecting a range of values to identify the lowest value is inefficient, especially in large spreadsheets. In Figure 2.13, =MIN(A2:A14) in cell D5 identifies that 50 is the lowest test score.

=MIN(number1,[number2],...)

The ***MAX function*** analyzes an argument list to determine the highest value, such as the highest score on a test. In Figure 2.13, =MAX(A2:A14) in cell D6 identifies 98 as the highest test score.

=MAX(number1,[number2],...)

TIP: NONADJACENT RANGES

In most basic aggregate functions such as SUM, MIN, MAX, and AVERAGE, you can use multiple ranges as arguments, such as finding the largest number within two nonadjacent (nonconsecutive) ranges. For example, you can find the highest test score where some scores are stored in cells A2:A14 and others are stored in cells K2:K14. Separate each range with a comma in the argument list, so that the formula is =MAX(A2:A14,K2:K14).

Use the COUNT Functions

Excel provides three basic count functions—COUNT, COUNTBLANK, and COUNTA— to count the cells in a range that meet a particular criterion. The ***COUNT function*** tallies the number of cells in a range that contain values you can use in calculations, such as numerical and date data, but excludes blank cells or text entries from the tally. In Figure 2.13, the selected range spans 13 cells; however, =COUNT(A2:A14) in cell D7 returns 11, the number of cells that contain numerical data. It does not count the cell containing the text *N/A* or the blank cell.

The ***COUNTBLANK function*** tallies the number of cells in a range that are blank. In Figure 2.13, =COUNTBLANK(A2:A14) in cell D8 identifies that one cell in the range A2:A14 is blank. The ***COUNTA function*** tallies the number of cells in a range that are not blank, that is, cells that contain data, whether a value, text, or a formula. In Figure 2.13, =COUNTA(A2:A14) in cell D9 returns 12, indicating that the range A2:A14 contains 12 cells that contain some form of data. It does not count the blank cell; however, it will count cells that contain text such as cell A6.

=COUNT(value1,[value2],...)

=COUNTBLANK(range)

=COUNTA(value1,[value2],...)

Perform Calculations with Quick Analysis Tools

Quick Analysis is a set of analytical tools you can use to apply formatting, create charts or tables, and insert basic functions. When you select a range of data, the Quick Analysis button displays adjacent to the bottom-right corner of the selected range. Click the Quick Analysis button to display the Quick Analysis gallery and select the analytical tool to meet your needs.

Figure 2.13 shows the Totals gallery options so that you can sum, average, or count the values in the selected range. Select % Total to display the percentage of the grand total of two or more columns. Select Running Total to provide a cumulative total at the bottom of multiple columns. Additional options can be seen by clicking the right expansion arrow.

Using Date Functions

In order to maximize the use of dates and date functions in Excel, it is important to understand how they are handled in the program. Excel assigns serial numbers to dates. The date January 1, 1900 is the equivalent to the number 1. The number 2 is the equivalent of January 2, 1900 and so on. Basically, Excel adds 1 to every serial number as each day passes. Therefore the newer the date, the bigger the equivalent serial number. For example, assume today is January 1, 2018, and you graduate on May 6, 2018. To determine how many days until graduation, subtract today's date from the graduation date. Excel uses the serial numbers for these dates (43101 and 43226) to calculate the difference of 125 days.

Insert the TODAY Function

STEP 5 ⟩⟩ The *TODAY function* displays the current date in a cell. Excel updates the TODAY function results when you open or print the workbook. The TODAY() function does not require arguments, but you must include the parentheses. If you omit the parentheses, Excel displays #NAME? in the cell with a green triangle in the top-left corner of the cell. When you click the cell, an error icon appears that you can click for more information.

=TODAY()

Insert the NOW Function

The *NOW function* uses the computer's clock to display the current date and military time that you last opened the workbook. (Military time expresses time on a 24-hour period where 1:00 is 1 a.m. and 13:00 is 1 p.m.) The date and time will change every time the workbook is opened. Like the TODAY function, the NOW function does not require arguments, but you must include the parentheses. Omitting the parentheses creates a #NAME? error.

=NOW()

Quick Concepts

4. What visual features help guide you through typing a function directly in a cell? *p. 496*

5. What type of data do you enter in a Function Arguments dialog box, and what are four things the dialog box tells you? *p. 497*

6. What is the difference between the AVERAGE and MEDIAN functions? *pp. 499–500*

7. What is a nested function, and why would you create one? *p. 499*

Hands-On Exercises

Watch the Video
for this Hands-On
Exercise!

MyITLab®
HOE2 Training

Skills covered: Insert a Function • Insert a Function Using Formula AutoComplete • Use the Insert Function Dialog Box • Use the SUM Function • Use the AVERAGE and MEDIAN Functions • Use the MIN and MAX Functions • Use the COUNT Functions • Use the TODAY Function

2 Function Basics

The Townsend Mortgage Company worksheet contains an area in which you will enter summary statistics. In addition, you will include the current date.

STEP 1 ►► USE THE SUM FUNCTION

The first summary statistic you calculate is the total value of the houses bought by the borrowers. You will use the SUM function. Refer to Figure 2.14 as you complete Step 1.

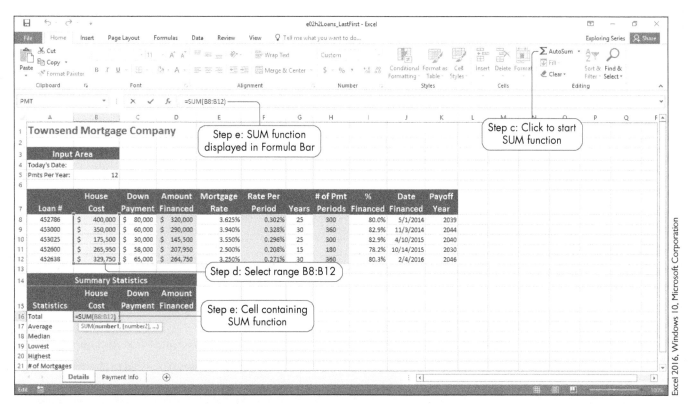

FIGURE 2.14 SUM Function Calculates Total House Cost

a. Open *e02h1Loans_LastFirst* if you closed it at the end of Hands-On Exercise 1 and save it as **e02h2Loans_LastFirst**, changing h1 to h2.

b. Ensure that the Details worksheet is active and click **cell B16**, the cell where you will enter a formula for the total house cost.

c. Click **AutoSum** Σ AutoSum ▾ in the Editing group on the Home tab.

Excel anticipates the range of cells containing values you want to sum based on where you enter the formula—in this case, A8:D15. This is not the correct range, so you must enter the correct range.

> **TROUBLESHOOTING:** AutoSum, like some other commands in Excel, contains two parts: the main command button and an arrow. Click the main command button when instructed to click Sum to perform the default action. Click the arrow when instructed to click the Sum arrow for additional options. If you accidentally clicked the arrow instead of Sum, press Esc to cancel the SUM function from being completed and try Step c again.

d. Select the **range B8:B12**, the cells containing house costs.

As you use the semi-selection process, Excel enters the range in the SUM function.

> **TROUBLESHOOTING:** If you entered the function without changing the arguments, repeat Steps b–d or edit the arguments in the Formula Bar by deleting the default range, typing B8:B12 between the parentheses and pressing Enter.

e. Click **Enter**.

Cell B16 contains the function = SUM(B8:B12), and the result is $1,521,200.

f. Save the workbook.

STEP 2 » USE THE AVERAGE FUNCTION

Before copying the functions to calculate the total down payments and amounts financed, you want to calculate the average house cost of the houses bought by the borrowers in your list. Refer to Figure 2.15 as you complete Step 2.

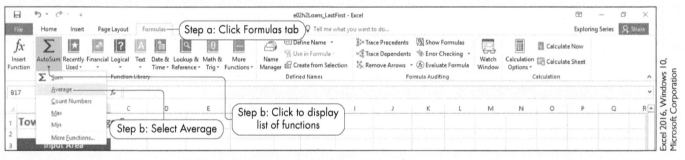

FIGURE 2.15 AVERAGE Function Calculates Average House Cost

a. Click the **Formulas tab** and click **cell B17**, the cell where you will display the average cost of the houses.

b. Click the **AutoSum arrow** in the Function Library group and select **Average**.

Excel selects cell B16, which is the total cost of the houses. You need to change the range.

c. Select the **range B8:B12**, the cells containing the house costs.

The function is =AVERAGE(B8:B12).

d. Press **Enter**, making cell B18 the active cell.

The average house cost is $304,240.

e. Save the workbook.

You realize that extreme house costs may distort the average. Therefore, you decide to identify the median house cost to compare it to the average house cost. Refer to Figure 2.16 as you complete Step 3.

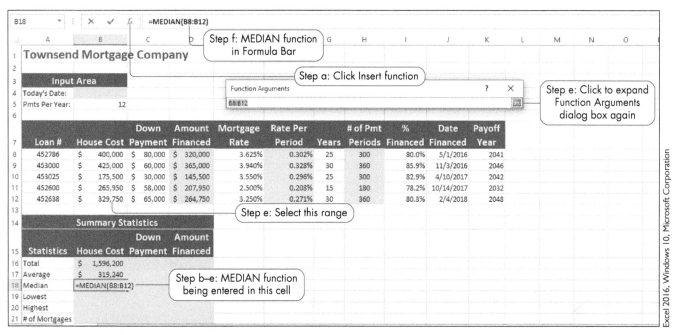

FIGURE 2.16 MEDIAN Function Calculates the Median House Cost

a. Ensure that cell B18 is the active cell. Click **Insert Function** f_x between the Name Box and the Formula Bar, or in the Function Library group on the Formulas tab.

The Insert Function dialog box opens. Use this dialog box to select the MEDIAN function because it is not available on the Ribbon.

b. Type **median** in the *Search for a function box* and click **Go**.

Excel displays a list of functions in the *Select a function* list. The MEDIAN function is selected at the top of the list; the bottom of the dialog box displays the syntax and the description.

c. Read the MEDIAN function description and click **OK**.

The Function Arguments dialog box opens. It contains one required argument, Number1, representing a range of cells containing values. It has an optional argument, Number2, which you can use if you have nonadjacent ranges that contain values.

d. Click **Collapse Dialog Box** 🔲 to the right of the Number1 box.

You collapsed the Function Arguments dialog box so that you can select the range.

e. Select the **range B8:B12** and click **Expand Dialog Box** 🔲 in the Function Arguments dialog box.

The Function Arguments dialog box expands, displaying B8:B12 in the Number1 box.

f. Click **OK** to accept the function arguments and close the dialog box.

Half of the houses purchased cost more than the median, $329,750, and half of the houses cost less than this value. Notice the difference between the median and the average: The average is lower because it is affected by the lowest-priced house, $175,500.

g. Save the workbook.

STEP 4 ›› USE THE MIN, MAX, AND COUNT FUNCTIONS

Erica wants to know the least and most expensive houses so that she can analyze typical customers of the Townsend Mortgage Company. You will use the MIN and MAX functions to obtain these statistics. In addition, you will use the COUNT function to tally the number of mortgages in the sample. Refer to Figure 2.17 as you complete Step 4.

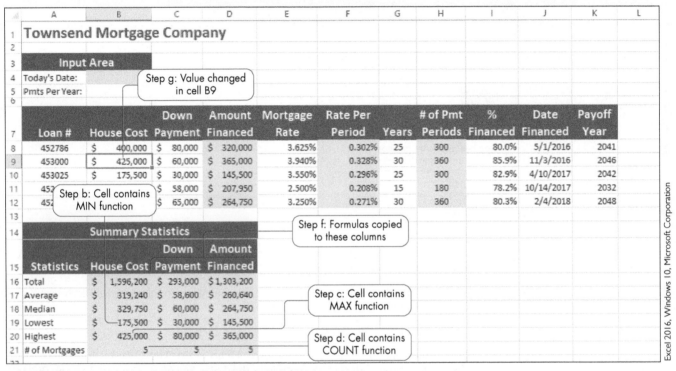

FIGURE 2.17 MIN, MAX, and COUNT Function Results

a. Click **cell B19**, the cell to display the cost of the lowest-costing house.

b. Click the **AutoSum arrow** in the Function Library group, select **MIN**, select the **range B8:B12**, and then press **Enter**.

The MIN function identifies that the lowest-costing house is $175,500.

c. Click **cell B20**. Click the **AutoSum arrow** in the Function Library group, select **MAX**, select the **range B8:B12**, and then press **Enter**.

The MAX function identifies that the highest-costing house is $400,000.

d. Click **cell B21**. Type **=COUNT(B8:B12)** and press **Enter**.

As you type the letter C, Formula AutoComplete suggests functions starting with C. As you continue typing, the list of functions narrows. After you type the beginning parenthesis, Excel displays the function ScreenTip, indicating the arguments for the function. The range B8:B12 contains five cells.

e. Select the **range B16:B21**.

You want to select the range of original statistics to copy the cells all at one time to the next two columns.

f. Drag the fill handle to the right by two columns to copy to the range C16:D21. Click **cell D21**.

Because you used relative cell references in the functions, the range in the function changes from =COUNT(B8:B12) to =COUNT(D8:D12).

g. Click **cell B9** and, change the cell value to **425000**, and click **Enter**.

The results of all formulas and functions change, including the total, average, and max house costs.

h. Save the workbook.

STEP 5 ➠ **USE THE TODAY FUNCTION**

Before finalizing the worksheet you will insert the current date. You will use the TODAY function to display the current date. Refer to Figure 2.18 as you complete Step 5.

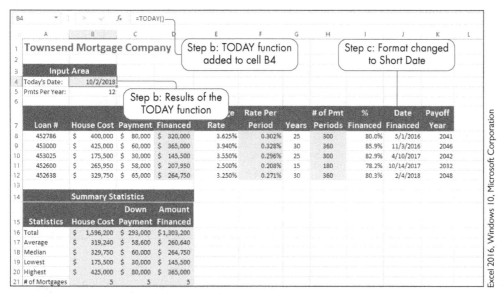

FIGURE 2.18 Insert the Current Date with the TODAY Function

a. Click **cell B4**, the cell to contain the current date.

b. Click **Date & Time** in the Function Library group, select **TODAY** to display the Function Arguments dialog box, and then click **OK** to close the dialog box.

The Function Arguments dialog box opens, although no arguments are necessary for this function. Excel displays TODAY() in the Edit formula bar, and inserts the current date in Short Date format, such as 6/1/2018, based on the computer system's date.

c. Click the **Format arrow** from the Cells group and select **AutoFit Column Width**.

d. Save the workbook. Keep the workbook open if you plan to continue with the next Hands-On Exercise. If not, close the workbook and exit Excel.

Logical, Lookup, and Financial Functions

As you prepare complex spreadsheets using functions, you will frequently use three function categories: logical, lookup and reference, and finance. Logical functions test the logic of a situation and return a particular result. Lookup and reference functions are useful when you need to look up a value in a list to identify the applicable value. Financial functions are useful to anyone who plans to take out a loan or invest money.

In this section, you will learn how to use the logical, lookup, and financial functions.

Determining Results with the IF Function

STEP 3 The most common logical function is the *IF function*, which tests specified criteria to see if it is true or false, then returns one value when a condition is met, or is true, and returns another value when the condition is not met, or is false. For example, a company gives a $500 bonus to employees who sold *over* $10,000 in merchandise in a week, but no bonus to employees who did not sell over $10,000 in merchandise. Figure 2.19 shows a worksheet containing the sales data for three representatives and their bonuses, if any.

F2				fx	=IF(E2>B$2,B$3,0)	Result if condition is false	
	A	B	C	D	E	F	G
1	Input Are Condition to be tested			Sales Rep	Sales	Bonus	
2	Sales Goal	$10,000.00		Tiffany	$11,000.00	$500.00	
3	Bonus	$ 500.00		Jose	$10,000.00	$ -	
4				Rex	$ 9,000.00	$ -	
5			Result if condition is true				

Excel 2016, Windows 10, Microsoft Corporation

FIGURE 2.19 Function to Calculate Bonus

The IF function has three arguments: (1) a condition that is tested to determine if it is either true or false, (2) the resulting value if the condition is true, and (3) the resulting value if the condition is false.

=IF(logical_test,[value_if_true],[value_if_false])

You might find it helpful to create two flowcharts to illustrate an IF function. First, construct a flowchart that uses words and numbers to illustrate the condition and results. For example, the left flowchart in Figure 2.20 illustrates the condition to see if sales are greater than $10,000, and the $500 bonus if the condition is true or $0 if the condition is false. Then, create a second flowchart—similar to the one on the right side of Figure 2.20—that replaces the words and values with actual cell references. Creating these flowcharts can help you construct the IF function that is used in cell F2 in Figure 2.19.

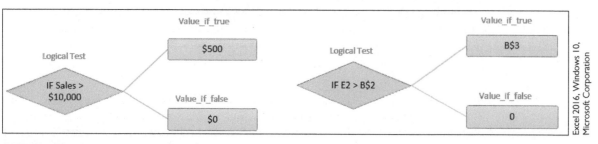

Excel 2016, Windows 10, Microsoft Corporation

FIGURE 2.20 Flowcharts Illustrating IF Function

Design the Logical Test

The first argument for the IF function is the logical test. The *logical test* contains either a value or an expression that evaluates to true or false. The logical test requires a comparison between at least two variables, such as the values stored in cells E2 and B2. In this example a salesperson receives a bonus IF he or she sells more than the $10,000 quota. The variable of total sales is in cell E2 and the constant of the sales quota is in cell B2. Therefore the logical test IF E2 > B2 translates into the following: if the amount of sales generated is greater than $10,000. Table 2.2 lists and describes in more detail the logical operators to make the comparison in the logical test.

In Figure 2.19, cell F2 contains an IF function where the logical test is E2>$B$2 to determine if Tiffany's sales in cell E2 are greater than the sales goal in cell B2. Copying the function down the column will compare each sales representative's sales with the $10,000 value in cell B2.

TABLE 2.2	Logical Operators
Operator	**Description**
=	Equal to
<>	Not equal to
<	Less than
>	Greater than
<=	Less than or equal to
>=	Greater than or equal to

Pearson Education, Inc.

Design the Value_If_True and Value_If_False Arguments

The second and third arguments of an IF function are value_if_true and value_if_false. When Excel evaluates the logical test, the result is either true or false. If the logical test is true, the value_if_true argument executes. If the logical test is false, the value_if_false argument executes. Only one of the last two arguments is executed; both arguments cannot be executed, because the logical test is either true or false but not both.

The value_if_true and value_if_false arguments can contain text, cell references, formulas, or constants. In Figure 2.19, cell F2 contains an IF function in which the value_if_true argument is B$3 and the value_if_false argument is 0. Because the logical test (E2>B$2) is true—that is, Tiffany's sales of $11,000 are greater than the $10,000 goal—the value_if_true argument is executed, and the result displays $500, the value that is stored in cell B3.

Jose's sales of $10,000 are *not* greater than $10,000, and Rex's sales of $9,000 are *not* greater than $10,000. Therefore, the value_if_false argument is executed and returns no bonus in cells F3 and F4.

> **TIP: AT LEAST TWO POSSIBLE RIGHT ANSWERS**
> Every IF function can have at least two right solutions to produce the same results. Since the logical test is a comparative expression, it can be written two ways. For example, comparing whether E2 is greater than B2 can be written using greater than (E2>B2) or the reverse can also be compared to see if B2 is less than E2 (B2<E2). Depending on the logical test, the value if true and value if false arguments will switch.

Figure 2.21 illustrates several IF functions, how they are evaluated, and their results. The input area contains values that are used in the logical tests and results. You can create this worksheet with the input area and IF functions to develop your understanding of how IF functions work.

⊿	A	B	C
1	Input Values		
2	$ 1,000.00		
3	$ 2,000.00		
4	10%		
5	5%		
6	$ 250.00		
7			
8	IF Function	Evaluation	Result
9	=IF(A2=A3,A4,A5)	$1,000 is equal to $2,000: FALSE	5%
10	=IF(A2<A3,A4,A5)	$1,000 is less than $2,000: TRUE	10%
11	=IF(A2<>A3,"Not Equal","Equal")	$1,000 and $2,000 are not equal: TRUE	Not Equal
12	=IF(A2>A3,A2*A4,A2*A5)	$1,000 is greater than $2,000: FALSE	$ 50.00
13	=IF(A2>A3,A2*A4,MAX(A2*A5,A6))	$1,000 is greater than $2,000: FALSE	$ 250.00
14	=IF(A2*A4=A3*A5,A6,0)	$100 (A2*A4) is equal to $100 (A3*A5): TRUE	$ 250.00

FIGURE 2.21 Sample IF Functions

- **Cell A9.** The logical test A2=A3 compares the values in cells A2 and A3 to see if they are equal. Because $1,000 is not equal to $2,000, the logical test is false. The value_if_false argument is executed, which displays 5%, the value stored in cell A5.

- **Cell A10.** The logical test A2<A3 determines if the value in cell A2 is less than the value in A3. Because $1,000 is less than $2,000, the logical test is true. The value_if_true argument is executed, which displays the value stored in cell A4, which is 10%.

- **Cell A11.** The logical test A2<>A3 determines if the values in cells A2 and A3 are not equal. Because $1,000 and $2,000 are not equal, the logical test is true. The value_if_true argument is executed, which displays the text Not Equal.

- **Cell A12.** The logical test A2>A3 is false. The value_if_false argument is executed, which multiplies the value in cell A2 ($1,000) by the value in cell A5 (5%) and displays $50. The parentheses in the value_if_true (A2*A4) and value_if_false (A2*A5) arguments are optional. They are not required but may help you read the function arguments better.

- **Cell A13.** The logical test A2>A3 is false. The value_if_false argument, which contains a nested MAX function, is executed. The MAX function, MAX(A2*A5,A6), multiplies the values in cells A2 ($1,000) and A5 (5%) and returns the higher of the product ($50) and the value stored in cell A6 ($250).

- **Cell A14.** The logical test A2*A4=A3*A5 is true. The contents of cell A2 ($1,000) are multiplied by the contents of cell A4 (10%) for a result of $100. That result is then compared to the result of A3*A5, which is also $100. Because the logical test is true, the function returns the value of cell A6 ($250).

TIP: TEXT AND NESTED FUNCTIONS IN IF FUNCTIONS

You can use text within a formula. For example, you can build a logical test comparing the contents of cell A1 to specific text, such as A1="Input Values". The IF function in cell A11 in Figure 2.21 uses "Not Equal" and "Equal" in the value_if_true and value_if_false arguments. When you use text in a formula or function, you must enclose the text in quotation marks. However, do not use quotation marks around formulas, cell references, or values. You can also nest functions in the logical test, value_if_true, and value_if_false arguments of the IF function. When you nest functions as arguments, make sure the nested function contains the required arguments for it to work and that you nest the function in the correct argument to calculate accurate results. For example, cell C13 in Figure 2.21 contains a nested MAX function in the value_if_false argument.

Using Lookup Functions

You can use lookup and reference functions to quickly find data associated with a specified value. For example, when you order merchandise on a website, the webserver looks up the shipping costs based on weight and distance; or at the end of a semester, your professor uses your average, such as 88%, to look up the letter grade to assign, such as B+. There are numerous lookup functions in Excel, including HLOOKUP, INDEX, LOOKUP, MATCH, and VLOOKUP. Each lookup function can be used to identify and return information based, in part, on how the data is organized.

Use the VLOOKUP function

STEP 1 »» The **VLOOKUP function** accepts a value and looks for the value in the left column of a specified table array and returns another value located in the same row from a specified column. Use VLOOKUP to search for exact matches or for the nearest value that is less than or equal to the search value, such as assigning a B grade for a class average between 80% and 89%. The VLOOKUP function has the following three required arguments and one optional argument: (1) lookup_value, (2) table_array, (3) col_index_num, and (4) range_lookup.

=VLOOKUP(lookup_value,table_array,col_index_num,[range_lookup])

Figure 2.22 shows a partial grade book that contains a vertical lookup table, as well as the final scores and letter grades. The function in cell F3 is =VLOOKUP(E3,$A$3:$B$7,2).

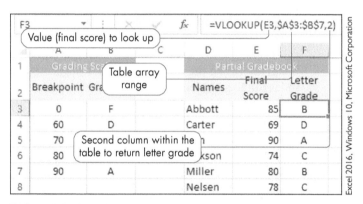

FIGURE 2.22 VLOOKUP Function for Grade Book

The **lookup value** is the cell reference of the cell that contains the value to look up. The lookup value for the first student is cell E3, which contains 85. The **table array** is the range that contains the lookup table: $A$3:$B$7. The table array range must be absolute, the value you want to look up must be located in the first column, and cannot include column labels for the lookup table. The **column index number** is the column number in the lookup table that contains the return values. In this example, the column index number is 2, which corresponds to the letter grades in column B.

TIP: USING VALUES IN FORMULAS
You know to avoid using values in formulas because the input values in a worksheet cell might change. However, as shown in Figure 2.22, the value 2 is used in the col_index_number argument of the VLOOKUP function. The 2 refers to a particular column within the lookup table and is an acceptable use of a number within a formula.

The last argument in the VLOOKUP function is the optional ***range_lookup***. This argument determines how the VLOOKUP function handles lookup values that are not an exact match for the data in the lookup table. By default, the range_lookup is set to TRUE, which is appropriate to look up values in a range. Omitting the optional argument or typing TRUE in it enables the VLOOKUP function to find the nearest value that is less than or equal in the table to the lookup value. For this reason, the first column in a VLOOKUP table array should be sorted from smallest to largest (or A to Z alphabetically) when defaulting to TRUE.

To look up an exact match, enter FALSE in the range_lookup argument. For example, if you are looking up product numbers, you must find an exact match to display the price. The function would look like this: =VLOOKUP(D15,$A$1:$B$50,2,FALSE). The function returns a value for the first lookup value that matches the first column of the lookup table. If no exact match is found, the function returns #N/A.

Here is how the VLOOKUP function works:

1. The first argument of the function evaluates the value to be located in the left column of lookup table.

2. Excel searches the first column of the lookup table until it (a) finds an exact match (if possible) or (b) identifies the correct range if an exact match is not required.

3. If Excel finds an exact match, it moves across the table to the column designated by the column index number on that same row, and returns the value stored in that cell. If the last argument is TRUE or omitted, then Excel is looking for an approximate value (NOT an exact value). In this example, if the lookup value is larger than the first number in the first column of the table, it looks to the next value to see if the lookup value is larger and will continue to do so until reaching the largest number in the column. When Excel detects that the lookup value is not greater than the next breakpoint, it stays on that row. It then uses the column index number to identify the column containing the value to return for the lookup value. Because Excel goes sequentially through the breakpoint values, it is mandatory that the first column values are arranged from the lowest value to the highest value for ranges when the range_lookup argument is TRUE or omitted.

In Figure 2.22, the VLOOKUP function assigns letter grades based on final scores. Excel identifies the lookup value (85 in cell E3) and compares it to the values in the first column of the lookup table (range A3:B7). The last argument is omitted, so Excel tries to find an exact match of 85 or an approximate match; and because the table contains breakpoints rather than every conceivable score and the first column of the lookup table is arranged from the lowest to the highest breakpoints, Excel detects that 85 is greater than 80 but is not greater than 90. Therefore, it stays on the 80 row. Excel looks at the second column (column index number of 2) and returns the letter grade of B. The B grade is then displayed in cell F3.

Create the Lookup Table

A ***lookup table*** is a range containing a table of values and text from which data can be retrieved. The table should contain at least two rows and two columns, not including headings. Figure 2.23 illustrates a college directory with three columns. The first column contains professors' names. You look up a professor's name in the first column to see his or her office (second column) and phone extension (third column).

Name	Office	Extension
Brazil, Estivan	GT 218b	7243
Fiedler, Zazilia	CS 417	7860
Lam, Kaitlyn	SC 124a	7031
Rodriquez, Lisa	GT 304	7592
Yeung, Braden	CS 414	7314

FIGURE 2.23 College Directory Lookup Table Analogy

It is important to plan the table so that it conforms to the way in which Excel can utilize the data in it. Excel cannot interpret the structure of Table 2.3. If the values you look up are exact values, you can arrange the first column in any logical order. However, to look up an approximate value in a range (such as the range 80–89), you must arrange data from the lowest to the highest value and include only the lowest value in the range (such as 80) instead of the complete range (as demonstrated in Table 2.3). The lowest value for a category or in a series is the **breakpoint**. Table 2.4 shows how to construct the lookup table in Excel. The first column contains the breakpoints—such as 60, 70, 80, and 90—or the lowest values to achieve a particular grade. The lookup table contains one or more additional columns of related data to retrieve.

TABLE 2.3 Grading Scale	
Range	Grade
90–100	A
80–89	B
70–79	C
60–69	D
Below 60	F

TABLE 2.4 Grades Lookup Table	
Range	Grade
0	F
60	D
70	C
80	B
90	A

You can nest functions as arguments inside the VLOOKUP function. For example, Figure 2.24 illustrates shipping amounts that are based on weight and location (Boston or Chicago). In the VLOOKUP function in cell C3, the lookup_value argument looks up the weight of a package in cell A3. That weight (14 pounds) is compared to the data in the table array argument, which is $E$3:$G$5. To determine which column of the lookup table to use, an IF function is nested as the column_index_number argument. The nested IF function compares the city stored in cell B3 to the text Boston. If cell B3 contains Boston, it returns 2 to use as the column_index_number to identify the shipping value for a package that is going to Boston. If cell B3 does not contain Boston (i.e., the only other city in this example is Chicago), the column_index_number is 3.

C3			fx	=VLOOKUP(A3,$E$3:$G$5,IF(B3="Boston",2,3))			
	A	B	C	D	E	F	G	H
1	Customer Data				Lookup Data			
2	Weight	Location	Shipping		Weight	Boston	Chicago	
3	14	Boston	$ 19.95		0	$ 9.95	$ 12.95	
4	4	Chicago	$ 12.95		5	$ 14.95	$ 16.95	
5	8	Boston	$ 14.95		10	$ 19.95	$ 22.95	

FIGURE 2.24 IF Function Nested in VLOOKUP Function

Use the HLOOKUP Function

Lookup functions are not limited to only vertical tables. In situations in which data is better organized horizontally, you can design a lookup table where the first row contains the values for the basis of the lookup or the breakpoints, and additional rows contain data to be retrieved. With a horizontal lookup table, use the **HLOOKUP function**. Table 2.5 shows how quarterly sales data would look in a horizontal lookup table.

TABLE 2.5 Horizontal Lookup Table				
Region	**Qtr1**	**Qtr2**	**Qtr3**	**Qtr4**
North	3495	4665	4982	5010
South	8044	7692	7812	6252
East	5081	6089	5982	6500
West	4278	4350	4387	7857

Pearson Education, Inc.

The syntax is almost the same as the syntax for the VLOOKUP function, except the third argument is row_index_num instead of col_index_num.

=HLOOKUP(lookup_value,table_array,row_index_num,[range_lookup])

Calculating Payments with the PMT Function

STEP 2)) Excel contains several financial functions to help you perform calculations with monetary values. If you take out a loan to purchase a car, you need to know the monthly payment, which depends on the price of the car, the down payment, and the terms of the loan, in order to determine if you can afford the car. The decision is made easier by developing the worksheet in Figure 2.25 and by changing the various input values as indicated.

B9		:	×	✓	fx	=PMT(B6,B8,-B3)

	A	B	C	D
1	Purchase Price	$25,999.00		
2	Down Payment	$ 5,000.00		
3	Amount to Finance	$20,999.00	Periodic interest	
4	Payments per Year	12	rate calculation	
5	Interest Rate (APR)	3.500%		
6	Periodic Rate (Monthly)	0.292%		
7	Term (Years)	5	Total number of	
8	No. of Payment Periods	60	payment periods	
9	Monthly Payment	$382.01		
10				

Excel 2016, Windows 10, Microsoft Corporation

FIGURE 2.25 Car Loan Worksheet

Creating a loan model helps you evaluate options. You realize that the purchase of a $25,999 car is prohibitive because the monthly payment is $382.01. Purchasing a less expensive car, coming up with a substantial down payment, taking out a longer-term loan, or finding a better interest rate can decrease your monthly payments.

The **PMT function** calculates payments for a loan with a fixed amount at a fixed periodic rate for a fixed time period. The PMT function uses three required arguments and up to two optional arguments: (1) rate, (2) nper, (3) pv, (4) fv, and (5) type.

=PMT(rate,nper,pv,[fv],[type])

The **rate** is the interest rate per payment period. If the annual percentage rate (APR) is 12% and you make monthly payments, the periodic rate is 1% (12%/12 months). With the same APR and quarterly payments, the periodic rate is 3% (12%/4 quarters). Divide the APR by the number of payment periods in one year. However, instead of calculating the periodic interest rate within the PMT function, you can calculate it in a separate cell and refer to that cell in the PMT function, as is done in cell B6 of Figure 2.25.

The **nper** is the total number of payment periods. The term of a loan is usually stated in years; however, you make several payments per year. For monthly payments, you make 12 payments per year. To calculate the nper, multiply the number of years by the number of payments in one year. You can either calculate the number of payment periods in the PMT function, or calculate the number of payment periods in cell B8 and use that calculated value in the PMT function.

The **pv** is the present value of the loan. The result of the PMT function is a negative value because it represents your debt. However, you can display the result as a positive value by typing a minus sign in front of the present value cell reference in the PMT function.

TIP: FINANCIAL FUNCTIONS AND NEGATIVE VALUES

When utilizing the PMT and other financial functions in Excel, you will often receive negative numbers. This happens because Excel understands accounting cash flow and the negative value represents a debt or outgoing monetary stream. It is important to understand why this happens and also to understand in some situations this should be a positive number, for example, if you are the company that granted the loan. In this situation you would receive an incoming cash flow, which should be a positive number. In contrast, if you are the requester of a loan, the payment should be negative as you will have a cash outflow each payment period. This can be manipulated by changing the pv argument of the PMT function between positive and negative values or by adding—in front of the PMT function.

Quick Concepts

8. Describe the three arguments for an IF function. **p. 509**

9. How should you structure a vertical lookup table if you need to look up values in a range? **pp. 512–513**

10. What are the first three arguments of a PMT function? Why would you divide by or multiply an argument by 12? **p. 515**

Hands-On Exercises

Watch the Video for this Hands-On Exercise!

MyITLab®
HOE3 Training

3 Logical, Lookup, and Financial Functions

Erica wants you to complete another model that she might use for future mortgage data analysis. As you study the model, you realize you need to incorporate logical, lookup, and financial functions.

STEP I ›› USE THE VLOOKUP FUNCTION

Rates vary based on the number of years to pay off the loan. Erica created a lookup table for three common mortgage years, and she entered the current APR. The lookup table will provide efficiency later when the rates change. You will use the VLOOKUP function to display the correct rate for each customer based on the number of years of the respective loans. Refer to Figure 2.26 as you complete Step 1.

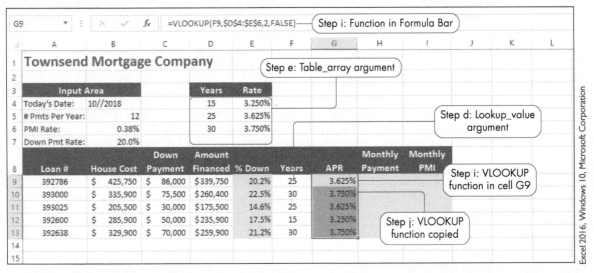

FIGURE 2.26 VLOOKUP Function to Determine APR

a. Open *e02h2Loans_LastFirst* if you closed it at the end of Hands-On Exercise 2 and save it as **e02h3Loans_LastFirst**, changing h2 to h3.

b. Click the **Payment Info worksheet tab** to display the worksheet containing the data to complete. Click **cell G9**, the cell that will store the APR for the first customer.

c. Click the **Formulas tab**, click **Lookup & Reference** in the Function Library group, and then select **VLOOKUP**.

The Function Arguments dialog box opens.

d. Ensure that the insertion point is in the Lookup_value box, click the **Collapse Dialog Box**, click **cell F9** to enter F9 in the Lookup_value box, and then click the **Expand Dialog Box** to return to Function Arguments dialog box.

Cell F9 contains the value you need to look up from the table: 25 years.

e. Press **Tab**, click **Collapse Dialog Box** to the right of the Table_array box, select the **range D4:E6**, and then click **Expand Dialog Box** to return to the Function Arguments dialog box.

This is the range that contains that data for the lookup table. The Years values in the table are arranged from lowest to highest. Do *not* select the column labels for the range.

Anticipate what will happen if you copy the formula down the column. What do you need to do to ensure that the cell references always point to the exact location of the table? If your answer is to make the table array cell references absolute, then you answered correctly.

f. Press **F4** to make the range references absolute.

The Table_array box now contains $D$4:$E$6.

g. Press **Tab** and type **2** in the Col_index_num box.

The second column of the lookup table contains the Rates that you want to return and display in the cells containing the formulas.

h. Press **Tab** and type **False** in the Range_lookup box.

To ensure an exact match to look up in the table, you enter *False* in the optional argument.

i. Click **OK**.

The VLOOKUP function uses the first loan's term in years (25) to find an exact match in the first column of the lookup table, and then returns the corresponding rate from the second column, which is 3.625%.

j. Copy the formula down the column.

Spot-check the results to make sure the function returned the correct APR based on the number of years.

k. Save the workbook.

The worksheet now has all the necessary data for you to calculate the monthly payment for each loan: the APR, the number of years for the loan, the number of payment periods in one year, and the initial loan amount. You will use the PMT function to calculate the monthly payment, which includes paying back the principal amount with interest. This calculation does not include escrow amounts, such as property taxes or insurance. Refer to Figure 2.27 as you complete Step 2.

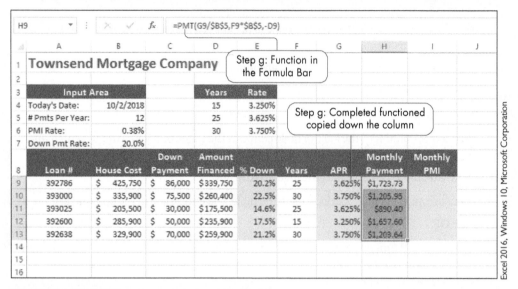

FIGURE 2.27 PMT Function to Calculate Monthly Payment

a. Click **cell H9**, the cell that will store the payment for the first customer.

b. Click **Financial** in the Function Library group, scroll through the list, and then select **PMT**.

   The Function Arguments dialog box opens.

> **TROUBLESHOOTING:** Make sure you select PMT, not PPMT. The PPMT function calculates the principal portion of a particular monthly payment, not the total monthly payment itself.

c. Type **G9/B5** in the Rate box.

   Think about what will happen if you copy the formula. The argument will be G10/B6 for the next customer. Are those cell references correct? G10 does contain the APR for the next customer, but B6 does not contain the correct number of payments in one year. Therefore, you need to make B5 an absolute cell reference because the number of payments per year does not vary.

d. Press **F4** to make the reference to cell B5 absolute.

e. Press **Tab** and type **F9*$B$5** in the Nper box.

   You calculate the nper by multiplying the number of years by the number of payments in one year. You must make B5 an absolute cell reference so that it does not change when you copy the formula down the column.

f. Press **Tab** and type **-D9** in the Pv box.

The bottom of the dialog box indicates that the monthly payment is 1723.73008 or $1,723.73.

> **TROUBLESHOOTING:** If the payment displays as a negative value, you probably forgot to type the minus sign in front of the D9 reference in the Pv box. Edit the function and type the minus sign in the correct place.

    g. Click **OK**. Copy the formula down the column.

    h. Save the workbook.

STEP 3 ⟫ USE THE IF FUNCTION

Lenders often want borrowers to have a 20% down payment. If borrowers do not put in 20% of the cost of the house as a down payment, they pay a private mortgage insurance (PMI) fee. PMI serves to protect lenders from absorbing loss if the borrower defaults on the loan, and it enables borrowers with less cash to secure a loan. The PMI fee is about 0.38% of the amount financed. Some borrowers have to pay PMI for a few months or years until the balance owed is less than 80% of the appraised value. The worksheet contains the necessary values in the input area. You use the IF function to determine which borrowers must pay PMI and how much they will pay. Refer to Figure 2.28 as you complete Step 3.

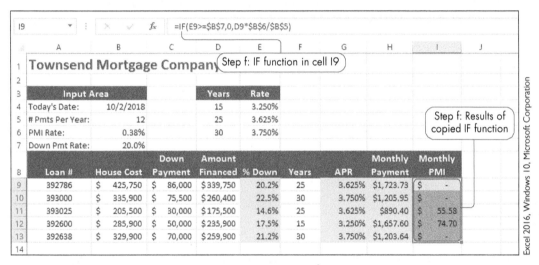

FIGURE 2.28 IF Function to Calculate Monthly PMI

    a. Click **cell I9**, the cell that will store the PMI, if any, for the first customer.

    b. Click **Logical** in the Function Library group and select **IF**.

    The Function Arguments dialog box opens. You will enter the three arguments.

    c. Type **E9>=$B$7** in the Logical_test box.

    The logical test compares the down payment percentage to see if the customer's down payment is at least 20%, the threshold stored in B7, of the amount financed. The customer's percentage cell reference is relative so that it will change when you copy it down the column; however, cell B7 must be absolute because it contains a value that should remain constant when the formula is copied to other cells.

    d. Press **Tab** and type **0** in the Value_if_true box.

If the customer makes a down payment that is at least 20% of the purchase price, the customer does not pay PMI, so a value of 0 will display whenever the logical test is true. The first customer paid 20% of the purchase price, so he or she does not have to pay PMI.

e. Press **Tab** and type **D9*$B$6/$B$5** in the Value_if_false box.

If the logical test is false, the customer must pay PMI, which is calculated by multiplying the amount financed (D9) by the periodic PMI rate (the result of dividing the yearly PMI (B6) by the number of payments per year (B5)).

f. Click **OK** and copy the formula down the column.

The first, second, and fifth customers paid 20% of the purchase price, so they do not have to pay PMI. The third and fourth customers must pay PMI because their respective down payments were less than 20% of the purchase price.

> **TROUBLESHOOTING:** If the results are not as you expected, check the logical operators. People often mistype < and > or forget to type = for >= situations. Correct any errors in the original formula and copy the formula again.

g. Set the worksheets to print on one page. Add a footer with your name on the left, sheet code in the middle, and the file name code on the right.

h. Save and close the file. Based on your instructor's directions, submit e02h3Loans_LastFirst.

Chapter Objectives Review

After reading this chapter, you have accomplished the following objectives:

1. Use relative, absolute, and mixed cell references in formulas.

- Use a relative cell address: A relative reference indicates a cell's location relative to the formula cell. When you copy the formula, the relative cell reference changes.
- Use an absolute cell reference: An absolute reference is a permanent pointer to a particular cell, indicated with $ before the column letter and the row number, such as $B$5. When you copy the formula, the absolute cell reference does not change.
- Use a mixed cell reference: A mixed reference contains part absolute and part relative reference, such as $B5 or B$5. Either the column or the row reference changes, while the other remains constant when you copy the formula.

2. Insert a function.

- A function is a predefined formula that performs a calculation. It contains the function name and arguments. Formula AutoComplete, function ScreenTips, and the Insert Function dialog box help you select and create functions. The Function Arguments dialog box guides you through the entering requirements for each argument.

3. Insert basic math and statistics functions.

- Use the SUM function: The SUM function calculates the total of a range of values. The syntax is =SUM(number1,[number2],...).
- Use the AVERAGE and MEDIAN functions: The AVERAGE function calculates the arithmetic mean of values in a range. The MEDIAN function identifies the midpoint value in a set of values.
- Use the MIN and MAX functions: The MIN function identifies the lowest value in a range, whereas the MAX function identifies the highest value in a range.
- Use the COUNT functions: The COUNT function tallies the number of cells in a range, that contain values, whereas the COUNTBLANK function tallies the number of blank cells in a range, and COUNTA tallies the number of cells that are not empty.

- Perform calculations with Quick Analysis tools: With the Quick Analysis tools you can apply formatting, create charts or tables, and insert basic functions.

4. Use date functions.

- Insert the TODAY function: The TODAY function displays the current date.
- Insert the NOW function: The NOW function displays the current date and time.

5. Determine results with the IF function.

- Design the logical test: The IF function is a logical function that evaluates a logical test using logical operators, such as <, >, and =, and returns one value if the condition is true and another value if the condition is false.
- Design the value_if_true and value_if_false arguments: The arguments can contain cell references, text, or calculations. If a logical test is true, Excel executes the value_if_true argument. If a logical test is false, Excel executes the value_if_false argument.
- You can nest or embed other functions inside one or more of the arguments of an IF function to create more complex formulas.

6. Use lookup functions.

- Use the VLOOKUP function: The VLOOKUP function contains the required arguments lookup_value, table_array, and col_index_num and one optional argument, range_lookup.
- Create the lookup table: Design the lookup table using exact values or the breakpoints for ranges. If using breakpoints, the breakpoints must be in ascending order.
- Use the HLOOKUP function: The HLOOKUP function looks up values by row (horizontally) rather than by column (vertically).

7. Calculate payments with the PMT function.

- The PMT function calculates periodic payments for a loan with a fixed interest rate and a fixed term. The PMT function requires the periodic interest rate, the total number of payment periods, and the original value of the loan.

Key Terms Matching

Match the key terms with their definitions. Write the key term letter by the appropriate numbered definition.

a. Absolute cell reference

b. Argument

c. AVERAGE function

d. COUNT function

e. IF function

f. Logical test

g. Lookup table

h. MAX function

i. MEDIAN function

j. MIN function

k. Mixed cell reference

l. NOW function

m. PMT function

n. Relative cell reference

o. SUM function

p. Syntax

q. TODAY function

r. VLOOKUP function

1. _____ A set of rules that governs the structure and components for properly entering a function. **p. 495**

2. _____ Displays the current date. **p. 501**

3. _____ Indicates a cell's specific location; the cell reference does not change when you copy the formula. **p. 489**

4. _____ An input, such as a cell reference or value, needed to complete a function. **p. 495**

5. _____ Identifies the highest value in a range. **p. 500**

6. _____ Tallies the number of cells in a range that contain values. **p. 500**

7. _____ Looks up a value in a vertical lookup table and returns a related result from the lookup table. **p. 511**

8. _____ A range that contains data for the basis of the lookup and data to be retrieved. **p. 511**

9. _____ Calculates the arithmetic mean, or average, of values in a range. **p. 499**

10. _____ Identifies the midpoint value in a set of values. **p. 500**

11. _____ Displays the current date and time. **p. 501**

12. _____ Evaluates a condition and returns one value if the condition is true and a different value if the condition is false. **p. 508**

13. _____ Calculates the total of values contained in two or more cells. **p. 498**

14. _____ Calculates the periodic payment for a loan with a fixed interest rate and fixed term. **p. 515**

15. _____ Indicates a cell's location from the cell containing the formula; the cell reference changes when the formula is copied. **p. 488**

16. _____ Contains both an absolute and a relative cell reference in a formula; the absolute part does not change but the relative part does when you copy the formula. **p. 490**

17. _____ An expression that evaluates to true or false. **p. 509**

18. _____ Displays the lowest value in a range. **p. 500**

Multiple Choice

1. If cell E15 contains the formula =$C$5*J$15, what type of cell reference is the J$15 in the formula?

   (a) Relative reference

   (b) Absolute reference

   (c) Mixed reference

   (d) Syntax

2. What function would most efficiently accomplish the same thing as =(B5+C5+D5+E5+F5)/5?

   (a) =SUM(B5:F5)/5

   (b) =AVERAGE(B5:F5)

   (c) =MEDIAN(B5:F5)

   (d) =COUNT(B5:F5)

3. When you start to type =AV, what feature displays a list of functions and defined names?

   (a) Function ScreenTip

   (b) Formula AutoComplete

   (c) Insert Function dialog box

   (d) Function Arguments dialog box

4. A formula containing the entry =$B3 is copied to a cell one column to the right and two rows down. How will the entry appear in its new location?

   (a) =$B3

   (b) =B3

   (c) =$C5

   (d) =$B5

5. Which of the following functions should be used to insert the current date and time in a cell?

   (a) =TODAY()

   (b) =CURRENT()

   (c) =NOW()

   (d) =DATE

6. Which of the following is not an argument of the IF function?

   (a) value_if_true

   (b) value_if_false

   (c) logical_test

   (d) lookup_value

7. Which of the following is *not* true about the VLOOKUP function?

   (a) The lookup table must be in ascending order.

   (b) The lookup table must be in descending order.

   (c) The default match type is approximate.

   (d) The match type must be false when completing an exact match.

8. The function =PMT(C5,C7,-C3) is stored in cell C15. What must be stored in cell C5?

   (a) APR

   (b) Periodic interest rate

   (c) Loan amount

   (d) Number of payment periods

9. Which of the following is *not* an appropriate use of the SUM function?

   (a) =SUM(B3:B45)

   (b) =SUM(F1:G10)

   (c) =SUM(A8:A15,D8:D15)

   (d) =SUM(D15-C15)

10. What is the keyboard shortcut to create an absolute reference?

   (a) F2

   (b) F3

   (c) F4

   (d) Alt

Practice Exercises

1 Hamilton Heights Auto Sales

You are the primary loan manager for Hamilton Heights Auto Sales, an auto sales company located in Missouri. In order to most efficiently manage the auto loans your company finances, you have decided to create a spreadsheet to perform several calculations. You will insert the current date, calculate down payment and interest rates based on credit score, calculate periodic payment amounts, and complete the project with basic summary information. Refer to Figure 2.29 as you complete this exercise.

A2	fx	Date						
	A	B	C	D	E	F	G	H
1		Hamilton Heights Auto Sales						
2	Date	10/2/2018						
3			Auto Finance Worksheet					
4	Vin #	Purchase Price	Credit Rating	Down Payment	Amount Financed		Rate	Payment
5	619600647	$ 23,417.00	579	$ 2,341.70	$ 21,075.30		4.00%	$388.13
6	464119439	$ 23,732.00	763	$ -	$ 23,732.00		3.00%	$426.43
7	122140305	$ 44,176.00	657	$ 4,417.60	$ 39,758.40		3.50%	$723.27
8	276772526	$ 42,556.00	827	$ -	$ 42,556.00		2.75%	$759.96
9	335963723	$ 24,305.00	652	$ 2,430.50	$ 21,874.50		3.50%	$397.94
10	401292230	$ 27,847.00	676	$ 2,784.70	$ 25,062.30		3.50%	$455.93
11		$ 186,033.00			$ 29,009.75			
12								
13	Credit Score	APR		Down Payment		Credit Score Threshold		
14	500	4.00%		10%		750		
15	650	3.50%						
16	700	3.25%		Payments Per Year		Total # of Payments		
17	750	3.00%		12		60		
18	800	2.75%						
19	850	2.25%						

Excel 2016, Windows 10, Microsoft Corporation

FIGURE 2.29 Hamilton Heights Auto Sales

a. Open *e02p1AutoSales* and save it as **e02p1AutoSales_LastFirst**.

b. Click cell **B2**, click the **Formulas tab**, click **Date & Time** in the Function Library group, select **NOW**, and then click **OK** to enter today's date in the cell.

c. Click cell **D5** on the Formulas tab, click **Logical** in the Function Library group, and select **IF**.

d. Type **C5<=$E$14** in the Logical_test box, type **$D$14*B5** in the Value_if_true box, type **0** in the Value_if_false box, and then click **OK**.

This uses the IF function to calculate the required down payment based on credit score. If the customer has a credit score higher than 750 a down payment is not required. All clients with credits scores lower than 750 must pay a required 10% down payment in advance.

e. Use the fill handle to copy the contents of **cell D5** down the column, click **Auto Fill Options** to the lower-right of the copied cells, and then click **Fill Without Formatting** to ensure that the **Bottom Double border** remains applied to cell D10.

f. Calculate the Amount Financed by doing the following:
   - Click **cell E5** and type **=B5-D5**.
   - Use **cell E5's fill handle** to copy the function down the column.
   - Apply **Bottom Double border** to cell E10.

g. Calculate the Rate by doing the following:
   - Click **cell F5**. Click **Lookup & Reference** in the Function Library group and select **VLOOKUP**.
   - Type **C5** in the Lookup_value box, type **$A$14:$B$19** in the Table_array box, type **2** in the Col_index_num box, and then click **OK**
   - Double-click **cell F5's fill handle** to copy the function down the column.
   - Click **Auto Fill Options**, and click **Fill Without Formatting**.

h. Calculate the required periodic payment by doing the following:
   - Click **cell G5**, click **Financial** in the Function Library Group, and then click **PMT**.
   - Type **F5/$D$17** in the Rate box, type **$E$17** in the Nper box, type **–E5** in the Pv box, and then click **OK**.
   - Double-click **cell G5's** fill handle to copy the function down the column.
   - Click the **Auto Fill Options** button, and click **Fill Without Formatting**.

i. Select the **range B5:B10**, click the **Quick Analysis button**, click **TOTALS**, and select **Sum** from the Quick Analysis Gallery.

j. Click **cell E11** and type **=AVERAGE(E5:E10)** to calculate the average amount financed.

k. Create a footer with your name on the left side, the sheet name code in the center, and the file name on the right side.

l. Save and close the workbook. Based on your instructor's directions, submit e02p1AutoSales_LastFirst.

2 Lockridge Marketing Analytics

As a business analyst for Lockridge Marketing Analytics, you have been tasked with awarding performance bonuses. You prepare a model to calculate employee bonuses based on average customer satisfaction survey results. The survey is based on a scale of 1 to 5 with 5 being the highest rating. Employees with survey results where ratings are between 1 and 2.9 do not receive bonuses, scores between 3 and 3.9 earn a 2% one-time bonus on their monthly salary, and scores of 4 or higher receive a 5% bonus. In addition, you calculate basic summary data for reporting purposes. Refer to Figure 2.30 as you complete this exercise.

J10 | fx

	A	B	C	D	E	F
1	Lockridge Marketing Analytics					
2						
3	**Inputs and Constants**				**Bonus Data**	
4	Today:	10/2/2018		**Rating**	1	3
5	Employees Surveyed	6		**Bonus**	0%	2%
6						
7						
8						
9	**Survey Code**	**Current Salary**	**Monthly Salary**	**Survey Score**	**Rating Bonus**	**Monthly Take Home**
10	38078	$ 50,000	$ 4,166.67	5	$ 208.33	$ 4,375.00
11	41105	$ 75,250	$ 6,270.83	3.5	$ 125.42	$ 6,396.25
12	39752	$ 67,250	$ 5,604.17	4.2	$ 280.21	$ 5,884.38
13	37872	$ 45,980	$ 3,831.67	3	$ 76.63	$ 3,908.30
14	40616	$ 58,750	$ 4,895.83	4.2	$ 244.79	$ 5,140.63
15	40347	$ 61,000	$ 5,083.33	4.5	$ 254.17	$ 5,337.50
16						
17						
18	**Statistics**					
19	Lowest Bonus	$ 76.63				
20	Average Bonus	$ 198.26				
21	Highest Bonus	$ 280.21				

Excel 2016, Windows 10, Microsoft Corporation

FIGURE 2.30 Lockridge Marketing Analytics

a. Open *e02p2Bonus* and save it as **e02p2Bonus_LastFirst**.

b. Click **cell B4**, click the **Formulas tab**, click **Date & Time** in the Function Library group, select **TODAY**, and then click **OK** to enter today's date in the cell.

c. Click **cell B5**, click the **AutoSum arrow** in the Function Library group, and then select **Count Numbers**. Select the **range A10:A15** and press **Enter**.

d. Click **cell C10**, type **=B10/12**, press **Ctrl+Enter**, and double-click the **fill handle**.

e. Enter the Rating Bonus based on survey average by doing the following:
  - Click **cell E10** and type **=C10***.
  - Click **Lookup & Reference** in the Function Library group and select **HLOOKUP**.
  - Type **D10** in the Lookup_value box, type **E$4:G$5** in the Table_array box, type **2** in the Col_index_num box, and then click **OK**.
  - Double-click the **cell E10 fill handle** to copy the formula down the Rating Bonus column.

f. Calculate each employee's monthly take-home by doing the following:
  - Click **cell F10** and type **=C10+E10**.
  - Double-click the **cell F10 fill handle**.

g. Calculate basic summary statistics by doing the following:
  - Click **cell B19**, click the **Formulas tab**, click the **AutoSum arrow**, and then select **MIN**.
  - Select the **range E10:E15** and then press **Enter**.
  - In **cell B20**, click the **AutoSum arrow**, select **AVERAGE**, select the **range E10:E15**, and then press **Enter**.
  - In **cell B21**, click the **AutoSum arrow**, select **MAX**, select the **range E10:E15**, and then press **Enter**.

h. Create a footer with your name on the left side, the sheet name in the center, and the file name code on the right side.

i. Save and close the workbook. Based on your instructor's directions, submit e02p2Bonus_LastFirst.

Mid-Level Exercises

1 Metropolitan Zoo Gift Shop Weekly Payroll

ANALYSIS CASE

As manager of the gift shop at the Metropolitan Zoo, you are responsible for managing the weekly payroll. Your assistant developed a partial worksheet, but you need to enter the formulas to calculate the regular pay, overtime pay, gross pay, taxable pay, withholding tax, FICA, and net pay. In addition, you want to include total pay columns and calculate some basic statistics. As you construct formulas, make sure you use absolute and relative cell references correctly in formulas.

a. Open the *e02m1Payroll* workbook and save it as **e02m1Payroll_LastFirst**.

b. Study the worksheet structure and read the business rules in the Notes section.

c. Use IF functions to calculate the regular pay and overtime pay based on a regular 40-hour workweek in **cells E5** and **F5**. Pay overtime only for overtime hours. Calculate the gross pay based on the regular and overtime pay. Abram's regular pay is $398. With 8 overtime hours, Abram's overtime pay is $119.40.

d. Create a formula in **cell H5** to calculate the taxable pay. Multiply the number of dependents by the deduction per dependent and subtract that from the gross pay. With two dependents, Abram's taxable pay is $417.40.

e. Use a VLOOKUP function in **cell I5** to identify and calculate the federal withholding tax. With a taxable pay of $417.40, Abram's tax rate is 25% and the withholding tax is $104.35. The VLOOKUP function returns the applicable tax rate, which you must then multiply by the taxable pay.

f. Calculate FICA in **cell J5** based on gross pay and the FICA rate, and calculate the net pay in cell K5.

g. Copy all formulas down their respective columns.

h. Use Quick Analysis tools to calculate the total regular pay, overtime pay, gross pay, taxable pay, withholding tax, FICA, and net pay on **row 17**.

i. Apply **Accounting Number Format** to the **range C5:C16**. Apply **Accounting Number Format** to the first row of monetary data and to the total row. Apply the **Comma style** to the monetary values for the other employees. Underline the last employee's monetary values and use the Format Cells dialog box to apply Top and Double Bottom borders for the totals.

j. Insert appropriate functions to calculate the average, highest, and lowest values in the Summary Statistics area (the **range I21:K23**) of the worksheet. Format the # of hours calculations as **Number format** with one decimal and the remaining calculations with **Accounting Number Format**.

k. Insert a new sheet named **Overtime**. List the number of overtime hours for the week. Calculate the yearly gross amount spent on overtime assuming the same number of overtime hours per week. Add another row with only half the overtime hours (using a formula). What is your conclusion and recommendation on overtime? Format this worksheet.

l. Insert a footer with your name on the left side, the sheet name in the center, and the file name code on the right side of both worksheets.

m. Save and close the workbook. Based on your instructor's directions, submit e02m1Payroll_LastFirst.

2 Mortgage Calculator

As a financial consultant, you work with a family who plans to purchase a $35,000 car. You want to create a worksheet containing variable data (the price of the car, down payment, date of the first payment, and borrower's credit rating) and constants (sales tax rate, years, and number of payments in one year). Borrowers pay 0.5% sales tax on the purchase price of the vehicle and their credit rating determines the required down payment percentage and APR. Your worksheet needs to perform various calculations.

a. Start a new Excel workbook, save it as **e02m2Loan_LastFirst**, and then rename Sheet1 **Payment**.

b. Type **Auto Loan Calculator** in cell A1, and then merge and center the title on the first row in the **range A1:F1**. Apply **bold, 18 pt** font size, and **Gold, Accent 4, Darker 25%** font color.

c. Type the labels in the **range A3:A12**. For each label, such as *Negotiated Cost of Vehicle*, merge the cells, such as the **range A4:B4**. Use the Format Painter to copy the formatting to the remaining nine labels. Next type and format the Inputs and Constants values in **column C**.

d. Type **Credit, Down Payment**, and **APR** in the **range A14:C14**, type the four credit ratings in the first column, the required down payment percentages in the second column, and the respective APRs in the third column. Next format the percentages, and then indent the percentages in the cells as needed.

e. Type labels in the Intermediate Calculations *and* Outputs sections in **column E**.

f. Enter formulas in the Intermediate Calculations and Outputs sections to calculate the following:

   • **APR** based on credit rating: Use a Lookup function that references the borrower's credit rating and the table array in range. Include the range_lookup argument to ensure an exact match.

   • **Minimum down payment required**: Use a lookup function and calculation. Use the credit rating as the lookup value, and the **table array A15:C18**. Include the range_lookup argument to ensure an exact match. Multiply the function results by the negotiated cost of the house.

   • **Sales tax**: Multiply the negotiated cost of the vehicle by the sales tax rate.

   • **Total down payment**: The sum of the minimum down payment required and any additional down payment made.

   • **Amount of the loan**: The difference between the negotiated cost of the house and the total down payment.

   • **Monthly payment**: Principal and interest using the PMT function.

g. Format each section with fill color, bold, underline, number formats, borders, and column widths as needed.

h. Insert a footer with your name on the left side, the sheet name in the center, and the file name code on the right side of both sheets.

i. Save and close the workbook. Based on your instructor's directions, submit e02m2Loan_LastFirst.

3 Facebook and Blackboard

COLLABORATION CASE

FROM SCRATCH

Social media extends past friendships to organizational and product "fan" pages. Organizations such as Lexus, Pepsi, and universities create pages to provide information about their organizations. Some organizations even provide product details, such as for the Lexus ES350. Facebook includes a wealth of information about Microsoft Office products. People share information, pose questions, and reply with their experiences.

a. Log in to your Facebook account. If you do not have a Facebook account, sign up for one and add at least two classmates as friends. Search for Microsoft Excel 2016 and click **Like**.

b. Review postings on the Microsoft Excel wall. Notice that some people post what they like most about Excel or how much it has improved their productivity. Post a note about one of your favorite features about Excel that you have learned so far or how you have used Excel in other classes or on the job.

c. Click the **Discussions link** on the Microsoft Excel Facebook page and find topics that relate to IF or HLOOKUP functions. Post a response to one of the discussions. Take a screenshot of your posting and insert it into a Word document. Save the Word document **as e02m3_LastFirst**.

d. Create a team of three students. Create one discussion that asks people to describe their favorite use of any of the nested functions used in this chapter. Each team member should respond to the posting. Monitor the discussion and, when you have a few responses, capture a screenshot of the dialogue and insert it into your Word document.

e. Go to www.youtube.com and search for one of these Excel topics: absolute references, mixed references, semi-selection, IF function, VLOOKUP function, or PMT function.

f. Watch several video clips and find one of particular interest to you.

g. Post the URL on your Facebook wall. Specify the topic and describe why you like this particular video.

h. Watch videos from the links posted by other students on their Facebook walls. Comment on at least two submissions. Point out what you like about the video or any suggestions you have for improvement.

i. Insert screenshots of your postings in a Word document, if required by your instructor. Save and close the file. Based on your instructor's directions submit e02m3_LastFirst.

Beyond the Classroom

Auto Finance

After graduating from college and obtaining your first job, you have decided to purchase a new vehicle. Before purchasing the car, you want to create a worksheet to estimate the monthly payment based on the purchase price, APR, down payment, and years. Your monthly budget is $500 and you will use conditional logic to automatically determine if you can afford the cars you are evaluating. Open the workbook *e02b1CarLoan* and save it as **e02b1CarLoan_LastFirst**.

Insert a function to automatically enter the current date in cell A4. Starting in cell B12 enter a formula to calculate the down payment for each vehicle price range based on the down payment percentage listed in cell D4. Be sure to use the appropriate absolute or mixed reference and copy the formula to complete range B13:B16. Before calculating the periodic payment for each vehicle, you will need to research the current vehicle interest rates. Conduct an Internet search to determine the current interest rate for a five-year auto loan and enter the value in cell D5. In cell C12 type a function that calculates the periodic payment for the first vehicle based on the input information in range D4:D7. Be sure to use the appropriate absolute or mixed reference and copy the formula to complete range C12:C16. In column D, use an IF function to determine if the first vehicle is financially viable; display either Test Drive or NA based on the criteria in cell D8. Be sure to use the appropriate absolute or mixed reference and copy the formula to complete range D12:D16.

Include a footer with your name on the left side, the date in the center, and the file name on the right side. Save and close the workbook. Based on your instructor's directions, submit e02b1CarLoan_LastFirst.

Park City Condo Rental

You and some friends are planning a Labor Day vacation to Park City, Utah. You have secured a four-day condominium that costs $1,200. Some people will stay all four days; others will stay part of the weekend. One of your friends constructed a worksheet to help calculate each person's cost of the rental. The people who stay Thursday night will split the nightly cost evenly. To keep the costs down, everyone agreed to pay $30 per night per person for Friday, Saturday, and/or Sunday nights. Depending on the number of people who stay each night, the group may owe more money. Kyle, Ian, Isaac, and Daryl agreed to split the difference in the total rental cost and the amount the group members paid. Open the workbook *e02b2ParkCity*, and save it as **e02b2ParkCity_LastFirst**.

Review the worksheet structure, including the assumptions and calculation notes at the bottom of the worksheet. Check the formulas and functions, making necessary corrections. With the existing data, the number of people staying each night is 5, 8, 10, and 7, respectively. The total paid given the above assumptions is $1,110, giving a difference of $90 to be divided evenly among the first four people. Kyle's share should be $172.50. In the cells containing errors, insert comments to describe the error and fix the formulas. Verify the accuracy of formulas by entering an IF function in cell I1 to ensure that the totals match. Nick, James, and Body inform you they cannot stay Sunday night, and Rob wants to stay Friday night. Change the input accordingly. The updated total paid is now $1,200, and the difference is $150. Include a footer with your name on the left side, the date in the center, and the file name on the right side. Save and close the workbook. Based on your instructor's directions, submit e02b2ParkCity_LastFirst.

Capstone Exercise

You are an account manager for Inland Jewelers, a regional company that makes custom class rings for graduating seniors. Your supervisor requested a workbook to report on new accounts created on payment plans. The report should provide details on total costs to the student as well as payment information. Each ring financed has a base price that can fluctuate based on ring personalization.

Insert Current Date

You open the starting workbook you previously created, and insert the current date and time.

a. Open the *e02c1ClassRing* workbook, and then save it as **e02c1ClassRing_LastFirst**.

b. Insert a function in **cell B2** to display the current date and format as a **Long Date**.

c. Set column B's width to **Autofit**.

Calculate Cost

You are ready to calculate the cost of each class ring ordered. The rings are priced based on their base metal as displayed in the range A15:B19.

a. Insert a lookup function in **cell C5** to display the ring cost for the first student.

b. Copy the function from **cell C5** down through **C11** to complete column C.

c. Apply **Accounting Number Format** to **column C**.

Determine the Total Due

You will calculate the total due for each student's order. The total is the base price of the ring plus an additional charge for personalization if applicable.

a. Insert an IF function in **cell E5** to calculate the total due. If the student has chosen to personalize the ring, there is an additional charge of 5% located in **cell B21** that must be applied; if not, the student pays only the base price. Use appropriate relative and absolute cell references.

b. Copy the function from **cell E5** down through **E11** to complete column E.

c. Apply **Accounting Number Format** to **column E**.

Calculate the Monthly Payment

Your next step is to calculate the periodic payment for each student's account. The payments are based on the years financed in column F and the annual interest rate in cell B22. All accounts are paid on a monthly basis.

a. Insert the function in **cell G5** to calculate the first student's monthly payment, using appropriate relative and absolute cell references.

b. Copy the formula down the column.

c. Apply **Accounting Number Format** to **column G**.

Finalize the Workbook

You perform some basic statistical calculations and finalize the workbook with formatting and page setup options.

a. Calculate totals in **cells C12**, **E12**, and **G12**.

b. Apply **Accounting Number Format** to the **cells C12, E12**, and **G12**.

c. Set **0.3"** left and right margins and ensure that the page prints on only one page.

d. Insert a footer with your name on the left side, the sheet name in the center, and the file name on the right side.

e. Save and close the workbook. Based on your instructor's directions, submit e02c1ClassRing_LastFirst.

Excel

Charts

LEARNING OUTCOME | You will create charts and insert sparklines to represent data visually.

OBJECTIVES & SKILLS: After you read this chapter, you will be able to:

Chart Basics

OBJECTIVE 1: SELECT THE DATA SOURCE   534
Select an Adjacent Range, Select a Nonadjacent Range
OBJECTIVE 2: CHOOSE A CHART TYPE   536
Create a Clustered Column Chart, Create a Bar Chart, Change the Chart Type, Create a Line Chart, Create a Pie Chart, Create a Combo Chart, Create an Area Chart, Create a Scatter Chart, Create a Stock Chart
OBJECTIVE 3: MOVE, SIZE, AND PRINT A CHART   548
Move a Chart to a New Chart Sheet, Move a Chart Within a Worksheet, Size a Chart

HANDS-ON EXERCISE 1:
Chart Basics   552

Chart Elements

OBJECTIVE 4: ADD, EDIT, AND FORMAT CHART ELEMENTS   559
Edit and Format Chart Titles; Add and Format Axes Titles; Format Axes; Add, Position, and Format Data Labels; Format and Position the Legend; Apply a Quick Layout; Format the Chart Area; Format the Plot Area; Format a Data Series; Format the Gridlines; Format a Data Point

HANDS-ON EXERCISE 2:
Chart Elements   569

Chart Design and Sparklines

OBJECTIVE 5: APPLY A CHART STYLE AND COLORS   574
Apply a Chart Style, Change Colors
OBJECTIVE 6: MODIFY THE DATA SOURCE   575
Apply Chart Filters, Switch Row and Column Data
OBJECTIVE 7: CREATE AND CUSTOMIZE SPARKLINES   577
Insert a Sparkline, Customize Sparklines

HANDS-ON EXERCISE 3:
Chart Design and Sparklines   580

CASE STUDY | Computer Job Outlook

You are an academic advisor for the School of Computing at a private university in Seattle, Washington. You will visit high schools over the next few weeks to discuss the computing programs at the university and to inform students about the job outlook in the computing industry. Your assistant, Doug Demers, researched growing computer-related jobs in the *Occupational Outlook Handbook* published by the Bureau of Labor Statistics on the U.S. Department of Labor's website. In particular, Doug listed seven jobs, the number of those jobs in 2010, the projected number of jobs by 2020, the growth in percentage increase and number of jobs, and the 2010 median pay. This dataset shows an 18%–31% increase in computer-related jobs in that 10-year time period.

To prepare for your presentation to encourage students to enroll in your School of Computing, you will create several charts that depict the job growth in the computer industry. You know that different charts provide different perspectives on the data. After you complete the charts, you will be able to use them in a variety of formats, such as presentations, fliers, and brochures.

Depicting Data Visually

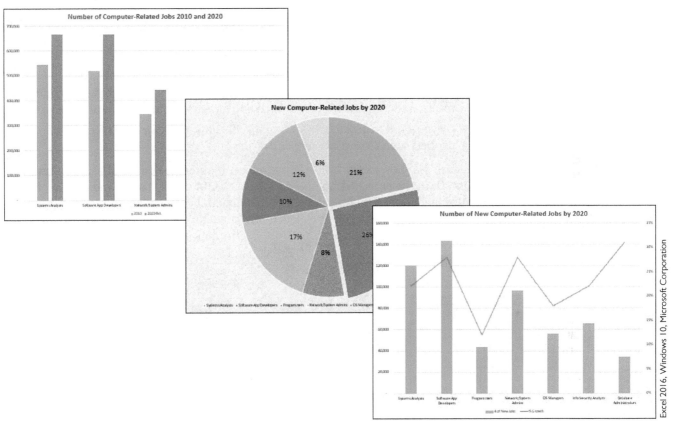

FIGURE 3.1 Computer Job Outlook Charts

Excel 2016, Windows 10, Microsoft Corporation

CASE STUDY | Computer Job Outlook

Starting File	File to be Submitted
e03h1Jobs	e03h3Jobs_LastFirst

Chart Basics

A ***chart*** is a visual representation of numerical data that compares data and reveals trends or patterns to help people make informed decisions. An effective chart depicts data in a clear, easy-to-interpret manner and contains enough data to be useful without overwhelming your audience.

In this section, you will select the data source, choose the best chart type to represent numerical data, and designate the chart's location.

Selecting the Data Source

Look at the structure of the worksheet—the column labels, the row labels, the quantitative data, and the calculated values. Before creating a chart, make sure the worksheet data are organized so that the values in columns and rows use the same value system (such as dollars or units), make sure labels are descriptive, and delete any blank rows or columns that exist in the dataset. Decide what you want to convey to your audience by answering these questions:

- Does the worksheet hold a single set of data, such as average snowfall at one ski resort, or multiple sets of data, such as average snowfall at several ski resorts?

- Do you want to depict data for one specific time period or over several time periods, such as several years or decades?

Figure 3.2 shows a worksheet containing computer-related job titles, the number of jobs in 2010, the projected number of jobs by 2020, other details, and a chart. Row 3 contains labels merged and centered over individual column labels in row 5. Row 4 is blank and hidden. It is a good practice to insert a blank row between merged labels and individual column labels to enable you to sort the data correctly.

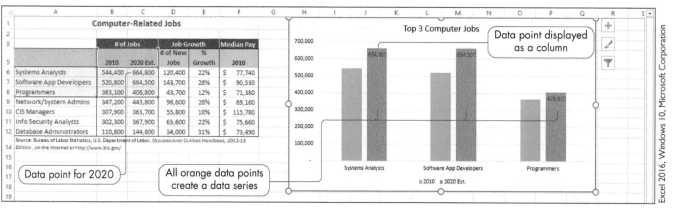

FIGURE 3.2 Dataset and Chart

Each cell containing a value is a ***data point***. For example, the value 664,800 in cell C6 is a data point for the estimated number of Systems Analysts in 2020. Each data point in the worksheet creates an individual data point in the chart. A group of related data points that display in row(s) or column(s) in the worksheet create a ***data series***. For example, the values 664,800, 664,500, and 406,800 comprise the number of estimated jobs by 2020 data series, which is indicated by the orange columns in the chart.

Identify the data range by selecting values and labels that you want to include in the chart. If the values and labels are not stored in adjacent cells, hold Ctrl while selecting the nonadjacent ranges. Do not select worksheet titles or subtitles; doing so would add unnecessary data to the chart. To create the chart in Figure 3.2, select the range A5:C8. It is important to select parallel ranges. A parallel range is one that consists of the same starting and end point as another similar range. For example, the range C5:C12 is a parallel range to A5:A12. Including the column headings on row 5 (even though cell A5 is blank) is necessary to include the years in the legend at the bottom of the chart area.

Excel transforms the selected data into a chart. A chart may include several chart elements or components. Table 3.1 lists and describes some of these elements. Figure 3.3 shows a chart area that contains these elements.

TABLE 3.1 Chart Elements

Chart Element	Description
Chart area	The container for the entire chart and all of its elements.
Plot area	Region containing the graphical representation of the values in the data series. Two axes form a border around the plot area.
X-axis	The horizontal border that provides a frame of reference for measuring data left to right.
Y-axis	The vertical border that provides a frame of reference for measuring data up and down.
Legend	A key that identifies the color, gradient, picture, texture, or pattern assigned to each data series in a chart. For example, blue might represent values for 2010, and orange might represent values for 2020.

Pearson Education, Inc.

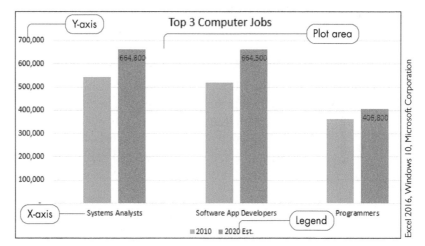

FIGURE 3.3 Chart Elements

Excel refers to the axes as the category axis and value axis. The ***category axis*** is the axis that displays descriptive labels for the data points plotted in a chart. The category axis labels are typically text contained in the first column of worksheet data (such as job titles) used to create the chart. The ***value axis*** is the axis that displays incremental numbers to identify the approximate values (such as number of jobs or revenue) of data points in a chart.

Choosing a Chart Type

You can create different charts from the same dataset; each chart type tells a different story. Select a chart type that appropriately represents the data and tells a story. For example, one chart might compare the number of computer-related jobs between 2010 and 2020, and another chart might indicate the percentage of new jobs by job title. The most commonly used chart types are column, bar, line, pie, and combo (see Table 3.2). Each chart type is designed to provide a unique perspective to the selected data.

TABLE 3.2 Common Chart Types

Chart	Chart Type	Description
	Column	Displays values in vertical columns where the height represents the value; the taller the column, the larger the value. Categories display along the horizontal (category) axis.
	Bar	Displays values in horizontal bars where the length represents the value; the longer the bar, the larger the value. Categories display along the vertical (category) axis.
	Line	Displays category data on the horizontal axis and value data on the vertical axis. Appropriate to show continuous data to depict trends over time, such as months, years, or decades.
	Pie	Shows proportion of individual data points to the total or whole of all those data points.
	Combo	Combines two chart types (such as column and line) to plot different data types (such as values and percentages)

Pearson Education, Inc.

Quick Analysis. When you select a range of adjacent cells (such as the range A5:C12) and position the pointer over that selected range, Excel displays Quick Analysis in the bottom-right corner of the selected area. However, Quick Analysis does not display when you select nonadjacent ranges, such as ranges A6:A12 and D6:D12. Quick Analysis displays thumbnails of recommended charts based on the data you selected so that you can create a chart quickly.

> **To create a chart using Quick Analysis, complete the following steps:**
>
> 1. Select the data and click Quick Analysis.
> 2. Click Charts in the Quick Analysis gallery (see Figure 3.4).
> 3. Point to each recommended chart thumbnail to see a preview of the type of chart that would be created from the selected data.
> 4. Click the thumbnail of the chart you want to create.

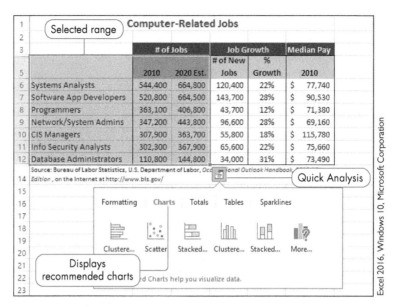

FIGURE 3.4 Quick Analysis Tool

Insert Tab. The Insert tab contains commands for creating a variety of charts. You must use the Insert tab to create a chart when you select nonadjacent ranges, but you can also use the Insert tab to create a chart when you select adjacent ranges. Clicking a particular chart on the Insert tab displays a gallery of icons representing more specific types of charts.

To create a chart using the Insert tab, complete the following steps:

1. Select the data and click the Insert tab.
2. Complete one of the following steps to select the chart type:
   - Click the chart type (such as Column) in the Charts group and click a chart subtype (such as Clustered Column) from the chart gallery (see Figure 3.5).
   - Click Recommended Charts in the Charts group to open the Insert Chart dialog box, click a thumbnail of the chart you want in the Recommended Charts tab or click the All Charts tab (see Figure 3.6) and click a thumbnail, and then click OK.

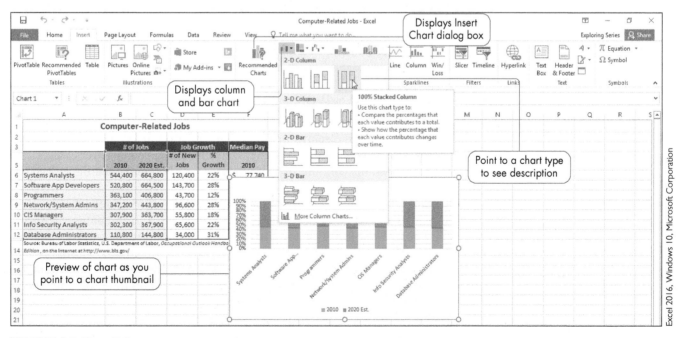

FIGURE 3.5 Chart Gallery

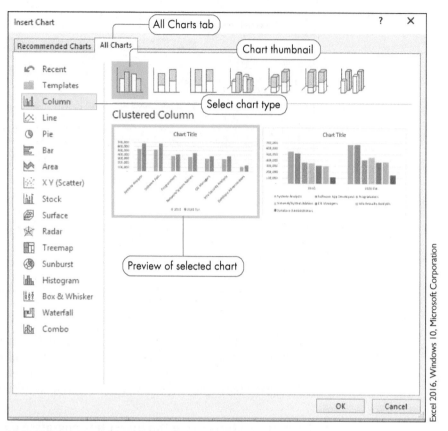

FIGURE 3.6 Insert Chart Dialog Box

TIP: RECOMMENDED VS. LIST OF ALL CHARTS

If you are unsure which type of chart would be a good choice for the selected data, click Recommended Charts in the Chart group. Excel will analyze the selected data and display thumbnails of recommended charts in the Insert Chart dialog box. Click a thumbnail to see a larger visualization of how your selected data would look in that chart type. The dialog box displays a message indicating the purpose of the selected chart, such as *A clustered bar chart is used to compare values across a few categories. Use it when the chart shows duration or when the category text is long.*

Click the All Charts tab in the Insert Chart dialog box to display a list of all chart types. After you click a type on the left side of the dialog box, the top of the right side displays specific subtypes, such as Clustered Column. When you click a subtype, the dialog box displays an image of that subtype using the selected data.

Create a Column Chart

STEP 1 ➤➤ A *column chart* compares values across categories, such as job titles, using vertical columns. The vertical axis displays values, and the horizontal axis displays categories. Column charts are most effective when they are limited to seven or fewer categories. If more categories exist, the columns appear too close together, making it difficult to read the labels.

The column chart in Figure 3.7 compares the number of projected jobs by job title for 2020 using the non-adjacent ranges A5:A9 and C5:C9 in the dataset shown in Figure 3.5. The first four job titles stored in the range A6:A9 form the category axis, and the increments of the estimated number of jobs in 2020 in range C6:C9 form the value axis. The height of each column in the chart represents the value of individual data points. For example, the Systems Analysts column is taller than the Programmers column, indicating that more jobs are projected for Systems Analysts than Programmers.

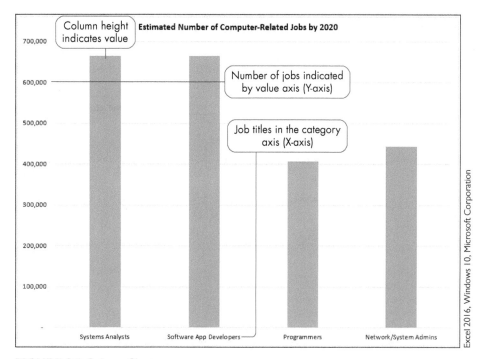

FIGURE 3.7 Column Chart

A ***clustered column chart*** compares groups—or clusters—of columns set side by side. The clustered column chart facilitates quick comparisons across data series, and it is effective for comparing several data points among categories. Figure 3.8 shows a clustered column chart created from the adjacent range A5:C9 in the dataset shown in Figure 3.5. By default, the job titles in the range A6:A9 appear on the category axis, and the yearly data points appear as columns with the value axis showing incremental numbers. Excel assigns a different color to each yearly data series and includes a legend so that you know what color represents which data series. The 2010 data series is light blue, and the 2020 data series is dark blue. This chart makes it easy to compare the predicted job growth from 2010 to 2020 for each job title and then to compare the trends among job titles.

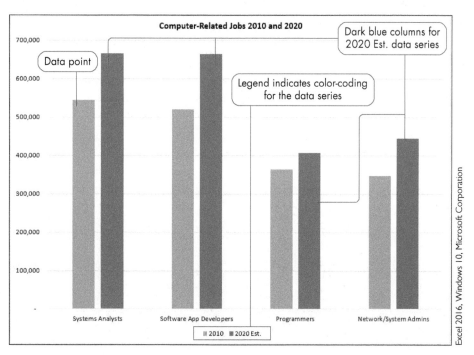

FIGURE 3.8 Clustered Column Chart

Figure 3.9 shows a clustered column chart in which the categories and data series are reversed. The years appear on the category axis, and the job titles appear as color-coded data series in the legend. This chart gives a different perspective from that in Figure 3.8 in that the chart in Figure 3.9 compares the number of jobs within a given year.

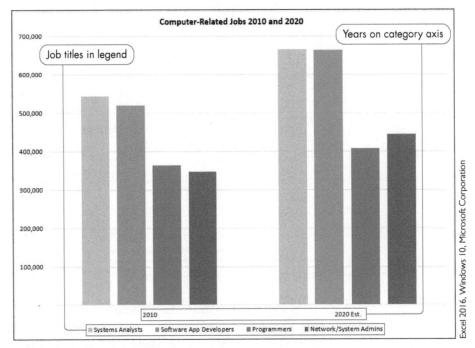

FIGURE 3.9 Clustered Column Chart: Category Axis and Legend Reversed

A **stacked column chart** shows the relationship of individual data points to the whole category. A stacked column chart displays only one column for each category. Each category within the stacked column is color-coded for one data series. Use the stacked column chart when you want to compare total values across categories, as well as to display the individual category values. Figure 3.10 shows a stacked column chart in which a single column represents each categorical year, and each column stacks color-coded data-point segments representing the different jobs. The stacked column chart enables you to compare the total number of computer-related jobs for each year. The height of each color-coded data point enables you to identify the relative contribution of each job to the total number of jobs for a particular year. A disadvantage of the stacked column chart is that the segments within each column do not start at the same point, making it more difficult to compare individual segment values across categories.

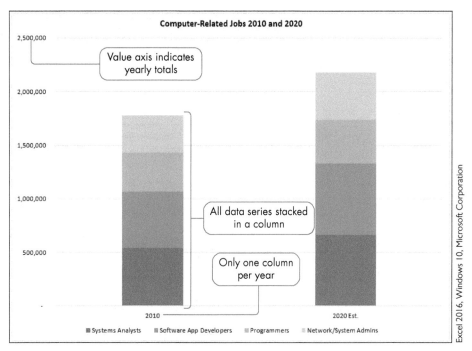

FIGURE 3.10 Stacked Column Chart

When you create a stacked column chart, make sure data are additive: Each column represents a sum of the data for each segment. Figure 3.10 correctly uses years as the category axis and the jobs as data series. For each year, Excel adds the number of jobs, and the columns display the total number of jobs. For example, the estimated total number of the four computer-related jobs in 2020 is about 2,180,000. Figure 3.11 shows a meaningless stacked column chart because the yearly number of jobs by job title is *not* additive. Adding the number of current actual jobs to the number of estimated jobs in the future does not make sense. It is incorrect to state that about 1,200,000 Systems Analysts jobs exist. Be careful when constructing stacked column charts to ensure that they lead to logical interpretation of data.

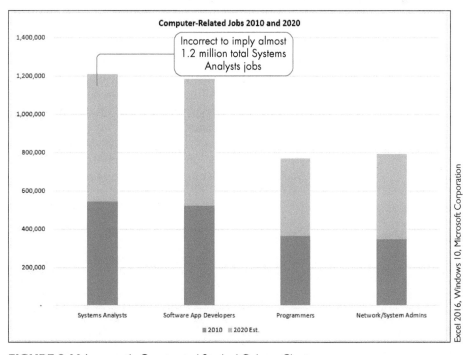

FIGURE 3.11 Incorrectly Constructed Stacked Column Chart

A **100% stacked column chart** converts individual data points (values) into percentages of the total value, similar to a pie chart. Each data series is a different color of the stack, representing a percentage. The total of each column is 100%. This type of chart depicts contributions to the whole. For example, the chart in Figure 3.12 illustrates that Systems Analysts account for 30% of the computer-related jobs represented by the four job categories in both 2010 and 2020.

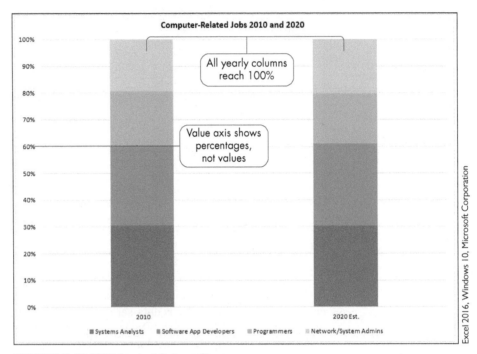

FIGURE 3.12 100% Stacked Column Chart

TIP: AVOID 3-D CHARTS

Avoid creating 3-D charts, because the third dimension is a superficial enhancement that usually distorts the charted data. For example, some columns appear taller or shorter than they actually are because of the angle of the 3-D effect, or some columns might be hidden by taller columns in front of them.

Create a Bar Chart

STEP 2 ▶▶ A **bar chart** compares values across categories using horizontal bars. The horizontal axis displays values, and the vertical axis displays categories (see Figure 3.13). Bar charts and column charts tell a similar story: they both compare categories of data. A bar chart is preferable when category names are long, such as *Software App Developers*. A bar chart enables category names to appear in an easy-to-read format, whereas a column chart might display category names at an awkward angle or in a smaller font size. The overall decision between a column and a bar chart may come down to the fact that different data may look better with one chart type than the other.

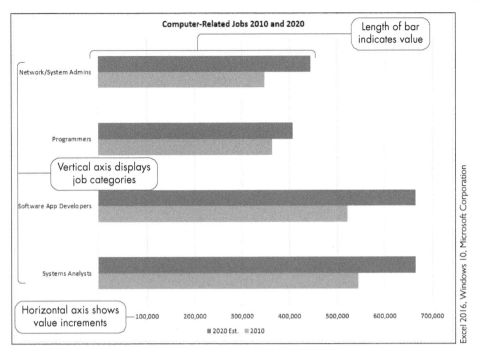

Computer-Related Jobs 2010 and 2020

Length of bar indicates value

Vertical axis displays job categories

Horizontal axis shows value increments

Network/System Admins

Programmers

Software App Developers

Systems Analysts

100,000 200,000 300,000 400,000 500,000 600,000 700,000

■ 2020 Est. ■ 2010

Excel 2016, Windows 10, Microsoft Corporation

FIGURE 3.13 Clustered Bar Chart

Change the Chart Type

After you create a chart, you may decide that the data would be better represented by a different type of chart. For example, you might decide a bar chart would display the labels better than a column chart, or you might want to change a clustered bar chart to a stacked bar chart to provide a different perspective for the data. Use the Change Chart Type feature to change a chart to a different type of chart.

> **To change the type of an existing chart, complete the following steps:**
>
> 1. Select the chart and click the Design tab.
> 2. Click Change Chart Type in the Type group to open the Change Chart Type dialog box (which is similar to the Insert Chart dialog box).
> 3. Click the All Charts tab within the dialog box.
> 4. Click a chart type on the left side of the dialog box.
> 5. Click a chart subtype on the right side of the dialog box and click OK.

Create a Line Chart

A *line chart* displays lines connecting data points to show trends over equal time periods. Excel displays each data series with a different line color. The category axis (X-axis) represents time, such as 10-year increments, whereas the value axis (Y-axis) represents a value, such as money or quantity. A line chart enables you to detect trends because the line continues to the next data point. To show each data point, choose the Line with Markers chart type. Figure 3.14 shows a line chart indicating the number of majors from 2005 to 2020 (estimated) at five-year increments. The number of Arts majors remains relatively constant, but the number of Tech & Computing majors increases significantly over time, especially between the years 2010 and 2020.

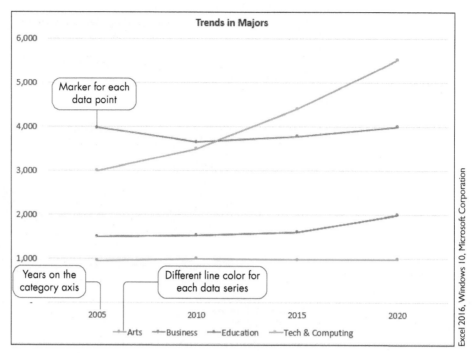

FIGURE 3.14 Line Chart

Create a Pie Chart

STEP 4 ▶▶ A **pie chart** shows each data point as a proportion to the whole data series. The pie chart displays as a circle, or "pie," where the entire pie represents the total value of the data series. Each slice represents a single data point. The larger the slice, the larger percentage that data point contributes to the whole. Use a pie chart when you want to convey percentage. Unlike column, bar, and line charts that typically chart multiple data series, pie charts represent a single data series only.

The pie chart in Figure 3.15 divides the pie representing the estimated number of new jobs into seven slices, one for each job title. The size of each slice is proportional to the percentage of total computer-related jobs depicted in the worksheet for that year. For example, Systems Analysts account for 21% of the estimated total number of new computer-related jobs in 2020. Excel creates a legend to indicate which color represents which pie slice. When you create a pie chart, limit it to about seven data points. Pie charts with too many slices appear too busy to interpret, or shades of the same color scheme become too difficult to distinguish.

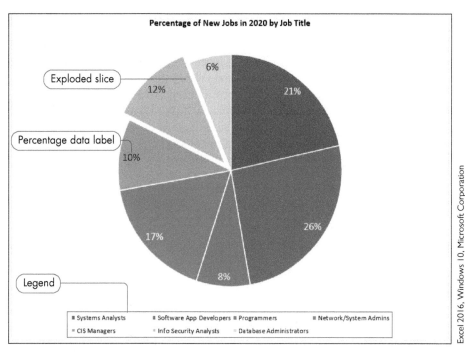

FIGURE 3.15 Pie Chart

Create a Combo Chart

STEP 5 ⟫ A ***combo chart*** is a chart that combines two chart types, such as column and line charts. This type of chart is useful to show two different but related data types. For example, you might want to show the number of new jobs in columns and the percentage growth of new jobs in a line within the same chart (see Figure 3.16). A combo chart has a primary and a secondary axis. The primary axis displays on the left side of the chart. In this case, the primary axis indicates the number of jobs represented in the columns. The secondary axis displays on the right side of the chart. In this case, the secondary axis indicates the percentage of new jobs created as represented by the line.

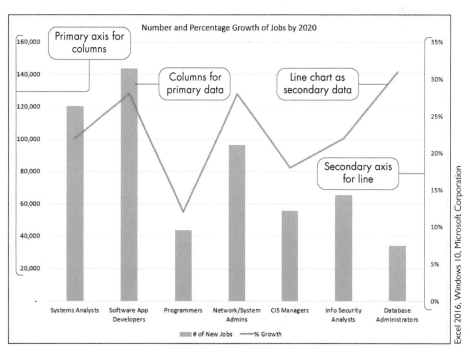

FIGURE 3.16 Combo Chart

Create Other Chart Types

Excel provides a variety of other types of charts. Two other chart types that are used for specialized analysis are X Y (scatter) charts and stock charts.

An **X Y (scatter) chart** shows a relationship between two numerical variables using their X and Y coordinates. Excel plots one variable on the horizontal X-axis and the other variable on the vertical Y-axis. Scatter charts are often used to represent data in educational, scientific, and medical experiments. Figure 3.17 shows the relationship between the number of minutes students view a training video and their test scores. The more minutes of a video a student watches, the higher the test score.

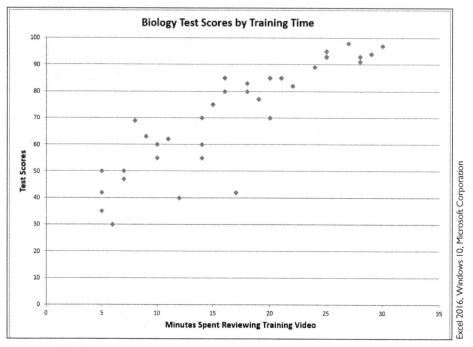

FIGURE 3.17 X Y (Scatter) Chart

A **stock chart** shows fluctuations in stock prices. Excel has four stock subtypes: High-Low-Close, Open-High-Low-Close, Volume-High-Low-Close, and Volume-Open-High-Low-Close. The High-Low-Close stock chart marks a stock's trading range on a given day with a vertical line from the lowest to the highest stock prices. Rectangles mark the opening and closing prices. Figure 3.18 shows three days of stock prices for a particular company.

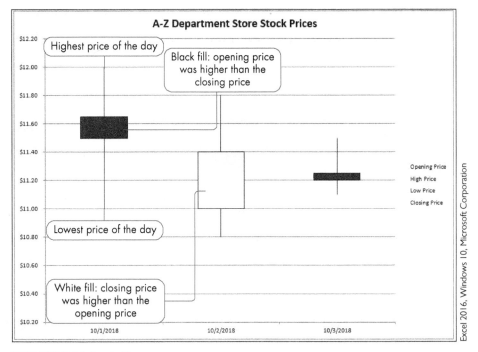

FIGURE 3.18 Stock Chart

The rectangle represents the difference in the opening and closing prices. If the rectangle has a white fill, the closing price is higher than the opening price. If the rectangle has a black fill, the opening price is higher than the closing price. In Figure 3.18, on October 1, the opening price was $11.65, and the closing price was $11.50, indicated by the top and bottom of the black rectangle. A line below the rectangle indicates that the lowest trading price is lower than the opening and closing prices. The lowest price was $11.00 on October 1. A line above the rectangle indicates that the highest trading price is higher than the opening and closing prices. The highest price was $12.00 on October 1. If no line exists below the rectangle, the lowest price equals either the opening or closing price, and if no line exists above the rectangle, the highest price equals either the opening or closing price.

TIP: ARRANGE DATA FOR A STOCK CHART

To create an Open-High-Low-Close stock chart, you must arrange data with Opening Price, High Price, Low Price, and Closing Price as column labels in that sequence. If you want to create other variations of stock charts, you must arrange data in a structured sequence required by Excel.

Table 3.3 lists and describes some of the other types of charts you can create in Excel.

TABLE 3.3 Other Chart Types

Chart	Chart Type	Description
	Area	Similar to a line chart in that it shows trends over time; however, the area chart displays colors between the lines to help illustrate the magnitude of changes.
	Surface	Represents numeric data and numeric categories. Displays trends using two dimensions on a continuous curve.
	Radar	Uses each category as a spoke radiating from the center point to the outer edges of the chart. Each spoke represents each data series, and lines connect the data points between spokes, similar to a spider web. A radar chart compares aggregate values for several data series. For example, a worksheet could contain the number of specific jobs for 2015, 2016, 2017, and 2018. Each year would be a data series containing the individual data points (number of specific jobs) for that year. The radar chart would aggregate the total number of jobs per year for all four data series.
	Histogram	A histogram is similar to a column chart. The category axis shows bin ranges (intervals) where data is aggregated into bins, and the vertical axis shows frequencies. For example, your professor might want to show the number (frequency) of students who earned a score within each grade interval, such as 60-69, 70-79, 80-89, and 90-100.

Pearson Education, Inc.

Moving, Sizing, and Printing a Chart

STEP 3 Excel inserts the chart as an embedded object in the current worksheet, often to the right of, but sometimes on top of and covering up, the data area. After you insert a chart, you usually need to move it to a different location and adjust its size. If you need to print a chart, decide whether to print the chart only or the chart and its data source.

Move a Chart

When you create a chart, Excel displays the chart in the worksheet, often on top of existing worksheet data. Therefore, you should move the chart so that it does not cover up data. If you leave the chart in the same worksheet, you can print the data and chart on the same page.

To move a chart on an active worksheet, complete the following steps:

1. Point to the chart area to display the Chart Area ScreenTip and the pointer includes the white arrowhead and a four-headed arrow.
2. Drag the chart to the desired location.

You might want to place the chart in a separate worksheet, called a *chart sheet*. A chart sheet contains a single chart only; you cannot enter data and formulas on a chart sheet. If you want to print or view a full-sized chart, move the chart to its own chart sheet.

To move a chart to another sheet or a chart sheet, complete the following steps:

1. Select the chart.
2. Click the Design tab and click Move Chart in the Location group (or right-click the chart and select Move Chart) to open the Move Chart dialog box (see Figure 3.19).
3. Select one of these options to indicate where you want to move the chart:
   - Click *New sheet* to move the chart to its own sheet. The default chart sheet for the first chart is Chart1, but you can rename it in the Move Chart dialog box or similarly to the way you rename other sheet tabs.
   - Click *Object in*, click the *Object in* arrow, and select the worksheet to which you want to move the chart.
4. Click OK.

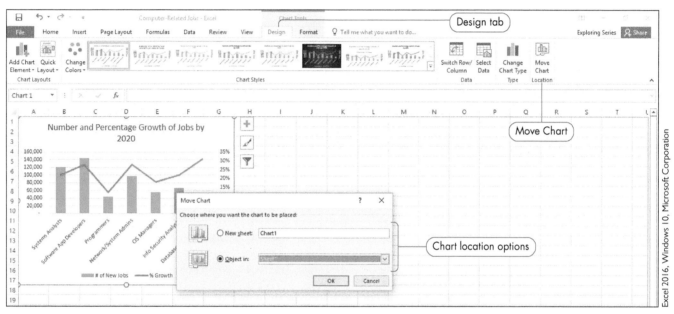

FIGURE 3.19 Design Tab and Move Chart Dialog Box

Size a Chart

If you move a chart to a chart sheet, the chart is enlarged to fill the entire sheet. If you keep a chart embedded within a worksheet, you might want to size the chart to fit in a particular range or to ensure the chart elements are proportional. Use the sizing handles or the Format tab on the Ribbon to change the size of the chart.

To change the chart size with sizing handles, complete the following steps:

1. Select the chart. Excel displays a line border and sizing handles around the chart when you select it. **Sizing handles** are eight circles that display around the four corners and outside middle sections of a chart when you select it.
2. Point to the outer edge of the chart where the sizing handles are located until the pointer changes to a two-headed arrow.
3. Drag the border to adjust the chart's height or width. Drag a corner sizing handle to increase or decrease the height and width of the chart at the same time. Press and hold Shift as you drag a corner sizing handle to change the height and width proportionately.

To change the chart size on the Ribbon, complete the following steps:

1. Select the chart.
2. Click the Format tab.
3. Change the value in the Height and Width boxes in the Size group (see Figure 3.20).

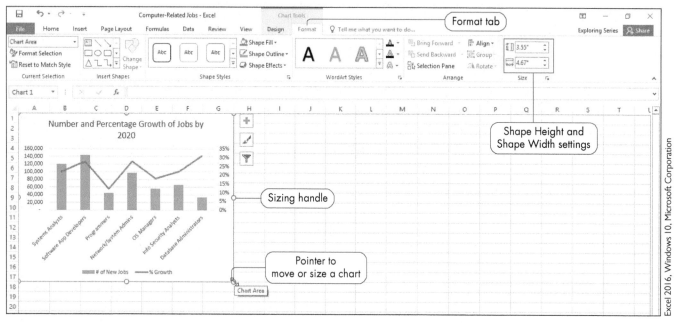

FIGURE 3.20 Sizing a Chart

Print a Chart

After you create a chart, you may want to print it. If you embedded a chart on the same sheet as the data source, you need to decide if you want to print the data only, the data and the chart, or the chart only.

To print the data only, complete the following steps:

1. Select the data.
2. Click the File tab and click Print.
3. Click the first arrow in the Settings section and select Print Selection.
4. Click Print.

To print only the chart as a full page, complete the following steps:

1. Select the chart if it is on a worksheet that also contains data.
2. Click the File tab and click Print.
3. Make sure the default setting is Print Selected Chart.
4. Click Print.

If the data and chart are on the same worksheet, print the worksheet contents to print both, but do not select either the chart or the data before displaying the Print options. The preview shows you what will print. Make sure it displays what you want to print before clicking Print.

If you moved the chart to a chart sheet, the chart is the only item on that worksheet. When you display the print options, the default is Print Active Sheets, and the chart will print as a full-page chart.

Quick Concepts

1. Why should you not include aggregates, such as totals or averages, along with individual data points in a chart? *p. 535*

2. Describe the purpose of each of these chart types: (a) column, (b) bar, (c) line, (d) pie, and (e) combo. *p. 536*

3. How can you use Quick Analysis to create a chart? *p. 536*

4. How do you decide whether to move a chart within the worksheet where you created it or move it to a chart sheet? *p. 548*

Hands-On Exercises

Watch the Video for this Hands-On Exercise!

Skills covered: Select an Adjacent Range • Create a Clustered Column Chart • Move a Chart to a New Chart Sheet • Select a Nonadjacent Range • Create a Bar Chart • Change the Chart Type • Move a Chart Within a Worksheet • Size a Chart • Create a Pie Chart • Create a Combo Chart

1 Chart Basics

Doug Demers, your assistant, gathered data about seven computer-related jobs from the *Occupational Outlook Handbook* online. He organized the data into a structured worksheet that contains the job titles, the number of jobs in 2010, the projected number of jobs by 2020, and other data. Now you are ready to transform the data into visually appealing charts.

STEP 1 ➤➤ CREATE A CLUSTERED COLUMN CHART

You want to compare the number of jobs in 2010 to the projected number of jobs in 2020 for all seven computer-related professions that Doug entered into the worksheet. You decide to create a clustered column chart to depict this data. After you create this chart, you will move it to its own chart sheet. You will format the charts in Hands-On Exercise 2. Refer to Figure 3.21 as you complete Step 1.

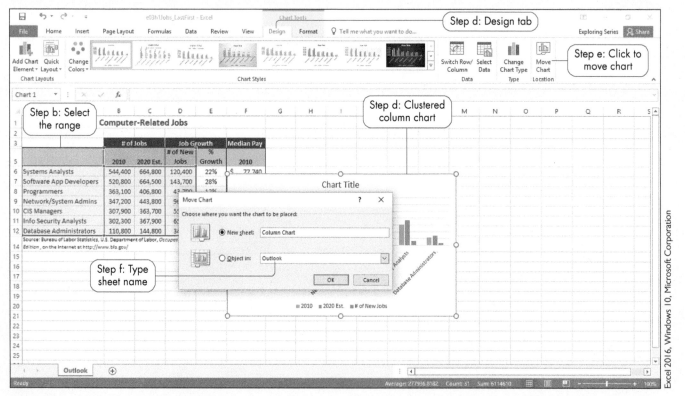

FIGURE 3.21 Clustered Column Chart

a. Open *e03h1Jobs* and save it as **e03h1Jobs_LastFirst**.

> **TROUBLESHOOTING:** If you make any major mistakes in this exercise, you can close the file, open *e03h1Jobs* again, and then start this exercise over.

b. Select the **range A5:D12**.

You selected the job titles, the number of jobs in 2010, the projected number of jobs in 2020, and the number of new jobs. Because you are selecting three data series (three columns of numerical data), you must also select the column headings on row 5.

c. Click **Quick Analysis** at the bottom-right corner of the selected range and click **Charts**.

The Quick Analysis gallery displays recommended charts based on the selected range.

d. Point to **Clustered Column** (the third thumbnail in the Charts gallery) to see a preview of what the chart would look like and click **Clustered Column**.

Excel inserts a clustered column chart based on the selected data. The Design tab displays on the Ribbon while the chart is selected.

e. Click **Move Chart** in the Location group.

The Move Chart dialog box opens for you to specify where to move the chart.

f. Click **New sheet**, type **Column Chart**, and then click **OK**. Save the workbook.

Excel moves the clustered column chart to a new sheet called Column Chart.

STEP 2 >> CREATE A BAR CHART

You want to create a bar chart to depict the number of jobs in 2010 and the number of new jobs that will be created by 2020. Finally, you want to change the chart to a stacked bar chart to show the total jobs in 2020 based on the number of jobs in 2010 and the number of new jobs. Refer to Figure 3.22 as you complete Step 2.

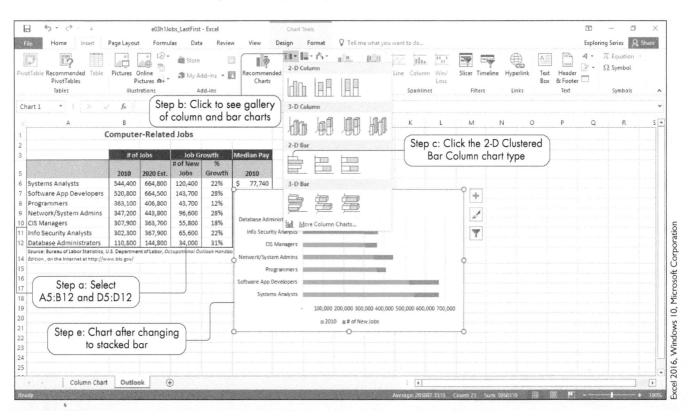

FIGURE 3.22 Bar Chart

a. Click the **Outlook sheet tab**, select the **range A5:B12**, press and hold **Ctrl**, and then select the **range D5:D12**.

You used Ctrl to select nonadjacent ranges: the job title labels, the number of jobs in 2010, and the number of new jobs.

> **TIP: PARALLEL RANGES**
> Nonadjacent ranges should be parallel so that the legend will correctly reflect the data series. This means that each range should contain the same number of related cells. For example, A5:A12, B5:B12, and D5:D12 are parallel ranges. Even though cell A5 is blank, you must select it to have a parallel range with the other two selected ranges that include cells on row 5.

b. Click the **Insert tab** and click **Insert Column or Bar Chart** in the Charts group.

The gallery shows both column and bar chart thumbnails.

c. Click **Clustered Bar** in the 2-D Bar section to create a clustered bar chart.

Excel inserts the clustered bar chart in the worksheet.

d. Click **Change Chart Type** in the Type group on the Design tab.

The Change Chart Type dialog box opens. The left side of the dialog box lists all chart types. The top-right side displays thumbnails of various bar charts, and the lower section displays a sample of the selected chart.

e. Click **Stacked Bar** in the top center of the dialog box and click **OK**. Save the workbook.

Excel displays the number of jobs in 2010 in blue and stacks the number of new jobs in orange into one bar per job title. This chart tells the story of how the total projected number of jobs in 2020 is calculated: the number of existing jobs in 2010 (blue) and the number of new jobs (orange).

STEP 3 ⟫ MOVE AND SIZE A CHART

The bar chart is displayed in the middle of the worksheet. You decide to position it below the job outlook data and adjust its size to make it larger so that it is as wide as the dataset and a little taller for better proportions. Refer to Figure 3.23 as you complete Step 3.

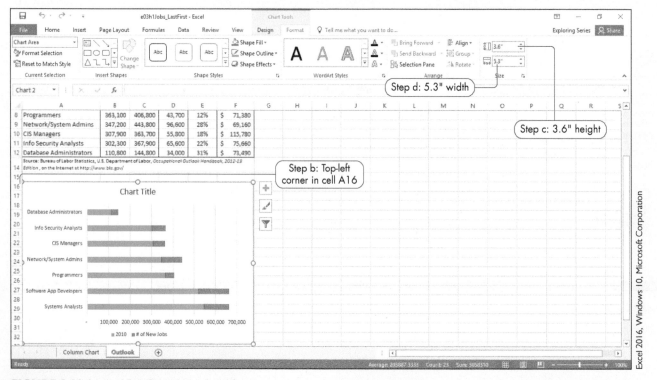

FIGURE 3.23 Stacked Bar Chart Moved and Sized

a. Point to an empty part of the chart area.

The pointer displays a four-headed arrow with the regular white arrowhead, and the Chart Area ScreenTip displays.

> **TROUBLESHOOTING:** Make sure you see the Chart Area ScreenTip as you perform Step b. If you move the pointer to another chart element—such as the legend—you will move or size that element instead of moving the entire chart.

b. Drag the chart so that the top-left corner of the chart appears in **cell A16**.

You positioned the chart below the worksheet data.

c. Click the **Format tab**, select the value in the **Shape Height box**, type **3.6**, and then press **Enter**.

The chart is now 3.6" tall.

d. Select the value in the **Shape Width box**, type **5.3**, and then press **Enter**. Save the workbook.

The chart is now 5.3" wide.

STEP 4 ❯❯ **CREATE A PIE CHART**

You decide to create a pie chart that depicts the percentage of new jobs by job title calculated from the total number of new jobs created for the seven job titles Doug researched. After creating the pie chart, you will move it to its own sheet. Refer to Figure 3.24 as you complete Step 4.

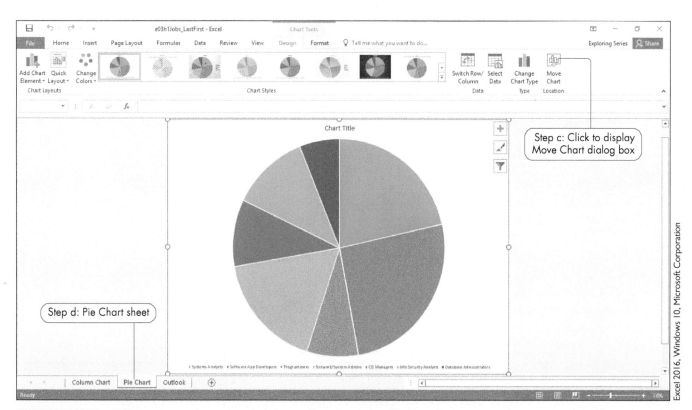

FIGURE 3.24 Pie Chart

a. Select the **range A6:A12**, press and hold **Ctrl**, then select the **range D6:D12**.

> **TROUBLESHOOTING:** Do not select cells A5 and D5 this time because you are creating a pie chart. When creating a chart from a single data series (e.g., # of New Jobs), you do not need to select the column headings.

b. Click the **Insert tab**, click **Insert Pie or Doughnut Chart** in the Charts group, and then select **Pie** in the 2-D Pie group on the gallery.

The pie chart displays in the worksheet.

c. Click **Move Chart** in the Location group on the Design tab.

The Move Chart dialog box opens.

d. Click **New sheet**, type **Pie Chart**, and then click **OK**. Save the workbook.

Excel creates a new sheet called Pie Chart. The pie chart is the only object on that sheet.

STEP 5 ➤➤ **CREATE A COMBO CHART**

You want to create a combo chart that shows the number of new jobs in columns and the percentage of new jobs created in a line on the secondary axis. Although the number of new jobs may appear low as represented by the smallest column (such as 34,000 new database administrators), the actual percentage of new jobs created between 2010 and 2020 may be significant as represented by the steep incline of the orange line (such as 31% growth for database administrators). Refer to Figure 3.25 as you complete Step 5.

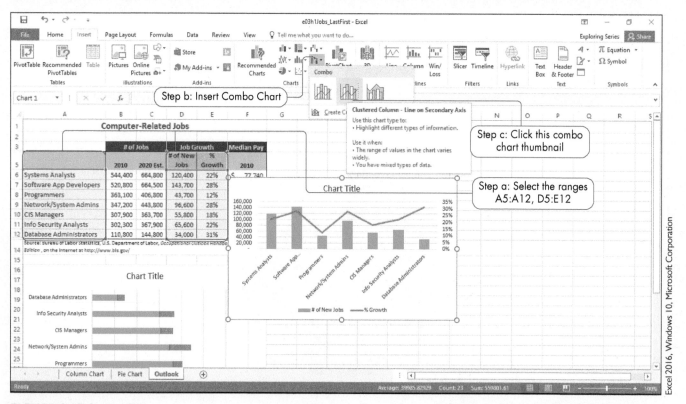

FIGURE 3.25 Combo Chart

a. Click the **Outlook sheet tab**, select the **range A5:A12**, press and hold **Ctrl**, then select the **range D5:E12**.

b. Click the **Insert tab** and click **Insert Combo Chart** in the Charts group.

   The Combo Chart gallery of thumbnails displays.

c. Click the **Clustered Column – Line on Secondary Axis thumbnail**, which is the middle thumbnail.

   Excel creates a combo chart based on the thumbnail you selected. The number of new jobs displays in blue columns, and the percentage growth displays as an orange line.

d. Click **Move Chart** in the Location group on the Design tab, click **New sheet**, type **Combo Chart**, and then click **OK**.

e. Save the workbook. Keep the workbook open if you plan to continue with the next Hands-On Exercise. If not, close the workbook, and exit Excel.

Chart Elements

After creating a chart, you should add appropriate chart elements. A ***chart element*** is a component that completes or helps clarify the chart. Some chart elements, such as chart titles, should be included in every chart. Other elements are optional. Table 3.4 describes the chart elements, and Figure 3.26 illustrates several chart elements.

TABLE 3.4	Chart Elements
Element	**Description**
Axis title	Label that describes the category or value axes. Display axis titles, such as In Millions of Dollars or Top 7 Computer Job Titles, to clarify the axes. Axis titles are not displayed by default.
Chart title	Label that describes the entire chart. It should reflect the purpose of the chart. For example, Houses Sold is too generic, but Houses Sold in Seattle in 2018 indicates the what (Houses), the where (Seattle), and the when (2018). The default text is Chart Title.
Data label	Descriptive label that shows the exact value or name of a data point. Data labels are not displayed by default.
Data table	A grid that contains the data source values and labels. If you embed a chart on the same worksheet as the data source, you might not need to include a data table. Only add a data table with a chart that is on a chart sheet.
Error bars	Visuals that indicate the standard error amount, a percentage, or a standard deviation for a data point or marker. Error bars are not displayed by default.
Gridlines	Horizontal or vertical lines that display in the plot area, designed to help people identify the values plotted by the visual elements, such as a column.
Legend	A key that identifies the color, gradient, picture, texture, or pattern assigned to each data series. The legend is displayed by default for some chart types.
Trendline	A line that depicts trends or helps forecast future data, such as estimating future sales or number of births in a region. Add a trendline to column, bar, line, stock, scatter, and bubble charts. Excel will analyze the current trends and display a line indicating future values based on those trends.

Pearson Education, Inc.

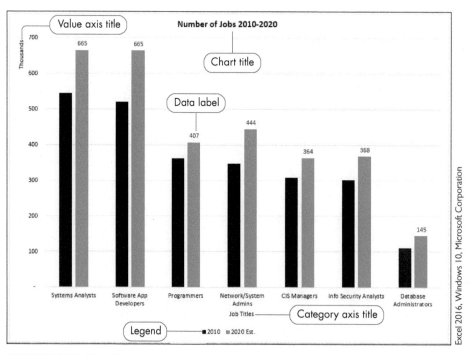

FIGURE 3.26 Chart Elements

Excel 2016, Windows 10, Microsoft Corporation

In this section, you will learn how to add, edit, and format chart elements. Specifically, you will learn how to type a chart title, add axis titles, add data labels, and position the legend. Furthermore, you will learn how to format these elements as well as format axes, position the legend, and add gridlines. Finally, you will learn how to format the chart area, plot area, data series, and a data point.

Adding, Editing, and Formatting Chart Elements

After you create a chart, you usually need to add elements to provide labels to describe the chart. Adding descriptive text for labels provides information for the reader to comprehend the chart without knowing or seeing the underlying data. When you create a chart, one or more elements may display by default. For example, when you created the charts in Hands-On Exercise 1, Excel displayed a placeholder for the chart title and displayed a legend so that you know which color represents each data series.

When a chart is selected, three icons display to the right of the chart: Chart Elements, Chart Styles, and Chart Filters. In addition, the Design tab contains the Chart Layouts group that allows you to add and customize chart elements and change the layout of the chart.

When you point to a chart element, Excel displays a ScreenTip with the name of that element. To select a chart element, click it when you see the ScreenTip, or click the Format tab, click the Chart Elements arrow in the Current Selection group, and select the element from the list.

Edit, Format, and Position the Chart Title

STEP 1 ›› Excel includes the placeholder text *Chart Title* above the chart. You should replace that text with a descriptive title. In addition, you might want to format the chart title by applying bold and changing the font, font size, font color, and fill color.

> **To edit and format the chart title, complete the following steps:**
> 1. Select the chart title.
> 2. Type the text you want to appear in the title and press Enter.
> 3. Click the Home tab.
> 4. Apply the desired font formatting, such as increasing the font size and applying bold.
> 5. Click the chart to deselect the chart title.

> **TIP: FONT COLOR**
> The default font color for the chart title, axes, axes titles, and legend is Black, Text 1, Lighter 35%. If you want these elements to stand out, change the color to Black, Text 1 or another solid color.

By default, the chart title displays centered above the plot area. Although this is a standard location for the chart, you might want to position it elsewhere.

To change the position of the chart title, complete the following steps:

1. Select the chart title and click Chart Elements to the right of the chart.
2. Point to the Chart Title and click the triangle on the right side of the menu option, Chart Title (see Figure 3.27).
3. Select one of the options:
   - Above Chart: Centers the title above the plot area, decreasing the plot area size to make room for the chart title.
   - Centered Overlay: Centers the chart title horizontally without resizing the plot area; the title displays over the top of the plot area.
   - More Options: Opens the Format Chart Title task pane to apply fill, border, and alignment settings. A *task pane* is a window of options to format and customize chart elements. The task pane name and options change based on the selected chart element. For example, when you double-click the chart title, the Format Chart Title task pane displays.
4. Click Chart Elements to close the menu.

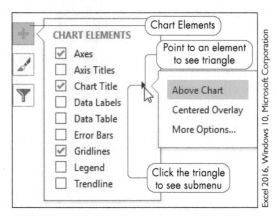

FIGURE 3.27 Chart Elements List

TIP: LINKING A CHART TITLE OR AN AXIS TITLE TO A CELL
Instead of typing text directly in the Chart Title or Axis Title placeholder, you can link the title to a label in a cell. Click the Chart Title or Axis Title placeholder, type = in the Formula Bar, click the cell containing the label you want for the title, and then press Enter. Excel will enter the sheet name and cell reference, such as =Outlook!$A$1, in the Formula Bar. If you change the worksheet label, Excel will also change the title in the chart.

Add, Format, and Position Axis Titles

STEP 2 ⟩⟩ Axis titles are helpful to provide more clarity about the value or category axis. Axis titles also help you conform to ADA compliance requirements. For example, if the values are abbreviated as 7 instead of 7,000,000 you should indicate the unit of measurement on the value axis as In Millions. You might want to further clarify the labels on the category axis by providing a category axis title, such as Job Titles.

To add an axis title, complete the following steps:

1. Select the chart and click Chart Elements to the right of the chart.
2. Point to Axis Titles and click the triangle on the right side.
3. Select one or more of these options:
   - Primary Horizontal: Displays a title for the primary horizontal axis.
   - Primary Vertical: Displays a title for the primary vertical axis.
   - Secondary Horizontal: Displays a title for the secondary horizontal axis in a combo chart.
   - Secondary Vertical: Displays a title for the secondary vertical axis in a combo chart.
   - More Options: Opens the Format Axis Title task pane to apply fill, border, and alignment settings.
4. Click Chart Elements to close the menu.

To use the Design tab to add a chart element, complete the following steps:

1. Click the Design tab.
2. Click Add Chart Element in the Chart Layouts group.
3. Point to an element and select from that element's submenu (see Figure 3.28).

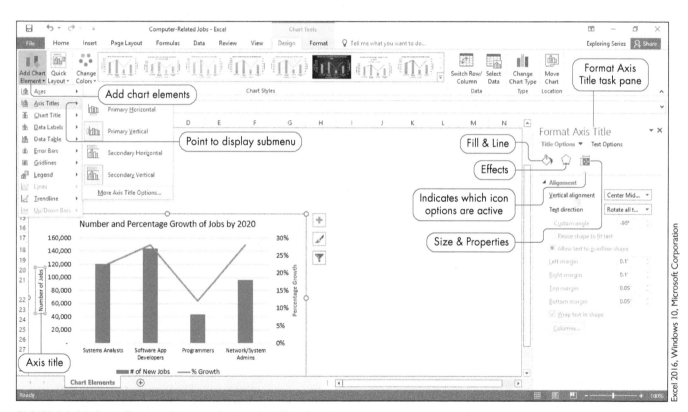

FIGURE 3.28 Chart Elements Menu and Format Axis Title Task Pane

The horizontal axis title displays below the category labels, and the rotated vertical axis title displays on the left side of the value axis. After including an axis title, click the title, type the text for the title, and then press Enter similarly to editing text for a chart title. You might want to apply font formatting (such as font size and color) to the axis titles similarly to formatting a chart title. Use the Format Axis Title task pane to customize and format the axis title.

To position and format the axis title, complete the following:

1. Double-click the axis title to open the Format Axis Title task pane (refer to Figure 3.28). Each task pane has categories, such as Title Options and Text Options. Below these categories are icons, such as Fill & Line, Effects, and Size & Properties.
2. Click Title Options and click the Size & Properties icon. The options in the task pane change to display options related to the icon you click. A thin horizontal gray line separates the icons from the options. The line contains a partial triangle that points to the icon that is active to indicate which options are displayed. Figure 3.28 shows the triangle is pointing to Size & Properties.
3. Change the *Vertical alignment* or *Horizontal alignment* option to the desired position.
4. Click other icons, such as Fill & Line, and select the desired options.
5. Close the Format Axis Title task pane.
6. Click the Home tab and apply font formatting, such as Font Color.

TIP: REMOVE AN ELEMENT

To remove an element, click Chart Elements and click a check box to deselect the check box. Alternatively, click Add Chart Element in the Chart Layouts group on the Chart Tools Design tab, point to the element name, and then select None. You can also select a chart element and press Delete to remove it.

Format the Axes

Based on the data source values and structure, Excel determines the start, incremental, and end values that display on the value axis when you create the chart. However, you might want to adjust the value axis so that the numbers displayed are simplified or fit better on the chart. For example, when working with large values such as 4,567,890, the value axis displays increments, such as 4,000,000 and 5,000,000. You can simplify the value axis by displaying values in millions, so that the values on the axis are 4 and 5 with the word Millions placed by the value axis to indicate the units. Use the Format Axis task pane to specify the bounds, units, display units, labels, and number formatting for an axis.

To format an axis, complete the following steps:

1. Double-click the axis to open the Format Axis task pane (see Figure 3.29).
2. Click the Axis Options icon, and complete any of the following steps:
   - Change the bounds, units, and display units. The Minimum Bound sets the starting value, and the Maximum Bound sets the ending value on the value axis. The Major Units specifies the intervals of values on the value axis. The Display units converts the values, such as to Millions.
   - Click Tick Marks to change the major and minor tick marks.
   - Click Labels to change the label position.
   - Click Number to change the category, specify the number of decimal places, select how negative numbers display. The Category option specifies the number formatting, such as Currency. Depending on the category, other options may display, such as Decimal places so that you can control the number of decimal places on the value axis.
3. Close the Format Axis task pane.
4. Click the Home tab and apply font formatting, such as Font Color.

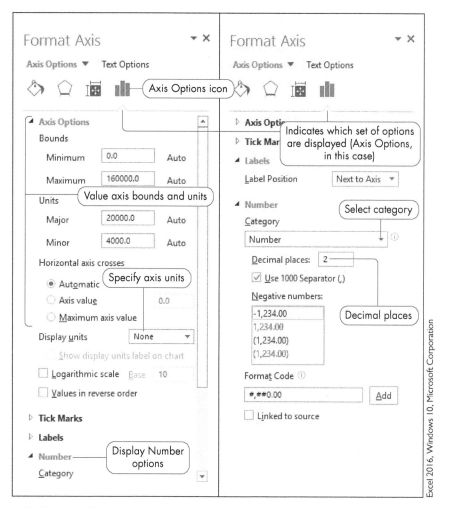

FIGURE 3.29 Format Axis Task Pane

TIP: DISPLAYING OPTIONS WITHIN TASK PANES

A diagonal black triangle next to a category, such as Axis Options, indicates that all of a category's options are displayed (expanded). A triangle with a white fill, such as the one next to Tick Marks, indicates that the category options are not displayed (collapsed).

Add, Position, and Format Data Labels

STEP 3 »» A data label is descriptive text that shows the exact value or name of a data point. Data labels are useful to indicate specific values for data points you want to emphasize. Typically, you would add data labels only to specific data points, and not all data points. Use either Chart Elements or the Design tab to display data labels.

To add and position data labels, complete the following steps:

1. Select the chart and click Chart Elements to the right of the chart.
2. Click the Data Labels check box to display data labels.
3. Click the arrow to the right of the Data Labels item to select the position, such as Center or Outside End.
4. Click Chart Elements to close the menu.

By default, Excel adds data labels to all data series. If you want to display data labels for only one series, select the data labels for the other data series and press Delete. In Figure 3.26, data labels are included for the 2020 data series but not the 2010 data series. When you select a data label, Excel selects all data labels in that data series. Use the Format Data Labels task pane to customize and format the data labels. You can also apply font formatting (such as font size and color) to the data labels similarly to formatting a chart title.

To format the data labels, complete the following steps:

1. Double-click a data label to open the Format Data Labels task pane (see Figure 3.30).
2. Click the Label Options icon.
3. Click Label Options to customize the labels, and complete any of the following steps:
   - Select the Label Contains option. The default is Value, but you might want to display additional label contents, such as Category Name. For example, you might want to add data labels to a pie chart to indicate both Percentage and Category Names.
   - Select the Label Position option, such as Center or Inside End.
4. Click Number and apply number formatting if the numeric data labels are not formatted.
5. Close the Format Data Labels task pane.
6. Click the Home tab and apply font formatting, such as Font Color.

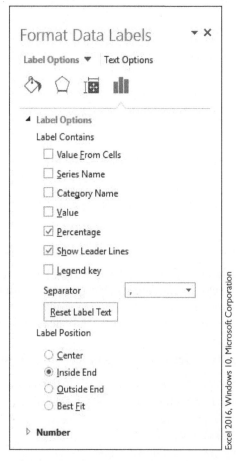

FIGURE 3.30 Format Data Labels Task Pane

Position and Format the Legend

When you create a multiple series chart, the legend displays, providing a key to the color-coded data series. Position the legend to the right, top, bottom, or left of the plot area, similarly to choosing the position for a chart title using Chart Elements. Make sure that the columns, bars, or lines appear proportionate and well balanced after you position the legend. Use the Format Legend task pane to customize and format the legend.

To format the legend, complete the following steps:

1. Double-click the legend to open the Format Legend task pane.
2. Click the Legend Options icon.
3. Select the position of the legend: Top, Bottom, Left, Right, or Top Right.
4. Click the Fill & Line icon, click Border, and set border options if you want to change the border settings for the legend.
5. Close the Format Legend task pane.
6. Click the Home tab and apply font formatting, such as Font Color.

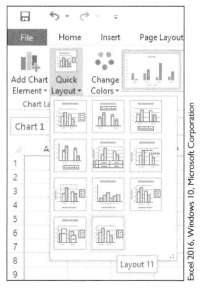

FIGURE 3.31 Quick Layout Gallery

Add and Format Gridlines

Gridlines are horizontal or vertical lines that span across the plot area of the chart to help people identify the values plotted by the visual elements, such as a column. Excel displays horizontal gridlines for column, line, scatter, stock, surface, and bubble charts and vertical gridlines for bar charts. Click either Chart Elements or Add Chart Elements in the Chart Layouts group on the Design tab to add gridlines.

Format gridlines by double-clicking a gridline to open the Format Major Gridlines task pane. You can change the line type, color, and width of the gridlines.

TIP: ALTERNATIVE FOR OPENING FORMAT TASK PANES

Another way to display a task pane is to right-click the chart element and choose Format <element>, where <element> is the specific chart element. If you do not close a task pane after formatting a particular element, such as gridlines, and then click another chart element, the task pane will change so that you can format that particular chart element.

Format the Chart Area, Plot Area, and Data Series

STEP 4 ❯❯ Apply multiple settings, such as fill colors and borders, at once using the Format task pane for an element. To open a chart element's task pane, double-click the chart element. Figure 3.32 displays the Format Chart Area, Format Plot Area, and Format Data Series task panes with different fill options selected to display the different options that result. All three task panes include the same fill and border elements. For example, you might want to change the fill color of a data series from blue to green. After you select a fill option, such as *Gradient fill*, the remaining options change in the task pane.

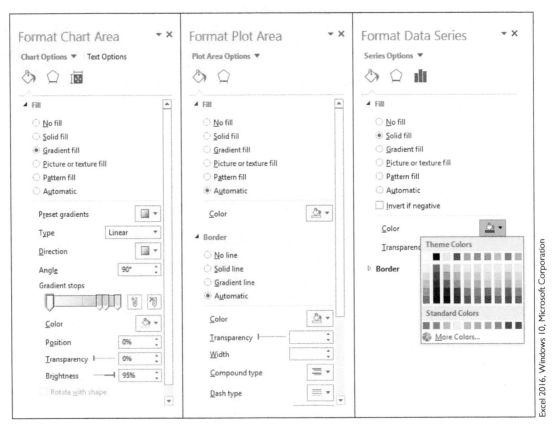

FIGURE 3.32 Format Task Panes

Format a Data Point

STEP 4 ❯❯ Earlier in this chapter, you learned that a data point reflects a value in a single cell in a worksheet. You can select that single data point in a chart and format it differently from the rest of the data series. Select the data point you want to format, display the Format Data Point task pane, and make the changes you want. For example, you might want to focus a person's attention on a particular slice by separating one or more slices from the rest of the chart in an ***exploded pie chart*** (refer to Figure 3.15).

To format a pie slice data point, complete the following steps:

1. Click within the pie chart, pause, and then click the particular slice you want to format.
2. Right-click the selected pie slice and select Format Data Point to open the Format Data Point task pane.
3. Click the Fill & Line icon and click the desired option (such as Solid fill) in the Fill category.
4. Click the Color arrow and select a color for a solid fill; select a *Preset gradient*, type, color, and other options for a gradient fill; or insert a picture or select a texture for a picture or texture fill.
5. Click the Series Options icon and drag the Point Explosion to the right to explode the selected pie slice, such as to 12% (see Figure 3.33).
6. Close the Format Data Point task pane.

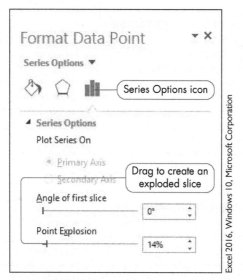

FIGURE 3.33 Format Data Point Task Pane

TIP: DRAG TO EXPLODE A PIE SLICE

Another way to explode a pie slice is to select the specific slice and then drag it away from the pie.

Use the Chart Tools Format Tab

The Format tab contains options to select a chart element, insert shapes, apply shape styles, apply WordArt styles, arrange objects, and specify the size of an object. Table 3.5 lists and describes the groups on the Format tab.

TABLE 3.5	Chart Tools Format Tab
Group	**Description**
Current Selection	Selects a chart element, displays the task pane to format the selected element, and clears custom formatting of the selected element.
Insert Shapes	Inserts a variety of shapes in a chart.
Shape Styles	Specifies a shape style, fill color, outline color, and shape effect.
WordArt Styles	Adds artistic style, text fill, and text effects to an object.
Arrange	Brings an object forward or backward to layer multiple objects; aligns, groups, and rotates objects.
Size	Adjusts the height and width of the selected object.

Pearson Education, Inc.

Quick Concepts

5. List at least four types of appropriate labels that describe chart elements. What types of things can you do to customize these labels? ***p. 558***

6. What is the purpose of exploding a slice on a pie chart? ***p. 567***

7. What are some of the fill options you can apply to a chart area or a plot area? ***p. 566***

Hands-On Exercises

Skills covered: Edit and Format Chart Titles • Add and Format Axes Titles • Format Axes • Add, Position, and Format Data Labels • Format the Chart Area • Format a Data Point

2 Chart Elements

You want to enhance the computer job column, bar, and pie charts by adding some chart elements. In particular, you will enter a descriptive chart title for each chart, add and format axis titles for the bar chart, add and format data labels for the pie chart, and change fill colors in the pie chart.

STEP 1 ▶▶ EDIT AND FORMAT CHART TITLES

When you created the column, bar, and pie charts in Hands-On Exercise 1, Excel displayed *Chart Title* at the top of each chart. You will add a title that appropriately describes each chart. In addition, you want to format the chart titles by applying bold and enlarging the font sizes. Refer to Figure 3.34 as you complete Step 1.

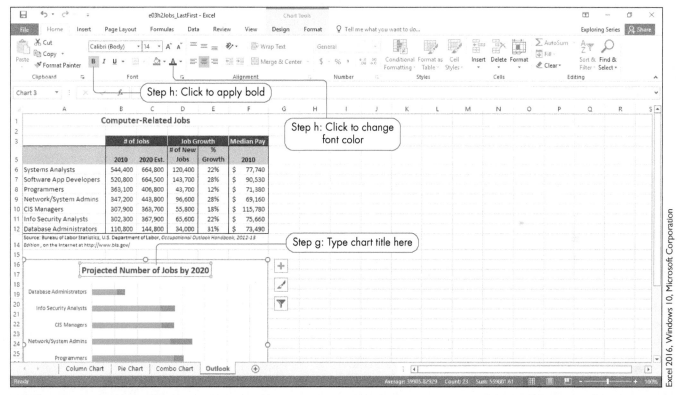

FIGURE 3.34 Formatted Chart Title

a. Open *e03h1Jobs_LastFirst* if you closed it at the end of the Hands-On Exercise 1, and save it as **e03h2Jobs_LastFirst**, changing h1 to h2.

b. Make sure the Combo Chart sheet is the active sheet, select the **Chart Title** placeholder, type **Number of New Computer-Related Jobs by 2020**, and then press **Enter**.

As you type a chart title, Excel displays the text in the Formula Bar. The text does not appear in the chart title until after you press Enter.

> **TROUBLESHOOTING:** If you double-click a title and type directly into the title placeholder, do not press Enter after typing the new title. Doing so will add a blank line.

c. Click the **Home tab**, click **Bold**, click the **Font Color arrow**, and then select **Black, Text 1**.

You applied font formats so that the chart title stands out.

d. Click the **Pie Chart sheet tab**, select the **Chart Title** placeholder, type **New Computer-Related Jobs by 2020**, and then press **Enter**.

Excel displays the text you typed for the chart title.

e. Click the **Home tab**, click **Bold**, click the **Font Size arrow** and select **18**, and then click the **Font Color arrow** and select **Black, Text 1**.

You formatted the pie chart title so that it stands out.

f. Click the **Column Chart sheet tab**, select the **Chart Title** placeholder, type **Number of Computer-Related Jobs 2010 and 2020**, and then press **Enter**. Click **Bold**, click the **Font Size arrow**, and then select **18**. Click the **Font Color arrow** and click **Black, Text 1** font color to the chart title.

g. Click the **Outlook sheet tab**, select the **Chart Title** placeholder, type **Projected Number of Jobs by 2020**, and then press **Enter**.

h. Click **Bold**, click the **Font Size arrow**, and then select **14**. Click the **Font Color arrow** and click **Dark Blue** in the Standard Colors section. Save the workbook.

You formatted the bar chart title to have a similar font color as the worksheet title.

STEP 2 **»** **ADD AND FORMAT AXIS TITLES AND FORMAT AXES**

For the bar chart, you want to add and format a title to describe the job titles on the vertical axis. In addition, you want to simplify the horizontal axis values to avoid displaying *,000* for each increment and add the title *Thousands*. Refer to Figure 3.35 as you complete Step 2.

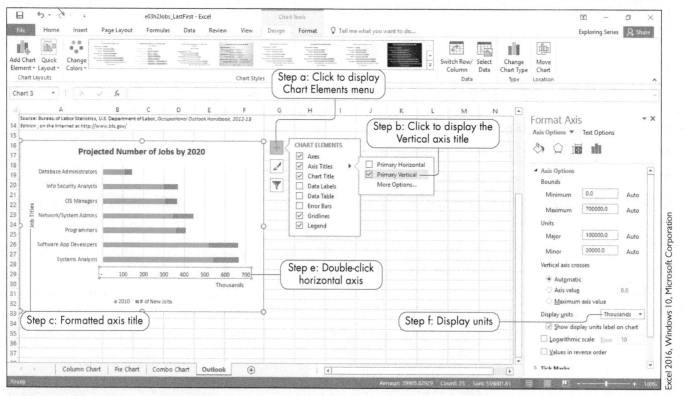

FIGURE 3.35 Formatted Axis Titles and Axes

a. Ensure that the bar chart is selected in the Outlook worksheet and click **Chart Elements** to the right of the chart.

Excel displays the Chart Elements menu.

b. Point to **Axis Titles**, click the **Axis Titles arrow**, and then click the **Primary Vertical check box** to select it. Close the menu.

Excel displays Axis Title on the left side of the vertical axis.

c. Ensure that the Axis Title placeholder is selected, type **Job Titles**, and then press **Enter**.

d. Click **Font Color** to apply the default Dark Blue font color to the selected axis title.

e. Point to the **horizontal axis**. When you see the ScreenTip, Horizontal (Value) Axis, double-click the values on the horizontal axis.

The Format Axis task pane opens for you to format the value axis.

f. Click the **Display units arrow** and select **Thousands**.

> **TROUBLESHOOTING:** If the Display units is not shown, click the Axis Options icon, and click Axis Options to display the options.

The axis now displays values such as 700 instead of 700,000. The title Thousands displays in the bottom-right corner of the horizontal axis.

g. Click the **Home tab**, select the title **Thousands**, and then apply **Dark Blue font color** in the Font group. Close the Format Axis task pane. Save the workbook.

STEP 3 ⟫ ADD AND FORMAT DATA LABELS

The pie chart includes a legend to identify which color represents each computer-related job; however, it does not include numerical labels to help you interpret what percentage of all computer-related jobs will be hired for each position. You want to insert and format percentage value labels. Refer to Figure 3.36 as you complete Step 3.

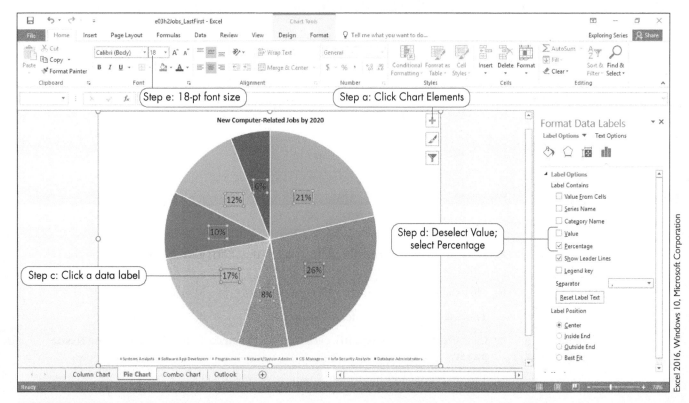

FIGURE 3.36 Formatted Data Labels

a. Click the **Pie Chart sheet tab** and click **Chart Elements**.

b. Click the **Data Labels arrow** and select **Center**. Close the Chart Elements menu.

You added data labels to the pie slices. The default data labels show the number of new jobs in the pie slices.

c. Right-click one of the data labels and select **Format Data Labels** to open the Format Data Label task pane.

d. Click **Label Options**, click the **Percentage check box** to select it, and then click the **Value check box** to deselect it. Close the Format Data Labels task pane.

Typically, pie chart data labels show percentages instead of values.

e. Change the font size to **18** to make the data labels larger. Save the workbook.

You want to apply a texture fill to the chart area and change the fill colors for the Software Apps Developers and the Database Administrators slices. Refer to Figure 3.37 as you complete Step 4.

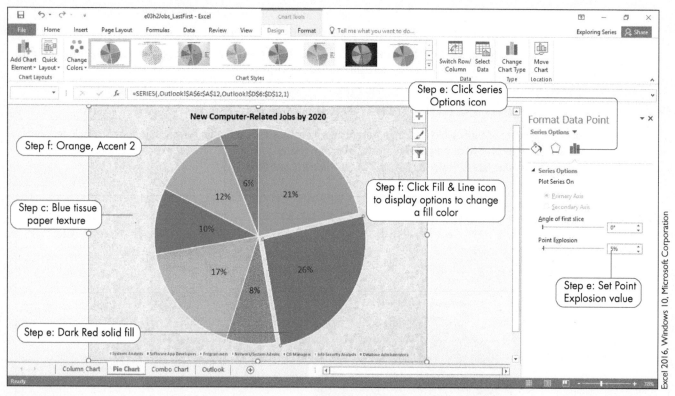

FIGURE 3.37 Formatted Chart Area and Data Point

a. Point to the **chart area** (the white space in the chart) and double-click when you see the Chart Area ScreenTip.

b. Click the **Fill & Line icon** in the Format Chart Area task pane and click **Fill**.

The task pane displays different fill options.

c. Click **Picture or texture fill**, click the **Texture arrow**, and then click **Blue tissue paper**.

The chart area now has the blue tissue paper texture fill.

d. Click the **26% Orange, Accent 2 slice**, pause, and then click the **26% Orange, Accent 2 slice** again to select just that data point (slice).

The first click selects all slices of the pie. The second click selects only the Software App Developers slice so that you can format that data point. Because you did not close the Format Chart Area task pane after Step c, Excel changes to the Format Data Point task pane when you select a data point.

e. Complete the following steps to format the selected data point:

- Click the **Fill & Line icon**, click **Solid fill**, click the **Color arrow**, and then click **Dark Red** in the Standard Colors section.
- Click the **Series Options icon** in the Format Data Point task pane and click the **Point Explosion increment** to **5%**.

You changed the fill color and exploded the slice for the selected data point.

f. Click the **6% Database Administrators slice**, click the **Fill & Line icon** in the Format Data Point task pane, click **Solid fill**, click the **Color arrow**, and then click **Orange, Accent 2**. Close the Format Data Point task pane.

The new color for the Database Administrators slice makes it easier to read the percentage data label.

g. Save the workbook. Keep the workbook open if you plan to continue with the next Hands-On Exercise. If not, close the workbook and exit Excel.

Chart Design and Sparklines

After you add and format chart elements, you might want to experiment with other features to enhance a chart. The Chart Tools Design tab contains two other groups: Chart Styles and Data. These groups enable you to apply a different style or color scheme to a chart or manipulate the data that are used to build a chart. You can also click Chart Styles and Chart Filters to the right of a chart to change the design of a chart.

At times, you might want to insert small visual chart-like images within worksheet cells to illustrate smaller data series rather than a large chart to illustrate several data points. Excel enables you to create small chart-like images in close proximity to individual data points to help you visualize the data.

In this section, you will learn how to apply chart styles and colors, filter chart data, and insert and customize miniature charts (sparklines) within individual cells.

Applying a Chart Style and Colors

STEP 1 ⟩⟩ A **chart style** is a collection of formatting that controls the color of the chart area, plot area, and data series. Styles, such as flat, 3-D, or beveled, also affect the look of the data series. Figure 3.38 shows the options when you click Chart Styles to the right of the chart, and Figure 3.39 shows the Chart Styles gallery that displays when you click Chart Styles on the Design tab. The styles in the Chart Styles gallery reflect what is available for the currently selected chart, such as a pie chart. If you select a different type of chart, the gallery will display styles for that particular type of chart.

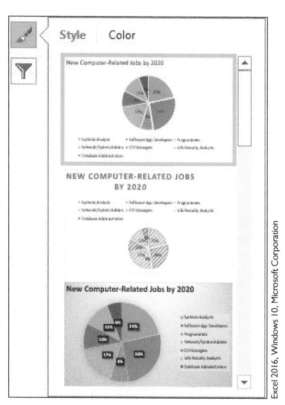

Excel 2016, Windows 10, Microsoft Corporation

FIGURE 3.38 Chart Styles

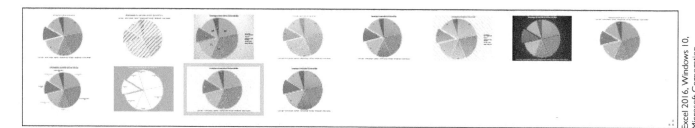

Excel 2016, Windows 10, Microsoft Corporation

FIGURE 3.39 Chart Styles Gallery

> **TIP: CHOOSING APPROPRIATE CHART STYLES**
> When choosing a chart style, make sure the style complements the chart data and is easy to read. Also, consider whether you will display the chart onscreen in a presentation or print the chart. If you will display the chart in a presentation, consider selecting a style with a black background.

To change the color scheme of the chart, complete the following steps:

1. Click Chart Styles to the right of the chart.
2. Click Color or click Change Colors in the Chart Styles group on the Design tab.
3. Select from the Colorful and Monochromatic sections.

Modifying the Data Source

The data source is the range of worksheet cells that are used to construct a chart. Although you should select the data source carefully before creating a chart, you may decide to alter that data source after you create and format the chart. The Data group on the Design tab is useful for adjusting the data source. Furthermore, you can apply filters to display or hide a data series without adjusting the entire data source.

Apply Chart Filters

STEP 2 >> A *chart filter* controls which data series and categories are visible in a chart. By default, all the data you selected to create the chart are used to construct the data series and categories. However, you can apply a chart filter to focus on particular data. For example, you might want to focus on just one job title at a time. Click Chart Filters to the right of the chart to display the options (see Figure 3.40). A check mark indicates the data series or categories currently displayed in the chart. Click a check box to deselect or hide a data series or a category.

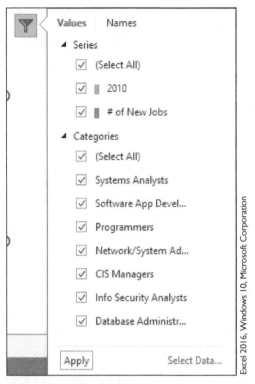

FIGURE 3.40 Chart Filter Options

Click Select Data in the Data group on the Design tab to open the Select Data Source dialog box (see Figure 3.41). This dialog box is another way to filter which categories and data series are visible in your chart. Furthermore, this dialog box enables you to change the chart data range, as well as add, edit, or remove data that is being used to create the chart. For example, you might want to add another data series or remove an existing data series from the chart.

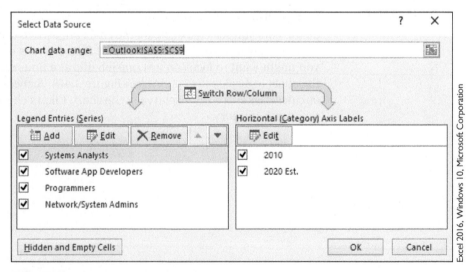

FIGURE 3.41 Select Data Source Dialog Box

Switch Row and Column Data

You might want to switch data used to create the horizontal axis and the legend to give a different perspective and to change the focus on the data. For example, you might want to display years as data series to compare different years for categories, and then you might want to switch the data to show years on the category axis to compare job titles within the same year. In Figure 3.42, the chart on the left uses the job titles to build the data series and legend, and the years display on the horizontal axis. The chart on the right shows the results after switching the data: the job titles build the horizontal axis, and the years build the data series and legend.

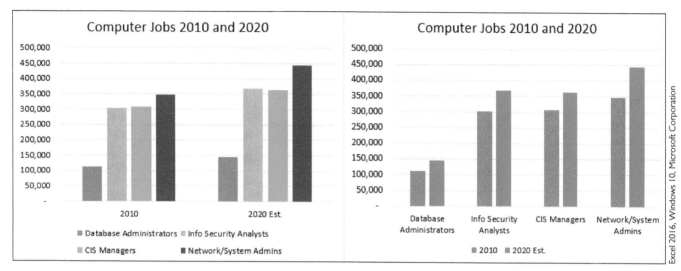

FIGURE 3.42 Original Chart and Chart with Switched Rows/Columns

> **To switch the row and column data, complete the following steps:**
> 1. Select the chart.
> 2. Click Switch Row/Column in the Data group on the Design tab.

Creating and Customizing Sparklines

A ***sparkline*** is a small line, column, or win/loss chart contained in a single cell. The purpose of a sparkline is to present a condensed, simple, succinct visual illustration of data. Unlike a regular chart, a sparkline does not include any of the standard chart labels, such as a chart title, axis label, axis titles, legend, or data labels. Inserting sparklines next to data helps to create a visual "dashboard" to help you understand the data quickly without having to look at a full-scale chart.

Figure 3.43 shows three sample sparklines: line, column, and win/loss. The line sparkline shows trends over time, such as each student's trends in test scores. The column sparkline compares test averages. The win/loss sparkline depicts how many points a team won or lost each game.

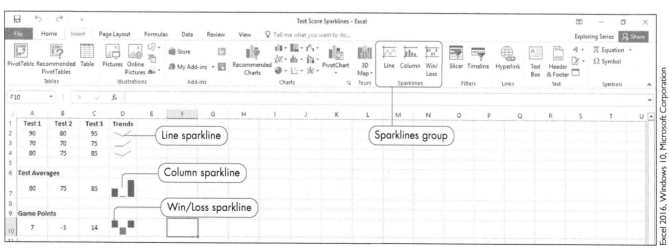

FIGURE 3.43 Sample Sparklines

Insert a Sparkline

 Before creating a sparkline, identify the data range you want to depict (such as A2:C2 for the first person's test score) and where you want to place the sparkline (such as cell D2).

To insert a sparkline, complete the following steps:

1. Click the Insert tab.
2. Click Line, Column, or Win/Loss in the Sparklines group. The Create Sparklines dialog box opens (see Figure 3.44).
3. Type the cell references containing the values in the Data Range box or select the range.
4. Enter or select the range where you want the sparkline to display in the Location Range box and click OK. The default cell location is the active cell unless you change it.

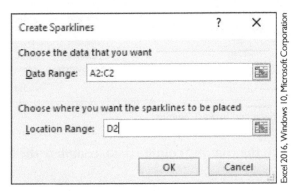

FIGURE 3.44 Create Sparklines Dialog Box

Customize a Sparkline

After you insert a sparkline, the Sparkline Tools Design tab displays (see Figure 3.45), with options to customize the sparkline. Table 3.6 lists and describes the groups on the Sparkline Tools Design tab.

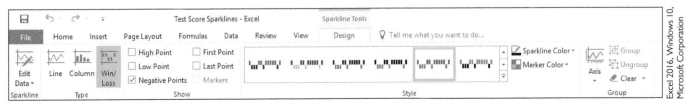

FIGURE 3.45 Sparkline Tools Design Tab

TABLE 3.6	Sparkline Tools Design Tab
Group	**Description**
Sparkline	Edits the location and data source for a group or individual data point that generates a group of sparklines or an individual sparkline.
Type	Changes the selected sparkline type (line, column, win/loss).
Show	Displays points, such as the high points, or markers within a sparkline.
Style	Changes the sparkline style, similar to a chart style, changes the sparkline color, or changes the marker color.
Group	Specifies the horizontal and vertical axis settings, groups objects together, ungroups objects, and clears sparklines.

Quick Concepts

8. What are two ways to change the color scheme of a chart? *p. 575*

9. How can you change a chart so that the data in the legend are on the X-axis and the data on the X-axis are in the legend? *pp. 576–577*

10. What is a sparkline, and why would you insert one? *p. 577*

Hands-On Exercises

Skills covered: Apply a Chart Style • Apply Chart Filters • Insert a Sparkline • Customize Sparklines

3 Chart Design and Sparklines

Now that you have completed the pie chart, you want to focus again on the bar chart. You are not satisfied with the overall design and want to try a different chart style. In addition, you would like to include sparklines to show trends for all jobs between 2010 and 2020.

STEP I ❯❯ APPLY A CHART STYLE

You want to give more contrast to the bar chart. Therefore, you will apply the Style 2 chart style. That style changes the category axis labels to all capital letters and displays data labels inside each segment of each bar. Refer to Figure 3.46 as you complete Step 1.

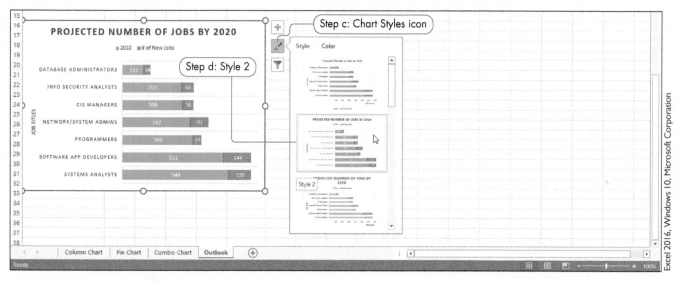

FIGURE 3.46 Chart Style Applied

a. Open *e03h2Jobs_LastFirst* if you closed it at the end of the Hands-On Exercise 2, and save it as **e03h3Jobs_LastFirst**, changing h2 to h3.

b. Click the **Outlook sheet tab** and click the bar chart to select it.

c. Click **Chart Styles** to the right of the chart.

The gallery of chart styles opens.

d. Point to **Style 2**. When you see the ScreenTip that identifies Style 2, click **Style 2**. Click **Chart Styles** to close the gallery. Save the workbook.

Excel applies the Style 2 chart style to the chart, which displays value data labels in white font color within each stack of the bar chart. The chart title and the category labels display in all capital letters. The legend displays above the plot area.

When you first created the clustered column chart, you included the number of new jobs as well as the number of 2010 jobs and the projected number of 2020 jobs. However, you decide that the number of new jobs is implied by comparing the 2010 to the 2020 jobs. Therefore, you want to set a chart filter to exclude the number of new jobs. Refer to Figure 3.47 as you complete Step 2.

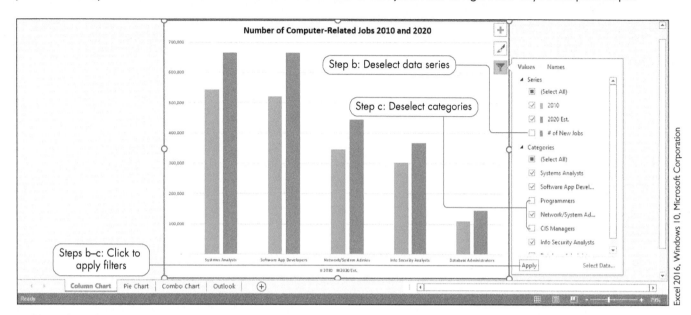

FIGURE 3.47 Chart Filters

a. Click the **Column Chart sheet tab** and click **Chart Filters** on the right of the chart area.

b. Point to the various filter options to see a preview of the filtered data. Click the **# of New Jobs check box** in the Series group to deselect it and click **Apply** at the bottom of the filter window.

   The number of new jobs (gray) data series no longer displays in the clustered column chart.

c. Click the **Programmers check box** to deselect the category, click the **CIS Managers check box** to deselect it, and then click **Apply**. Click **Chart Filters** to close the menu. Save the workbook.

   The Programmers and CIS Managers categories no longer display in the clustered column chart.

You want to insert sparklines to show the trends between 2010 and 2020. After inserting the sparklines, you want to display the high points to show that all jobs will have major increases by 2020. Refer to Figure 3.48 as you complete Step 3.

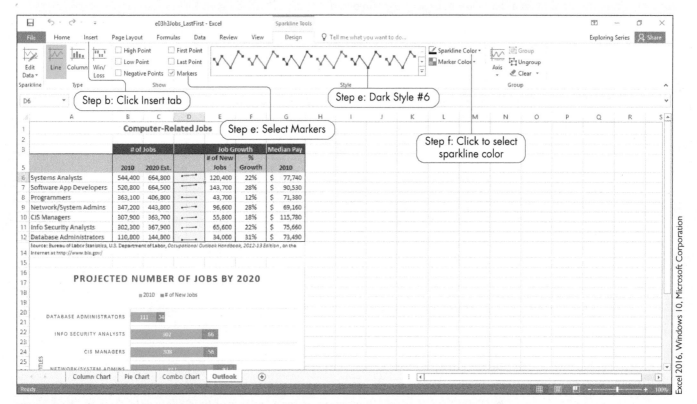

FIGURE 3.48 Sparkline Tools Design Tab

a. Click the **Outlook sheet tab**, select **cell D6**, click the **Insert arrow** in the Cells group, and then select **Insert Sheet Columns**.

You inserted a new column so that you can place the sparklines close to the data you want to visualize.

b. Click the **Insert tab** and click **Line** in the Sparklines group.

c. Select the **range B6:C12** to enter that range in the Data Range box.

You selected multiple rows at one time to create a group of sparklines.

d. Press **Tab** and select the **range D6:D12** to enter that range in the Location Range box. Click **OK**.

Excel inserts sparklines in the range D6:D12 with each sparkline representing data on its respective row. The Sparkline Tools Design tab displays.

e. Click the **Markers check box** in the Show group to select it and click **Sparkline Style Dark #6** in the Style group.

f. Click **Sparkline Color** in the Style group and click **Red** in the Standard Colors section.

g. Click **Axis** in the Group group and click **Same for All Sparklines** in the Vertical Axis Minimum Value Options section. Click **Axis** again and click **Same for All Sparklines** in the Vertical Axis Maximum Value Options section.

Because the sparklines look identical in trends, you changed the axis settings to set the minimum and maximum values as relative to the sparkline values in the entire selected range of rows rather than the default setting that bases the minimum and maximum for each row.

h. Save and close the file. Based on your instructor's directions, submit e03h3Jobs_LastFirst.

Chapter Objectives Review

After reading this chapter, you have accomplished the following objectives:

1. Select the data source.

- Decide which data you want to include in a chart. Each value is a data point, and several related data points create a data series in a chart.
- Select the range of data, including appropriate labels. The labels become the legend and the category axis.

2. Choose a chart type.

- After selecting a range, click Quick Analysis and click Charts to display a gallery of recommended chart types.
- Create a column chart: A clustered column chart compares groups of side-by-side columns where the height of the column indicates its value. The taller the column, the larger the value. A stacked column chart shows relationships of individual data points to the whole.
- Create a bar chart: A bar chart compares values across categories using horizontal bars where the width of the bar indicates its value. The wider the bar, the larger the value. A stacked bar chart shows relationships of individual data points to the whole.
- Change the chart type: After creating a chart, you might want to change it to a different type by clicking Change Chart Type in the Type group on the Design tab.
- Create a line chart: A line chart compares trends over time. Values are displayed on the value axis, and time periods are displayed on the category axis.
- Create a pie chart: A pie chart indicates the proportion to the whole for one data series. The size of the slice indicates the size of the value. The larger the pie slice, the larger the value.
- Create a combo chart: A combo chart combines elements of two chart types, such as column and line, to depict different data, such as individual data points compared to averages or percentages.
- Create other chart types: An X Y (scatter) chart shows a relationship between two numerical variables. A stock chart shows fluctuations in prices of stock, such as between the opening and closing prices on a particular day.

3. Move, size, and print a chart.

- Move a chart: The Move Chart dialog box enables you to select a new sheet and name the new chart sheet. To move a chart within a worksheet, click and drag the chart to the desired area.
- Size a chart: Adjust the chart size by dragging a sizing handle or specifying exact measurements in the Size group on the Format tab.
- Print a chart: To print a chart with its data series, the chart needs to be on the same worksheet as the data source. To ensure both the data and the chart print, make sure the chart is not selected. If the chart is on its own sheet or if you select the chart on a worksheet containing other data, the chart will print as a full-sized chart.

4. Add, edit, and format chart elements.

- Click Chart Elements to add elements. Chart elements include a chart title, axis titles, data labels, legend, gridlines, chart area, plot area, data series, and data point.
- Edit, format, and position the chart title: The default chart title is Chart Title, but you should edit it to provide a descriptive title for the chart. Apply font formats, such as bold and font size, to the chart title. Position the chart title above the chart, centered and overlaid, or in other locations.
- Add, format, and position axis titles: Display titles for the value and category axes to help describe the axes better. Apply font formats, such as bold and font size, to the axis titles.
- Format the axes: Change the unit of display for the value axis, such as converting values to In Millions.
- Add, position, and format data labels: Data labels provide exact values for a data series. Select the position of the data labels and the content of the data labels. Apply font formats, such as bold and font size, to the data labels.
- Position and format the legend: Position the legend to the right, top, bottom, or left of the plot area. Change the font size to adjust the label sizes within the legend.
- Add and format gridlines: Gridlines help the reader read across a column chart. Adjust the format of the major and minor gridlines.
- Format the chart area, plot area, and data series: The Format task panes enable you to apply fill colors, select border colors, and apply other settings.
- Format a data point: Format a single data point, such as changing the fill color for a single pie slice or specifying the percentage to explode a slice in a pie chart. Apply font formats, such as bold and font size, to the data points.
- Use the Chart Tools Format tab: Use this tab to select a chart element and insert and format shapes.

5. Apply a chart style and colors.

- Apply a chart style: This feature applies predetermined formatting, such as the background color and the data series color.

6. Modify the data source.

- Add or remove data from the data source to change the data in the chart.
- Apply chart filters: The Select Data Source dialog box enables you to modify the ranges used for the data series. When you deselect a series, Excel removes that series from the chart.
- Switch row and column data: You can switch the way data is used to create a chart by switching data series and categories.

7. Create and customize sparklines.

- Create a sparkline: A sparkline is a miniature chart in a cell representing a single data series.
- Customize a sparkline: Change the data source, location, and style. Display markers and change line or marker colors.

Key Terms Matching

Match the key terms with their definitions. Write the key term letter by the appropriate numbered definition.

a. Axis title
b. Bar chart
c. Category axis
d. Chart area
e. Chart title
f. Clustered column chart
g. Combo chart
h. Data label
i. Data point
j. Data series

k. Gridline
l. Legend
m. Line chart
n. Pie chart
o. Plot area
p. Sizing handle
q. Sparkline
r. Task pane
s. Value axis
t. X Y (scatter) chart

1. _____ Chart that groups columns side by side to compare data points among categories. **p. 539**

2. _____ Miniature chart contained in a single cell. **p. 577**

3. _____ Chart type that shows trends over time in which the value axis indicates quantities and the horizontal axis indicates time. **p. 543**

4. _____ Label that describes the entire chart. **p. 558**

5. _____ Label that describes either the category axis or the value axis. **p. 558**

6. _____ Key that identifies the color, gradient, picture, texture, or pattern fill assigned to each data series in a chart. **p. 535**

7. _____ Chart type that compares categories of data horizontally. **p. 542**

8. _____ Chart that shows each data point in proportion to the whole data series. **p. 544**

9. _____ Numeric value that describes a single value on a chart. **p. 534**

10. _____ Chart that contains two chart types, such as column and line, to depict two types of data, such as individual data points and percentages. **p. 545**

11. _____ A circle that enables you to adjust the height or width of a selected chart. **p. 549**

12. _____ Horizontal or vertical line that extends from the horizontal or vertical axis through the plot area. **p. 566**

13. _____ Chart type that shows the relationship between two variables. **p. 546**

14. _____ Group of related data points that display in row(s) or column(s) in a worksheet. **p. 534**

15. _____ Window of options to format and customize chart elements. **p. 560**

16. _____ Provides descriptive labels for the data points plotted in a chart. **p. 535**

17. _____ Section of a chart that contains graphical representation of the values in a data series. **p. 535**

18. _____ A container for the entire chart and all of its elements. **p. 535**

19. _____ An identifier that shows the exact value of a data point in a chart. **p. 558**

20. _____ Displays incremental numbers to identify approximate values, such as dollars or units, of data points in a chart. **p. 535**

Multiple Choice

1. Which type of chart is the *least* appropriate for depicting yearly rainfall totals for five cities for four years?

   (a) Pie chart
   (b) Line chart
   (c) Column chart
   (d) Bar chart

2. Look at the stacked bar chart in Figure 3.35. Which of the following is a category on the category axis?

   (a) Thousands
   (b) Job Titles
   (c) CIS Managers
   (d) 700

3. Which of the following is not a type of sparkline?

   (a) Line
   (b) Bar
   (c) Column
   (d) Win-Loss

4. If you want to show exact values for a data series in a bar chart, which chart element should you display?

   (a) Chart title
   (b) Legend
   (c) Value axis title
   (d) Data labels

5. The value axis currently shows increments such as 50,000 and 100,000. What option would you select to display the values in increments of 50 and 100?

   (a) More Primary Vertical Axis Title Options
   (b) Show Axis in Thousands
   (c) Show Axis in Millions
   (d) Show Right to Left Axis

6. You want to create a single chart that shows the proportion of yearly sales for five divisions for each year for five years. Which type of chart can accommodate your needs?

   (a) Pie chart
   (b) Surface chart
   (c) Clustered bar chart
   (d) 100% stacked column chart

7. Currently, a column chart shows values on the value axis, years on the category axis, and state names in the legend. What should you do if you want to organize data with the states on the category axis and the years shown in the legend?

   (a) Change the chart type to a clustered column chart.
   (b) Click Switch Row/Column in the Data group on the Design tab.
   (c) Click Layout 2 in the Chart Layouts group on the Design tab and apply a different chart style.
   (d) Click Legend in the Labels group on the Layout tab and select Show Legend at Bottom.

8. What do you click to remove a data series from a chart so that you can focus on other data series?

   (a) Chart Elements
   (b) Chart Series
   (c) Chart Filters
   (d) Chart Styles

9. Which of the following does not display automatically when you create a clustered column chart?

   (a) Data labels
   (b) Chart title placeholder
   (c) Gridlines
   (d) Legend

10. After you create a line type sparkline, what option should you select to display dots for each data point?

    (a) High Point
    (b) Negative Point
    (c) Sparkline Color
    (d) Markers

Practice Exercises

1 Hulett Family Utility Expenses

Your cousin, Alex Hulett, wants to analyze his family's utility expenses for 2018. He gave you his files for the electric, gas, and water bills for the year. You created a worksheet that lists the individual expenses per month, along with yearly totals per utility type and monthly totals. You will create some charts to depict the data. Refer to Figure 3.49 as you complete this exercise.

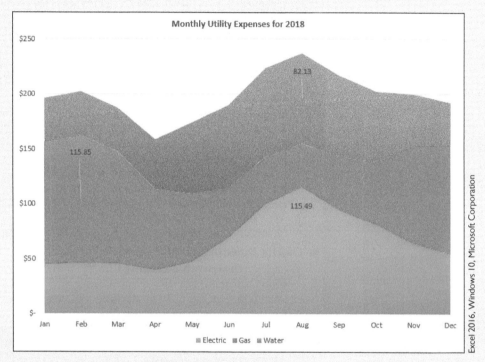

FIGURE 3.49 Hulett Family Utility Expenses

a. Open *e03p1Utilities* and save it as **e03p1Utilities_LastFirst**.

b. Select the **range A4:E17**, click **Quick Analysis**, click **Charts**, and then click **Clustered Column**.

c. Click **Chart Filters** to the right of the chart and do the following:
  • Deselect the **Monthly Totals check box** in the Series group.
  • Scroll through the Categories group and deselect the **Yearly Totals check box**.
  • Click **Apply** to remove totals from the chart. Click **Chart Filters** to close the menu.

d. Point to the **chart area**. When you see the Chart Area ScreenTip, drag the chart so that the top-left corner of the chart is in **cell A21**.

e. Click the **Format tab** and change the size by doing the following:
  • Click in the **Shape Width box** in the Size group, type **6"**, and then press **Enter**.
  • Click in the **Shape Height box** in the Size group, type **3.5"**, and then press **Enter**.

f. Click the **Design tab**, click **Quick Layout** in the Chart Layouts group, and then click **Layout 3**.

g. Select the **Chart Title placeholder**, type **Monthly Utility Expenses for 2018**, and then press **Enter**.

h. Click the chart, click the **More button** in the Chart Styles group, and then click **Style 6**.

i. Click **Copy** on the Home tab, click **cell A39**, and then click **Paste**. With the second chart selected, do the following:

- Click the **Design tab**, click **Change Chart Type** in the Type group, click **Line** on the left side of the dialog box, select **Line with Markers** in the top-center section, and then click **OK**.
- Click the **Electric data series line** to select it and click the highest marker to select only that marker. Click **Chart Elements** and click **Data Labels**.
- Repeat and adapt the previous bulleted step to add a data label to the highest markers for Gas and Water. Click **Chart Elements** to close the menu.
- Select the chart, copy it, and then paste it in **cell A57**.

j. Ensure that the third chart is selected and do the following:

- Click the **Design tab**, click **Change Chart Type** in the Type group, select **Area** on the left side, click **Stacked Area**, and then click **OK**.
- Click **Move Chart** in the Location group, click **New sheet**, type **Area Chart**, and then click **OK**.
- Select each data label and change the font size to **12**. Move each data label up closer to the top of the respective shaded area.
- Select the value axis and change the font size to **12**.
- Right-click the value axis and select **Format Axis**. Scroll down in the Format Axis task pane, click **Number**, click in the **Decimal places box**, and then type **0** . Close the Format Axis task pane.
- Change the font size to **12** for the category axis and the legend.

k. Click the **Expenses sheet tab**, select the line chart, and do the following:

- Click the **Design tab**, click **Move Chart** in the Location group, click **New sheet**, type **Line Chart**, and then click **OK**.
- Change the font size to **12** for the value axis, category axis, data labels, and legend.
- Format the vertical axis with zero decimal places.
- Right-click the **chart area**, select **Format Chart Area**, click **Fill**, click **Gradient fill**, click the **Preset gradients arrow**, and then select **Light Gradient – Accent 1**. Close the Format Chart Area task pane.

l. Click the **Expenses sheet**, select the **range B5:D16** and do the following:

- Click the **Insert tab**, click **Line** in the Sparkline group, click in the **Location Range box**, type **B18:D18**, and then click **OK**.
- Click the **High Point check box** to select it and click the **Low Point check box** to select it in the Show group with all three sparklines selected.

m. Create a footer with your name on the left side, the sheet name code in the center, and the file name code on the right of each sheet.

n. Save and close the file. Based on your instructor's directions, submit e03p1Utilities_LastFirst.

2 Trends in Market Value of Houses on Pine Circle

You live in a house on Pine Circle, a quiet cul-de-sac in a suburban area. Recently, you researched the market value and square footage of the five houses on Pine Circle. Now, you want to create charts to visually depict the data to compare values for the houses in the cul-de-sac. Refer to Figure 3.50 as you complete this exercise.

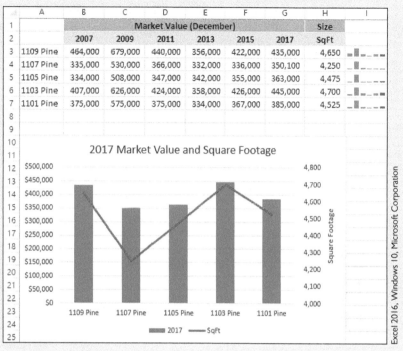

	A	B	C	D	E	F	G	H	I
1		Market Value (December)						Size	
2		2007	2009	2011	2013	2015	2017	SqFt	
3	1109 Pine	464,000	679,000	440,000	356,000	422,000	435,000	4,650	
4	1107 Pine	335,000	530,000	366,000	332,000	336,000	350,100	4,250	
5	1105 Pine	334,000	508,000	347,000	342,000	355,000	363,000	4,475	
6	1103 Pine	407,000	626,000	424,000	358,000	426,000	445,000	4,700	
7	1101 Pine	375,000	575,000	375,000	334,000	367,000	385,000	4,525	

FIGURE 3.50 Market Values

a. Open *e03p2Pine* and save it as **e03p2Pine_LastFirst**.

b. Select the **range A2:G7**, click **Quick Analysis**, click **Charts**, and then click **Line**.

c. Click **Move Chart** in the Location group, click **New sheet**, type **Line**, and then click **OK**.

d. Select the **Chart Title placeholder** and do the following:
   • Type **Market Value of Pine Circle Houses** and press **Enter**.
   • Apply bold to the chart title, change the font size to **20**, and then select **Olive Green, Accent 3, Darker 50% font color**.

e. Click the **value axis** on the left side of the chart and do the following:
   • Change the font size to 12 and select **Olive Green, Accent 3, Darker 50% font color**.
   • Double-click the value axis to open the Format Axis task pane.
   • Type **300000** in the Minimum Bounds box and press **Enter**. The Maximum Bounds box should change to 700000 automatically.
   • Scroll down in the Format Axis task pane and click **Number** to display those options.
   • Click the **Category arrow** and select **Currency**.
   • Close the Format Axis task pane.

f. Click **Chart Elements**, click the **Axis Titles triangle**, and then click the **Primary Vertical check box** to select it. Type **December Market Values** in the **Axis Title placeholder** and press **Enter**.

g. Make sure the Chart Elements menu is showing, click the **Gridlines triangle**, and then click the **Primary Minor Horizontal check box** to select it.

h. Click the blue **1109 Pine data series line**, click the **Data Labels check box** to select it, and then click **Chart Elements** to close the menu.

i. Click the data labels you just created, click the **Home tab**, click the **Font Color arrow**, and then select **Blue** in the Standard Colors section.

j. Select the category axis, change the font size to **12**, and select **Olive Green, Accent 3, Darker 50% font color**.

k. Right-click the legend and select **Format Legend**. Click **Top** in the Legend Position section of the Format Legend task pane and close the task pane.

l. Click the **Pine Circle sheet tab** and select the **ranges A2:A7** and **G2:H7**.

m. Click the **Insert tab**, click **Insert Combo Chart** in the Charts group, and then click the **Clustered Column – Line on Secondary Axis thumbnail**.

n. Do the following to the chart:
- Move and resize the chart to fill the **range A10:H25**.
- Select the **Chart Title placeholder**, type **2017 Market Value and Square Footage**, and then press **Enter**.
- Double-click the value axis on the left side, scroll down in the Format Axis task pane, click **Number**, click the **Category arrow**, and then select **Currency**.
- Click **Chart Elements**, click the **Axis Titles triangle**, click the **Secondary Vertical check box** to select it, type **Square Footage**, and then press **Enter**. Close the Format Axis Title task pane.

o. Select the **range B3:G7**, click the **Insert tab**, click **Column** in the Sparklines group, make sure B3:G7 displays in the Data Range box, type **I3:I7** in the Location Range box, and then click **OK**.

p. Customize the sparklines by doing the following:
- Click **More** in the Style group and select **Sparkline Style Accent 6, Darker 25%**.
- Click **Last Point** in the Show group.

q. Create a footer with your name on the left side, the sheet name code in the center, and the file name code on the right of both sheets.

r. Save and close the file. Based on your instructor's directions, submit e03p2Pine_LastFirst.

Mid-Level Exercises

1 Airport Passenger Counts

ANALYSIS CASE

As an analyst for the airline industry, you track the number of passengers at the top five major U.S. airports: Atlanta, Chicago, Los Angeles, Dallas/Fort Worth, and Denver. You researched passenger data at http://www.aci-na.org. One worksheet you created lists the number of total yearly passengers at the top five airports for a six-year period. To prepare for an upcoming meeting, you need to create a clustered column chart to compare the number of passengers at each airport. Next, you will create a bar chart to compare the passenger count for the latest year of data available and then emphasize the airport with the largest number of passenger traffic. Finally, you want to insert sparklines to visually represent trends in passengers at each airport over the six-year period. You can then refer to the sparklines and clustered column chart to write a paragraph analyzing the trends to detect.

a. Open *e03m1Airports* and save it as **e03m1Airports_LastFirst**.

b. Create a clustered column chart for the **range A4:G9**. Position and resize the chart to fit in the **range A15:G34**.

c. Customize the chart by doing the following:
- Swap the data on the category axis and in the legend.
- Apply the **Style 6 chart style**.
- Select **Color 12** in the Monochromatic section of the Change Colors gallery.
- Apply the **Light Gradient – Accent 1** preset gradient fill to the chart area.
- Change the fill color of the 2013 data series to **Dark Blue** and change the fill color of the 2008 data series to **Blue, Accent 5, Lighter 60%**.

- Use Help and add a solid **Blue border** around the legend.

d. Type **Passengers by Top U.S. Airports** as the chart title. Change the font color to **Blue**.

e. Adjust the value axis by doing the following:

- Change the display units to **Millions** for the value axis.
- Edit the axis title to display **Millions of Passengers**.

f. Display data labels above the columns for the 2013 data series only.

g. Create a clustered bar chart for the **range A5:A9** and **G5:G9** and then do the following:
- Move the bar chart to a chart sheet named **Bar Chart**.
- Enter **Passengers at Top 5 U.S. Airports in 2013** as the chart title.
- Apply the **Style 3 chart style**.
- Change the font color to **Dark Blue** on the chart title, category axis, and the value axis.
- Format the Atlanta data point with **Dark Blue fill color**.

h. Display the Passenger worksheet and insert **Line sparklines** in the **range H5:H9** to illustrate the data in the **range B5:G9**. This should insert a sparkline to represent yearly data for each airport.

i. Customize the sparklines by doing the following:
- Show the high and low points in each sparkline.
- Apply **Black, Text 1 color** to the high point marker in each sparkline.
- Apply **Dark Red color** to the low point marker in each sparkline.

j. Click **cell A36** and compose a paragraph that analyzes the trends depicted by the airport sparklines. Notice the overall trends in decreased and increased number of passengers and any unusual activity for an airport. Spell-check the worksheet and correct any errors.

k. Set **0.2"** left and right margins and scale to fit to 1 page for the Passenger worksheet.

l. Insert a footer with your name on the left side, the sheet name code in the center, and the file name code on the right on all worksheets.

m. Save and close the file. Based on your instructor's directions, submit e03m1Airports_LastFirst.

2 Grade Analysis

You are a teaching assistant for Dr. Monica Unice's introductory psychology class. You have maintained her grade book all semester, entering three test scores for each student and calculating the final average. You created a section called Final Grade Distribution that contains calculations to identify the number of students who earned an A, B, C, D, or F. Dr. Unice wants you to create a chart that shows the percentage of students who earn each letter grade. Therefore, you decide to create and format a pie chart. You will also create a bar chart to show a sample of the students' test scores. Furthermore, Dr. Unice wants to see if a correlation exists between attendance and students' final grades; therefore, you will create a scatter chart depicting each student's percentage of attendance with his or her respective final grade average.

a. Open *e03m2Psych* and save it as **e03m2Psych_LastFirst**.

b. Create a pie chart from the Final Grade Distribution data located below the student data in the **range F38:G42** and move the pie chart to its own sheet named **Grades Pie**.

c. Customize the pie chart with these specifications:
   - Apply the **Style 7 chart style.**
   - Type **PSY 2030 Final Grade Distribution - Fall 2018** for the chart title.
   - Explode the B grade slice by **10%**.
   - Remove the legend.

d. Add centered data labels and customize the labels with these specifications:
   - Display these data labels: **Percentage** and **Category Name**. Remove other data labels.
   - Change the font size to **20** and apply **Black, Text 1** font color.

e. Create a clustered bar chart using the **range A7:D12** and move the bar chart to its own sheet named **Students Bar Chart**.

f. Customize the bar chart with these specifications:
   - Apply the **Style 5 chart style**.
   - Type **Sample Student Test Scores** for the chart title.
   - Position the legend on the right side.
   - Add data labels in the Outside End position for the Final Exam data series.
   - Arrange the categories in reverse order so that Atkin is listed at the top and Ethington is listed at the bottom of the bar chart.

DISCOVER 🔍

DISCOVER 🔍

g. Create a scatter chart using the **range E7:F33**, the attendance record and final averages from the Grades worksheet. Move the scatter chart to its own sheet named **Scatter Chart**.

h. Apply these label settings to the scatter chart:
   - Remove the legend.
   - Type **Attendance-Final Average Relationship** for the chart title.
   - Add the following primary horizontal axis title: **Percentage of Attendance**.
   - Add the following primary vertical axis title: **Student Final Averages**.

DISCOVER 🔍

i. Use Help to learn how to apply the following axis settings:
   - Vertical axis: 40 minimum bound, 100 maximum bound, 10 major units, and a number format with zero decimal places
   - Horizontal axis: 40 minimum bound, 100 maximum bound, automatic units

j. Change the font size to **12** on the vertical axis title, vertical axis, horizontal axis title, and horizontal axis. Bold the chart title and the two axes titles.

k. Add the **Parchment texture fill** to the plot area.

l. Insert a linear trendline.

m. Insert Line sparklines in the **range H8:H33** using the three tests score columns. Change the sparkline color to **Purple** and show the low points.

n. Insert a footer with your name on the left, the sheet name code in the center, and the file name code on the right on all the sheets.

o. Save and close the file. Based on your instructor's directions, submit e03m2Psych_LastFirst.

3 Box Office Movies

You and two of your friends like to follow the popularity of new movies at the theater. You will research current movies that have been showing for four weeks and decide which movies on which to report. Work in teams of three for this activity. After obtaining the data, your team will create applicable charts to illustrate the revenue data. Team members will critique each other's charts.

a. Have all three team members log in to a chat client and engage in a dialogue about which movies are currently playing. Each member should research a different theater to see what is playing at that theater. Decide on six movies that have been in theaters for at least four weeks to research. Save a copy of your instant message dialogue and submit based on your instructor's directions.

b. Divide the six movies among the three team members. Each member should research the revenue reported for two movies for the past four weeks. Make sure your team members use the same source to find the data.

Student 1:

c. Create a new Excel workbook and enter appropriate column labels and the four-week data for all six movies. Name Sheet1 **Data**.

d. Format the data appropriately. Save the workbook as **e03m3Movies_GroupName**. Upload the workbook to a shared location, such as OneDrive, invite the other students to share this location, and send a text message to the next student.

Student 2:

e. Create a line chart to show the trends in revenue for the movies for the four-week period.

f. Add a chart title, format the axes appropriately, select a chart style, and then apply other formatting.

g. Move the chart to its own sheet named **Trends**. Save the workbook, upload it to the shared location, and send a text message to the next student.

Student 3:

h. Add a column to the right of the four-week data and total each movie's four-week revenue.

i. Create a pie chart depicting each movie's percentage of the total revenue for your selected movies.

j. Add a chart title, explode one pie slice, add data labels showing percentages and movie names, and then apply other formatting.

k. Move the chart to its own sheet named **Revenue Chart**. Save the workbook, upload it to the shared location, and send a text message to the next student.

Student 1:

l. Critique the charts. Insert a new worksheet named **Chart Critique** that provides an organized critique of each chart. Type notes that list each team member's name and specify what each student's role was in completing this exercise.

m. Save the workbook, upload it to the shared location, and send a text message to the next student.

Student 2:

n. Read the critique of the line chart and make any appropriate changes for the line chart. On the critique worksheet, provide a response to each critique and why you made or did not make the suggested change.

o. Save the workbook, upload it to the shared location, and send a text message to the next student.

Student 3:

p. Read the critique of the pie chart and make any appropriate changes for the pie chart. On the critique worksheet, provide a response to each critique and why you made or did not make the suggested change.

q. Save and close the file. Based on your instructor's directions, submit e03m3Movies_GroupName.

Beyond the Classroom

Historical Stock Prices

GENERAL CASE ✓

FROM SCRATCH

You are interested in investing in the stock market. First, you need to research the historical prices for a particular stock. Launch a Web browser, go to finance.yahoo.com, type a company name, such as Apple, and then select the company name from a list of suggested companies. Click the Historical Prices link. Copy the stock data (date, high, low, open, close, volume) for a six-month period and paste it in a new workbook, adjusting the column widths to fit the data. Save the workbook as **e03b1StockData_LastFirst**. Rename Sheet1 **Data**. Display data for only the first date listed for each month; delete rows containing data for other dates. Sort the list from the oldest date to the newest date. Use Help if needed to learn how to sort data and how to create a Volume-Open-High-Low-Close chart. Then rearrange the data columns in the correct sequence. Format the data and column labels.

Insert a row to enter the company name and insert another row to list the company's stock symbol, such as AAPL. Copy the URL from the Web browser and paste it as a source below the list of data and the date you obtained the data. Merge the cells containing the company name and stock symbol through the last column of data and word-wrap the URL.

Create a Volume-Open-High-Low-Close chart on a new chart sheet named **Stock Chart**. Type an appropriate chart title. Set the primary vertical axis (left side) unit measurement to millions and include an axis title **Volume in Millions**. Include a secondary vertical axis (right side) title **Stock Prices**. Apply the Currency number style with 0 decimal places for the secondary axis values. Change the font size to 11 and the font color to Black, Text 1 on the vertical axes and category axis. Hide the legend.

Use Help to research how to insert text boxes. Insert a text box that describes the stock chart: white fill rectangles indicate the closing price was higher than the opening price; black fill rectangles indicate the closing price was lower than the opening price; etc. Create a footer with your name, the sheet name code, and the file name code on both worksheets. Save and close the file. Based on your instructor's directions, submit e03b1StockData_LastFirst.

Harper County Houses Sold

DISASTER RECOVERY ✚

You want to analyze the number of houses sold by type (e.g., rambler, two story, etc.) in each quarter in Harper County. You entered quarterly data for 2018, calculated yearly total number of houses sold by each type, and quarterly total number of houses sold. You asked an intern to create a stacked column chart for the data, but the chart contains a lot of errors.

Open *e03b2Houses* and save it as **e03b2Houses_LastFirst**. Identify the errors and poor design for the chart. Below the chart, list the errors and your corrections in a two-column format. Then correct the problems in the chart. Link the chart title to the cell containing the most appropriate label in the worksheet. Create a footer with your name, the sheet name code, and the file name code. Adjust the margins and scaling to print the worksheet data, including the error list, and the chart on one page. Save and close the file. Based on your instructor's directions, submit e03b2Houses_LastFirst.

Capstone Exercise

You are an analyst for the airline industry. You created a workbook that lists overall airline arrival statistics for several years. In particular, you listed the percentage and number of on-time arrivals, late arrivals, canceled flights, and diverted flights based on information provided by the Bureau of Transportation Statistics. You want to create charts and insert sparklines that show the trends to discuss with airline and airport managers.

Insert and Format Sparklines

The first dataset shows the percentages. You want to insert sparklines that show the trends in the five-year data. The sparklines will help show any trends in on-time arrivals compared to late arrivals, canceled flights, and diverted flights.

a. Open the *e03c1Arrivals* workbook and save it as **e03c1Arrivals_LastFirst**.

b. Insert Line sparklines in the **range G4:G7**, using the data for the five years.

c. Display the high and low points for the sparklines.

d. Change the high point marker color to **Green**.

Create a Pie Chart

You want to focus on the arrival percentages for 2014. Creating a pie chart will help people visualize the breakdown of all operations for that year. After you create the chart, you will move it to its own chart sheet and edit the chart title to reflect 2014 flight arrivals.

a. Select the **range A4:A7** and the **range F4:F7**.

b. Create a pie chart and move it to a chart sheet named **Pie Chart**.

c. Change the chart title to **2014 Flight Arrivals**.

Add and Format Chart Elements

You want to format the chart by applying a different chart style and positioning the legend above the plot area. Furthermore, you need to add data labels so that you will know the percentages for the arrival categories. Finally, you want to emphasize the canceled flights in Dark Red and explode the late arrival pie slice.

a. Apply the **Style 12 chart style** to the pie chart.

b. Format the chart title with **Blue font color**.

c. Position the legend between the chart title and the plot area.

d. Add data labels to the Best Fit position and display.

e. Apply bold to the data labels and change the font size to **12**.

f. Format the Canceled data point with **Dark Red fill color** and format the Late Arrival data point in **Green**.

g. Explode the Late Arrival data point by **5%**.

Create and Size a Column Chart

To provide a different perspective, you will create a clustered column chart using the actual number of flights. The Total Operations row indicates the total number of reported (scheduled) flights. After creating the chart, you will position and size the chart below the source rows.

a. Create a clustered column chart using the **range A10:F15** in the Arrivals sheet.

b. Edit the chart title: **On-Time and Late Flight Arrivals.**

c. Position the clustered column chart so that the top-left corner is in **cell A20**.

d. Change the width to **5.75"** and the height to **3.5"**.

Format the Column Chart

Now that you have created the column chart, you realize that some data seems irrelevant. You will filter out the unneeded data, format the value axis to remove digits, insert a vertical axis title, apply a color change, and format the chart area.

a. Apply chart filters to remove the canceled, diverted, and total operations data.

b. Select the value axis, set **500000** for the Major unit, display the axis units **in Millions**, select category **Number** format with **1** decimal place.

c. Add a primary vertical axis title **Number of Flights.**

d. Apply the **Color 2 chart color** to the chart.

e. Apply the **Light Gradient – Accent 3** fill to the chart area.

Finalizing the Workbook

You want to prepare the workbook in case someone wants to print the data and charts. The margins and scaling have already been set. You just need to insert a footer.

a. Create a footer on each worksheet with your name, the sheet name code, and the file name code.

b. Save and close the file. Based on your instructor's direction, submit e03c1Arrivals_LastFirst.

Excel

Datasets and Tables

LEARNING OUTCOME — You will demonstrate how to manage and analyze large sets of data.

OBJECTIVES & SKILLS: After you read this chapter, you will be able to:

Large Datasets

OBJECTIVE 1: FREEZE ROWS AND COLUMNS   599
Freeze Rows and Columns
OBJECTIVE 2: PRINT LARGE DATASETS   600
Display and Change Page Breaks, Set and Clear
a Print Area, Print Titles, Control Print Page Order

HANDS-ON EXERCISE 1:
Large Datasets   604

Excel Tables

**OBJECTIVE 3: UNDERSTAND THE BENEFITS OF DATA
TABLES**   609
OBJECTIVE 4: DESIGN AND CREATE TABLES   609
Create a Table; Rename a Table; Add and Delete
Fields; Add, Edit, and Delete Records; Remove
Duplicate Rows
OBJECTIVE 5: APPLY A TABLE STYLE   614
Apply a Table Style

HANDS-ON EXERCISE 2:
Excel Tables   616

Table Manipulation

**OBJECTIVE 6: CREATE STRUCTURED REFERENCES
IN FORMULAS**   621
Create a Structured Reference in a Formula

OBJECTIVE 7: SORT DATA   622
Sort One Field, Sort Multiple Fields,
Create a Custom Sort
OBJECTIVE 8: FILTER DATA   624
Apply Text Filters, Apply Number Filters,
Apply Date Filters, Apply a Custom Filter

HANDS-ON EXERCISE 3:
Table Manipulation   629

Table Aggregation and Conditional Formatting

OBJECTIVE 9: ADD A TOTAL ROW   636
Add a Total Row
OBJECTIVE 10: APPLYING CONDITIONAL FORMATTING   638
Apply Conditional Formatting with the
Quick Analysis Tool; Apply Highlight Cells Rules;
Specify Top/Bottom Rules; Display Data Bars,
Color Scales, and Icon Sets
OBJECTIVE 11. CREATE A NEW RULE   643
Use Formulas in Conditional Formatting,
Manage Rules

HANDS-ON EXERCISE 4:
Table Aggregation and Conditional Formatting   646

CASE STUDY | Reid Furniture Store

Vicki Reid owns Reid Furniture Store in Portland, Oregon. She divided her store into four departments: Living Room, Bedroom, Dining Room, and Appliances. All merchandise is categorized into one of these four departments for inventory records and sales. Vicki has four sales representatives: Chantalle Desmarais, Jade Gallagher, Sebastian Gruenewald, and Ambrose Sardelis. The sales system tracks which sales representative processed each transaction.

The business has grown rapidly, and Vicki hired you to analyze the sales data in order to increase future profits. For example, which department generates the most sales? Who is the leading salesperson? Do most customers purchase or finance? Are sales promotions necessary to promote business, or will customers pay the full price?

You downloaded March 2018 data from the sales system into an Excel workbook. To avoid extraneous data that is not needed in the analysis, you did not include customer names, accounts, or specific product numbers. The downloaded file contains transaction numbers, dates, sales representative names, departments, general merchandise descriptions, payment types, transaction types, and the total price.

Everything possible/
Shutterstock

Managing Large Volumes of Data

	A	B	C	D	E	F	G	H	I	J	K	L	M
1	**Reid Furniture Store**												
2	Monthly Transactions:			March 2018									
3	Down Payment Requirement:			25%									
4													
5	Trans_No	Operator	Sales_First	Sales_Last	Date	Department	Furniture		Pay_Type	Trans_Type	Amount		
6	2018-001	KRM	Sebastian	Gruenewald	3/1/2018	Bedroom	Mattress		Finance	Promotion	2,788		
7	2018-002	RKM	Sebastian	Gruenewald	3/1/2018	Bedroom	Mattress		Finance	Promotion	3,245		
8	2018-003	MAP	Jade	Gallagher	3/1/2018	Living Room	Sofa, Loveseat, Chair Package		Finance	Promotion	10,000		
9	2018-004	MAP	Jade	Gallagher	3/1/2018	Living Room	End Tables		Finance	Promotion	1,000		
10	2018-005	MAP	Jade	Gallagher	3/1/2018	Appliances	Washer and Dryer		Finance	Promotion	2,750		
11	2018-006	COK	Ambrose	Sardelis	3/1/2018	Living Room	Sofa, Loveseat, Chair Package		Finance	Promotion	12,000		
12	2018-006	COK	Ambrose	Sardelis	3/1/2018	Living Room	Sofa, Loveseat, Chair Package		Finance	Promotion	12,000		
13	2018-007	MAP	Jade	Gallagher	3/1/2018	Dining Room	Dining Room Table		Finance	Promotion	3,240		
14	2018-008	COK	Chantalle	Desmarais	3/1/2018	Dining Room	Dining Room Table		Finance	Promotion	4,080		
15	2018-009	KRM	Sebastian	Gruenewald	3/1/2018	Appliances	Washer and Dryer		Finance	Promotion	2,750		
16	2018-010	MAP	Jade	Gallagher	3/2/2018	Dining Room	Dining Room Table and Chairs		Finance	Standard	6,780		
17	2018-011	COK	Chantalle	Desmarais	3/2/2018	Dining Room	Dining Room Table and Chairs		Finance	Standard	10,000		
18	2018-012	KRM	Ambrose	Sardelis	3/2/2018	Appliances	Washer		Paid in Full	Promotion	1,100		
19	2018-013	COK	Chantalle	Desmarais	3/3/2018	Living Room	Recliners		Finance	Standard	2,430		
20	2018-014	COK	Jade	Gallagher	3/3/2018	Dining Room	Dining Room Table and Chairs		Paid in Full	Standard	4,550		
21	2018-015	MAP	Chantalle	Desmarais	3/3/2018	Living Room	Sofa, Loveseat, Chair Package		Finance	Standard	6,784		
22	2018-016	MAP	Jade	Gallagher	3/4/2018	Appliances	Dishwasher		Paid in Full	Standard	640		
23	2018-017	MAP	Jade	Gallagher	3/4/2018	Appliances	Refrigerator, Oven, Microwave Combo		Finance	Promotion	8,490		
24	2018-018	KRM	Sebastian	Gruenewald	3/4/2018	Appliances	Refrigerator, Oven, Microwave Combo		Finance	Promotion	6,780		

March Totals | March Individual | (+)

Ready ████████ 100%

	A	B	C	D	E	F	G	H	I	J	K	L	M	N	O
1	**Reid Furniture**														
2	Monthly Transactions:			March 2018											
3	Down Payment Requirement:			25%											
4															
5	Trans_No	Date	Sales_First	Sales_Last	Department	Furniture		Pay_Type	Trans_Type	Amou	Down_Pa	Owe			
6	2018-001	3/1/2018	Sebastian	Gruenewald	Bedroom	Mattress		Finance	Promotion	2,788	697.00	2,091.00			
7	2018-002	3/1/2018	Sebastian	Gruenewald	Bedroom	Mattress		Finance	Promotion	3,245	811.25	2,433.75			
8	2018-003	3/1/2018	Jade	Gallagher	Living Room	Sofa, Loveseat, Chair Package		Finance	Promotion	10,000	2,500.00	7,500.00			
9	2018-004	3/1/2018	Jade	Gallagher	Living Room	End Tables		Finance	Promotion	1,000	250.00	750.00			
10	2018-005	3/1/2018	Jade	Gallagher	Appliances	Washer and Dryer		Finance	Promotion	2,750	687.50	2,062.50			
11	2018-006	3/1/2018	Ambrose	Sardelis	Living Room	Sofa, Loveseat, Chair Package		Finance	Promotion	12,000	3,000.00	9,000.00			
12	2018-007	3/1/2018	Jade	Gallagher	Dining Room	Dining Room Table		Finance	Promotion	3,240	810.00	2,430.00			
13	2018-008	3/1/2018	Chantalle	Desmarais	Dining Room	Dining Room Table		Finance	Promotion	4,080	1,020.00	3,060.00			
14	2018-009	3/1/2018	Sebastian	Gruenewald	Appliances	Washer and Dryer		Finance	Promotion	2,750	687.50	2,062.50			
15	2018-010	3/2/2018	Jade	Gallagher	Dining Room	Dining Room Table and Chairs		Finance	Standard	6,780	1,695.00	5,085.00			
16	2018-011	3/2/2018	Chantalle	Desmarais	Dining Room	Dining Room Table and Chairs		Finance	Standard	10,000	2,500.00	7,500.00			
17	2018-012	3/2/2018	Ambrose	Sardelis	Appliances	Washer		Paid in Full	Promotion	1,100	1,100.00	-			
18	2018-013	3/3/2018	Chantalle	Desmarais	Living Room	Recliners		Finance	Standard	2,430	607.50	1,822.50			
19	2018-014	3/3/2018	Jade	Gallagher	Dining Room	Dining Room Table and Chairs		Paid in Full	Standard	4,550	4,550.00	-			
20	2018-015	3/3/2018	Chantalle	Desmarais	Living Room	Sofa, Loveseat, Chair Package		Finance	Standard	6,784	1,696.00	5,088.00			
21	2018-016	3/4/2018	Jade	Gallagher	Appliances	Dishwasher		Paid in Full	Standard	640	640.00	-			
22	2018-017	3/4/2018	Jade	Gallagher	Appliances	Refrigerator, Oven, Microwave Combo		Finance	Promotion	8,490	2,122.50	6,367.50			
23	2018-018	3/4/2018	Sebastian	Gruenewald	Appliances	Refrigerator, Oven, Microwave Combo		Finance	Promotion	6,780	1,695.00	5,085.00			
24	2018-019	3/5/2018	Jade	Gallagher	Living Room	Sofa		Paid in Full	Standard	2,500	2,500.00	-			

March Totals | **March Individual** | (+)

Ready ████████ 100%

Excel 2016, Windows 10, Microsoft Corporation

FIGURE 4.1 Reid Furniture Store Datasets

CASE STUDY | Reid Furniture Store

Starting File	File to be Submitted
e04h1Reid	**e04h4Reid_LastFirst**

Large Datasets

So far you have worked with worksheets that contain small datasets, a collection of structured, related data in a limited number of columns and rows. In reality, you will probably work with large datasets consisting of hundreds or thousands of rows and columns of data. When you work with small datasets, you can usually view most or all of the data without scrolling. When you work with large datasets, you probably will not be able to see the entire dataset onscreen even on a large, widescreen monitor set at high resolution. You might want to keep the column and row labels always in view, even as you scroll throughout the dataset. Figure 4.2 shows Reid Furniture Store's March 2018 sales transactions. Because it contains a lot of transactions, the entire dataset is not visible. You could decrease the zoom level to display more transactions; however, doing so decreases the text size onscreen, making it hard to read the data.

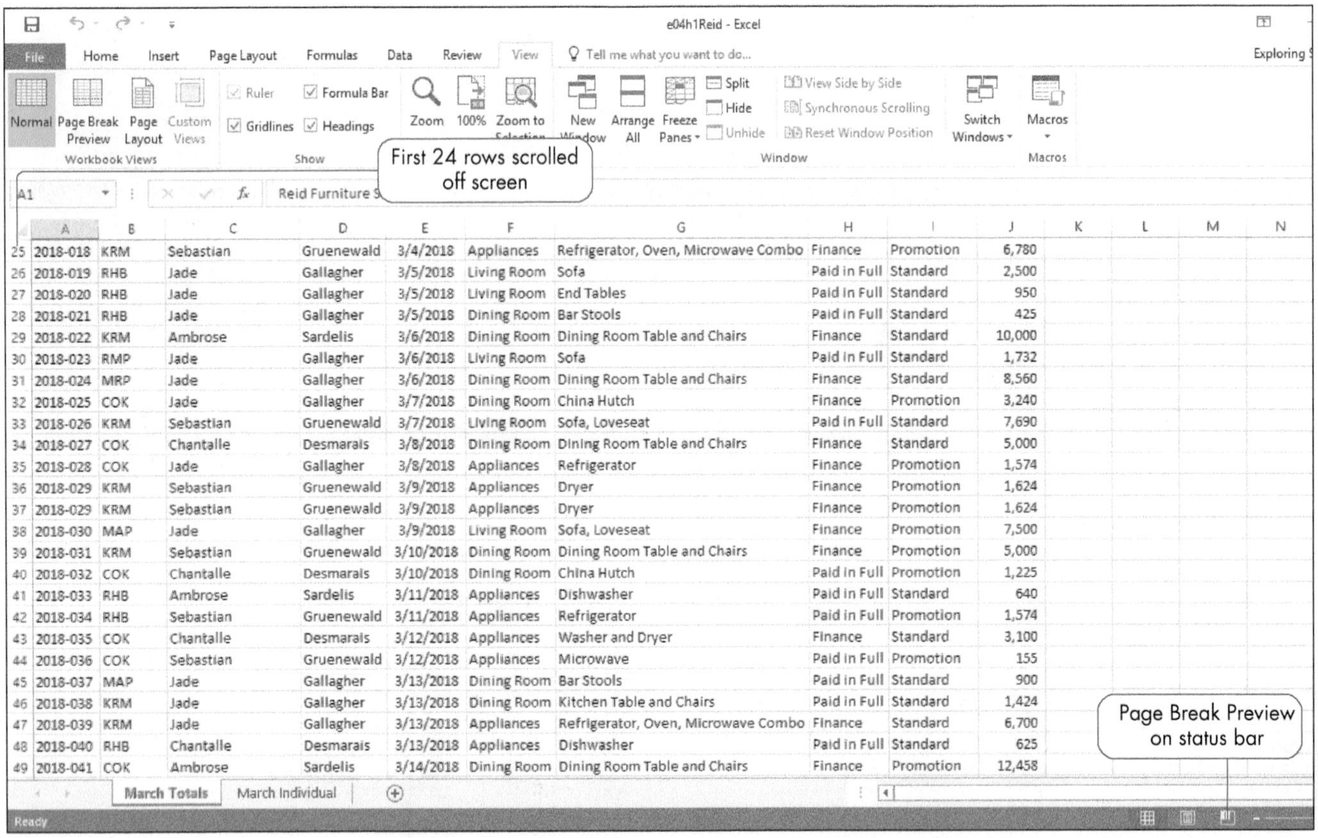

FIGURE 4.2 Large Dataset

As you work with larger datasets, realize that the data will not always fit on one page when it is printed. You will need to preview the automatic page breaks and probably insert some manual page breaks in more desirable locations, or you might want to print only a selected range within the large dataset to distribute to others.

In this section, you will learn how to keep labels onscreen as you scroll through a large dataset. In addition, you will learn how to manage page breaks, print only a range instead of an entire worksheet, and print column labels at the top of each page of a large dataset.

TIP: GO TO A SPECIFIC CELL

You can navigate through a large worksheet by using the Go To command. Click Find & Select in the Editing group on the Home tab and select Go To (or press F5 or Ctrl+G) to display the Go To dialog box, enter the cell address in the Reference box, and then press Enter to go to the cell. You can also click in the Name Box, type the cell reference, and then press Enter to go to a specific cell.

Freezing Rows and Columns

STEP I ›› When you scroll to parts of a dataset not initially visible, some rows and columns, such as headings, disappear from view. When the row and column labels scroll off the screen, you may not remember what each column or row represents. You can keep labels onscreen by freezing them. ***Freezing*** is the process of keeping rows and/or columns visible onscreen at all times even when you scroll through a large dataset. Table 4.1 describes the three freeze options.

TABLE 4.1 Freeze Options

Option	Description
Freeze Panes	Keeps both rows and columns above and to the left of the active cell visible as you scroll through a worksheet.
Freeze Top Row	Keeps only the top row visible as you scroll through a worksheet.
Freeze First Column	Keeps only the first column visible as you scroll through a worksheet.

To freeze one or more rows and columns, use the Freeze Panes option. Before selecting this option, make the active cell one row below and one column to the right of the rows and columns you want to freeze. For example, to freeze the first five rows and the first column, make cell B6 the active cell before clicking the Freeze Panes option. As Figure 4.3 shows, Excel displays a horizontal line below the last frozen row (row 5) and a vertical line to the right of the last frozen column (column F). Unfrozen rows (such as rows 6–14) and unfrozen columns (such as columns G and H) are no longer visible as you scroll down and to the right, respectively.

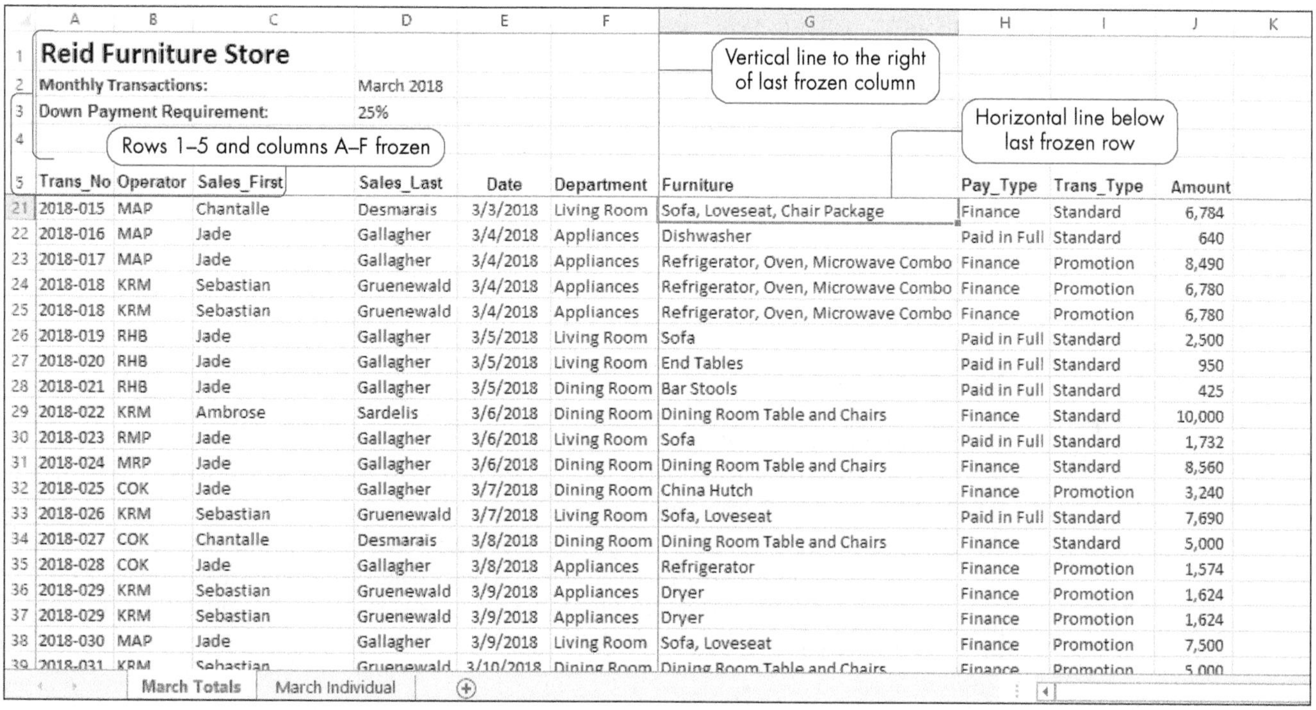

	A	B	C	D	E	F	G	H	I	J	K
1	Reid Furniture Store										
2	Monthly Transactions:			March 2018							
3	Down Payment Requirement:			25%							
4											
5	Trans_No	Operator	Sales_First	Sales_Last	Date	Department	Furniture	Pay_Type	Trans_Type	Amount	
21	2018-015	MAP	Chantalle	Desmarais	3/3/2018	Living Room	Sofa, Loveseat, Chair Package	Finance	Standard	6,784	
22	2018-016	MAP	Jade	Gallagher	3/4/2018	Appliances	Dishwasher	Paid in Full	Standard	640	
23	2018-017	MAP	Jade	Gallagher	3/4/2018	Appliances	Refrigerator, Oven, Microwave Combo	Finance	Promotion	8,490	
24	2018-018	KRM	Sebastian	Gruenewald	3/4/2018	Appliances	Refrigerator, Oven, Microwave Combo	Finance	Promotion	6,780	
25	2018-018	KRM	Sebastian	Gruenewald	3/4/2018	Appliances	Refrigerator, Oven, Microwave Combo	Finance	Promotion	6,780	
26	2018-019	RHB	Jade	Gallagher	3/5/2018	Living Room	Sofa	Paid in Full	Standard	2,500	
27	2018-020	RHB	Jade	Gallagher	3/5/2018	Living Room	End Tables	Paid in Full	Standard	950	
28	2018-021	RHB	Jade	Gallagher	3/5/2018	Dining Room	Bar Stools	Paid in Full	Standard	425	
29	2018-022	KRM	Ambrose	Sardelis	3/6/2018	Dining Room	Dining Room Table and Chairs	Finance	Standard	10,000	
30	2018-023	RMP	Jade	Gallagher	3/6/2018	Living Room	Sofa	Paid in Full	Standard	1,732	
31	2018-024	MRP	Jade	Gallagher	3/6/2018	Dining Room	Dining Room Table and Chairs	Finance	Standard	8,560	
32	2018-025	COK	Jade	Gallagher	3/7/2018	Dining Room	China Hutch	Finance	Promotion	3,240	
33	2018-026	KRM	Sebastian	Gruenewald	3/7/2018	Living Room	Sofa, Loveseat	Paid in Full	Standard	7,690	
34	2018-027	COK	Chantalle	Desmarais	3/8/2018	Dining Room	Dining Room Table and Chairs	Finance	Standard	5,000	
35	2018-028	COK	Jade	Gallagher	3/8/2018	Appliances	Refrigerator	Finance	Promotion	1,574	
36	2018-029	KRM	Sebastian	Gruenewald	3/9/2018	Appliances	Dryer	Finance	Promotion	1,624	
37	2018-029	KRM	Sebastian	Gruenewald	3/9/2018	Appliances	Dryer	Finance	Promotion	1,624	
38	2018-030	MAP	Jade	Gallagher	3/9/2018	Living Room	Sofa, Loveseat	Finance	Promotion	7,500	
39	2018-031	KRM	Sebastian	Gruenewald	3/10/2018	Dining Room	Dining Room Table and Chairs	Finance	Promotion	5,000	

FIGURE 4.3 Freeze Panes Set

To unlock the rows and columns from remaining onscreen as you scroll, click Freeze Panes in the Window group and select Unfreeze Panes, which only appears on the menu when you have frozen rows and/or columns. After you unfreeze the panes, the Freeze Panes option appears instead of Unfreeze Panes on the menu again.

When you freeze panes and press Ctrl+Home, the first unfrozen cell is the active cell instead of cell A1. For example, with column F and rows 1 through 5 frozen in Figure 4.3, pressing Ctrl+Home makes cell G6 the active cell. If you want to edit a cell in the frozen area, click the particular cell to make it active and edit the data.

Printing Large Datasets

For a large dataset, some columns and rows may print on several pages. Analyzing the data on individual printed pages is difficult when each page does not contain column and row labels. To prevent wasting paper, always use Print Preview. Doing so enables you to adjust page settings until you are satisfied with how the data will print.

The Page Layout tab (see Figure 4.4) contains options to help you prepare large datasets to print. Previously, you changed the page orientation, set different margins, and adjusted the scaling. In addition, you can manage page breaks, set the print area, and print titles.

FIGURE 4.4 Page Setup Options

Display and Change Page Breaks

STEP 2 >> Based on the paper size, orientation, margins, and other settings, Excel identifies how much data can print on a page. Then it displays a ***page break***, indicating where data will start on another printed page. To identify where these automatic page breaks will occur, click Page Break Preview on the status bar or in the Workbook Views group on the View tab. In Page Break Preview, Excel displays watermarks, such as Page 1, indicating the area that will print on a specific page. Blue dashed lines indicate where the automatic page breaks occur, and solid blue lines indicate manual page breaks.

If the automatic page breaks occur in an undesirable location, you can insert a manual page break. For example, if you have a worksheet listing sales data by date, the automatic page break might occur within a group of rows for one date, such as between two rows of data for 3/1/2018. To make all rows for that date appear together, you can either insert a page break above the first data row for that date or decrease the margins so that all 3/1/2018 transactions fit at the bottom of the page.

To set a manual break at a specific location, complete the following steps:

1. Click the cell that you want to be the first row and column on a new printed page. For example, if you click cell D50, you create a page for columns A through C, and then column D starts a new page.
2. Click the Page Layout tab.
3. Click Breaks in the Page Setup group and select Insert Page Break. Excel displays a solid blue line in Page Break Preview or a dashed line in Normal view to indicate the manual page breaks you set. Figure 4.5 shows a worksheet with both automatic and manual page breaks.

To remove a manual page break, complete the following steps:

1. Click a cell below a horizontal page break or a cell to the right of a vertical page break.
2. Click Breaks in the Page Setup group and select Remove Page Break.

To reset all page breaks back to the automatic page breaks, complete the following steps:

1. Click Breaks in the Page Setup group.
2. Select Reset All Page Breaks.

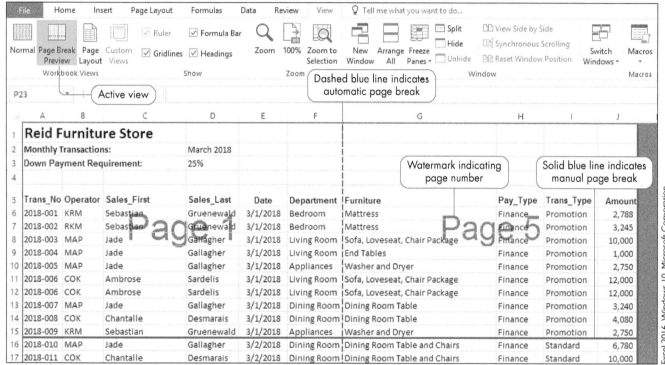

FIGURE 4.5 Page Breaks in Page Break Preview

TIP: USING THE POINTER TO MOVE PAGE BREAKS
To use the pointer to adjust a page break, point to the page break line to see the two-headed arrow and drag the line to the location where you want the page break to occur.

Set and Clear a Print Area

STEP 3 ›› The default Print settings send an entire dataset on the active worksheet to the printer. However, you might want to print only part of the worksheet data. If you display the worksheet in Page Break view, you can identify which page(s) you want to print. Then click the File tab and select Print. Under Settings, type the number(s) of the page(s) you want to print. For example, to print page 2 only, type 2 in the Pages text box and in the *to* text box.

You can further restrict what is printed by setting the ***print area***, which is the range of cells that will print. For example, you might want to print only an input area or just the transactions that occurred on a particular date.

> **To set a print area, complete the following steps:**
>
> 1. Select the range you want to print.
> 2. Click the Page Layout tab and click Print Area in the Page Setup group.
> 3. Select Set Print Area.

In Page Break Preview, the print area has a white background and solid blue border; the rest of the worksheet has a gray background (see Figure 4.6). In Normal view or Page Layout view, the print area is surrounded by thin gray lines.

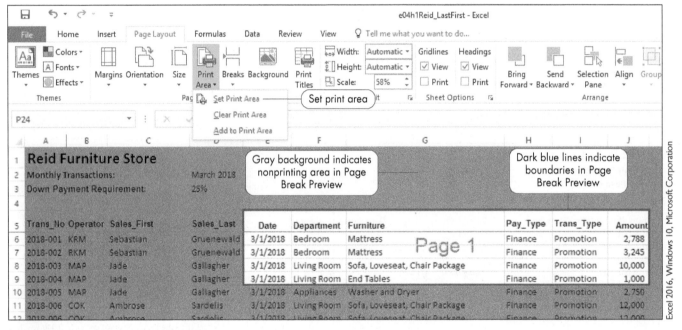

FIGURE 4.6 Print Area in Page Break Preview

To add print areas where each print area will print on a separate page, select the range you want to print, click Print Area, and then select Add to Print Area. To clear the print area, click Print Area in the Page Setup group and select Clear Print Area.

TIP: PRINT A SELECTION

Another way to print part of a worksheet is to select the range you want to print. Click the File tab and click Print. Click the first arrow in the Settings section and select Print Selection. This provides additional flexibility compared to using a defined print area in situations in which you may be required to print materials outside a consistent range of cells.

Print Titles

STEP 4 ›› When you print large datasets, it is helpful if every page contains descriptive column and row labels. When you click Print Titles in the Page Setup group on the Page Layout tab, Excel opens the Page Setup dialog box with the Sheet tab active so that you can select which row(s) and/or column(s) to repeat on each page of a printout (see Figure 4.7).

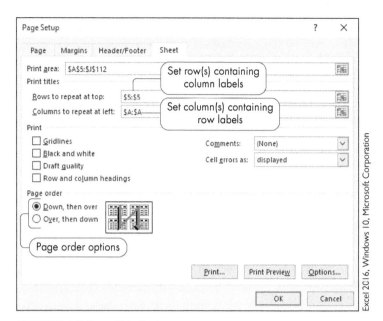

FIGURE 4.7 Sheet Tab Options

To repeat rows or columns at the top or left of each page when printed, select the row(s) that contain the labels or titles (such as row 5) in the *Rows to repeat at top* box to display $5:$5. To print the row labels at the left side of each page, select the column(s) that contain the labels or titles (such as column A) in the *Columns to repeat at left* box to display AA.

Control Print Page Order

Print order is the sequence in which the pages are printed. By default, the pages print in this order: top-left section, bottom-left section, top-right section, and bottom-right section. However, you might want to print the entire top portion of the worksheet before printing the bottom portion. To change the print order, open the Page Setup dialog box, click the Sheet tab, and then select the desired Page order option (refer to Figure 4.7).

Quick Concepts

1. What is the purpose of freezing panes in a worksheet? *p. 599*

2. Why would you want to insert page breaks instead of using the automatic page breaks? *p. 600*

3. What steps should you take to ensure that column labels display on each printed page of a large dataset? *pp. 602–603*

Hands-On Exercises

 Watch the Video for this Hands-On Exercise!

 MyITLab® HOE1 Training

Skills covered: Freeze Rows and Columns • Display and Change Page Breaks • Set and Clear a Print Area • Print Titles

1 Large Datasets

You want to review the large dataset that shows the March 2018 transactions for Reid Furniture Store. You will view the data and adjust some page setup options so that you can print necessary labels on each page.

STEP 1 ›› FREEZE ROWS AND COLUMNS

Before printing the March 2018 transaction dataset, you want to view the data. The dataset contains more rows than will display onscreen at the same time. You decide to freeze the column and row labels to stay onscreen as you scroll through the transactions. Refer to Figure 4.8 as you complete Step 1.

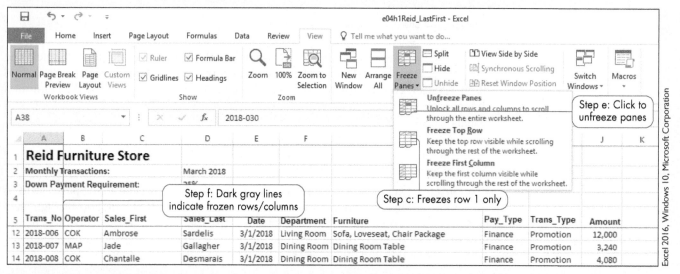

FIGURE 4.8 Freeze Panes Activated

a. Open *e04h1Reid* and save it as **e04h1Reid_LastFirst**.

> **TROUBLESHOOTING:** If you make any major mistakes in this exercise, you can close the file, open *e04h1Reid* again, and then start this exercise over.

The workbook contains two worksheets: March Totals (for Hands-On Exercises 1–3) and March Individual (for Hands-On Exercise 4).

b. Press **Page Down** four times to scroll through the dataset. Then press **Ctrl+Home** to go back to the top of the worksheet.

After you press Page Down, the column labels in row 5 scroll off the screen, making it challenging to remember what type of data are in some columns.

c. Click the **View tab**, click **Freeze Panes** in the Window group, and then select **Freeze Top Row**.

A dark gray horizontal line displays between rows 1 and 2.

d. Press **Page Down** to scroll down through the worksheet.

As rows scroll off the top of the Excel window, the first row remains frozen onscreen. The title by itself is not helpful; you need to freeze the column labels as well.

TROUBLESHOOTING: Your screen may differ from Figure 4.8 due to different Windows resolution settings. If necessary, continue scrolling right and down until you see columns and rows scrolling offscreen.

---

e. Click **Freeze Panes** in the Window group and select **Unfreeze Panes**.

f. Click **cell B6**, the cell below the row and one column to the right of what you want to freeze. Click **Freeze Panes** in the Window group and select **Freeze Panes**.

Excel displays a vertical line between columns A and B, indicating that column A is frozen, and a horizontal line between rows 5 and 6, indicating the first five rows are frozen.

g. Press **Ctrl+G**, type **Q112** in the Reference box of the Go To dialog box, and then click **OK** to make cell Q112 the active cell.

Rows 6 through 96 and columns B and C are not visible because they scrolled off the screen. Note that the results will vary slightly based on screen resolution.

h. Save the workbook.

You plan to print the dataset so that you and Vicki Reid can discuss the transactions in your weekly meeting. Because the large dataset will not fit on one page, you want to see where the automatic page breaks are and then insert a manual page break. Refer to Figure 4.9 as you complete Step 2.

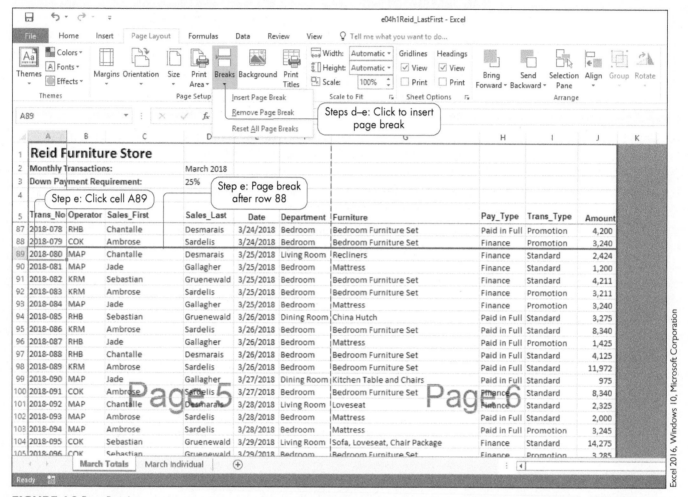

FIGURE 4.9 Page Breaks

a. Press **Ctrl+Home** to move to **cell B6**, the first cell in the unfrozen area. Click the **View tab** and click **Page Break Preview** in the Workbook Views group or on the status bar.

Excel displays blue dashed lines to indicate the automatic page breaks.

b. Scroll down until you see row 44 below the frozen column labels.

The automatic horizontal page break is between rows 46 and 47 (or between rows 45 and 46). You do not want transactions for a particular day to span between printed pages, so you need to move the page break up to keep all 3/13/2018 transactions together.

c. Click **cell A45**, the first cell containing 3/13/2018 data and the cell to start the top of the second page.

d. Click the **Page Layout tab**, click **Breaks** in the Page Setup group, and then select **Insert Page Break**.

You inserted a page break between rows 44 and 45 so that the 3/13/2018 transactions will be on one page.

e. Click **cell A89**, click **Breaks** in the Page Setup group, and then select **Insert Page Break**.

You inserted a page break between rows 88 and 89 to keep the 3/25/2018 transactions on the same page.

f. Save the workbook.

You want to focus on the transactions for only March 1, 2018. To avoid printing more data than you need, you will set the print area to print transactions for only that day. Refer to Figure 4.10 as you complete Step 3.

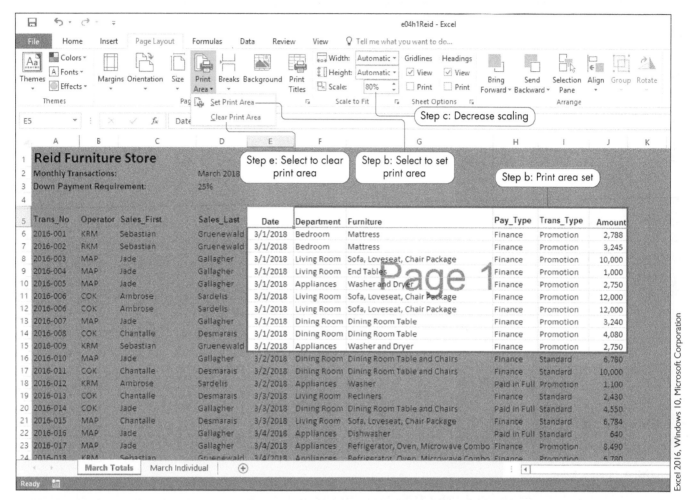

FIGURE 4.10 Print Area Set

a. Select the **range E5:J15**, the range of data for March 1, 2018.

b. Click the **Page Layout tab**, click **Print Area** in the Page Setup group, and then select **Set Print Area**.

Excel displays the print area with a border. The rest of the worksheet displays with a gray background.

c. Click **cell E5** and click the **Scale arrow** down four times to display 80% in the Scale to Fit group.

The selected print area will print on one page.

d. Press **Ctrl+P** to see that only the print area will print. Press **Esc**.

e. Click **Print Area** in the Page Setup group and select **Clear Print Area**.

f. Save the workbook.

Only the first page will print both row and column labels. Pages 2 and 3 will print the remaining row labels, page 4 will print the remaining column labels, and pages 5 and 6 will not print either label. You want to make sure the column and row labels print on all pages. To do this, you will print titles. Refer to Figure 4.11 as you complete Step 4.

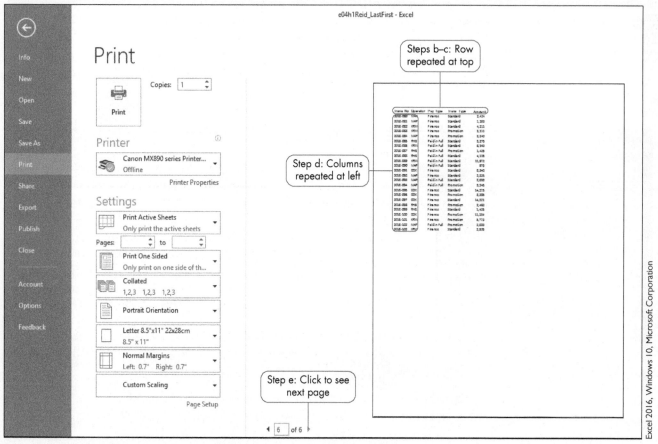

FIGURE 4.11 Print Titles

a.   Click **Print Titles** in the Page Setup group.

The Page Setup dialog box opens, displaying the Sheet tab.

b.   Click **Collapse Dialog Box** on the right side of the *Rows to repeat at top* box.

Clicking Collapse Dialog Box reduces the dialog box so that you can select a range in the worksheet easily.

c.   Click the **row 5 heading** and click **Expand Dialog Box** within the *Page Setup: Rows to repeat at top* dialog box.

You selected the fifth row, which contains the column labels, and expanded the Page Setup dialog box back to its full size.

d.   Click in the **Columns to repeat at left box**, type **A:B**, click the **Over, then down** Page order, and then click **Print Preview**.

You have manually entered the columns that contain the heading you want to repeat.

e.   Click **Next Page** at the bottom of the Print Preview. Click **Next Page** until the sixth page displays.

Figure 4.11 shows a preview of the sixth page. The column labels and the first two columns appear on all pages.

f.   Click the **Back arrow**.

g.   Save the workbook. Keep the workbook open if you plan to continue with the next Hands-On Exercise. If not, close the workbook, and exit Excel.

Excel Tables

All organizations maintain lists of data. Businesses maintain inventory lists, educational institutions maintain lists of students and faculty, and governmental entities maintain lists of contracts. Although more complicated related data should be stored in a database management program, such as Access, you can manage basic data structure in Excel tables. A ***table*** is a structured range that contains related data organized in a method that increases the capability to manage and analyze information.

In this section, you will learn table terminology and rules for structuring data. You will create a table from existing data, manage records and fields, and remove duplicates. You will then apply a table style to format the table.

Understanding the Benefits of Data Tables

When dealing with large datasets it is imperative that documents are strategically organized to maintain data integrity and ease of use. Thus far you have worked with the manipulation of data ranges, and while you can use many tools in Excel to analyze simple data ranges, tables provide many additional analytical and time saving benefits. Using tables in Excel can help create and maintain data structure. ***Data structure*** is the organization method used to manage multiple data points within a dataset. For example, a dataset of students may include names, grades, contact information, and intended majors of study. The data structure of this dataset would define how the information is stored, organized, and accessed. Although you can manage and analyze data structure as a range in Excel, a table provides many advantages:

- Column headings remain onscreen without having to use Freeze Panes.
- Filter arrows let you sort and filter efficiently.
- Table styles easily format table rows and columns with complementary fill colors.
- Calculated columns let you create and edit formulas that copy down the columns automatically.
- A calculated total row lets you implement a variety of summary functions.
- You can use structured references instead of cell references in formulas.
- You can export table data to a SharePoint list.

Designing and Creating Tables

A table is a group of related data organized in a series of rows and columns that is managed independently from any other data on the worksheet. Once a data range is converted into a table, each column represents a ***field***, which is an individual piece of data, such as last names or quantities sold. Each field should represent the smallest possible unit of data. For example, instead of a Name field, separate name data into First Name and Last Name fields. Instead of one large address field, separate address data into Street Address, City, State, and ZIP Code fields. Separating data into the smallest units possible enables you to manipulate the data in a variety of ways for output. Each row in a table represents a ***record***, which is a collection of related data about one entity. For example, all data related to one particular transaction form a record in the Reid Furniture Store worksheet.

You should plan the structure before creating a table. The more thoroughly you plan, the fewer changes you will have to make to gain information from the data in the table after you create it. To help plan your table, follow these guidelines:

- Enter field (column) names on the top row of the table.
- Keep field names short, descriptive, and unique. No two field names should be identical.

- Format the field names so that they stand out from the data.
- Enter data for each record on a row below the field names.
- Do not leave blank rows between records or between the field names and the first record.
- Delete any blank columns between fields in the dataset.
- Make sure each record has something unique, such as a transaction number or ID.
- Insert at least one blank row and one blank column between the table and other data, such as the main titles. When you need multiple tables in one workbook, a best practice is to place each table on a separate worksheet.

Create a Table

STEP 1 ⟩⟩ While it is possible to create a table from random unorganized data, it is a best practice first to plan the data structure. When your worksheet data is structured correctly, you can easily create a table. Furthermore, by taking the time to create an organized data structure you will ensure that the data can be used to identify specific information easily, is easy to manage, and is scalable.

To create a table from existing data, complete the following steps:

1. Click within the existing range of data.
2. Click the Insert tab and click Table in the Tables group. The Create Table dialog box opens (see Figure 4.12), prompting you to enter the range of data.
   - Select the range for the *Where is the data for your table* box if Excel does not correctly predict the range.
   - Select the *My table has headers* check box if the existing range contains column labels.
3. Click OK to create the table.

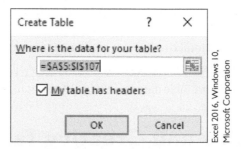

FIGURE 4.12 Create Table Dialog Box

TIP: QUICK ANALYSIS TABLE CREATION

You can also create a table by selecting a range, clicking the Quick Analysis button, clicking Tables (see Figure 4.13) in the Quick Analysis gallery, and then clicking Table. While Quick Analysis is efficient for tasks such as creating a chart, it may take more time to create a table because you have to select the entire range first. Some people find that it is faster to create a table on the Insert tab.

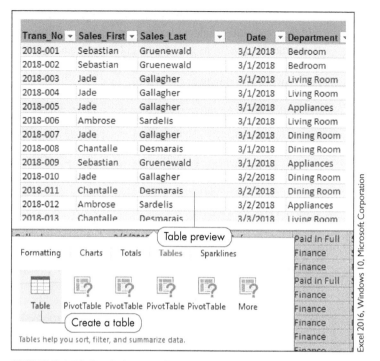

FIGURE 4.13 Quick Analysis Gallery

After you create a table, the Table Tools Design tab displays. Excel applies the default Table Style Medium 2 style to the table, and each cell in the header row has filter arrows (see Figure 4.14). This book uses the term *filter arrows* for consistency.

> **TIP: FILTER ARROWS**
> Click the Filter Button check box in the Table Style Options group on the Design tab to display or hide the filter arrows (see Figure 4.14). For a range of data instead of a table, click Filter in the Sort & Filter group on the Data tab to display or hide the filter arrows.

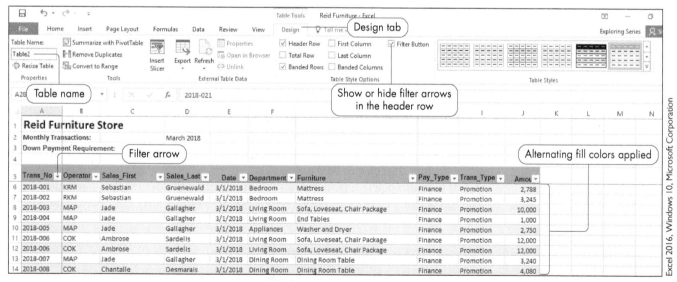

FIGURE 4.14 Excel Table in Default Format

Instead of converting a range to a table, you can create a table structure first and add data to it later. Select an empty range and follow the previously listed steps to create the range for the table. The default column headings are Column1, Column2, and so on. Click each default column heading and type a descriptive label. Then enter the data into each row of the newly created table.

> **TIP: CONVERTING A TABLE TO A RANGE**
> To convert a table back to a range, click within the table range, click the Table Tools Design tab, click Convert to Range in the Tools group, and then click Yes in the message box asking, *Do you want to convert the table to a normal range?*

Rename a Table

 By default, when a table is created, Excel assigns a name automatically. For example, the first table created in a worksheet will be named Table1. The default nomenclature does not provide descriptive information and, as a best practice, you should change the default name to something more meaningful.

To change the table name, complete the following steps:

1. Click the Table Name box in the Properties group of the Table Tools Design tab.
2. Type a new name using the same rules you applied when assigning range names, and press Enter.

Once a name has been assigned to a table, it can be used when building functions in place of the traditional absolute reference.

Add and Delete Fields

 After creating a table, you may need to insert a new field. For example, you might want to add a field for product numbers to the Reid Furniture Store transaction table.

To insert a field, complete the following steps:

1. Click in any data cell (other than the cell containing the field name) in a field that will be to the right of the new field. For example, to insert a new field between the fields in columns A and B, click any cell in column B.
2. Click the Home tab and click the Insert arrow in the Cells group.
3. Select Insert Table Columns to the Left.

If you want to add a field at the end of the right side of a table, click in the cell to the right of the last field name and type a label. Excel will extend the table to include that field and will format the cell as a field name.

You can also delete a field if you no longer need any data for that particular field. Although deleting records and fields is easy, you must make sure not to delete data erroneously. If you accidentally delete data, click Undo immediately.

To delete a field, complete the following steps:

1. Click a cell in the field that you want to delete.
2. Click the Delete arrow in the Cells group on the Home tab.
3. Select Delete Table Columns.

Add, Edit, and Delete Records

STEP 4 »» After you begin storing data in your newly created table, you might want to add new records, such as adding a new client or a new item to an inventory table. One of the advantages to using tables in Excel is the ability to easily add, edit, or delete records within the dataset.

> **To add a record to a table, complete the following steps:**
>
> 1. Click a cell in the record below which you want the new record inserted. If you want to add a new record below the last record, click the row containing the last record.
> 2. Click the Home tab and click the Insert arrow in the Cells group.
> 3. Select Insert Table Rows Above to insert a row above the current row, or select Insert Table Row Below if the current row is the last one and you want a row below it.

You can also add a record to the end of a table by clicking in the row immediately below the table and typing. Excel will extend the table to include that row as a record in the table and will apply consistent formatting.

You might need to change data for a record. For example, when a client moves, you need to change the client's address. You edit data in a table the same way you edit data in a regular worksheet cell.

Finally, you can delete records. For example, if you maintain an inventory of artwork in your house and sell a piece of art, delete that record from the table.

> **To delete a record from the table, complete the following steps:**
>
> 1. Click a cell in the record that you want to delete.
> 2. Click the Home tab and click the Delete arrow in the Cells group.
> 3. Select Delete Table Rows.

Remove Duplicate Rows

STEP 5 »» A table might contain duplicate records, which can give false results when totaling or performing other calculations on the dataset. For a small table, you might be able to detect duplicate records by scanning the data. For large tables, it is more difficult to identify duplicate records by simply scanning the table with the eye.

> **To remove duplicate records, complete the following steps:**
>
> 1. Click within the table and click the Design tab.
> 2. Click Remove Duplicates in the Tools group to display the Remove Duplicates dialog box (see Figure 4.15). As an alternate method, you can also click the Data tab and click Remove Duplicates in the Data Tools group to open the Remove Duplicates dialog box.
> 3. Click Select All to set the criteria to find a duplicate for every field in the record and click OK. If you select individual column(s), Excel looks for duplicates in the specific column(s) only and deletes all but one record of the duplicated data. Excel will display a message box informing you of how many duplicate rows it removed.

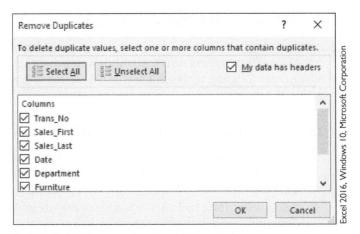

FIGURE 4.15 Remove Duplicates Dialog Box

Applying a Table Style

STEP 6 ⟫ When you create a table, it is automatically formatted with a table style of alternating colored rows and a bold style for the header row. ***Table styles*** control the fill color of the header row (the row containing field names) and rows of records. In addition, table styles specify bold and border lines. You can change the table style to a color scheme that complements your organization's color scheme or to emphasize data in the header rows or columns. Click the More button in the Table Styles group to display the Table Styles gallery (see Figure 4.16). To see how a table style will format your table using Live Preview, point to a style in the Table Styles gallery. After you identify a style you want, click it to apply it to the table.

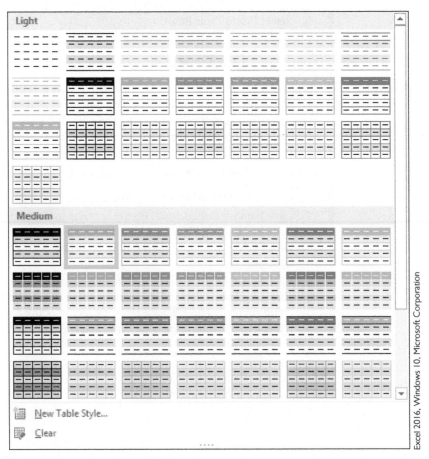

FIGURE 4.16 Table Styles Gallery

After you select a table style, you can control what the style formats. The Table Style Options group contains check boxes to select specific format actions in a table. Table 4.2 lists the options and the effect of each check box. Avoid overformatting the table. Applying too many formatting effects may obscure the message you want to present with the data.

TABLE 4.2	Table Style Options
Check Box	**Action**
Header Row	Displays the header row (field names) when checked; removes field names when not checked. Header Row formatting takes priority over column formats.
Total Row	Displays a total row when selected. Total Row formatting takes priority over column formats.
First Column	Applies a different format to the first column so that the row headings stand out. First Column formatting takes priority over Banded Rows formatting.
Last Column	Applies a different format to the last column so that the last column of data stands out; effective for aggregated data, such as grand totals per row. Last Column formatting takes priority over Banded Rows formatting.
Banded Rows	Displays alternate fill colors for even and odd rows to help distinguish records.
Banded Columns	Displays alternate fill colors for even and odd columns to help distinguish fields.
Filter Button	Displays a filter button on the right side of each heading in the header row.

Pearson Education, Inc.

Quick Concepts

4. List at least four guidelines for planning a table in Excel. ***pp. 609–610***

5. Why would you convert a range of data into an Excel table? ***p. 610***

6. What are six options you can control after selecting a table style? ***p. 615***

Hands-On Exercises

Skills covered: Create a Table • Rename a Table • Add and Delete Fields • Add, Edit, and Delete Records • Remove Duplicate Rows • Apply a Table Style

2 Excel Tables

You want to convert the March Totals data to a table. As you review the table, you will delete the unnecessary Operator field, add two new fields, insert a missing furniture sale transaction, and remove duplicate transactions. Finally, you will enhance the table appearance by applying a table style.

STEP 1 ›› CREATE A TABLE

Although Reid Furniture Store's March transaction data are organized in an Excel worksheet, you know that you will have additional functionality if you convert the range to a table. Refer to Figure 4.17 as you complete Step 1.

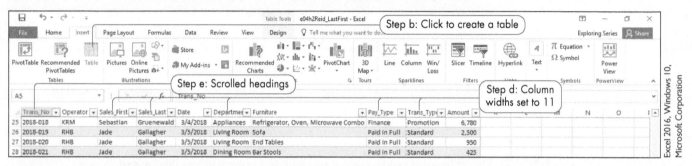

FIGURE 4.17 Range Converted to a Table

a. Open *e04h1Reid_LastFirst* if you closed it at the end of Hands-On Exercise 1, and save it as **e04h2Reid_LastFirst**, changing h1 to h2. Click **Normal** on the status bar.

b. Click in any cell within the transactional data, click the **Insert tab**, and then click **Table** in the Tables group.

The Create Table dialog box opens. The *Where is the data for your table?* box displays =$A$5:$J$112. Keep the *My table has headers* check box selected so that the headings on the fifth row become the field names for the table.

c. Click **OK** and click **cell A5**.

Excel creates a table from the data range and displays the Design tab, filter arrows, and alternating fill colors for the records. The columns widen to fit the field names, although the wrap text option is still applied to those cells.

d. Set the column width to **11** for the Sales_First, Sales_Last, Department, Pay_Type, and Trans_Type fields.

e. Unfreeze the panes and scroll through the table.

With a regular range of data, column labels scroll off the top of the screen if you do not freeze panes. When you scroll within a table, the table's header row remains onscreen by moving up to where the Excel column (letter) headings usually display (see Figure 4.17). Note that it will not retain the bold formatting when scrolling.

f. Save the workbook.

After creating the table, you will change the name from the default "Table1" to a more descriptive title that meets your business standards. Refer to Figure 4.18 as you complete Step 2.

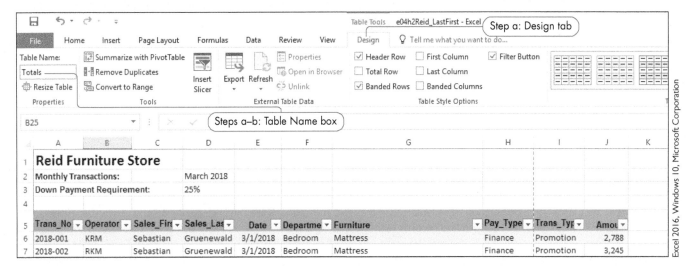

FIGURE 4.18 Rename the Table

a. Click the **Design tab**, and click the **Table Name box** in the Properties group.

b. Type **Totals** in the Table Name box and press **Enter**.

When a table is created, Excel assigns the default name "table" and a sequential number based on the number of tables in the document. For example, if there were two tables in the document the default name for the second table would be "Table2." In this step you have added a custom name that will be used throughout the rest of the project.

The original range included a column for the data entry operators' initials. You will delete this column because you do not need it for your analysis. In addition, you want to add a field to display down payment amounts in the future. Refer to Figure 4.19 as you complete Step 3.

FIGURE 4.19 Newly Created Fields

a. Click any cell containing a value in the Operator column.

You need to make a cell active in the field you want to remove.

b. Click the **Home tab**, click the **Delete arrow** in the Cells group, and then select **Delete Table Columns**.

Excel deletes the Operator column and may adjust the width of other columns.

c. Set the widths of columns E, F, and G to AutoFit. Click **cell J5**, the first blank cell on the right side of the field names.

d. Type **Down_Pay** and press **Ctrl+Enter**.

Excel extends the table formatting to column J automatically. A filter arrow appears for the newly created field name, and alternating fill colors appear in the rows below the field name. The fill color is the same as the fill color for other field names; however, the font color is White, Background 1, instead of Black Text 1.

e. Click **cell K5**, type **Owed**, and then press **Ctrl+Enter**.

f. Click **cell I5**, click **Format Painter** in the Clipboard group, and then select the **range J5:K5** to copy the format. Save the workbook.

STEP 4 》》 ADD RECORDS

As you review the March 2018 transaction table, you notice that two transactions are missing: 2018-068 and 2018-104. After finding the paper invoices, you are ready to add records with the missing transaction data. Refer to Figure 4.20 as you complete Step 4.

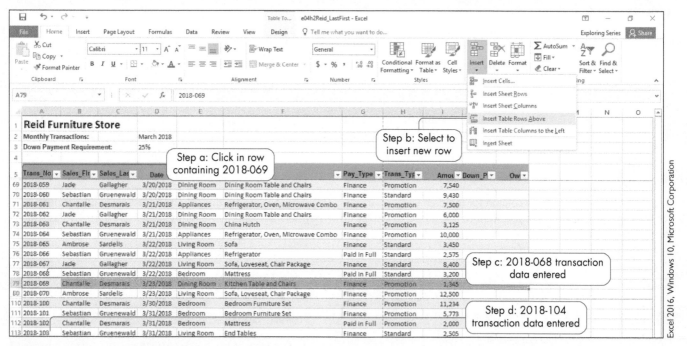

FIGURE 4.20 Missing Records Added

a. Click **cell A78**.

The missing record 2018-068 needs to be inserted between 2018-067 on row 77 and 2018-069 on row 78.

b. Click the **Home tab**, click the **Insert arrow** in the Cells group, and then select **Insert Table Rows Above**.

Excel inserts a new table row on row 78, between the 2018-067 and 2018-069 transactions.

c. Enter the following data in the respective fields on the newly created row:

2018-068, Sebastian, Gruenewald, 3/22/2018, Bedroom, Mattress, Paid in Full, Standard, 3200

d. Click **cell A114** and enter the following data in the respective fields:

2018-104, Ambrose, Sardelis, 3/31/2018, Appliances, Refrigerator, Paid in Full, Standard, 1500

When you start typing 2018-104 in the row below the last record, Excel immediately includes and formats row 114 as part of the table. Review Figure 4.20 to ensure that you inserted the records in the correct locations. In the figure, rows 81–109 are hidden to display both new records in one screenshot.

e. Save the workbook.

STEP 5 » REMOVE DUPLICATE ROWS

You noticed that the 2018-006 transaction is duplicated on rows 11 and 12 and that the 2018-018 transaction is duplicated on rows 24 and 25. You think the table may contain other duplicate rows. To avoid having to look at the entire table row by row, you will have Excel find and remove the duplicate rows for you. Refer to Figure 4.21 as you complete Step 5.

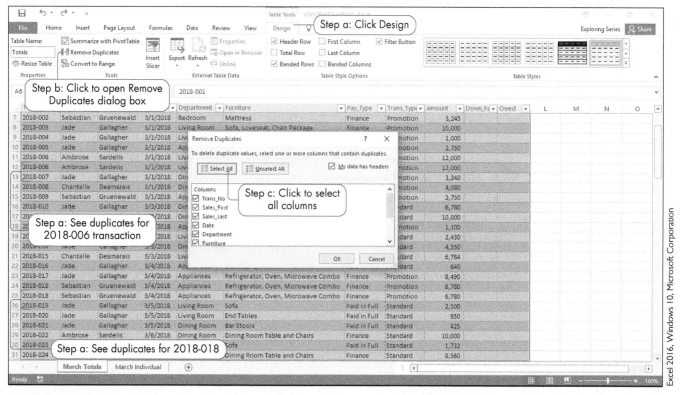

FIGURE 4.21 Remove Duplicate Records

a. Click a cell in the table. Scroll to see rows 11 and 12. Click the **Design tab**.

The records on rows 11 and 12 are identical. Rows 24 and 25 are also duplicates. You need to remove the extra rows.

b. Click **Remove Duplicates** in the Tools group.

The Remove Duplicates dialog box opens.

c. Click **Select All**, make sure the *My data has headers* check box is selected, and then click **OK**.

Excel displays a message box indicating *5 duplicate records found and removed; 104 unique values remain.*

d. Click **OK** in the message box. Click **cell A109** to view the last record in the table. Save the workbook.

Transaction 2018-104 is located on row 109 after the duplicate records are removed.

Now that you have finalized the fields and added missing records to the March 2018 transaction table, you want to apply a table style to format the table. Refer to Figure 4.22 as you complete Step 6.

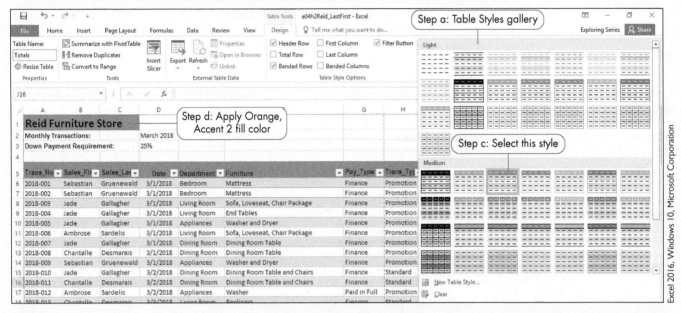

FIGURE 4.22 Table Style Applied

a. Click a cell in the table. Click the **Design tab** and click **More** in the Table Styles group to open the Table Styles gallery.

b. Point to the fourth style on the second row in the Light section.

Live Preview shows the table with the Table Style Light 10 style but does not apply it.

c. Click **Table Style Medium 3**, the third style on the first row in the Medium section.

Excel formats the table with the Medium 3 table style, which applies Orange, Accent 2 fill color to the table header row and Orange, Accent 2, Lighter 80% fill color to every other record.

d. Press **Ctrl+Home**. Select the **range A1:C1**, click the **Fill Color arrow** in the Font group on the Home tab, and then click **Orange, Accent 2**.

You applied a fill color for the title to match the fill color of the field names on the header row in the table.

e. Save the workbook. Keep the workbook open if you plan to continue with the next Hands-On Exercise. If not, close the workbook, and exit Excel.

Table Manipulation

Along with maintaining data structure, tables have a variety of options to enhance and manipulate data, in addition to managing fields, adding records, and applying table styles. You can build formulas and functions, arrange records in different sequences to get different perspectives on the data, and restrict the onscreen appearance of data using filtering. For example, you can arrange the transactions by sales representative. Furthermore, you can display only particular records instead of the entire dataset to focus on a subset of the data. For example, you might want to focus on the financed transactions.

In this section, you will learn how to create structured references, and how to sort records by text, numbers, and dates in a table. In addition, you will learn how to filter data based on conditions you set.

Creating Structured References in Formulas

STEP 1 ▶▶ Your experience in building formulas involves using cell references, such as =SUM(B1:B15) or =H6*$B$3. Cell references in formulas help to identify where the content is on a worksheet, but does not tell the user what the content represents. An advantage to Excel tables is that they use structured references to clearly indicate which type of data is used in the calculations. A **structured reference** is a tag or use of a table element, such as a field heading, as a reference in a formula. As shown in Figure 4.23, structured references in formulas clearly indicate which type of data is used in the calculations.

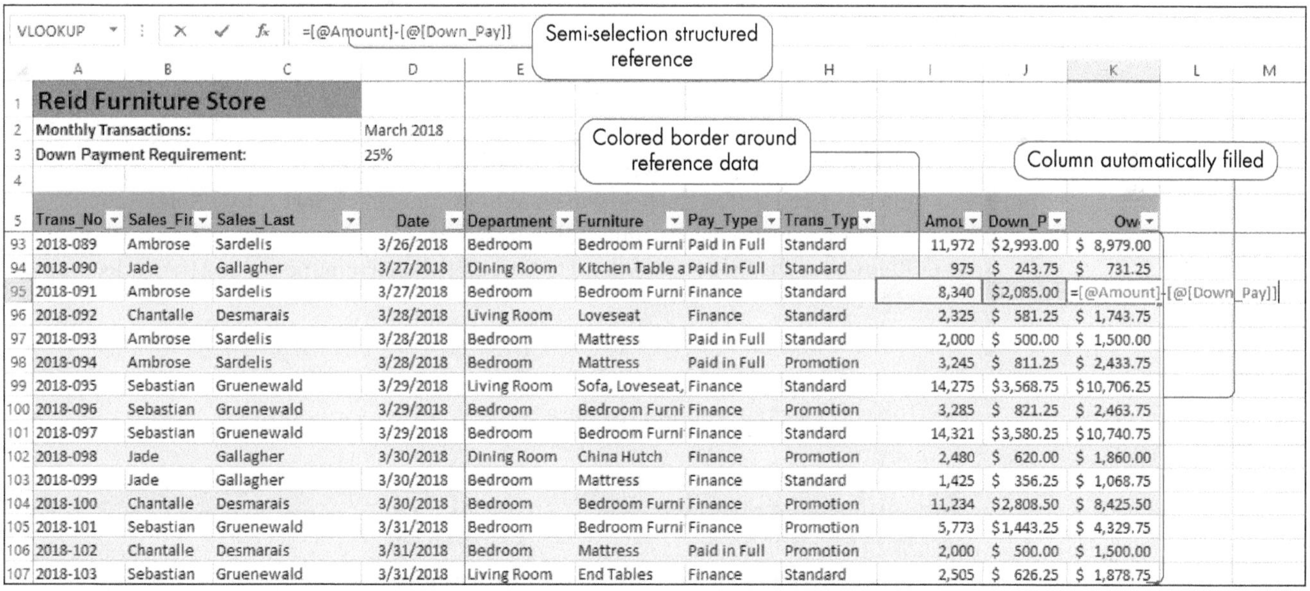

FIGURE 4.23 Structured Reference

When creating a formula in a table using structured references, field headings are set off by brackets around column headings or field names, such as =[Amount]–[Down_Pay]. The use of field headings without row references in a structured formula is called an **unqualified reference**. After you type the equal sign to begin your formula, type an opening bracket, and then Formula AutoComplete displays a list of field headings. Type or double-click the column name from the list and type the closing bracket. Excel displays a colored border around the referenced column that coordinates with the structured reference in the formula, similar to Excel identifying cell references and their worksheet placement. When you enter a formula using structured references, Excel copies the formula down the rest of the table column automatically, compared to typing references in formulas and using the fill handle to copy the formula down a column.

You can also use the semi-selection process to create a formula. As you click cells to enter a formula in a table, Excel builds a formula like this: =[@Amount]−[@Down_Pay], where the @ indicates the current row. If you use the semi-selection process to create a formula outside the table, the formula includes the table and field names, such as =Table1[@Amount]−Table1[@Down_Pay]. Table1 is the name of the table; Amount and Down_Pay are field names. This structured formula that includes references, such as table name, is called a *fully qualified structured reference*. When you build formulas *within* a table, you can use either unqualified or fully qualified structured references. If you need to use table data in a formula *outside* the table boundaries, you must use fully qualified structured references.

Sorting Data

Sometimes if you rearrange the order of records, new perspective is gained making the information easier to understand. In Figure 4.2, the March 2018 data are arranged by transaction number. You might want to arrange the transactions so that all of the transactions for a particular sales representative are together. *Sorting* is the process of arranging records by the value of one or more fields within a table. Sorting is not limited to data within tables; normal data ranges can be sorted as well.

Sort One Field

STEP 2 ⟫ You can sort data in a table or a regular range in a worksheet. For example, you could sort by transaction date or department.

To sort by only one field, complete one of the following steps:

- Click in a cell within the field you want to sort and click Sort & Filter in the Editing group on the Home tab, and select a desired sort option.
- Click in a cell within the field you want to sort and click Sort A to Z, Sort Z to A, or Sort in the Sort & Filter group on the Data tab.
- Right-click the field to sort, point to Sort on the shortcut menu, and then select the type of sort you want.
- Click the filter arrow in the header row and select the desired sort option.

Table 4.3 lists sort options by data type.

TABLE 4.3	Sort Options	
Data Type	**Options**	**Explanation**
Text	Sort A to Z	Arranges data in alphabetical order.
	Sort Z to A	Arranges data in reverse alphabetical order.
Dates	Sort Oldest to Newest	Displays data in chronological order, from oldest to newest.
	Sort Newest to Oldest	Displays data in reverse chronological order, from newest to oldest.
Values	Sort Smallest to Largest	Arranges values from the smallest value to the largest.
	Sort Largest to Smallest	Arranges values from the largest value to the smallest.
Color	Sort by Cell Color	Arranges data together for cells containing a particular fill color.
	Sort by Font Color	Arranges data together for cells containing a particular font color.

Sort Multiple Fields

STEP 3 >> After sorting, if a second sort is applied the original sort will be removed. However, at times, sorting by only one field does not yield the desired outcome. Using multiple level sorts enables like records in the primary sort to be further organized by additional sort levels. For example, you could sort by date of transaction and then by last name. Excel enables you to sort data on 64 different levels.

> **To perform a multiple level sort, complete the following steps:**
> 1. Click in any cell in the table.
> 2. Click Sort in the Sort & Filter group on the Data tab to display the Sort dialog box.
> 3. Select the primary sort level by clicking the Sort by arrow, selecting the field to sort by, and then clicking the Order arrow and selecting the sort order from the list.
> 4. Click Add Level, select the second sort level by clicking the Then by arrow, select the column to sort by, click the Order arrow, and then select the sort order from the list.
> 5. Continue to click Add Level and add sort levels until you have entered all sort levels (see Figure 4.24). Click OK.

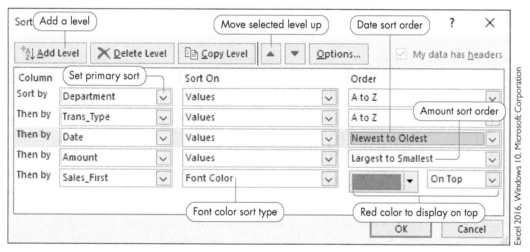

FIGURE 4.24 Sort Dialog Box

Create a Custom Sort

STEP 4 >> Excel arranges data in alphabetical or numerical order. For example, days of the week are sorted alphabetically: Friday, Monday, Saturday, Sunday, Thursday, Tuesday, and Wednesday. However, you might want to create a custom sort sequence. For example, you can create a custom sort to arrange days of the week in order from Sunday to Saturday.

> **To create a custom sort sequence, complete the following steps:**
> 1. Click Sort in the Sort & Filter group on the Data tab.
> 2. Click the Order arrow and select Custom List to display the Custom Lists dialog box (see Figure 4.25).
> 3. Select an existing sort sequence in the Custom lists box, or select NEW LIST.
> 4. Type the entries in the desired sort sequence in the List entries box, pressing Enter between entries.
> 5. Click Add and click OK.

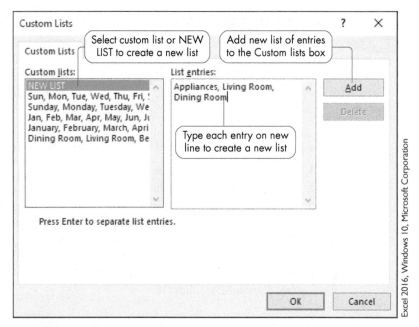

FIGURE 4.25 Custom Lists Dialog Box

TIP: NAME SORTS

Always check the data to determine how many levels of sorting you need to apply. If your table contains several people with the same last name but different first names, you would first sort by the Last Name field, then sort by First Name field. All the people with the last name Desmarais would be grouped together and further sorted by first name, such as Amanda and then Bradley.

Filtering Data

In some situations you might want to display only a subset of the data available, for example, the data to show transactions for only a particular sales representative. In these situations, you could apply a filter to achieve the desired results. In Excel, you have the ability to filter using various criteria such as date, value, text, and color. **Filtering** is the process of specifying conditions to display only those records that meet certain conditions.

TIP: COPYING BEFORE FILTERING DATA

Often, you need to show different filters applied to the same dataset. You can copy the worksheet and filter the data on the copied worksheet to preserve the original dataset.

Apply Text Filters

 When you apply a filter to a text field, the filter menu displays each unique text item. You can select one or more text items from the list to be filtered. Once completed only the selected text will be displayed.

To apply a text filter, complete the following steps:

1. Click any cell in the range of data to be filtered.
2. Click the Data tab and click Filter in the Sort & Filter group to display the filter arrows.
3. Click the filter arrow for the column you will filter.
4. Deselect the (Select All) check mark and click the check boxes for the text you would like to remain visible in the dataset. Click OK.

You can also select Text Filters to see a submenu of additional options, such as Begins With, to select all records for which the name begins with the letter G, for example.

Figure 4.26 shows the Sales_Last filter menu with two names selected. Excel displays records for these two reps only. The records for the other sales reps are hidden but not deleted. The filter arrow displays a filter icon, indicating which field is filtered. Excel displays the row numbers in blue, indicating that you applied a filter. The missing row numbers indicate hidden rows of data. When you remove the filter, all the records display again.

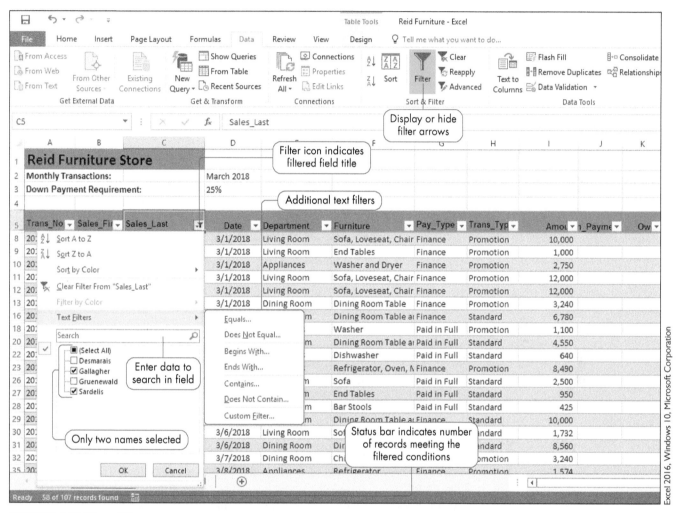

FIGURE 4.26 Filtered Text

Apply Number Filters

STEP 6 » Excel contains a variety of number filters that enable you to display specific numbers, or a range of numbers such as above average or top 10 values. When you filter a field of numbers, you can select specific numbers. Or, you might want to filter numbers by a range, such as numbers greater than $5,000 or numbers between $4,000 and $5,000. If the field contains a large number of unique entries, you can click in the Search box and enter a value to display all matching records. For example, if you enter $7, the list will display only values that start with $7. The filter submenu enables you to set a variety of number filters. In Figure 4.27, the amounts are filtered to show only those that are above the average amount. In this situation, Excel calculates the average amount as $4,512. Only records above that amount display.

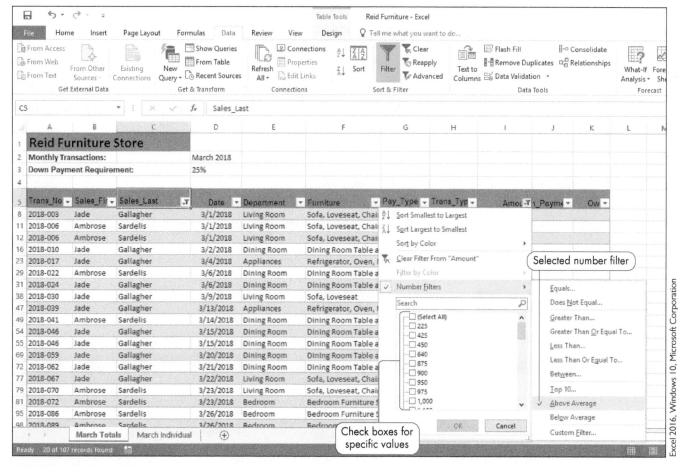

FIGURE 4.27 Filtered Numbers

The Top 10 option enables you to specify the top records. Although the option name is Top 10, you can specify the number or percentage of records to display. For example, you can filter the list to display only the top five or the bottom 7%. Figure 4.28 shows the Top 10 AutoFilter dialog box.

To filter using the custom Top 10 AutoFilter, complete the following steps:

1. Click anywhere in the range or table, click the Data tab, and click Filter in the Sort & Filter group.
2. Click the filter arrow for the column that contains the data you would like to manipulate, point to Number Filters, and select Top 10.
3. Choose Top or Bottom value, click the last arrow to select either Items or Percent, and click OK.

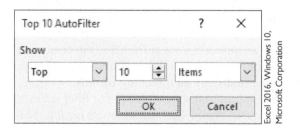

FIGURE 4.28 Top 10 AutoFilter Dialog Box

Apply Date Filters

STEP 7 ⟫⟫ When you filter a field of dates, you can select specific dates or a date range, such as dates after 3/15/2018 or dates between 3/1/2018 and 3/7/2018. The submenu enables you to set a variety of date filters. For more specific date options, point to Date Filters, point to *All Dates in the Period*, and then select a period, such as Quarter 2 or October. Figure 4.29 shows the Date Filters menu.

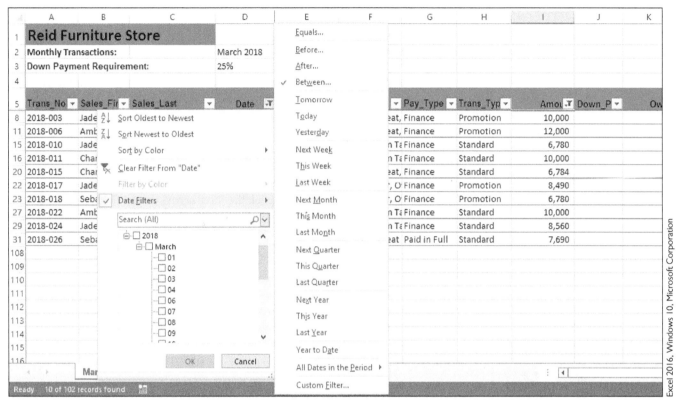

FIGURE 4.29 Filtered Dates

Apply a Custom Filter

Suppose as the manager of a furniture store, you are only interested in marketing directly to people who spent between $500 and $1,000 in the last month. To quickly identify the required data, you could use a custom AutoFilter. If you select options such as Greater Than or Between, Excel displays the Custom AutoFilter dialog box (see Figure 4.30). You can also select Custom Filter from the menu to display this dialog box, which is designed for more complex filtering requirements.

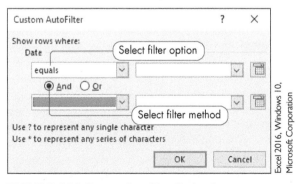

FIGURE 4.30 Custom AutoFilter Dialog Box

The dialog box indicates the column being filtered. To set the filters, click the arrows to select the comparison type, such as equals or contains. Click the arrow on the right to select a specific text, value, or date entry, or type the data yourself. For ranges of dates or values, click And, and then specify the comparison operator and value or date for the next condition row. For text, click Or. For example, if you want both Gallagher and Desmarais, you must select Or because each data entry contains either Gallagher or Desmarais but not both at the same time.

When filtering, you can use wildcards to help locate information in which there are multiple criteria and no custom filters. For example, to select all states starting with New, type *New** in the second box; this will obtain results such as New York or New Mexico. The asterisk (*) is used in exchange for the text after "New" and can represent any number of characters. Therefore this wildcard filter would return states New York, New Mexico, and New Hampshire because they all begin with the word "New." If you want a wildcard for only a single character, type the question mark (?). For example when filtering departments, "R?om" would return any department with room in the name as would "Room*."

Clear Filters

You can remove the filters from one or more fields to expand the dataset again. To remove only one filter and keep the other filters, click the filter arrow for the field from which you wish to clear the filter and select Clear Filter From.

> **To remove all filters and display all records in a dataset, complete one of the following steps:**
>
> - Click Clear in the Sort & Filter group on the Data tab.
> - Click Sort & Filter in the Editing group on the Home tab and select Clear.

Quick Concepts

7. What is the purpose of sorting data in a table? *p. 622*

8. What are two ways to arrange (sort) dates? *p. 622*

9. List at least five ways you can filter numbers. *p. 625*

10. Assume you are filtering a list and want to display records for people who live in Boston or New York. What settings do you enter in the Custom AutoFilter dialog box for that field? *p. 624*

Hands-On Exercises

Watch the Video
for this Hands-On
Exercise!

MyITLab®
HOE3 Training

3 Table Manipulation

You want to start analyzing the March 2018 transactions for Reid Furniture Store by calculating the totals owed, then sorting and filtering data in a variety of ways to help you understand the transactions better.

STEP 1 >> CREATE A STRUCTURED REFERENCE IN A FORMULA

First, you want to calculate the down payment owed by each customer. You will then calculate the total amount owed by subtracting the down payment from the total down payment. You will use structured references to complete these tasks. Refer to Figure 4.31 as you complete Step 1.

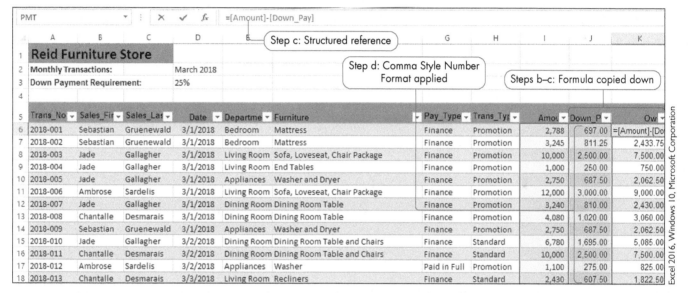

FIGURE 4.31 Create a Structured Reference

a. Open *e04h2Reid_LastFirst* if you closed it at the end of Hands-On Exercise 2. Save it as **e04h3Reid_LastFirst**, changing h2 to h3.

b. Click **cell J6**. Type the formula **=[Amount]*$D$3** and press **Enter**.

The down payment required is 25% of the total purchase price. Structured reference format is used for Amount to create the formula that calculates the customer's down payment. Excel copies the formula down the column.

c. Click **cell K6**. Type the formula **=[Amount]-[Down_Pay]** and press **Enter**.

The formula calculates the total value owed to the sales rep and copies the formula down the column.

d. Select the **range J6:K109** and apply the **Comma Style Number Format**.

e. Save the workbook.

You want to compare the number of transactions by sales rep, so you will sort the data by the Sales_Last field. After reviewing the transactions by sales reps, you then want to arrange the transactions to show the one with the largest purchase first and the smallest purchase last. Refer to Figure 4.32 as you complete Step 2.

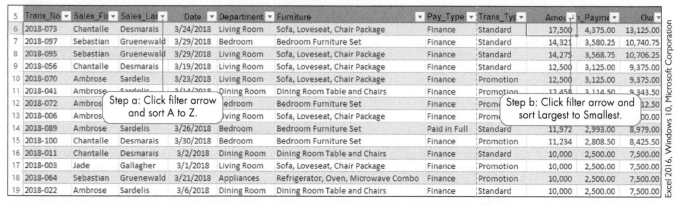

5	Trans_No	Sales_Fir	Sales_Las	Date	Department	Furniture	Pay_Type	Trans_Typ	Amou	1_Payme	Ow
6	2018-073	Chantalle	Desmarais	3/24/2018	Living Room	Sofa, Loveseat, Chair Package	Finance	Standard	17,500	4,375.00	13,125.00
7	2018-097	Sebastian	Gruenewald	3/29/2018	Bedroom	Bedroom Furniture Set	Finance	Standard	14,321	3,580.25	10,740.75
8	2018-095	Sebastian	Gruenewald	3/29/2018	Living Room	Sofa, Loveseat, Chair Package	Finance	Standard	14,275	3,568.75	10,706.25
9	2018-056	Chantalle	Desmarais	3/19/2018	Living Room	Sofa, Loveseat, Chair Package	Finance	Standard	12,500	3,125.00	9,375.00
10	2018-070	Ambrose	Sardelis	3/23/2018	Living Room	Sofa, Loveseat, Chair Package	Finance	Promotion	12,500	3,125.00	9,375.00
11	2018-041	Ambrose	Sardelis	3/14/2018	Dining Room	Dining Room Table and Chairs	Finance	Promotion	12,458	3,114.50	9,343.50
12	2018-072	Ambros	*Step a: Click filter arrow and sort A to Z.*		edroom	Bedroom Furniture Set	Finance	Prom	*Step b: Click filter arrow and sort Largest to Smallest.*		12.50
13	2018-006	Ambros			iving Room	Sofa, Loveseat, Chair Package	Finance	Prom			00.00
14	2018-089	Ambrose	Sardelis	3/26/2018	Bedroom	Bedroom Furniture Set	Paid in Full	Standard	11,972	2,993.00	8,979.00
15	2018-100	Chantalle	Desmarais	3/30/2018	Bedroom	Bedroom Furniture Set	Finance	Promotion	11,234	2,808.50	8,425.50
16	2018-011	Chantalle	Desmarais	3/2/2018	Dining Room	Dining Room Table and Chairs	Finance	Standard	10,000	2,500.00	7,500.00
17	2018-003	Jade	Gallagher	3/1/2018	Living Room	Sofa, Loveseat, Chair Package	Finance	Promotion	10,000	2,500.00	7,500.00
18	2018-064	Sebastian	Gruenewald	3/21/2018	Appliances	Refrigerator, Oven, Microwave Combo	Finance	Promotion	10,000	2,500.00	7,500.00
19	2018-022	Ambrose	Sardelis	3/6/2018	Dining Room	Dining Room Table and Chairs	Finance	Standard	10,000	2,500.00	7,500.00

FIGURE 4.32 Sorted Data

a. Click the **Sales_Last filter arrow** and select **Sort A to Z**.

Excel arranges the transactions in alphabetical order by last name, starting with Desmarais. Within each sales rep, records display in their original sequence by transaction number. If you scan the records, you can see that Gallagher completed the most sales transactions in March. The up arrow icon on the Sales_Last filter arrow indicates that records are sorted in alphabetical order by that field.

b. Click the **Amount filter arrow** and select **Sort Largest to Smallest**.

The records are no longer sorted by Sales_Last. When you sort by another field, the previous sort is not saved. In this case, Excel arranges the transactions from the one with the largest amount to the smallest amount, indicated by the down arrow icon in the Amount filter arrow.

c. Save the workbook.

You want to review the transactions by payment type (financed or paid in full). Within each payment type, you further want to compare the transaction type (promotion or standard). Finally, you want to compare costs within the sorted records by displaying the highest costs first. You will use the Sort dialog box to perform a three-level sort. Refer to Figure 4.33 as you complete Step 3.

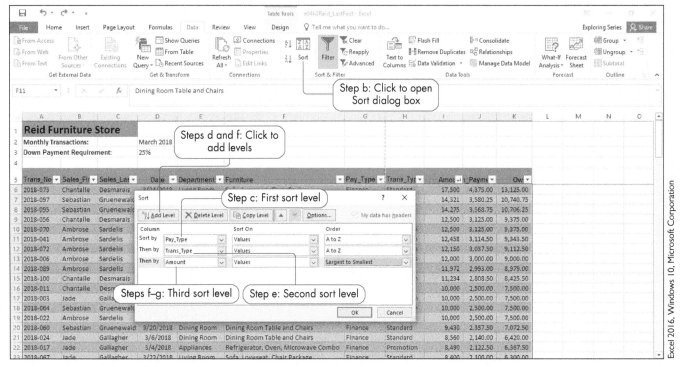

FIGURE 4.33 Three-Level Sort

a. Click inside the table and click the **Data tab**.

Both the Data and Home tabs contain commands to open the Sort dialog box.

b. Click **Sort** in the Sort & Filter group to open the Sort dialog box.

c. Click the **Sort by arrow** and select **Pay_Type**. Click the **Order arrow** and select **A to Z**.

You start by specifying the column for the primary sort. In this case, you want to sort the records first by the Payment Type column.

d. Click **Add Level**.

The Sort dialog box adds the Then by row, which adds a secondary sort.

e. Click the **Then by arrow** and select **Trans_Type**.

The default order is A to Z, which will sort in alphabetical order by Trans_Type. Excel will first sort the records by the Pay_Type (Finance or Paid in Full). Within each Pay_Type, Excel will further sort records by Trans_Type (Promotion or Standard).

f. Click **Add Level** to add another Then by row. Click the second **Then by arrow** and select **Amount**.

g. Click the **Order arrow** for the Amount sort and select **Largest to Smallest**.

Within the Pay_Type and Trans_Type sorts, this will arrange the records with the largest amount first in descending order to the smallest amount.

h. Click **OK** and scroll through the records. Save the workbook.

Most customers finance their purchases instead of paying in full. For the financed transactions, more than half were promotional sales. For merchandise paid in full, a majority of the transactions were standard sales, indicating that people with money do not necessarily wait for a promotional sale to purchase merchandise.

For the month of March you want to closely monitor sales of the Dining Room and Living Room departments. After completing the prior sort, you will add an additional level to create a custom sort of the department's data. Refer to Figure 4.34 as you complete Step 4.

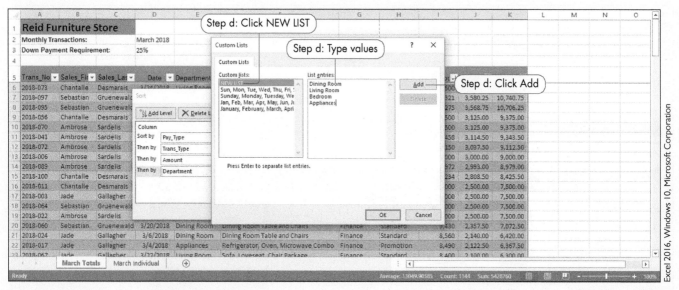

FIGURE 4.34 Custom Sort

a. Click inside the table and click **Sort** in the Sort & Filter group to open the Sort dialog box.

   The Sort dialog box will open with the prior sort criteria displayed.

b. Click the **last level added** in the prior step and click **Add Level**.

c. Select **Department**. Click the **Order arrow** and select **Custom List**.

   This will open the Custom Lists dialog box, enabling you to manually specify the sort order.

d. Click **NEW LIST** in the Custom lists box, click the **List entries box** and type **Dining Room, Living Room, Bedroom, Appliances**. Click **Add**, click **OK**, and click **OK** again to complete to return to the worksheet..

   After completing the custom list, the data in column E will be sorted by Dining Room, Living Room, Bedroom, and Appliances as the last step within the custom sort.

e. Save the workbook.

Now that you know Jade Gallagher had the most transactions for March, you will filter the table to focus on her sales. You notice that she sells more merchandise from the Dining Room department, so you will filter out the other departments. Refer to Figure 4.35 as you complete Step 5.

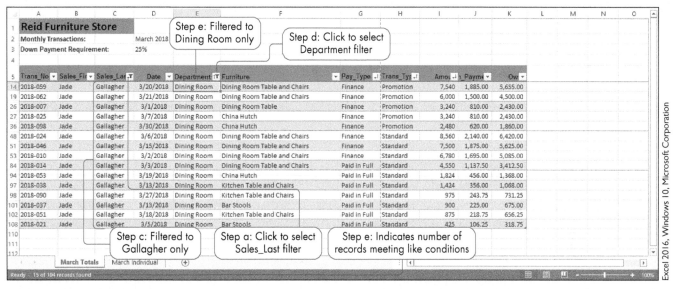

FIGURE 4.35 Apply Text Filters

a. Click the **Sales_Last filter arrow**.

The (Select All) check box is selected.

b. Click the **(Select All) check box** to deselect all last names.

c. Click the **Gallagher check box** to select it and click **OK**.

The status bar indicates that 33 out of 104 records meet the filtering condition. The Sales_Last filter arrow includes a funnel icon, indicating that this column is filtered.

d. Click the **Department filter arrow**.

e. Click the **(Select All) check box** to deselect all departments, click the **Dining Room check box** to focus on that department, and then click **OK**. Save the workbook.

The remaining 15 records show Gallagher's dining room sales for the month. The Department filter arrow includes a funnel icon, indicating that this column is also filtered.

Vicki is considering giving a bonus to employees who sold high-end dining room furniture during a specific time period (3/16/2018 to 3/31/2018). You want to determine if Jade Gallagher qualifies for this bonus. In particular, you are interested in how much gross revenue she generated for dining room furniture that cost at least $5,000 or more. Refer to Figure 4.36 as you complete Step 6.

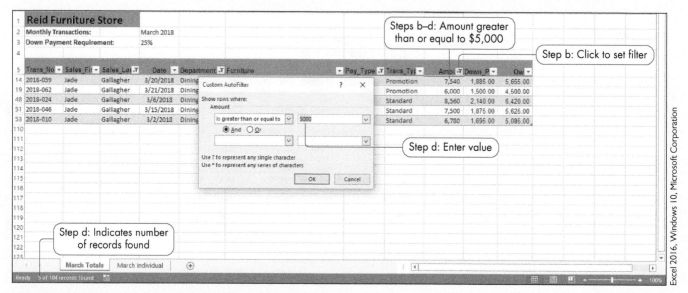

FIGURE 4.36 Filtered to Amounts Greater Than or Equal to $5,000

a. Select the **range I14:I108** of the filtered list and then view the status bar.

   The average transaction amount is $3,754 with 15 transactions (i.e., 15 filtered records).

b. Click the **Amount filter arrow**.

c. Point to **Number Filters** and select **Greater Than Or Equal To**.

   The Custom AutoFilter dialog box opens.

d. Type **5000** in the box to the right of *is greater than or equal to* and click **OK**. Save the workbook.

   When typing numbers, you can type raw numbers such as 5000 or formatted numbers such as $5,000. Out of Gallagher's original 15 dining room transactions, only 5 transactions (one-third of her sales) were valued at $5,000 or more.

Finally, you want to study Jade Gallagher's sales records for the last half of the month. You will add a date filter to identify those sales records. Refer to Figure 4.37 as you complete Step 7.

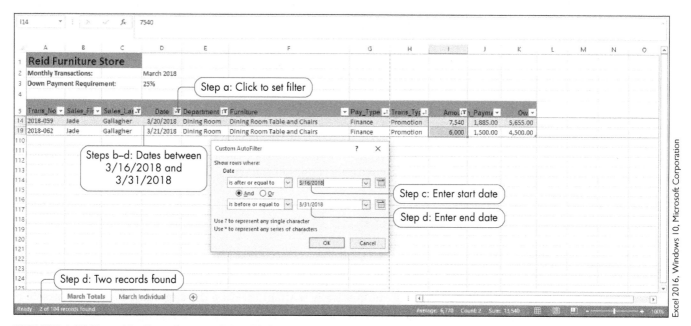

FIGURE 4.37 Filtered by Dates Between 3/16/2018 and 3/31/2018

a. Click the **Date filter arrow**.

b. Point to **Date Filters** and select **Between**.

The Custom AutoFilter dialog box opens. The default comparisons are *is after or equal to* and *is before or equal to*, ready for you to enter the date specifications.

c. Type **3/16/2018** in the box on the right side of *is after or equal to*.

You specified the starting date of the range of dates to include. You will keep the *And* option selected.

d. Type **3/31/2018** in the box on the right side of *is before or equal to*. Click **OK**.

Gallagher had only two dining room sales greater than $5,000 during the last half of March.

e. Save the workbook. Keep the workbook open if you plan to continue with the next Hands-On Exercise. If not, close the workbook, and exit Excel.

Table Aggregation and Conditional Formatting

In addition to sorting and filtering tables to analyze data, you might want to add fields that provide data aggregation such as Average or Sum of amount purchased. Furthermore, you might want to apply special formatting to cells that contain particular values or text using conditional formatting. ***Conditional formatting*** applies special formatting to highlight or emphasize cells that meet specific conditions. For example, a sales manager might want to highlight employees that have reached their sales goal, or a professor might want to highlight test scores that fall below the average. You can also apply conditional formatting to point out data for a specific date or duplicate values in a range.

In this section, you will learn how to add a total row to a table along with learning about the five conditional formatting categories and how to apply conditional formatting to a range of values based on a condition you set.

Adding a Total Row

STEP 1 >> At times, aggregating data provides insightful information. For regular ranges of data, you use basic statistical functions, such as SUM, AVERAGE, MIN, and MAX, to provide summary analysis for a dataset. An Excel table provides the advantage of being able to display a total row automatically without creating the aggregate function yourself. A ***total row*** displays below the last row of records in an Excel table and enables you to display summary statistics, such as a sum of values displayed in a column.

> **To display and use the total row, complete the following steps:**
>
> 1. Click any cell in the table.
> 2. Click the Design tab.
> 3. Click Total Row in the Table Style Options group. Excel displays the total row below the last record in the table. Excel displays Total in the first column of the total row.
> 4. Click a cell in the total row, click that cell's total row arrow, and then select the function result that you desire. Excel calculates the summary statistics for values, but if the field is text, the only summary statistic that can be calculated is Count.
> 5. Add a summary statistic to another column click in the empty cell for that field in the total row and click the arrow to select the desired function. Select None to remove the function.

Figure 4.38 shows the active total row with totals applied to the Amount, Down_Pay, and Owed fields. A list of functions displays to change the function for the last field.

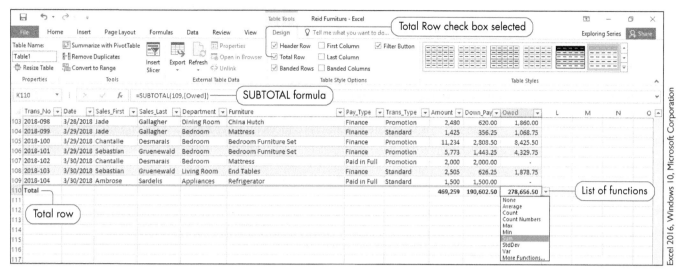

FIGURE 4.38 Total Row

The calculations on the total row use the SUBTOTAL function. The **SUBTOTAL function** calculates an aggregate value, such as totals or averages, for displayed values in a range, table, or database. If you click in a calculated total row cell, the SUBTOTAL function displays in the Formula Bar. The function for the total row looks like this: =SUBTOTAL(function_num,ref1). The function_num argument is a number that represents a function (see Table 4.4). The ref1 argument indicates the range of values to calculate. The SUBTOTAL function used to total the values in the Owed field would be =SUBTOTAL(109,[Owed]), where the number 109 represents the SUM function, and [Owed] represents the Owed field. A benefit of the SUBTOTAL function is that it subtotals data for filtered records, so you have an accurate total for the visible records.

=SUBTOTAL(function_num,ref1,...)

TABLE 4.4 Subtotal Function Numbers

Function	Function Number	Table Number
AVERAGE	1	101
COUNT	2	102
COUNTA	3	103
MAX	4	104
MIN	5	105
PRODUCT	6	106
STDEV.S	7	107
STDEV.P	8	108
SUM	9	109
VAR.S	10	110
VAR.P	11	111

TIP: FILTERING DATA AND SUBTOTALS
If you filter the data and display the total row, the SUBTOTAL function's 109 argument ensures that only the displayed data are summed; data for hidden rows are not calculated in the aggregate function.

Applying Conditional Formatting

Conditional formatting helps you and your audience understand a dataset better because it adds a visual element to the cells. The term is called conditional because the formatting only displays when a condition is met. This is similar logic to the IF function you have used. Remember with an IF function, you create a logical test that is evaluated. If the logical or conditional test is true, the function produces one result. If the logical or conditional test is false, the function produces another result. With conditional formatting, if the condition is true, Excel formats the cell automatically based on that condition. If the condition is false, Excel does not format the cell. If you change a value in a conditionally formatted cell, Excel examines the new value to see if it should apply the conditional format.

Apply Conditional Formatting with the Quick Analysis Tool

When you select a range and click the Quick Analysis button, the Formatting options display in the Quick Analysis gallery. Point to a thumbnail to see how it will affect the selected range (see Figure 4.39). You can also apply conditional formatting by clicking Conditional Formatting in the Styles group on the Home tab.

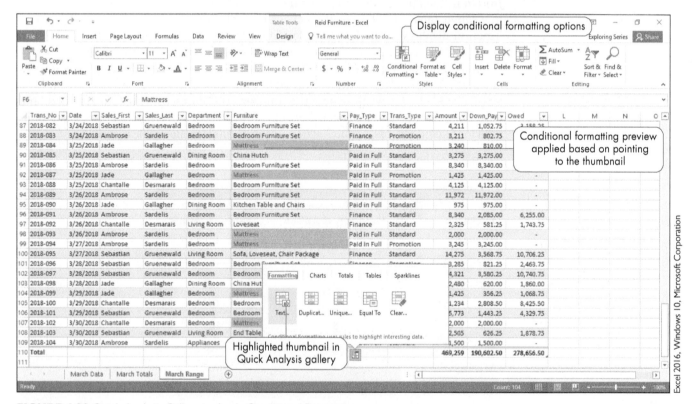

FIGURE 4.39 Quick Analysis Gallery to Apply Conditional Formatting

Table 4.5 describes the conditional formatting options in the Quick Analysis gallery.

TABLE 4.5	Conditional Formatting Options in Quick Analysis Gallery
Options	**Description**
Text Contains	Formats cells that contain the text in the first selected cell. In Figure 4.39, the first selected cell contains Mattress. If a cell contains Mattress and Springs, Excel would format that cell also because it contains Mattress.
Duplicate Values	Formats cells that are duplicated in the selected range.
Unique Values	Formats cells that are unique; that is, no other cell in the selected range contains the same data.
Equal To	Formats cells that are exactly like the data contained in the first selected cell.
Clear Format	Removes the conditional formatting from the selected range.

Table 4.6 lists and describes a number of different conditional formats that you can apply if you want more specific rules.

TABLE 4.6	Conditional Formatting Options
Options	**Description**
Highlight Cells Rules	Highlights cells with a fill color, font color, or border (such as Light Red Fill with Dark Red Text) if values are greater than, less than, between two values, equal to a value, or duplicate values; text that contains particular characters; or dates when a date meets a particular condition, such as *In the last 7 days*.
Top/Bottom Rules	Formats cells with values in the top 10 items, top 10%, bottom 10 items, bottom 10%, above average, or below average. You can change the exact values to format the top or bottom items or percentages, such as top 5 or bottom 15%.
Data Bars	Applies a gradient or solid fill bar in which the width of the bar represents the current cell's value compared relatively to other cells' values.
Color Scales	Formats different cells with different colors, assigning one color to the lowest group of values and another color to the highest group of values, with gradient colors to other values.
Icon Sets	Inserts an icon from an icon palette in each cell to indicate values compared to each other.

To apply a conditional format, complete the following steps:

1. Select the cells for which you want to apply a conditional format, click the Home tab, and click Conditional Formatting in the Styles group.
2. Select the conditional formatting category you want to apply.

Apply Highlight Cells Rules

STEP 2 ›› The Highlight Cells Rules category enables you to apply a highlight to cells that meet a condition, such as cells containing values greater than a particular value. This option contains predefined combinations of fill colors, font colors, and/or borders. For example, suppose you are a sales manager who developed a worksheet containing the sales for each day of a month. You are interested in sales between $5000 and $10,000. You might want to apply a conditional format to cells that contain values within the desired range. To apply this conditional formatting, you would select Highlight Cells Rules and then select Between. In the Between dialog box (see Figure 4.40), type 5000 in the first value box and 10000 in the second value box, select the type of conditional formatting, such as Light Red Fill with Dark Red Text, and then click OK to apply the formats.

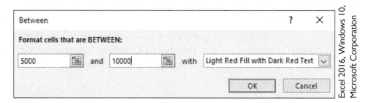

FIGURE 4.40 Between Dialog Box

Figure 4.41 shows two columns of data that contain conditional formats. The Department column is conditionally formatted to highlight text with a Light Red Fill with Dark Red Text for cells that contain Living Room, and the Amount column is conditionally formatted to highlight values between $5,000 and $10,000 with a Dark Red Border.

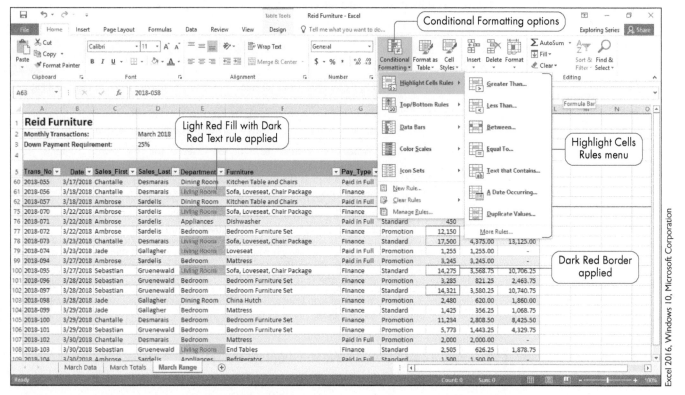

FIGURE 4.41 Highlight Cells Rules Conditional Formatting

Specify Top/Bottom Rules

STEP 3 ›› You might be interested in identifying the top five sales to reward the sales associates, or want to identify the bottom 15% of of sales for more focused marketing. The Top/Bottom Rules category enables you to specify the top or bottom number, top or bottom percentage, or values that are above or below the average value in a specified range. In Figure 4.42, the Amount column is conditionally formatted to highlight the top five amounts. (Some rows are hidden so that all top five values display in the figure.) Although the menu option is Top 10 Items, you can specify the exact number of items to format.

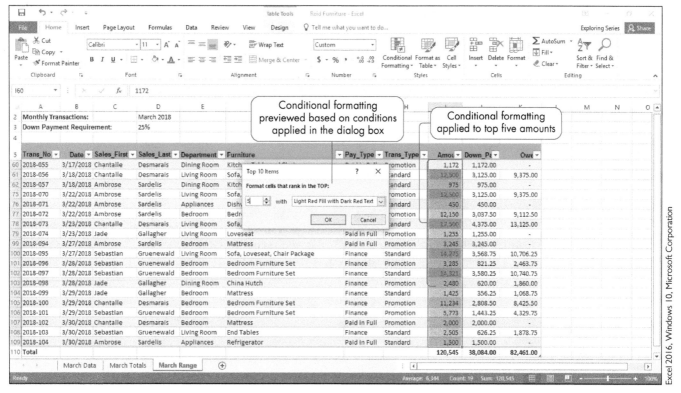

FIGURE 4.42 Top 10 Items Dialog Box

Display Data Bars, Color Scales, and Icon Sets

STEP 4 **Data bars** apply a gradient or solid fill bar in which the width of the bar represents the current cell's value compared relatively to other cells' values (see Figure 4.43). The width of the data bar represents the value in a cell, with a wider bar representing a higher value and a narrower bar a lower value. Excel locates the largest value and displays the widest data bar in that cell. Excel then finds the smallest value and displays the smallest data bar in that cell. Excel sizes the data bars for the remaining cells based on their values relative to the high and low values in the column. If you change the values, Excel updates the data bar widths. Excel uses the same color for each data bar, but each bar differs in size based on the value in the respective cells.

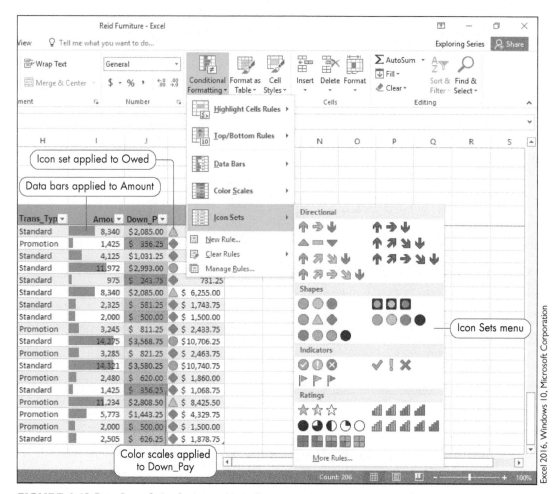

FIGURE 4.43 Data Bars, Color Scales, and Icon Sets

Color scales format cells with different colors based on the relative value of a cell compared to other selected cells. You can apply a two- or three-color scale. This scale assists in comparing a range of cells using gradations of those colors. The shade of the color represents higher or lower values. In Figure 4.43, for example, the red color scales display for the lowest values, the green color displays for the highest values, and gradients of yellow and orange represent the middle range of values in the Down_Pay column. Use color scales to understand variation in the data to identify trends, for example, to view good stock returns and weak stock returns.

Icon sets are symbols or signs that classify data into three, four, or five categories, based on the values in a range. Excel determines categories of value ranges and assigns an icon to each range. In Figure 4.43, a three-icon set was applied to the Owed column. Excel divided the range of values between the lowest value of $0 and the highest value of $13,125 into thirds. The red diamond icon displays for the cells containing values in the lowest third ($0 to $4,375), the yellow triangle icon displays for cells containing the values in the middle third ($4,376 to $8,750), and the green circle icon displays for cells containing values in the top third ($8,751 to $13,125). Most purchases fall into the lowest third.

TIP: DON'T OVERDO IT!
Although conditional formatting helps identify trends, you should use this feature wisely and sparingly. Apply conditional formatting only when you want to emphasize important data. When you decide to apply conditional formatting, think about which category is best to highlight the data.

Creating a New Rule

The default conditional formatting categories provide a variety of options. Excel also enables you to create your own rules to specify different fill colors, borders, or other formatting if you do not want the default settings. Excel provides three ways to create a new rule.

To create a new Conditional Formatting rule, complete one of the following steps:

- Click Conditional Formatting in the Styles group and select New Rule.
- Click Conditional Formatting in the Styles group, select Manage Rules to open the Conditional Formatting Rules Manager dialog box, and then click New Rule.
- Click Conditional Formatting in the Styles group, select a rule category such as Highlight Cells Rules, and then select More Rules.

When creating a new rule, the New Formatting Rule dialog box opens (see Figure 4.44) so that you can define the conditional formatting rule. First, select a rule type, such as *Format all cells based on their values*. The *Edit the Rule Description* section changes, based on the rule type you select. With the default rule type selected, you can specify the format style (2-Color Scale, 3-Color Scale, Data Bar, or Icon Sets). You can then specify the minimum and maximum values, the fill colors for color sets or data bars, or the icons for icon sets. After you edit the rule description, click OK to save your new conditional format.

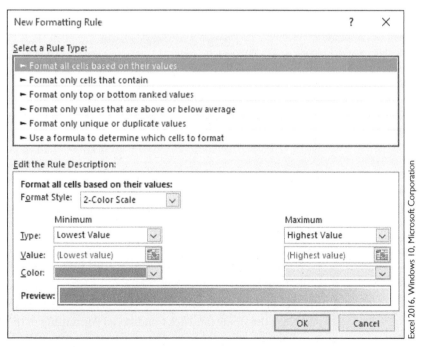

FIGURE 4.44 New Formatting Rule Dialog Box

If you select any rule type except the *Format all cells based on their values* rule, the dialog box contains a Format button. When you click Format, the Format Cells dialog box opens so that you can specify number, font, border, and fill formats to apply to your rule.

TIP: FORMAT ONLY CELLS THAT CONTAIN

When creating new Conditional Formatting rules, you have the option to format only cells that contain a specific value. This option provides a wide array of things you can format: values, text, dates, blanks, no blanks, errors, or no errors. Formatting blanks is helpful to see where you are missing data, and formatting cells containing errors helps you find those errors quickly. These options can be accessed from the Select a Rule Type box in the New Formatting Rule dialog box when creating a Conditional Formatting rule.

Use Formulas in Conditional Formatting

STEP 5 >> Suppose you want to format merchandise amounts of financed items *and* amounts that are $10,000 or more. You can use a formula to create a conditional formatting rule to complete the task. Figure 4.45 shows the Edit Formatting Rule dialog box and the corresponding conditional formatting applied to cells.

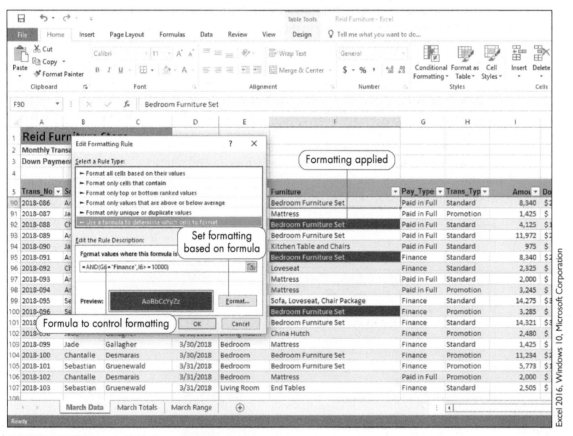

FIGURE 4.45 Formula Rule Created and Applied

To create a formula-based conditional formatting rule, complete the following steps:

1. Select the desired data range.
2. Click the Home tab, click Conditional Formatting in the Styles group, and click New Rule.
3. Select *Use a formula to determine which cells to format* and type the formula, using cell references in the first row, in the *Format values where this formula is true* box.

Once complete, Excel applies the general formula to the selected range, substituting the appropriate cell reference as it makes the comparisons. In the Figure 4.45 example, =AND(G6="Finance",I6>=10000) requires that the text in the Pay_Type column (column G) contain Finance and the Amount column (column I) contain a value that is greater than or equal to $10,000. The AND function requires that both logical tests be met to apply the conditional formatting. A minimum of two logical tests are required; however, you can include additional logical tests. Note that *all* logical tests must be true to apply the conditional formatting.

= AND(logical1,logical2,...)

Manage Rules

Periodically conditional formatting rules may need to be updated, moved, or completely deleted.

To edit or delete conditional formatting rules you create, click Conditional Formatting in the Styles group and select Manage Rules. The Conditional Formatting Rules Manager dialog box opens (see Figure 4.46). Click the *Show formatting rules for* arrow and select from *current selection, the entire worksheet,* or *this table.* Select the rule, click Edit Rule or Delete Rule, and click OK after making the desired changes. To remove conditional formatting from a range of cells, select the cells. Then click Conditional Formatting, point to Clear Rules, and select Clear Rules from Selected Cells.

> **To clear all conditional formatting from the entire worksheet, complete the following steps:**
>
> 1. Click Conditional Formatting in the Styles group on the Home tab.
> 2. Point to Clear Rules, and then select Clear Rules from Entire Sheet.

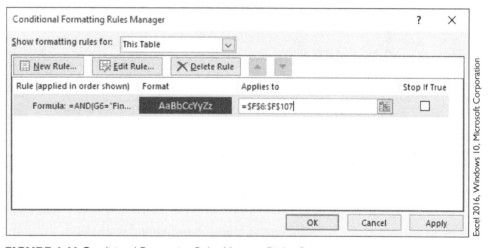

FIGURE 4.46 Conditional Formatting Rules Manager Dialog Box

Quick Concepts

11. How is conditional formatting similar to an IF function? *p. 638*

12. What conditional formatting would be helpful to identify the three movies with the highest revenue playing at theaters? *pp. 640–641*

13. How is data bar conditional formatting helpful when reviewing a column of data? *p. 641*

Hands-On Exercises

 Watch the Video for this Hands-On Exercise!

 MyITLab® HOE4 Training

4 Table Aggregation and Conditional Formatting

Vicki Reid wants to review the transactions with you. She is interested in Sebastian Gruenewald's sales record and the three highest transaction amounts. In addition, she wants to compare the down payment amounts visually. Finally, she wants you to analyze the amounts owed for sales completed by Sebastian.

STEP 1 ADD A TOTAL ROW

You want to see the monthly totals for the Amount, Down_Pay, and Owed columns. You will add a total row to calculate the values. Refer to Figure 4.47 as you complete Step 1.

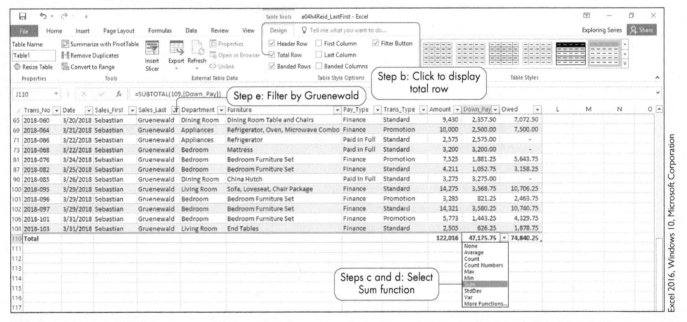

FIGURE 4.47 Add a Total Row

a. Open *e04h3Reid_LastFirst* if you closed it at the end of Hands-On Exercise 3. Save the workbook as **e04h4Reid_LastFirst**, changing h3 to h4.

b. Select the **March Individual worksheet**, click any cell inside the table, click the **Design tab**, and then click **Total Row** in the Table Style Options group.

Excel displays the total row after the last record. It sums the last field of values automatically. The total amount customers owe is $278,656.50.

c. Click the **Down_Pay cell** in row 110, click the **total arrow**, and then select **Sum**.

You added a total to the Down_Pay field. The total amount of down payment collected is $190,602.50. The formula displays as =SUBTOTAL(109,[Down_Pay]) in the Formula Bar.

d. Click the **Amount cell** in row 110, click the **total arrow**, and then select **Sum**.

You added a total to the Amount column. The total amount of merchandise sales is $469,259. The formula displays as =SUBTOTAL(109,[Amount]) in the Formula Bar.

e. Click the **Sales_Last filter arrow**, click the **(Select All) check box**, click the **Gruenewald check box** to select it, and then click **OK**.

The total row values change to display the totals for only Gruenewald: $122,016 (Amount), 47,175.75 (Down_Pay), and 74,840.25 (Owed). This is an advantage of using the total row, which uses the SUBTOTAL function, as opposed to if you had inserted the SUM function manually. The SUM function would provide a total for all data in the column, not just the filtered data.

f. Click the **Data tab** and click **Clear** in the Sort & Filter group to remove all filters.

g. Save the workbook.

STEP 2 ❱❱ **APPLY HIGHLIGHT CELLS RULES**

You want to identify Sebastian's sales for March 2018 without filtering the data. You will set a conditional format to apply a fill and font color so cells that document appliance sales stand out. Refer to Figure 4.48 as you complete Step 2.

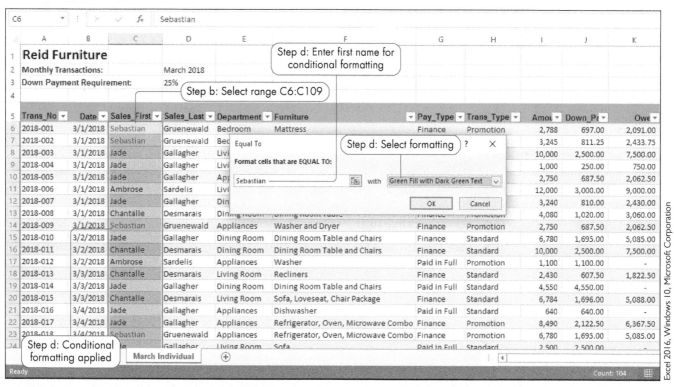

FIGURE 4.48 Conditional Formatting Rules Manager Dialog Box

a. Select **row headings 6 through 109** in the March Individual worksheet. Click the **Home tab**, click the **Fill Color arrow**, and then select **No Fill**.

You removed the previous table style. This will avoid having too many fill colors when you apply conditional formatting rules.

b. Select the **range C6:C109**.

c. Click **Conditional Formatting** in the Styles group, point to **Highlight Cells Rules**, and then select **Text that Contains**.

The Text that Contains dialog box opens.

d. Type **Sebastian** in the box, click the **with arrow**, and then select **Green Fill with Dark Green Text**. Click **OK**. Deselect the range and save the workbook.

Excel formats only cells that contain Sebastian with the fill and font color.

Vicki is now interested in identifying the highest three sales transactions in March. Instead of sorting the records, you will use the Top/Bottom Rules conditional formatting. Refer to Figure 4.49 as you complete Step 3.

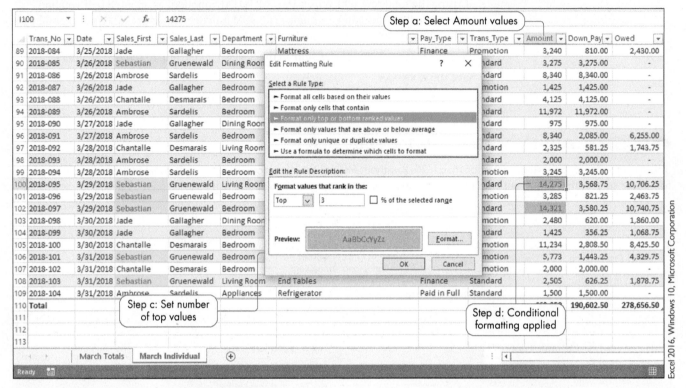

FIGURE 4.49 Top 3 Amounts Conditionally Formatted

a. Select the **range I6:I109**, the range containing the amounts.

b. Click **Conditional Formatting** in the Styles group, point to **Top/Bottom Rules**, and then select **Top 10 Items**.

The Top 10 Items dialog box opens.

c. Click the arrow to display **3** and click **OK**.

d. Scroll through the worksheet to see the top three amounts. Save the workbook.

STEP 4 >> DISPLAY DATA BARS

Vicki wants to compare all of the down payments. Data bars would add a nice visual element as she compares down payment amounts. Refer to Figure 4.50 as you complete Step 4.

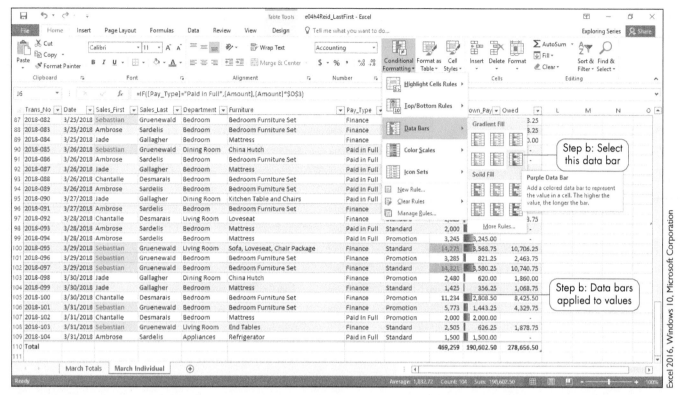

FIGURE 4.50 Data Bars Conditional Formatting

a. Select the **range J6:J109**, which contains the down payment amounts.

b. Click **Conditional Formatting** in the Styles group, point to **Data Bars**, and then select **Purple Data Bar** in the Gradient Fill section. Scroll through the list and save the workbook.

Excel displays data bars in each cell. The larger bar widths help Vicki quickly identify the largest down payments. However, the largest down payments are identical to the original amounts when the customers pay in full. This result illustrates that you should not accept the results at face value. Doing so would provide you with an inaccurate analysis.

Vicki's next request is to analyze the amounts owed by Sebastian's customers. In particular, she wants to highlight the merchandise for which more than $5,000 is owed. To do this, you realize you need to create a custom rule that evaluates both the Sales_First column and the Owed column. Refer to Figure 4.51 as you complete Step 5.

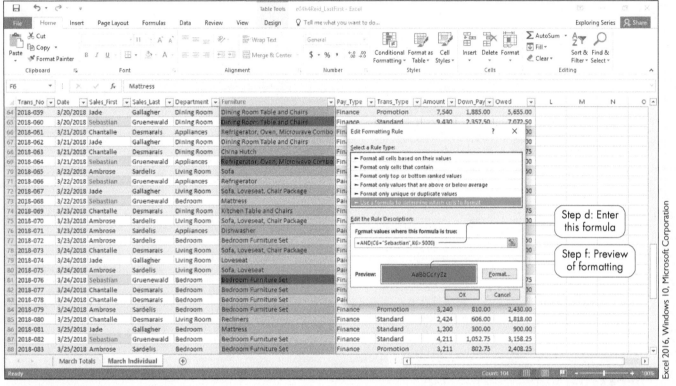

FIGURE 4.51 Custom Rule Created

a. Select the **range F6:F109**, which contains the furniture merchandise.

b. Click **Conditional Formatting** in the Styles group and select **New Rule**.

   The New Formatting Rule dialog box opens.

c. Select **Use a formula to determine which cells to format**.

d. Type **=AND(C6="Sebastian",K6>5000)** in the *Format values where this formula is true* box.

   Because you are comparing the contents of cell C6 to text, you must enclose the text within quotation marks.

e. Click **Format** to open the Format Cells dialog box.

f. Click the **Font tab**, and click **Bold** in the Font style list. Click the **Border tab**, click the **Color arrow**, select **Blue, Accent 5**, and then click **Outline**. Click the **Fill tab**, click **Blue, Accent 5 background color** (the second color from the right on the first row), and then click **OK**.

   Figure 4.51 shows the Edit Formatting Rule dialog box, but the options are similar to the New Formatting Rule dialog box.

g. Click **OK** in the New Formatting Rule dialog box and scroll through the list to see which amounts owed are greater than $5,000 for Sebastian only.

> **TROUBLESHOOTING:** If the results seem incorrect, click Conditional Formatting and select Manage Rules. Edit the rule you just created and make any corrections to the formula.

h. Save and close the file. Based on your instructor's directions, submit the file e04h4Reid_LastFirst.

Chapter Objectives Review

After reading this chapter, you have accomplished the following objectives:

1. Freeze rows and columns.
- The Freeze Panes setting freezes the row(s) above and the column(s) to the left of the active cell. When you scroll, those rows and columns remain onscreen.
- Use Unfreeze Panes to clear the frozen rows and columns.

2. Print large datasets.
- Display and change page breaks: Display the data in Page Break Preview to see the automatic page breaks. Dashed blue lines indicate automatic page breaks. You can insert manual page breaks, indicated by solid blue lines.
- Set and clear a print area: If you do not want to print an entire worksheet, select a range and set a print area.
- Print titles: Select rows to repeat at top and/or columns to repeat at left to print the column and row labels on every page of a printout of a large dataset.
- Control print page order: You can control the sequence in which the pages will print.

3. Understand the benefits of data tables.
- A table is a structured range that contains related data. Tables have several benefits over regular ranges. The column labels, called field names, display on the first row of a table. Each row is a complete set of data for one record.

4. Design and create tables.
- Plan a table before you create it. Create unique field names on the first row of the table and enter data below the field names, avoiding blank rows.
- Create a table: You can create a table from existing data. Excel applies the Table Style Medium 2 format and assigns a name, such as Table1, to the table. When the active cell is within a table, the Table Tools Design tab displays.
- Rename a table: When a table is created, Excel assigns a generic name and enables you to edit the default to a more suitable name.
- Add and delete fields: You can insert and delete table rows and columns to adjust the structure of a table.
- Add, edit, and delete records: You can add table rows, edit records, and delete table rows.
- Remove duplicate rows: Use the Remove Duplicates dialog box to remove duplicate records in a table. Excel will display a dialog box telling you how many records are deleted.

5. Apply a table style.
- Table styles control the fill color of the header row and records within the table.

6. Create structured references in formulas.
- Structured references use tags as field headings that can be used in formulas in place of cell references.

7. Sort data.
- Sort one field: You can sort text in alphabetical or reverse alphabetical order, values from smallest to largest or largest to smallest, and dates from oldest to newest or newest to oldest. Click the filter arrow and select the sort method from the list.
- Sort multiple fields: Open the Sort dialog box and add column levels and sort orders.
- Create a custom sort: You can create a custom sort for unique data, such as ensuring that the months sort in sequential order rather than alphabetical order.

8. Filter data.
- Filtering is the process of specifying conditions for displaying records in a table. Only records that meet those conditions display; the other records are hidden.
- Apply text filters: A text filter can find exact text, text that does not equal a condition, text that begins with a particular letter, and so forth.
- Apply number filters: A number filter can find exact values, values that do not equal a particular value, values greater than or equal to a value, and so on.
- Apply date filters: You can set filters to find dates before or after a certain date, between two dates, yesterday, next month, and so forth.
- Apply a custom filter: You can create a custom AutoFilter to filter values by options such as Greater Than, Less Than, or Before.
- Clear filters: If you do not need filters, you can clear the filters.

9. Add a total row.
- You can display a total row after the last record. You can add totals or select a different function, such as Average.

10. Apply conditional formatting.
- Apply conditional formatting with the Quick Analysis Tool: After selecting text, click Formatting in the Quick Analysis gallery to apply a conditional format.
- Apply a highlight cells rule: This rule highlights cell contents with a fill color, font color, and/or border color where the contents match a particular condition.
- Specify a top/bottom rule: This rule enables you to highlight the top or bottom x number of items or percentage of items.
- Display data bars, color scales, and icon sets: Data bars compare values within the selected range. Color scales indicate values that occur within particular ranges. Icon sets display icons representing a number's relative value compared to other numbers in the range.

11. Create a new rule.
- You can create conditional format rules. The New Formatting Rule dialog box enables you to select a rule type.
- Use formulas in conditional formatting: You can create rules based on content in multiple columns.
- Manage rules: Use the Conditional Formatting Rules Manager dialog box to edit and delete rules.

Key Terms Matching

Match the key terms with their definitions. Write the key term letter by the appropriate numbered definition.

a. Color scale
b. Conditional formatting
c. Data bar
d. Field
e. Filtering
f. Freezing
g. Icon set
h. Page break
i. Print area

j. Print order
k. Record
l. Sorting
m. Structured reference
n. SUBTOTAL function
o. Table
p. Table style
q. Total row

1. _____ A conditional format that displays a horizontal gradient or solid fill indicating the cell's relative value compared to other selected cells. **p. 640**

2. _____ The process of listing records or text in a specific sequence, such as alphabetically by last name. **p. 622**

3. _____ The process of specifying conditions to display only those records that meet those conditions. **p. 624**

4. _____ A set of rules that applies specific formatting to highlight or emphasize cells that meet specifications. **p. 636**

5. _____ A group of related fields representing one entity, such as data for one person, place, event, or concept. **p. 609**

6. _____ The rules that control the fill color of the header row, columns, and records in a table. **p. 614**

7. _____ An indication of where data will start on another printed page. **p. 600**

8. _____ A table row that appears below the last row of records in an Excel table and displays summary or aggregate statistics, such as a sum or an average. **p. 636**

9. _____ A conditional format that displays a particular color based on the relative value of the cell contents to the other selected cells. **p. 642**

10. _____ The sequence in which the pages are printed. **p. 603**

11. _____ A tag or use of a table element, such as a field label, as a reference in a formula. **p. 621**

12. _____ Symbols or signs that classify data into three, four, or five categories, based on the values in a range. **p. 642**

13. _____ The range of cells within a worksheet that will print. **p. 601**

14. _____ A predefined formula that calculates an aggregate value, such as totals, for values in a range, a table, or a database. **p. 637**

15. _____ The smallest data element contained in a table, such as first name, last name, address, and phone number. **p. 609**

16. _____ A structure that organizes data in a series of records (rows), with each record made up of a number of fields (columns). **p. 609**

17. _____ The process of keeping rows and/or columns visible onscreen at all times even when you scroll through a large dataset. **p. 599**

Multiple Choice

1. You have a large dataset that will print on several pages. You want to ensure that related records print on the same page with column and row labels visible and that confidential information is not printed. You should apply all of the following page setup options *except* which one to accomplish this task?

   (a) Set a print area.
   (b) Print titles.
   (c) Adjust page breaks.
   (d) Change the print page order.

2. You are working with a large worksheet. Your row headings are in column A. Which command(s) should be used to see the row headings and the distant information in columns X, Y, and Z?

   (a) Freeze Panes command
   (b) Hide Rows command
   (c) New Window command and cascade the windows
   (d) Split Rows command

3. Which statement is *not* a recommended guideline for designing and creating an Excel table?

   (a) Avoid naming two fields with the same name.
   (b) Ensure that no blank columns separate data columns within the table.
   (c) Leave one blank row between records in the table.
   (d) Include field names on the first row of the table.

4. Which of the following characters are wildcards in Excel? (Check all that apply.)

   (a) *
   (b) #
   (c) ?
   (d) $

5. What should you do to ensure that records in a table are unique?

   (a) Do nothing; a logical reason probably exists to keep identical records.
   (b) Use the Remove Duplicates command.
   (c) Look at each row yourself and manually delete duplicate records.
   (d) Find the duplicate records and change some of the data to be different.

6. Which Conditional Formatting rule is best suited to apply formatting to the top five values in a range of values?

   (a) Above Average
   (b) Greater Than
   (c) Top 10 Items
   (d) Between

7. Which date filter option enables you to restrict the view to only dates that occur in March of 2018?

   (a) Equals
   (b) Before
   (c) After
   (d) Between

8. Which of the following is an unqualified structured reference?

   (a) =[Purchase_Price]-[Down_Payment]
   (b) =Sales[Purchase_Price]-Sales[Down_Payment]
   (c) =Purchase_Price-Down_Payment
   (d) =[Sales]Purchase_Price-[Sales]Down_Payment

9. Which of the following is not an aggregate function that can be applied in a total row?

   (a) MAX
   (b) AVERAGE
   (c) COUNT
   (d) VLOOKUP

10. If you would like to set a conditional formatting rule based on the function =AND(G6="Finance", H7<7000), which formatting rule type is needed?

   (a) Format all cells based on their values
   (b) Format only cells that contain
   (c) Use a formula to determine which cells to format
   (d) Format only values that are above or below average

Practice Exercises

1 Collectables and Replacement Values

Marie Maier has collected dinnerware, from a fine china company, since 1986. Between 1986 and 2012, the company produced 30 colors, each with a unique name. Marie created a table in Word that lists the name, number, year introduced, and year retired (if applicable) for each color. She created another table in Word that lists the item number, item, replacement value, and source of information for each item in her collection. Her main sources for replacement values are Homer Laughlin (www.fiestafactorydirect.com), Replacements, Ltd. (www.replacements.com), eBay (www.ebay.com), and two local antique stores. She needs your help to convert the data to Excel tables, apply table formatting, delete duplicate records, insert functions, and sort and filter the data. Refer to Figure 4.52 as you complete this exercise.

	A	B	C	D	E	F	G	H
1	Color Number	Year Introduce	Year Retire	Status	Color	Item Number	Item	Replacement Value
31	102	2000	2010	Retired	Cinnabar	571	Canister Small	49.99 D
32	102	2000	2010	Retired	Cinnabar	830	5 Piece Place Setting	35.99 D
33	102	2000	2010	Retired	Cinnabar	484	Pitcher Large Disc	34.99 K
34	102	2000	2010	Retired	Cinnabar	467	Chop Plate	25.00 D
35	102	2000	2010	Retired	Cinnabar	497	Salt and Pepper Set	20.00 D
36	102	2000	2010	Retired	Cinnabar	465	Luncheon Plate	12.50 D
37	102	2000	2010	Retired	Cinnabar	439	Spoon Rest	11.99 Th
38	102	2000	2010	Retired	Cinnabar	570	Java Mug	9.99 R
39	102	2000	2010	Retired	Cinnabar	453	Mug	8.49 Th
40	102	2000	2010	Retired	Cinnabar	446	Tumbler	6.99 Th
41	103	1986	2005	Retired	Rose	494	Covered Coffee Server	75.00 K
42	103	1986	2005	Retired	Rose	495	Covered Casserole	65.00 D
43	103	1986	2005	Retired	Rose	489	Pyramid Candleholders	59.99 D
44	103	1986	2005	Retired	Rose	486	Sauceboat	39.99 E
45	103	1986	2005	Retired	Rose	830	5 Piece Place Setting	35.00 E
46	103	1986	2005	Retired	Rose	821	Sugar/Cream Tray Set	29.99 E
47	103	1986	2005	Retired	Rose	484	Pitcher Large Disc	24.99 E
48	103	1986	2005	Retired	Rose	478	AD Cup and Saucer	19.99 E
49	103	1986	2005	Retired	Rose	471	Bowl Large 1 qt	19.99 D
50	103	1986	2005	Retired	Rose	497	Salt and Pepper Set	18.00 E
51	103	1986	2005	Retired	Rose	467	Chop Plate	16.95 E
52	103	1986	2005	Retired	Rose	451	Rim Soup	12.50 E

FIGURE 4.52 Fiesta® Collection

a. Open *e04p1Collectables* and save it as **e04p1Collectables_LastFirst**.

b. Select the **range A2:D31** on the Colors Data sheet, click in the **Name Box**, type **Colors**, and then press **Enter** to assign the name *Colors* to the selected range.

c. Click **cell A2** on the Items sheet, click the **View tab**, click **Freeze Panes** in the Window group, and then select **Freeze Top Row**.

d. Click the **Insert tab**, click **Table** in the Tables group, and then click **OK** in the Create Table dialog box.

e. Click **More Styles** in the Table Styles group and click **Table Style Medium 5**.

f. Click the **Data tab**, click **Remove Duplicates** in the Data Tools group, and then click **OK** in the Remove Duplicates dialog box. Click **OK** in the message box that informs you that 6 duplicate values were found and removed; 356 unique values remain.

g. Click **cell A2**, click the **Home tab**, click **Sort & Filter** in the Editing group, and then select **Sort Smallest to Largest**.

h. Click **cell B2**, click the **Insert arrow** in the Cells group, and then select **Insert Table Columns to the Left**. Insert two more columns to the left. Do the following to insert functions and customize the results in the three new table columns:

- Type **Year Introduced** in **cell B1**, **Year Retired** in **cell C1**, and **Color** in **cell D1**.
- Click **cell B2**, type **=VLOOKUP([Color Number],colors,3,False)**, and then press **Enter**. Excel copies the function down the Year Introduced column. This function looks up each item's color number using the structured reference *[Color Number]*, looks up that value in the colors table, and then returns the year that color was introduced, which is in the third column of that table.
- Click **cell B2**, click **Copy**, click **cell C2**, and then click **Paste**. Change the *3* to **4** in the col_index_num argument of the pasted function and press **Enter**. Excel copies the function down the Year Retired column. This function looks up each item's color number using the structured reference *[Color Number]*, looks up that value in the colors table, and then returns the year that color was retired, if applicable, which is in the fourth column of that table. The function returns 0 if the retired cell in the lookup table is blank.

DISCOVER

- Click the **File tab**, click **Options**, click **Advanced**, scroll down to the Display options for this worksheet section, click the **Show a zero in cells that have zero value check box** to deselect it, and then click **OK**. The zeros disappear. (This option hides zeros in the active worksheet. While this is not desirable if you need to show legitimate zeros, this worksheet is designed to avoid that issue.)
- Click **cell C2**, click **Copy**, click **cell D2**, and then click **Paste**. Change the *4* to **2** in the col_index_num argument of the pasted function and press **Enter**. Excel copies the function down the Color column. This function looks up each item's color number using the structured reference *[Color Number]* to look up that value in the colors table and returns the color name, which is in the second column of that table.

i. Apply wrap text, horizontal centering, and **30.50 row height** to the column labels row. Adjust column widths to AutoFit. Center data horizontally in the Color Number, Year Introduced, Year Retired, and Item Number columns. Apply **Comma Style** to the Replacement Values. Deselect the data.

j. Click **Sort & Filter** in the Editing group and select **Custom Sort** to display the Sort dialog box. Do the following in the Sort dialog box:

- Click the **Sort by arrow** and select **Color**.
- Click **Add Level**, click the **Then by arrow**, and then select **Replacement Value**.
- Click the **Order arrow** and select **Largest to Smallest**.
- Click **Add Level**, click the **Then by arrow**, and select **Source**.
- Click the **Order arrow**, select **Custom List**, and type the following entries: **Ebay Auction, Downtown Antique Store, The Homer Laughlin China Co., Replacements LTD., Keith's Antique Store**. Click **Add** and click **OK**. Click **OK**.

k. Right-click the **Items sheet tab**, select **Move or Copy**, click **(move to end)**, click the **Create a copy check box** to select the option, and then click **OK**. Rename the copied sheet **Retired**.

l. Ensure that Retired is the active sheet. Insert a table column between the Year Retired and Color columns.

- Type **Status** in **cell D1** as the column label.
- Click **cell D2**, type **=IF([Year Retired]=0, "Current","Retired")**, and then press **Enter**. This function determines that if the cell contains a 0 (which is hidden), it will display the word *Current*. Otherwise, it will display *Retired*.

m. Click the **Status filter arrow**, deselect the **Current check box**, and then click **OK** to filter out the current colors and display only retired colors.

n. Click the **Design tab** and click **Total Row** in the Table Style Options group. Click **cell I358**, click the **Source total cell** (which contains a count of visible items), click the **Source total arrow**, and then select **None**. Click **cell H358**, the Replacement Value total cell, click the **Replacement Value total arrow**, and then select **Sum**.

o. Prepare the Retired worksheet for printing by doing the following:
- Set **0.2"** left and right page margins.
- Select the **range E1:I358**, click the **Page Layout tab**, click **Print Area** in the Page Setup group, and then select **Set Print Area**.
- Click **Print Titles** in the Page Setup group, click the **Rows to repeat at top Collapse Dialog Box**, click the **row 1 header**, and then click **Expand Dialog Box**. Click **OK**.
- Click the **View tab** and click **Page Break Preview** in the Workbook Views group. Decrease the top margin to avoid having only one or two records print on the last page.

p. Create a footer with your name on the left side, the sheet name code in the center, and the file name code on the right side of each worksheet.

q. Save and close the file. Based on your instructor's directions, submit e04p1Collectables_LastFirst.

2 Sunny Popcorn, Inc.

You are a financial analyst for Sunny Popcorn, Inc. and have been given the task of compiling a workbook to detail weekly sales information. The current information provided detailed sales rep information, flavors ordered, account type, and volume ordered. The owners are specifically interested in local sales that are generating at least $150.00 a week. To complete the document you will sort, filter, use table tools, and apply conditional formatting. Refer to Figure 4.53 as you complete this exercise.

	A	B	C	D	E	F	G	H
1	Sunny Popcorn Inc							
2	Date	10/6/2018						
3	Deposit	5%						
4								
5								
6	First Name	Last Name	Account type	Flavor	Volume in lbs	Price per lb	Deposit	Amount Due
22	Helen	Sanchez	Local	Regular	58	$2.25	$ 6.53	$ 123.98
23	Yoshio	Guo	Local	Cheese	88	$2.00	$ 8.80	$ 167.20
24	Yong	Lopez	Local	Regular	91	$2.25	$ 10.24	$ 194.51
25	Dalia	Azizi	Local	Regular	33	$2.25	$ 3.71	$ 70.54
26	Kyung	Rodriguez	Local	Carmel	99	$1.50	$ 7.43	$ 141.08
27	Jasmine	Bettar	Local	Cheese	67	$2.00	$ 6.70	$ 127.30
28	Yukio	He	Local	Low Salt	64	$2.25	$ 7.20	$ 136.80
29	Dai	Zhu	Local	Chocolate	62	$2.00	$ 6.20	$ 117.80
30	Nam	Sato	Local	Cheese	66	$2.00	$ 6.60	$ 125.40
31	Ryung	Inoue	Local	Chocolate	17	$2.00	$ 1.70	$ 32.30
32	Raul	Martinez	Local	Crunch	31	$2.25	$ 3.49	$ 66.26
33	Yoshio	Flores	Local	Low Salt	27	$2.25	$ 3.04	$ 57.71
34	Diego	Sun	Local	Low Salt	16	$2.25	$ 1.80	$ 34.20
35	Helen	Cho	Local	Cheese	48	$2.00	$ 4.80	$ 91.20
36	Yoshio	Seo	Local	Chocolate	32	$2.00	$ 3.20	$ 60.80
37	Sang	Allen	Local	Carmel	53	$1.50	$ 3.98	$ 75.53
38	Raj	Hong	Local	Cheese	41	$2.00	$ 4.10	$ 77.90
39	Javier	Hyat	Local	Cheese	100	$2.00	$ 10.00	$ 190.00
40	Brian	Hernandez	Local	Low Salt	16	$2.25	$ 1.80	$ 34.20

Sales ⊕

Ready

FIGURE 4.53 Sunny Popcorn Inc

a. Open *e04p2Popcorn* and save it as **e04p2Popcorn_LastFirst**.

b. Click **cell C7**, click the **Home tab**, click the **Sort & Filter arrow** in the Editing group, and select **Sort A to Z**. This sorts the data by account type in Column C.

c. Click the **Insert tab**, click **Table** in the Tables group, and click **OK** in the Create Table dialog box.

d. Click **Table Style Medium 3** in the Table Styles group on the Design tab.

e. Click cell **G7** and type **=[Price per lb]*[Volume in lbs]*$B$3** and press **Enter**.

f. Click cell **H7** and type **=[Price per lb]*[Volume in lbs]-[Deposit]** and press **Enter**

g. Select the **range G7:H106**, click the **Home tab**, and click **Accounting Number Format** in the Number group.

h. Click the **Design tab** and click **Total Row** in the Table Style Options group.

i. Click the **Deposit Total Row arrow**, and select **Sum**, click the **Volume in lbs Total Row arrow**, and then select **Average**. Apply **Number Style Format** to the results in **cell E107**.

j. Click the **filter arrow** of the Account type column, click the **Select All check box** to deselect it, click **Local**, and click **OK**.

k. Select the **range H22:H51**, click **Quick Analysis**, and then select **Greater Than**. Type **150.00** in the Format cells that are GREATER THAN box, select **Green Fill with Dark Green Text**, and click **OK**.

l. Select the **range E22:E51**, click **Quick Analysis**, and then select **Data Bars**.

m. Click the **Page Layout tab**, click the **Scale box** in the Scale to Fit group, and then type **85%**.

n. Create a footer with your name on the left side, the sheet name code in the center, and the file name code on the right side of each worksheet.

o. Save and close the file. Based on your instructor's directions, submit e04p2Popcorn_LastFirst.

Mid-Level Exercises

1 Crafton's Pet Supplies

You are the inventory manager for Crafton's Pet Supplies. You are currently preforming analysis to determine inventory levels, as well as the total value of inventory on hand. Your last steps will be to check the report for duplicate entries and format for printing.

a. Open *e04m1Inventory* and save it as **e04m1Inventory_LastFirst**.

b. Freeze the panes so that the column labels do not scroll offscreen.

c. Convert the data to a table and name the table **Inventory2018**.

d. Apply **Table Style Medium 3** to the table.

e. Sort the table by Warehouse (A to Z), then Department, and then by Unit Price (smallest to largest). Create a custom sort order for Department so that it appears in this sequence: Food & Health, Collars & Leashes, Toys, Clothes, Training, and Grooming.

f. Remove duplicate records from the table. Excel should find and remove one duplicate record.

g. Create an unqualified structured reference in column G to determine the value of the inventory on hand and apply **Accounting Number Format**. To calculate the inventory on hand multiply the **Unit Price** and the **Amount on Hand.**

h. Apply a **Total Row** to the Inventory2018 table, set the Inventory Value to Sum, and the Amount on Hand to Average. Format the results to display with two decimal points.

i. Create a new conditional formatting rule that displays any Inventory Value for the **Food & Health** department with a value of $30,000 or more as **Red Accent 2 fill color**. There will be two qualifying entries.

j. Ensure the warehouse information is not broken up between pages when printed. Add a page break to make sure that each warehouse prints on its own consecutive page.

k. Set the worksheet to **Landscape orientation**, and repeat row 1 labels on all pages.

l. Display the Inventory sheet in Page Break Preview.

m. Insert a footer with your name on the left side, the sheet name code in the center, and the file name code on the right side of all four sheets.

n. Save and close the file. Based on your instructor's directions, submit e04m1Inventory_LastFirst.

2 Artwork

You work for a gallery that is an authorized Greenwich Workshop fine art dealer (www.greenwichworkshop.com). Customers in your area are especially fond of James C. Christensen's art. Although customers can visit the website to see images and details about his work, they have requested a list of all his artwork. Your assistant prepared a list of artwork: art, type, edition size, release date, and issue price. In addition, you included a column to identify which pieces are sold out at the publisher, indicating the rare, hard-to-obtain artwork that is available on the secondary market. You now want to convert the data to a table so that you can provide information to your customers.

a. Open *e04m2FineArt* and save it as **e04m2FineArt_LastFirst**.

b. Convert the data to a table and apply **Table Style Medium 5**.

c. Add a row (below the record for *The Yellow Rose*) for this missing piece of art: **The Yellow Rose**, **Masterwork Canvas Edition**, **50** edition size, **May 2009** release date, **$895** issue price. Enter **Yes** to indicate the piece is sold out.

d. Sort the table by Type in alphabetical order and then by Release Date from newest to oldest.

e. Add a total row that shows the largest edition size and the most expensive issue price. Delete the Total label in **cell A205** and **cell H205**. Add a descriptive label in **cell C205** to reflect the content on the total row.

DISCOVER

f. Create a custom conditional format for the Issue Price column with these specifications:

- **4 Traffic Lights** icon set (Black, Red, Yellow, Green)
- **Red icon** when the number is greater than 1000
- **Yellow icon** when the number is less than or equal to 1000 and greater than 500
- **Green icon** when the number is less than or equal to 500 and greater than 250
- **Black icon** when the number is less than or equal to 250.

DISCOVER

g. Filter the table by the **Red Traffic Light** conditional formatting icon.

h. Answer the questions in the range D213:D217 based on the filtered data.

i. Set the print area to print the **range C1:H205**, select the **first row to repeat at the top of each printout**, set **1"** top and bottom margins, set **0.3"** left and right margins, and then select **Landscape orientation**. Set the option to fit the data to 1 page.

j. Wrap text, and horizontally center column labels and adjust column widths and row heights as needed.

k. Create a footer with your name on the left side, the sheet name code in the center, and the file name code on the right side.

l. Save and close the file. Based on your instructor's directions, submit e04m2FineArt_LastFirst.

3 Party Music

COLLABORATION CASE

FROM SCRATCH

You are planning a weekend party and want to create a mix of music so that most people will appreciate some of the music you will play at the party. To help you decide what music to play, you have asked five classmates to help you create a song list. The entire class should decide on the general format, capitalization style, and the sequence: Song, Artist, Genre, Released, and approximate song length.

a. Conduct online research to collect data for your favorite 25 songs.

b. Enter the data into a new workbook in the format, capitalization style, and sequence that was decided by the class.

c. Save the workbook as **e04m3PlayList_LastFirst**.

d. Upload the file to a shared folder on OneDrive or Dropbox that everyone in the class can access.

e. Download four workbooks from friends and copy and paste data from their workbooks into yours.

f. Convert the data to a table and apply a table style of your choice.

g. Detect and delete duplicate records. Make a note of the number of duplicate records found and deleted.

h. Sort the data by genre using the custom list: Pop, Rock, R&B, and Jazz, then by artist in alphabetical order, and then by release date with the oldest year first.

i. Set a filter to display songs that were released before 2018.

j. Display the total row and select the function to count the number of songs displayed.

k. Insert comments in the workbook to indicate which student's workbooks you used, the number of duplicate records deleted, and the number of filtered records.

l. Save and close the file. Based on your instructor's directions, submit e04m3PlayList_LastFirst.

Beyond the Classroom

Flight Arrival Status

As an analyst for an airport, you want to study the flight arrivals for a particular day. Select an airport and find its list of flight arrival data. Some airport websites do not list complete details, so search for an airport that does, such as Will Rogers World Airport or San Diego International Airport. Copy the column labels and arrival data (airline, flight number, city, gate, scheduled time, status, etc.) for one day and paste them in a new workbook. The columns may be in a different sequence from what is listed here. However, you should format the data as needed. Leave two blank rows below the last row of data and enter the URL of the webpage from which you got the data, the date, and the time. Save the workbook as **e04b1Flights_LastFirst**. Convert the list to a table and apply a table style.

Sort the table by scheduled time and then by gate number. Apply conditional formatting to the Status column to highlight cells that contain the text Delayed (or similar text). Add a total row to calculate the MODE for the gate number and arrival time. The MODE is the number that appears the most frequently in the dataset. You must select **More Functions** from the list of functions in the total row and search for and select **MODE**. Change the total row label in the first column from Total to **Most Frequent**. Use Help to refresh your memory on how to nest an IF function inside another IF function. Add a calculated column on the right side of the table using a nested IF function and structured references to display **Late** if the actual time was later than the scheduled time, **On Time or Early** if the actual time was earlier than or equal to the scheduled time, or **Incomplete** if the flight has not landed yet.

Name the worksheet **Arrival Time**. Copy the worksheet and name the copied worksheet **Delayed**. Filter the list by delayed flights. Include a footer with your name on the left side, the sheet name code in the center, and the file name code on the right side of both worksheets. Adjust the margins on both worksheets as necessary. Save and close the file. Based on your instructor's directions, submit e04b1Flights_LastFirst.

Dairy Farm

You are the product manager for Schaefer Dairy farm, a local organic farm that produces dairy products. Each month you must run an inventory report to identify and discard expired products before they are sold. Open *e04b2Dairy* and save it as **e04b2Dairy_LastFirst**. Convert the **range A5:E105** to a table, give the table a name, and apply a table style.

Freeze all data above row 6 and create a conditional formatting rule that highlights any package date that is 30 days or older than the manufacture date in B4. Sort the table first by the newly created highlight color then by department. Next, in column E create an IF function using structured referencing to determine the course of action for expired products. The function should display **discard** if the product is expired and nothing if the product is still sellable. Filter the table to display only items that should be discarded, then add a total row that counts the number of items to discard. Format the table so the column headings print at the top of each page and create a footer with your name, the sheet name code, and the file name code. Save and close the file. Based on your instructor's directions, submit e04b2Dairy_LastFirst.

Capstone Exercise

You work for Rockville Auto Sales and have been asked to aid in the development of a spreadsheet to manage sales and inventory information. You will start the task with a prior worksheet that contains vehicle information and sales data for 2018. You need to convert the data to a table. You will manage the large worksheet, prepare the worksheet for printing, sort and filter the table, include calculations, and then format the table.

Prepare the Large Worksheet as a Table

You will freeze the panes so that labels remain onscreen. You also want to convert the data to a table so that you can apply table options.

a. Open the *e04c1AutoSales* workbook and save it as **e04c1AutoSales_LastFirst**.

b. Freeze the first row on the Fleet Information worksheet.

c. Convert the data to a table, name the table **Inventory**, and apply the **Table Style Medium 19**.

d. Remove duplicate records.

Sort and Print the Table

To help the sales agents manage vehicle inventory, you will sort the data. Then you will prepare the large table to print.

a. Sort the table by Make in alphabetical order, add a second level to sort by Year, and a third level to sort by Sticker Price smallest to largest.

b. Repeat the field names on all pages.

c. Change page breaks so each vehicle make is printed on a separate page.

d. Add a footer with your name on the left side, the sheet name code in the center, and the file name code on the right side.

Add Calculated Fields and a Total Row

For tax purposes, the accounting department needs you to calculate the number of vehicles sold, the total value of sticker prices, and actual sales price for vehicles sold in the first quarter.

a. Click the Sales Information worksheet and convert the data to a table, name the table Sales, and apply the **Table Style Dark 11**.

b. Create a formula with structured references to calculate the percentage of the Sticker Price in column E.

c. Format the **range E2:E30** with **Percentage Style** Number Format.

d. Add a total row to display the Average of % of Sticker Price and Sum of Sticker Price and Sale Price.

e. Adjust the width of **columns B:E** to show the total values.

Apply Conditional Formatting

You want to help the office manager visualize the differences among the sales. To highlight sales trends, you will apply data bar conditional formatting to the % of Value column.

a. Apply **Data Bars conditional formatting** to the % of Sticker Price data.

b. Create a new conditional format that applies yellow fill and bold font to values that sold for less than 60% of the list price.

c. Edit the conditional format you created so that it formats values 70% or less.

Copy and Filter the Data

In order to isolate first quarter sales, you will filter the data. To keep the original data intact for the sales agents, you will copy the table data to a new sheet and use that sheet to display the filtered data.

a. Copy the Sales Information sheet and place the duplicate sheet to the right of the original sheet tab.

b. Rename the duplicate worksheet **First Quarter Sales**.

c. Rename the table **FirstQuarter**.

d. Display the filter arrows for the data.

e. Filter the data to display January, February, and March sales.

Finalize the Workbook

You are ready to finalize the workbook by adding a footer to the new worksheet and saving the final workbook.

a. Add a footer with your name on the left side, the sheet name code in the center, and the file name code on the right side.

b. Select **Landscape orientation** for all sheets and set appropriate margins so that the data will print on one page.

c. Save and close the file. Based on your instructor's directions, submit e04c1AutoSales_LastFirst.

Excel Application Capstone Exercise

You are a vice president for a publisher of software training books. Your division publishes three series that focus on Microsoft Office and Windows. You want to analyze the sales data and calculate author royalties. You will format the worksheet, insert formulas and functions to perform calculations, sort and filter data to review specific book sales, and prepare a chart that compares sales by series.

Format the Worksheet

Your assistant compiled the initial data and saved it in an Excel workbook. However, the column labels are hard to read because the full text does not display. You will use alignment and format options to make it easier to read the labels.

a. Open *eApp_Cap1_Publisher* and save it as **eApp_Cap1_Publisher_LastFirst**.

b. Select the **range A6:K6** on the Data worksheet.

c. Wrap the text and apply Center alignment to the selected range.

d. Change the row height to **30**.

Insert Formulas and Basic Functions

The Data worksheet contains the quantity of books sold, the number of books returned, and the unit price per book. You want to calculate the percentage of books that were returned from bookstores to your warehouse. Then you will also calculate the net sales, the amount of royalties to pay the authors, and the total author earnings. You want to insert functions to calculate the average, highest, and lowest net sales amounts. Use appropriate relative, absolute, and mixed references correctly in your formulas.

a. Click **cell F7** on the Data worksheet and insert a formula that calculates the percentage of books returned based on the number of books returned and the quantity sold. Copy the formula from cell F7 to the **range F8:F22**.

b. Click **cell H7** and insert a formula that calculates the net sales. This monetary amount reflects the number of books *not* returned and the unit price. Copy the formula from cell H7 to the **range H8:H22**.

c. Click **cell I7** and insert a formula that calculates the amount of the first author's royalties. An author's royalties are based on the Royalty Rate located in the Input Area and the respective Net Sales. Copy the formula from cell I7 to the **range I8:I22**.

d. Click **cell K7** and insert a formula that adds the first author's royalty amount to the bonus. Copy the formula from cell K7 to the **range K8:K22**.

e. Click **cell J2** and insert a function to calculate the average net sales.

f. Click **cell J3** and insert a function to calculate the highest net sales.

g. Click **cell J4** and insert a function to calculate the lowest net sales.

Move Data and Insert Functions

The legend that explains the abbreviations for each series would look better in a different location. You will insert a new column in the worksheet and insert a lookup function to display the full series names. Finally, you will replace the bonus with a function that calculates a bonus only if the return rate is less than 10%. Use relative, absolute, and mixed references correctly in your functions.

a. Select the **range L1:N2**, copy the selected data, and transpose the data when pasting it to **cell A2**. Delete the data in the **range L1:N2**.

b. Click **cell C6** and insert a column. Type **Series Name** in **cell C6**.

c. Click **cell C7** and insert a lookup function that identifies the series code, compares it to the series legend, and then returns the name of the series. Copy the function you entered from cell C7 to the **range C8:C22**.

d. Change the width of column C to **18**.

e. Click **cell K7** and insert an IF function that compares the percent returned for the first book to the return rate in the Input Area. If the percent returned is less than the return rate, the result is $500. Otherwise, the author receives no bonus. The only value you may type directly in the function is 0 where needed. Copy the function you entered from cell K7 to the **range K8:K22**.

Format Data

Most of the values were already formatted with Accounting Number Format, and when you inserted functions in the Net Sales area, Excel formatted the values for you because the source values were already formatted. However, you want to format the values in the Percent Returned and Bonus columns. In addition, you want to format the Series legend to match the other ranges at the top of the worksheet. You will merge and center the label and apply a border around the range.

a. Select the **range G7:G22** and apply the **Percent Style** format with one decimal place.

b. Select the **range K7:K22** and apply the **Accounting Number Format**.

c. Merge and center the label Series Legend in the **range A1:C1**.

d. Apply **Thick Outside Borders** to the **range A1:C4**.

Select Page Setup Options

Currently, the worksheet data would not fit on one printed page. You will change the orientation, scaling, and margins so that the data would fit on one page if you decide to print the worksheet.

a. Select **Landscape orientation**.

b. Adjust the scaling so that the data fits on one page.

c. Set **0.1"** left and right margins.

Insert a Table, Sort and Filter Data, and Apply Conditional Formatting

To preserve the integrity of the original data, you will work with a portion of the dataset in the Sales worksheet. First, you will convert the data to a table and apply a specific table style. Next, you will sort the data in a specific order and display the total net sales by series and within each series with the highest to lowest net sales. Then you will add a total row to display the total net sales. Finally, you want to apply a conditional format to focus on the book titles where 10% or more of the books were returned and then apply a filter to focus on the books with the lowest net sales.

a. Click the **Sales sheet tab** and convert the data to a table.

b. Apply **Table Style Light 9**.

c. Sort the data by Series Name in alphabetical order and then within Series Name, sort by Net Sales from largest to smallest.

d. Add a total row to display the sum of the Net Sales column. Change the column width to **14** for the Net Sales column.

e. Select the values in the Percent Returned column and apply conditional formatting to apply **Light Red Fill with Dark Red Text** for values that are greater than 9.9%.

f. Select the values in the Net Sales column and apply a filter to display only net sales that are less than $100,000.

Create a Column Chart

The Net Sales worksheet contains net sales organized by software and series. You will create a clustered column chart to compare the software sales across the series.

a. Click the **Net Sales sheet tab**.

b. Select the **range A3:D7** and create a clustered column chart.

c. Move the chart so that the top-left corner covers **cell A9**. Change the chart width to **4.66"** and the chart height to **2.9"**.

d. Link the chart title to **cell A1**.

e. Format the value axis to display whole numbers only.

f. Format the chart title, value axis, category axis, and legend with **Black, Text 1 font color**.

Create a Pie Chart

The Series Sales worksheet contains net sales organized by software and series. You will create a pie chart to determine the percentage of sales for each book within the Office Reference series.

a. Click the **Series Sales sheet tab**.

b. Select the **ranges A4:A7** and **C4:C7** and create a pie chart. Move the pie chart to a chart sheet named **Office Reference**. Move the Office Reference chart sheet to the right of the Series Sales sheet.

c. Change the chart title to **Office Reference Series**. Apply **bold** and change the font size to **18** for the chart title.

d. Apply the **Style 12** chart style and change the colors to **Color 4**.

e. Display data labels in the **Inside End** position. Display **Percentage** data labels; remove the Value data labels. Apply **bold**, change the font size to **18**, and then apply **White, Background 1** font color to the data labels.

f. Apply these fill colors: Excel data point **Green**, Access data point **Purple**, PowerPoint data point **Orange, Accent 2**.

Finish the Project

You want to insert a footer on each sheet.

a. Group the Data, Sales, Net Sales, and Series Sales sheet tabs.

b. Create a footer with your name on the left side, the sheet tab code in the center, and the file name code on the right side of each sheet.

c. Click the Office Reference chart sheet and create a footer with your name on the left side, the sheet tab code in the center, and the file name code on the right side.

d. Save and close the file. Based on your instructor's directions, submit eApp_Cap1_Publisher_LastFirst.

Glossary

100% stacked column chart A chart type that places (stacks) data in one column per category, with each column the same height of 100%.

Absolute cell reference A designation that indicates a constant reference to a specific cell location; the cell reference does not change when you copy the formula.

Access A relational database management system in which you can record and link data, query databases, and create forms and reports.

Accounting Number Format A number format that displays $ on the left side of a cell, formats a value with a comma for every three digits on the left side of the decimal point, and displays two digits to the right of the decimal point.

Action Center A location in Windows 10, accessed by an icon in the Notifications area on the taskbar, that provides status information, notifications, and recommended actions for various maintenance and security settings.

Active cell The current cell in a worksheet. It is indicated by a dark green border, and the Name Box shows the location of the active cell.

Add-in A custom program or additional command that extends the functionality of a Microsoft Office program.

Adjustment handle A yellow circle on a shape that is used to change the shape.

Aggregate function A calculation performed on an entire column of data that returns a single value. Includes functions such as Sum, Avg, and Count.

Align A feature that enables you to line up shapes and objects. You can align objects by lining up the sides, middles, or top/bottom edges of objects.

Alignment The placement of data within the boundaries of a cell. By default, text aligns on the left side, and values align on the right side of a cell.

Alignment guide A horizontal or vertical green bar that appears as you move an object, assisting with aligning the object with text or with another object.

Alt text An accessibility compliance feature where you enter text and a description for an objective, such as a table or a chart. A special reader can read the alt text to a user.

AND condition A condition in a query, returns only records that meet all criteria.

Animation A motion applied to text and objects.

Annotation A written note or drawing on a slide for additional commentary or explanation

APA (American Psychological Association) A writing style established by the American Psychological Association with rules and conventions for documenting sources and organizing a research paper (used primarily in business and the social sciences).

Application part A feature that enables you to add a set of common Access components to an existing database, such as a table, a form, and a report for a related task.

Area chart A chart type that emphasizes magnitude of changes over time by filling in the space between lines with a color.

Argument A positional reference contained within parentheses in a function such as a cell reference or value, required to complete a function and produce output.

Aspect Ratio The ratio of an object's width to its height.

Auto Fill A feature that helps you complete a sequence of months, abbreviated months, quarters, weekdays, weekday abbreviations, or values. Auto Fill also can be used to fill or copy a formula down a column or across a row.

AutoComplete A feature that searches for and automatically displays any other label in that column that matches the letters you type.

AutoNumber A number that automatically increments each time a record is added.

AutoRecover A feature that enables Word to recover a previous version of a document.

AVERAGE function A predefined formula that calculates the arithmetic mean, or average, of values in a range of cells.

Axis title A label that describes either the category axis or the value axis. Provides clarity, particularly in describing the value axis.

Back Up Database A utility that creates a duplicate copy of the entire database to protect from loss or damage.

Background The portion of a picture that can be deleted when removing the background of a picture.

Background Styles gallery A gallery providing both solid color and background styles for application to a theme.

Backstage view A component of Office that provides a concise collection of commands related to an open file.

Bar chart A chart type that compares values across categories using horizontal bars where the length represents the value; the longer the bar, the larger the value. In a bar chart, the horizontal axis displays values and the vertical axis displays categories.

Bibliography A list of works cited or consulted by an author in his or her work.

Bitmap image An image created by bits or pixels placed on a grid to form a picture.

Blog The chronological publication of personal thoughts and Web links.

Bookmark A method used to mark specific locations in a video.

Border A line that surrounds a paragraph, page, or a table or table element.

Border (Excel) A line that surrounds a cell or a range of cells to offset particular data from the rest of the data in a worksheet.

Border Painter A feature that enables you to choose border formatting and click on any table border to apply the formatting.

Breakpoint The lowest value for a category or in a series.

Brightness A picture correction that controls the lightness or darkness of a picture.

Bulleted list A graphic element that itemizes and separates paragraph text to increase readability; often used to identify lists.

Calculated field A field that displays the result of an expression rather than data stored in a field.

Callout A shape that be can used to add notes, often used in cartooning.

Cancel An icon between the Name Box and Formula Bar. When you enter or edit data, click Cancel to cancel the data entry or edit, and revert back to the previous data in the cell, if any. Cancel changes from gray to red when you position the pointer over it.

Caption A descriptive title for a table

Caption property A property that is used to create a more understandable label than a field name that displays in the top row in Datasheet view and in forms and reports.

Cascade Delete Related Records When the primary key value is deleted in a primary table, Access will automatically delete all records in related tables that contain values that match the primary key.

Cascade Update Related Fields An option that directs Access to automatically change all foreign key values in a related table when the primary key value is modified in a primary table.

Category axis The chart axis that displays descriptive labels for the data points plotted in a chart. The category axis labels are typically text contained in the first column of worksheet data (such as job titles) used to create the chart.

Cell The intersection of a column and row in a table, such as the intersection of column B and row 5.

Cell address The unique identifier of a cell, starting with the column letter and then the row number, such as C6.

Cell style A set of formatting applied to a cell to produce a consistent appearance for similar cells within a worksheet.

Center alignment Positions text horizontally in the center of a line, with an equal distance from both the left and right margins.

Chart A visual representation of numerical data.

Chart area A container for the entire chart and all of its elements, including the plot area, titles, legends, and labels.

Chart element A component of a chart that helps complete or clarify the chart.

Chart filter A setting that controls what data series and categories are displayed or hidden in a chart.

Chart sheet A sheet within a workbook that contains a single chart and no spreadsheet data.

Chart style A collection of formatting that controls the color of the chart area, plot area, and data series.

Chart title The label that describes the entire chart. The title is usually placed at the top of the chart area.

Chicago Manual of Style A writing style established by the University of Chicago with rules and conventions for preparing an academic paper for publication.

Citation A note recognizing a source of information or a quoted passage.

Clipboard An area of memory reserved to temporarily hold selections that have been cut or copied and allows you to paste the selections.

Cloud storage A technology used to store files and to work with programs that are stored in a central location on the Internet.

Clustered column chart A type of chart that groups, or clusters, columns set side by side to compare several data points among categories.

Codec (coder/decoder) A digital video compression scheme used to compress a video and decompress for playback.

Collapsed outline An Outline view that displays only the slide number, icon, and title of each slide in Outline view.

Color scale A conditional format that displays a particular color based on the relative value of the cell contents to the other selected cells.

Colors gallery A set of colors available for every theme.

Column A format that separates document text into side-by-side vertical blocks, often used in newsletters.

Column chart A type of chart that compares values vertically in columns where the height represents the value; the taller the column, the larger the value. In a column chart, the vertical axis displays values and the horizontal axis displays categories.

Column heading The alphabetical letter above a column in a worksheet. For example, B is the column heading for the second column.

Column index number The column number in the lookup table that contains the return values.

Column width The horizontal measurement of a column in a table or a worksheet. In Excel, it is measured by the number of characters or pixels.

Combo chart A chart that combines two chart types, such as column and line, to plot different types of data, such as quantities and percentages.

Comma Style A number format that formats a value with a comma for every three digits on the left side of the decimal point and displays two digits to the right of the decimal point.

Command A button or area within a group that you click to perform tasks.

Comment A note, annotation, or additional information to the author or another reader about the content of a document.

Comment balloon A small balloon that displays on the right side of a paragraph in which a comment has been made and provides access to the comment.

Compact and Repair Database A utility that reduces the size of a database and fixes any errors that may exist in the file.

Comparison Operator An operator such as greater than (>), less than (<), greater than or equal to (>=), and less than or equal to (<=), etc. used to limit query results that meet these criteria.

Compressed (zipped) folder A folder created with the Zip feature, contains a file or group of files. A compressed folder uses less drive space and can be transferred or shared with other users more quickly.

Compression A method applied to data to reduce the amount of space required for file storage.

Conditional formatting A set of rules that applies specific formatting to highlight or emphasize cells that meet specific conditions.

Connector A line with connection points at each end.

Constant A value that does not change.

Contextual tab A tab that contains a group of commands related to the selected object.

Contrast The difference between the darkest and lightest areas of a picture.

Control A text box, button, label, or other tool you use to add, edit, and display the data in a form or report.

Copy A command used to duplicate a selection from the original location and place a copy in the Office Clipboard.

Copyright The legal protection afforded to a written or artistic work.

Cortana Microsoft 10's personal assistant that helps search the Web and your PC, and can also assist with reminders, tasks, and other activities.

COUNT function A predefined formula that tallies the number of cells in a range that contain values you can use in calculations, such as numerical and date data, but excludes blank cells or text entries from the tally.

COUNTA function A predefined formula that tallies the number of cells in a range that are not blank, that is, cells that contain data, whether a value, text, or a formula.

COUNTBLANK function A predefined formula that tallies the number of cells in a range that are blank.

Cover page The first page of a report, including the report title, author or student, and other identifying information.

Criteria row A row in Query Design view that determines which records will be selected.

Crop The process of reducing an image size by eliminating unwanted portions of an image or other graphical object.

Current List A list that includes all citation sources you use in the current document.

Custom Web app A feature which enables users to create a database that you can build and then use and share with others through the Web.

Cut A command used to remove a selection from the original location and place it in the Office Clipboard.

Data bar Data bar formatting applies a gradient or solid fill bar in which the width of the bar represents the current cell's value compared relatively to other cells' values.

Data label An identifier that shows the exact value of a data point in a chart. Appears above or on a data point in a chart. May indicate percentage of a value to the whole on a pie chart.

Data point A numeric value that describes a single value in a chart or worksheet.

Data redundancy The unnecessary storing of duplicate data in two or more tables.

Data series A group of related data points that display in row(s) or column(s) in a worksheet.

Data source A list of information that is merged with a main document during a mail merge procedure.

Data structure The organization method used to manage multiple data points within a dataset.

Data table A grid that contains the data source values and labels to plot data in a chart. A data table may be placed below a chart or hidden from view.

Data type Determines the type of data that can be entered and the operations that can be performed on that data.

Database A collection of data organized as meaningful information that can be accessed, managed, stored, queried, sorted, and reported.

Database Management System (DBMS) A software system that provides the tools needed to create, maintain, and use a database.

Database Splitter A utility that puts the tables in one file (the back-end database), and the queries, forms, and reports in a second file (the front-end database).

Datasheet view A grid containing fields (columns) and records (rows) used to view, add, edit, and delete records.

Deck A collection of slides.

Design view A view which gives users a detailed view of the table's structure and is used to create and modify a table's design by specifying the fields it will contain, the fields' data types, and their associated properties.

Desktop The primary working area of Windows 10 that contains objects such as windows and icons.

Dialog box A box that provides access to more precise, but less frequently used, commands.

Dialog Box Launcher A button that when clicked opens a corresponding dialog box.

Disk Cleanup An administrative tool in Windows that is used to remove unnecessary files from the computer.

Distribute To divide or evenly spread selected shapes over a given area.

Document Inspector Checks for and removes certain hidden and personal information from a document.

Document properties Data elements that identify a document, such as author or comments.

Document theme A set of coordinating fonts, colors, and special effects that gives a stylish and professional look.

Draft view View that shows a great deal of document space, but no margins, headers, footers, or other special features.

Effects gallery A range of special effects for shapes used in the presentation.

Embed A method of storing an object from an external source within a presentation.

Endnote A citation that appears at the end of a document.

Enhanced ScreenTip A small message box that displays when you place the pointer over a command button. The purpose of the command, short descriptive text, or a keyboard shortcut if applicable will display in the box.

Enter An icon between the Name Box and Formula Bar. When you enter or edit data, click Enter to accept data typed in the active cell and keep the current cell active. Enter changes from gray to blue when you position the pointer over it.

Error bars Visual that indicates the standard error amount, a percentage, or a standard deviation for a data point or marker in a chart.

Excel An application that makes it easy to organize records, financial transactions, and business information in the form of worksheets.

Expanded outline An Outline view that displays the slide number, icon, title, and content of each slide in the Outline view.

Exploded pie chart A chart type in which one or more pie slices are separated from the rest of the pie chart for emphasis.

Expression A combination of elements that produce a value.

Expression Builder An Access tool that helps you create more complicated expressions.

Eyedropper tool A tool used to recreate an exact color.

Field The smallest data element contained in a table, such as first name, last name, address, and phone number.

Field property A characteristic of a field that determines how it will look and behave.

File Explorer The Windows app that is used to create folders and manage files and folders across various storage locations.

File History A utility in Windows that continuously makes copies of your important files so that you can recover them if you encounter a file problem.

File management The means of providing an organizational structure to file and folders.

Fill color The background color that displays behind the data in a cell so that the data stands out.

Fill handle A small green square at the bottom-right corner of the active cell. You can position the pointer on the fill handle and drag it to repeat the contents of the cell to other cells or to copy a formula in the active cell to adjacent cells down the column or across the row.

Filter A feature which allows users to specify conditions to display only those records that meet those conditions.

Filter By Form A more versatile method of selecting data, enabling users to display records based on multiple criteria.

Filtering The process of specifying conditions to display only those records that meet those conditions.

Firewall A software program included in Windows 10 that helps to protect against unauthorized access, or hacking, to your computer.

First line indent Marks the location to indent only the first line in a paragraph.

Flash Fill A feature that fills in data or values automatically based on one or two examples you enter using another part of data entered in a previous column in the dataset.

Flip To reverse the direction an object faces.

Flow chart An illustration showing the sequence of a project or plan containing steps.

Font A combination of typeface and type style.

Fonts gallery A gallery that pairs a title font with a body font.

Footer Information that displays at the bottom of a document page.

Footnote A citation that appears at the bottom of a page.

Foreground The portion of the picture that is kept when removing the background of a picture.

Foreign key A field in a related table that is the primary key of another table.

Form A database object that is used to add data into or edit data in a table.

Form letter A letter with standard information that you personalize with recipient information, which you might print or email to many people.

Form tool A tool used to create data entry forms for customers, employees, products, and other tables.

Form view A view that provides a simplified user interface primarily used for data entry; does not allow you to make changes to the layout.

Format Painter A feature that enables you to quickly and easily copy all formatting from one area to another in Word, PowerPoint, and Excel.

Formatting The process of modifying text by changing font and paragraph characteristics.

Formula A combination of cell references, operators, values, and/or functions used to perform a calculation.

Formula AutoComplete A feature that displays a list of functions and defined names that match letters as you type a formula.

Formula Bar An element located below the Ribbon and to the right of the Insert Function command. It shows the contents of the active cell. You enter or edit cell contents in the Formula Bar for the active cell.

Freeform shape A shape that combines both curved and straight-line segments.

Freezing The process of keeping rows and/or columns visible onscreen at all times even when you scroll through a large dataset.

Fully qualified structured reference A structured formula that contains the table name.

Function A predefined computation that simplifies creating a complex calculation and produces a result based on inputs known as arguments.

Function ScreenTip A small pop-up description that displays the function's arguments.

Gallery An area in Word which provides additional text styles. In Excel, the gallery provides a choice of chart styles, and in Power Point, the gallery provides transitions.

Gradient fill A fill that contains a blend of two or more colors or shades.

Grid Intersecting lines on a slide that enable you to align objects.

Gridline A horizontal or vertical line that extends from the horizontal or vertical axis through the plot area to guide the reader's eyes across the chart to identify values.

Group A subset of a tab that organizes similar tasks together.

Group (PowerPoint) Multiple objects connected so they are able to move as though they are a single object.

Grouping A method of summarizing data by the values of a field.

Guide A nonprinting, temporary vertical or horizontal line placed on a slide to enable you align objects or determine regions of the slide.

Hanging indent Aligns the first line of a paragraph at the left margin, indenting remaining lines in the paragraph.

Header An area with one or more lines of information at the top of each page.

Header row The first row in a data source, which contains labels describing the data in rows beneath.

Hierarchy A method used to organize text into levels of importance in a structure.

Histogram A chart that is similar to a column chart. The category axis shows bin ranges (intervals) where data is aggregated into bins, and the vertical axis shows frequencies.

HLOOKUP function A function that looks for a value in the top row of a specified table array and returns another value located in the same column from a specified row.

Horizontal alignment The placement of cell data between the left and right cell margins. By default, text is left-aligned, and values are right-aligned.

Icon A graphical link to a program, file, folder, or other item related to your computer.

Icon set Symbols or signs that classify data into three, four, or five categories, based on values in a range.

IF function A predefined formula that evaluates a condition and returns one value if the condition is true and a different value if the condition is false.

Indent A format that offsets data from its default alignment. For example, if text is left-aligned, the text may be indented or offset from the left side to stand out. If a value is right-aligned, it can be indented or offset from the right side of the cell.

Index An alphabetical listing of topics covered in a document, along with the page numbers on which the topic is discussed.

Infographic Informational graphic that is a visual representation of data or knowledge.

Infringement of copyright A situation that occurs when a right of the copyright owner is violated.

Input area A range of cells in a worksheet used to store and change the variables used in calculations.

Insert control An indicator that displays between rows or columns in a table; click the indicator to insert one or more rows or columns.

Insert Function An icon between the Name Box and Formula Bar. Click Insert Function to open the Insertion Function dialog box to search for and insert a particular function.

Insertion point Blinking bar that indicates where text that you next type will appear.

Insights A pane that presents outside resources, such as images, definitions, and other references.

Jump List List of program-specific shortcuts to recently opened files, the program name, an option to pin or unpin the program, and a close window option.

Justified alignment Spreads text evenly between the left and right margins, so that text begins at the left margin and ends uniformly at the right margin.

Kelvin The unit of measurement for absolute temperature used to measure the tone of an image.

Label Wizard A feature that enables you to easily create mailing labels, name tags, and other specialized tags.

Landscape orientation A document layout when a page is wider than it is tall.

Layout Determines the position of the objects or content on a slide.

Layout control A tool that provides guides to help keep controls aligned horizontally and vertically and give your form a uniform appearance.

Layout view A view that enables users to make changes to a layout while viewing the data in the form or report.

Left alignment Begins text evenly at the left margin, with a ragged right edge.

Left indent A setting that positions all text in a paragraph an equal distance from the left margin.

Legend A key that identifies the color, gradient, picture, texture, or pattern assigned to each data series in a chart.

Line chart A chart type that displays lines connecting data points to show trends over equal time periods, such as months, quarters, years, or decades.

Line spacing The vertical spacing between lines in a paragraph.

Line weight The width or thickness of a shape's outline.

Link A connection from the presentation to another location such as a storage device or website.

Live Layout Feature that enables you to watch text flow around an object as you move it, so you can position the object exactly as you want it.

Live Preview An Office feature that provides a preview of the results of a selection when you point to an option in a list or gallery. Using Live Preview, you can experiment with settings before making a final choice.

Lock Drawing Mode Enables the creation of multiple shapes of the same type.

Logical test An expression that evaluates to true or false.

Lookup table A range that contains data for the basis of the lookup and data to be retrieved.

Lookup value The cell reference of the cell that contains the value to look up.

Macro A stored series of commands that carry out an action; often used to automate simple tasks.

Mail Merge A process that combines content from a main document and a data source.

Main document A document that contains the information that stays the same for all recipients in a mail merge.

Margin The area of blank space that displays to the left, right, top, and bottom of a document or worksheet.

Markup A feature to help customize how tracked changes are displayed in a document.

Marquee A selection of multiple objects created by dragging a rectangle around all of the objects you want to select.

Master A slide view where the control of the layouts, background designs, and color combinations for handouts, notes pages, and slides can be set giving a presentation a consistent appearance.

Master List A database of all citation sources created in Word on a particular computer.

MAX function A predefined formula that identifies the highest value in a range.

MEDIAN function A predefined formula that identifies the midpoint value in a set of values.

Merge field An item that serves as a placeholder for the variable data that will be inserted into the main document during a mail merge procedure.

Microsoft Office A productivity software suite including a set of software applications, each one specializing in a particular type of output.

Microsoft Word A word processing software application used to produce all sorts of documents, including memos, newsletters, forms, tables, and brochures.

MIN function A predefined formula that displays the lowest value in a range.

Mini toolbar A toolbar that provides access to the most common formatting selections, such as adding bold or italic, or changing font type or color. Unlike the Quick Access Toolbar, the Mini toolbar is not customizable.

Mixed cell reference A designation that combines an absolute cell reference with a relative cell reference. The absolute part does not change but the relative part does when you copy the formula.

MLA (Modern Language Association) A writing style established by the Modern Language Association, with rules and conventions for preparing research papers (used primarily in the area of humanities).

Module An advanced object written using the VBA (Visual Basic for Applications) programming language.

Multimedia Various forms of media used to entertain or inform an audience.

Multiple Items form A form that displays multiple records in a tabular layout similar to a table's Datasheet view, with more customization options than a datasheet.

Multitable query Results contain fields from two or more tables, enabling you to take advantage of the relationships that have been set in your database.

Name Box An element located below the Ribbon, which displays the address of the active cell.

Narration Spoken commentary that is added to a presentation.

Navigation Pane An Access interface element that organizes and lists the objects in an Access database.

Nested function A function that contains another function embedded inside one or more of it's arguments.

New sheet An icon that, when clicked, inserts a new worksheet in the workbook.

Nonadjacent range A collection of multiple ranges (such as D5:D10 and F5:F10) that are not positioned in a contiguous cluster in an Excel worksheet.

Normal view (Excel) The default view of a worksheet that shows worksheet data but not margins, headers, footers, or page breaks.

Normal view (PowerPoint) The default PowerPoint workspace.

Notes Page view Used for entering and editing large amounts of text to which the speaker can refer when presenting.

Notification area An area on the far right of the taskbar, that includes the clock and a group of icons that relate to the status of a setting or program.

NOW function A predefined formula that calculates the current date and military time that you last opened the workbook using the computer's clock.

Nper Total number of payment periods.

Null The term Access uses to describe a blank field value.

Number format A setting that controls how a value appears in a cell.

Numbered list Sequences items in a list by displaying a successive number beside each item.

Object An item, such as a picture or text box, that can be individually selected and manipulated in a document.

Object (Access) A component created and used to make the database function (such as a table, query, form, or report).

One-to-many relationship When the primary key value in the primary table can match many of the foreign key values in the related table.

OneDrive Microsoft's cloud storage system. Saving files to OneDrive enables them to sync across all Windows devices and to be accessible from any Internet-connected device.

Opaque A solid fill, one with no transparency.

OR condition In a query, returns records meeting any of the specified criteria.

Order of operations A rule that controls the sequence in which arithmetic operations are performed. Also called the *order of precedence*.

Outline A method of organizing text in a hierarchy to depict relationships.

Outline view A structural view of a document that can be collapsed or expanded as necessary.

Outline view (PowerPoint) A view showing the presentation in an outline format displayed in levels according to the points and any subpoints on each slide.

Output area The range of cells in an Excel worksheet that contain formulas dependent on the values in the input area.

Page break An indication of where data will start on another printed page.

Page Break Preview A view setting that displays the worksheet data and page breaks within the worksheet.

Page Layout view A view setting that displays the worksheet data, margins, headers, and footers.

Paragraph spacing The amount of space before or after a paragraph.

Paste A command used to place a cut or copied selection into another location.

Paste Options button An icon that displays in the bottom-right corner immediately after using the Paste command. It enables the user to apply different paste options.

PDF (Portable Document Format) A file type that was created for exchanging documents independent of software applications and operating system environments.

PDF Reflow A Word feature that converts a PDF document into an editable Word document.

Percent Style A number format that displays a value as if it was multiplied by 100 and with the % symbol. The default number of decimal places is zero if you click Percent Style in the Number group or two decimal places if you use the Format Cells dialog box.

Photo Album A presentation containing multiple pictures organized into album pages.

Picture A graphic file that is retrieved from storage media or the Internet and placed in an Office project.

Picture fill Inserts an image from a file into a shape.

Pie chart A chart type that shows each data point in proportion to the whole data series as a slice in a circle. A pie chart depicts only one data series.

Pin A process to add a tile to the Start menu or icon to the taskbar.

Placeholder A container that holds text, images, graphs, or other objects to be used in a presentation.

Plagiarizing The act of using and documenting the works of another as one's own.

Plain text format (.txt) A file format that retains only text but no formatting when you transfer documents between applications or platforms.

Plot area The region of a chart containing the graphical representation of the values in one or more data series. Two axes form a border around the plot area.

Pmt function A function that calculates the periodic loan payment given a fixed rate, number of periods (also known as term), and the present value of the loan (the principal).

Point The smallest unit of measurement used in typography, 1/72 of an inch.

Pointing The process of using the pointer to select cells while building a formula. Also known as *semi-selection*.

Portable Document Format (PDF) A file type that was created for exchanging documents independent of software applications and operating system environment.

Portrait orientation A document layout when a page is taller than it is wide.

Poster Frame The image that displays on a slide when a video is not playing.

PowerPoint An application that enables you to create dynamic presentations to inform groups and persuade audiences.

PowerPoint presentation An electronic slide show that can be edited or delivered in a variety of ways.

PowerPoint show An unchangeable electronic slide show format used for distribution.

Presenter view Specialty view that delivers a presentation on two monitors simultaneously.

Primary key The field (or combination of fields) that uniquely identifies each record in a table.

Print area The range of cells within a worksheet that will print.

Print Layout view View that closely resembles the way a document will look when printed.

Print order The sequence in which the pages are printed.

Print Preview A view that enables you to see exactly what the report will look like when it is printed.

Property Sheet The location where you change settings such as number format and number of decimal places.

Public domain The rights to a literary work or property owned by the public at large.

PV A predefined formula that calculates the present value of a loan.

Query A question about the data stored in a database answers provided in a datasheet.

Quick access A component of File Explorer that contains shortcuts to the most frequently used folders. Folders can be pinned and removed from Quick access.

Quick Access Toolbar A toolbar located at the top-left corner of any Office application window, this provides fast access to commonly executed tasks such as saving a file and undoing recent actions.

Quick Analysis A set of analytical tools you can use to apply formatting, create charts or tables, and insert basic functions.

Quick Style A combination of formatting options that can be applied to a shape or graphic.

Radar chart A chart type that compares aggregate values of three or more variables represented on axes starting from the same point.

Range A group of adjacent or contiguous cells in a worksheet. A range can be adjacent cells in a column (such as C5:C10), in a row (such as A6:H6), or a rectangular group of cells (such as G5:H10).

Range_lookup An argument that determines how the VLOOKUP and HLOOKUP function handle lookup values that are not an exact match for the data in the lookup table.

Rate The periodic interest rate; the percentage of interest paid for each payment period; the first argument in the PMT function.

Read Mode View in which text reflows automatically between columns to make it easier to read.

Reading View Displays the slide show full screen, one slide at a time, complete with animations and transitions.

Real Time Typing A Word feature that shows where co-authors are working, and what their contributions are as they type.

Real-time co-authoring A Word feature that shows several authors simultaneously editing the document in Word or Word Online.

Recolor The process of changing a picture by adjusting the image's colors.

Record A group of related fields representing one entity, such as data for one person, place, event, or concept.

Record source The table or query that supplies the records for a form or report.

Recycle Bin Temporary storage for files deleted from the computer's hard drive or OneDrive.

Referential Integrity Rules in a database that are used to preserve relationships between tables when records are changed.

Relationship A connection between two tables using a common field.

Relative cell reference A designation that indicates a cell's relative location from the original cell containing the formula; the cell reference changes when the formula is copied.

Report A database document that outputs meaningful, professional-looking, formatted information from underlying tables or queries.

Report tool A tool used to instantly create a tabular report based on the table or query currently selected.

Report view A view that enables you to determine what a printed report will look like in a continuous onscreen page layout.

Report Wizard A feature that prompts you for input and then uses your answers to generate a customized report.

Resource Monitor A feature that displays how the computer is using its key resources such as the CPU and RAM.

Revision mark Markings that indicate where text is added, deleted, or formatted while the Track Changes feature is active.

Ribbon The command center of Office applications. It is the long bar located just beneath the title bar, containing tabs, groups, and commands.

Rich Text Format (.rtf) A file format that retains structure and most text formatting when transferring documents between applications or platforms.

Right alignment Begins text evenly at the right margin, with a ragged left edge.

Right indent A setting that positions all text in a paragraph an equal distance from the right margin.

Rotate To move an object around its axis.

Row heading A number to the left side of a row in a worksheet. For example, 3 is the row heading for the third row.

Row height The vertical measurement of the row in a worksheet.

Sans serif font A font that does not contain a thin line or extension at the top and bottom of the primary strokes on characters.

Saturation A characteristic of color that controls its intensity.

Search box A feature located on the taskbar. Combined with Cortana, or used alone, it provides a convenient way to search your computer or the Web.

Section A division to presentation content that groups slides meaningfully.

Section break An indicator that divides a document into parts, enabling different formatting for each section.

Select All The triangle at the intersection of the row and column headings in the top-left corner of the worksheet. Click it to select everything contained in the active worksheet.

Selection Filter A method of selecting that displays only the records that match a criterion you select.

Selection net A selection of multiple objects created by dragging a rectangle around all of the objects you wish to select.

Selection pane A pane designed to help select objects.

Semi-selection The process of using the pointer to select cells while building a formula. Also known as *pointing*.

Serif font A font that contains a thin line or extension at the top and bottom of the primary strokes on characters.

Shading A background color that appears behind text in a paragraph, page, or table element.

Shape A geometric or non-geometric object, such as a rectangle or an arrow, used to create an illustration or highlight information.

Sharpening A technique that enhances the edges of the content in a picture to make the boundaries more prominent.

Sheet tab A visual label that looks like a file folder tab. In Excel, a sheet tab shows the name of a worksheet contained in the workbook.

Sheet tab navigation Visual elements that help you navigate to the first, previous, next, or last sheet within a workbook.

Shortcut An icon on the desktop designated with a small arrow in the bottom-left corner, that provides a link a program.

Shortcut menu A menu that provides choices related to the selection or area at which you right-click.

Simple Markup A Word feature that simplifies the display of comments and revision marks, resulting in a clean, uncluttered look.

Simple Query Wizard Provides a step-by-step guide to help you through the query design process.

Sizing handle A series of faint dots on the outside border of a selected object; enables the user to adjust the height and width of the object.

Sizing handles (Excel) Eight circles that display on the outside border of a chart—one on each corner and one on each middle side—when the chart is selected; enables the user to adjust the height and width of the chart.

Sleep A power saving state that puts work and settings in memory and draws a small amount of power to allow the computer to resume full-power operation quickly.

Slide The most basic element of PowerPoint, similar to a page in Word.

Slide master The top slide in a hierarchy of slides based on the master.

Slide show A series of slides displayed onscreen for an audience.

Slide Show view Displays the completed presentation full screen to an audience as an electronic presentation.

Slide Sorter view Displays thumbnails of presentation slides enabling a view of multiple slides.

Slide pane The main workspace in PowerPoint, that displays the currently selected slide.

Slides pane Pane on the left side of Normal view that shows the slide deck with thumbnails.

Smart Lookup A feature that provides information about tasks or commands in Office, and can also be used to search for general information on a topic such as *President George Washington*.

SmartArt A diagram that presents information visually to effectively communicate a message.

SmartGuide A guide that displays when an object is moved that helps align objects in relation to other objects.

Snip A screenshot taken with the Snipping Tool accessory application in Windows.

Softening A technique that blurs the edges of the content in a picture to make the boundaries less prominent.

Sort A feature which lists records in a specific sequence.

Sorting The process of arranging records by the value of one or more fields within a table or data range.

Source A publication, person, or media item that is consulted in the preparation of a paper and given credit.

Sparkline A small line, column, or win/loss chart contained in a single cell to provide a simple visual illustrating one data series.

Split form A form that combines two views of the same record source—one section is displayed in a stacked layout and the other section is displayed in a tabular layout.

Spreadsheet An electronic file that contains a grid of columns and rows used to organize related data and to display results of calculations, enabling interpretation of quantitative data for decision making.

Stacked column chart A chart type that places stacks of data in segments on top of each other in one column, with each category in the data series represented by a different color.

Stacked layout A layout that displays fields in a vertical column.

Stacking order The order of objects placed on top of one another.

Start menu A feature that provides the main access to all programs on your computer.

Status bar A bar located at the bottom of the program window that contains information relative to the open file. It also includes tools for changing the view of the file and for changing the zoom size of onscreen file contents.

Status bar (Excel) The row at the bottom of the Excel window that displays instructions and other details about the status of a worksheet.

Stock chart A chart type that shows fluctuation in stock prices.

Storyboard A visual plan of a presentation that displays the content of each slide in the slide show.

Structured reference A tag or use of a table element, such as a field label, as a reference in a formula. Field labels are enclosed in square brackets, such as [Amount] within the formula.

Style A named collection of formatting characteristics that can be applied to text or paragraphs.

Style manual A guide to a particular writing style outlining required rules and conventions related to the preparation of papers.

Style set A combination of title, heading, and paragraph styles that can be used to format all of those elements in a document at one time.

SUBTOTAL function A predefined formula that calculates an aggregate value, such as totals, for displayed values in a range, a table, or a database.

SUM function A predefined formula that calculates the total of values contained in one or more cells.

Surface chart A chart type that displays trends using two dimensions on a continuous curve.

Symbol A character or graphic not normally included on a keyboard.

Syntax A set of rules that governs the structure and components for properly entering a function.

Tab Located on the Ribbon, each tab is designed to appear much like a tab on a file folder, with the active tab highlighted.

Tab stop A marker that specifies the position for aligning text in a column arrangement, often including a dot leader.

Table (Access) The location where all data is stored in a database; organizes data into columns and rows.

Table (Excel) A structured range that contains related data organized in a method that increases the capability to manage and analyze information.

Table alignment The horizontal position of a table between the left and right margins.

Table array The range that contains the lookup table.

Table of contents A page that lists headings in the order in which they appear in a document and the page numbers on which the entries begin.

Table style A named collection of color, font, and border designs that can be applied to a table.

Tabular layout A layout that displays fields horizontally.

Task Manager A tool that displays the programs and processes that are running on your computer. It is also used to close a non-responding program.

Task pane A window of options to format and customize chart elements. The task pane name and options change based on the selected chart element.

Task view A button on the taskbar that enables the user to view thumbnail previews of all open tasks in one glance.

Taskbar The horizontal bar at the bottom of the desktop that displays open applications, the Notification area, the Search box, and pinned apps or programs.

***Tell me what you want to do* box** Located to the right of the last tab, this box enables you to search for help and information about a command or task you want to perform and also presents you with a shortcut directly to that command.

Template A predesigned file that incorporates formatting elements, such as a theme and layouts, and may include content that can be modified.

Template (Access) A predefined database that includes professionally designed tables, forms, reports, and other objects that you can use to jumpstart the creation of your database.

Text Any combination of letters, numbers, symbols, and spaces not used in Excel calculations.

Text box A graphical object that contains text.

Text box (PowerPoint) An object that provides space for text anywhere on a slide; it can be formatted with a border, shading, and other characteristics.

Text pane A pane for text entry used for a SmartArt diagram.

Texture fill Inserts a texture such as canvas, denim, marble, or cork into a shape.

Theme A collection of design choices that includes colors, fonts, and special effects used to give a consistent look to a document, workbook, presentation, or database form or report.

Thesaurus A tool used to quickly find a synonym (a word with the same meaning as another).

Thumbnail A miniature view of a slide that appears in the Slidespane and Slide Sorter view.

Tile A rectangular icon on the Start menu that allow you to access programs and apps.

Title bar The long bar at the top of each window that displays the name of the folder, file, or program displayed in the open window and the application in which you are working.

TODAY function A predefined formula that displays the current date.

Toggle commands A button that acts somewhat like light switches that you can turn on and off. You select the command to turn it on, then select it again to turn it off.

Tone A characteristic of lighting that controls the temperature of a color. See also *Kelvin*.

Total row (Access) A method to display aggregate function results as the last row in Datasheet view of a table or query.

Total row (Excel) A table row that appears below the last row of records in an Excel table and displays summary or aggregate statistics, such as a sum or an average.

Totals query A way to display aggregate data when a query is run.

Track Changes A word feature that monitors all additions, deletions, and formatting changes you make in a document.

Transition A specific animation that is applied as na previous slide is repladed by a new slide while displayed in Slide Show view or Reading view.

Transparency The visibility of fill.

Trendline A line that depicts trends or helps forecast future data in a chart. For example, if the plotted data includes 2005, 2010, and 2015, a trendline can help forecast values for 2020 and beyond.

Ungroup To break a combined grouped object into individual objects.

Unqualified reference The use of field headings without row references in a structured formula.

Value A number that represents a quantity or a measurable amount.

Value axis The chart axis that displays incremental numbers to identify approximate values, such as dollars or units, of data points in a chart.

Variant A variation on a chosen design theme.

Vector graphic An image created by a mathematical statement.

Vertex The point where a curve ends or the point where two line segments meet in a shape.

Vertical alignment The placement of cell data between the top and bottom cell margins.

View The various ways a file can appear on the screen.

View controls Icons on the right side of the status bar that enable you to change to Normal, Page Layout, or Page Break view to display the worksheet.

Virtual desktop A way to organize and access groups of windows for different purposes.

VLOOKUP function A predefined formula that accepts a value, looks the value up in a vertical lookup table with data organized in columns, and returns a result.

Watermark Text or graphics that display behind text.

Web Layout view View that displays the way a document will look when posted on the Internet.

Wildcard A special character that can represent one or more characters in the criterion of a query.

Windows app A program that displays full screen without any borders or many controls. It is designed to be best viewed and used on smaller screens such as those on smartphone and tablets.

Windows Defender Antispyware and antivirus software included in Windows 10.

Windows Update A utility in Windows that provides a means to initiate updates and modifications pushed to the user that enhances Windows security or fixes problems.

Word An application that can produce all sorts of documents, including memos, newsletters, forms, tables, and brochures.

Word Online An online component of Office Online, it is a Web-based version of Word with sufficient capabilities to enable you to edit and format a document online.

Word processing software A computer application, such as Microsoft Word, used primarily with text to create, edit, and format documents.

Word wrap The feature that automatically moves words to the next line if they do not fit on the current line.

WordArt A feature that modifies text to include special effects, such as color, shadow, gradient, and 3-D appearance.

Workbook A collection of one or more related worksheets contained within a single file.

Works Cited A list of works cited or consulted by an author in his or her work; the list is titled Works Cited.

Worksheet A single spreadsheet that typically contains descriptive labels, numeric values, formulas, functions, and graphical representations of data.

Wrap text An Excel feature that makes data appear on multiple lines by adjusting the row height to fit the cell contents within the column width.

Writing style Writing a paper as directed by a style manual such as MLA or APA.

X Y (scatter) chart A chart type that shows a relationship between two variables using their X and Y coordinates. Excel plots one coordinate on the horizontal X-axis and the other variable on the vertical Y-axis. Scatter charts are often used to represent data in education, scientific, and medical experiments.

X-axis The horizontal border that provides a frame of reference for measuring data left to right on a chart.

Y-axis The vertical border that provides a frame of reference for measuring data up and down on a chart.

Zoom control A control that enables you to increase or decrease the size of the worksheet data onscreen.

Zoom slider A feature that displays at the far right side of the status bar. It is used to increase or decrease the magnification of the file.

Index

[ ] brackets, 498
= (equal sign), 418
 logical operator, 509
(pound signs), 431

A

absolute cell references, 489–490
 input area and, 489
ACCDE. *See* Access Database Executable
 (ACCDE)
accept Track Changes, 357–358
Access 2016, 66. *See also* database(s);
 form(s); queries; report(s); table(s)
 Database Tools tab, 672
 defined, 664
 External Data tab, 671–672
 fields, 668
 form, 669
 Form tools, 864–873
 macro object, 671
 module object, 671
 primary key, 668
 queries. *See* queries
 record, 668
 report, 670
 tables, 668
 template, 707
Access Database Executable (ACCDE), 667
accessibility compliance, 567
Accounting Number Format, 448, 449
Action Center, 40–42
active cell, 406
active voice, 941
adding
 animations, 957
 audio, 1158–1160
 axis title, 560–562
 captions, 996
 chart elements, 559–568
 data labels, 563–564
 fields, 612, 874–875
 field to report, 899–900
 gridlines, 566
 images by File Explorer, 1120
 pictures, 996
 records, 613
 records to desktop database,
 710–711
 records to table, 680–682
 sounds, 957
 split form, 872, 873
 subform, 870
 tables in presentations, 953
 transitions, 957
 videos, 1145–1149

add-ins, installing, 79–80
Add-Ins tab, 927
adjustment handle, 1045
Adobe Flash Media, 1145
Adobe Photoshop, 1119
aggregate functions, 837–844
 creating, 838–844
 and datasheets, 837–838
 defined, 837
alignment
 center, 206
 defined, 445
 guides, 241
 horizontal cell alignment, 446
 justified, 206
 left, 206
 objects, 1091–1094
 options, 445
 paragraph, 206–207
 picture, 239–241
 right, 206
 tables, 276–277
 vertical cell alignment, 446
 worksheets and, 444–445
AND condition, 774
Animation Painter feature, 957
animations
 adding, 957
 in presentations, 955–957
annotating slide shows, 967
APA (American Psychological
 Association), 335
application part
 databases, 711–712
application software, 4
area chart, 548
arguments
 combining, 290
 defined, 289, 495, 828
 logical test, 509
 nest functions as, 499, 510
 value_if_false, 509–510
 value_if_true, 509–510
arranging
 objects, 1089–1094
arrows
 move down one cell, 407
 move left one cell, 407
 move right one cell, 407
 move up one cell, 407
artistic effects, of pictures, 1128
audio
 adding, 1158–1160
 animating sequence, 1160–1161
 hiding sound icon, 1159
 inserting from file, 1158–1159

 playing sound over multiple slides,
 1161–1162
 recording, 1159–1160
 settings, 1160–1162
AutoComplete, 409
 Formula AutoComplete, 495
Auto Fill, 409
 worksheets, 409–411
AutoRecover, 176
AVERAGE function, 499
axes
 formatting, 562–563
 X-, 535
 Y-axis, 535
axis title, 558
 adding, 560–562
 formatting, 560–562
 linking to cell, 560
 positioning, 560–562

B

backgrounds
 creation from pictures, 1131–1133
 forms, 879
 picture, removing, 1121–1123
 removing, 242
 in worksheets, 458
Background Styles gallery, 1021
Backstage view, 104–106
 customizing application
 options, 105
back up databases, 683–684
bar chart, 542–543
bibliography
 defined, 338
 research papers, 338–340
bitmap images, 1118
blank desktop database, 708
blog
 defined, 374
bold argument names, 496
bookmarks
 videos, 1152
Border Painter, 292
borders
 cells, 447
 defined, 212, 291
 paragraph, 212–213
 sampler, 294
 tables, document, 291–294
brackets [ ], 498
breakpoint, 513
brightness
 of pictures, 1124, 1167
built-in functions, 828–831

bulleted lists, 213–215
business documents
    fonts for, 202

C

calculated field/result
    common errors, 817–818
    defined, 812
    queries, 812–816
    totals query, 842–843
    verifying, 819
callout
    defined, 1045
Cancel icon, 405
captions
    adding, 996
    defined, 295
    Photo Album, 1167
    tables, document, 295–296
Cascade Delete Related Records, 756
Cascade Update Related Fields, 756
category axis, 535
cell references
    absolute, 489–490
    in formulas, 417–418, 488–491
    mixed, 490
    relative, 488
    toggle between relative, absolute, mixed
        cell references (F4), 491
cells, 406
    active, 406
    address, 406
    borders, 447
    chart title linking to, 560
    clearing contents, 412
    defined, 270, 406
    deleting, 273, 428–429
    displaying formulas in, 420–421
    editing contents, 412
    Format Cells dialog box, 445, 449
    horizontal alignment, 446
    indenting contents, 446–447
    inserting, 427–428
    line break in, 446
    linking to axis title, 560
    merge options, 445–446
    merging, 273–274
    number formats, 447–449
    rotate data, 446
    splitting, 273–274
    unmerge, 445
    vertical alignment, 446
    wrap text feature, 446
cell style, 444
center alignment, 206
chart area, 535
    formatting, 566
chart elements, 558–568
    adding, 559–568
    axis title, 558
    chart title, 558
    data label, 558

data table, 558
    defined, 558
    editing, 559–568
    error bars, 558
    formatting, 559–568
    gridlines, 558
    images/textures, 567
    legend, 558
    removing, 562
    trendline, 558
chart filter, 575–576
chart(s)
    area, 548
    bar, 542–543
    basics, 534–535
    changing, 543
    clustered column, 539–540
    column, 538–542
    combo, 545
    data source, 534–535
    defined, 534
    design, 574–579
    elements, 535
    histogram, 548
    Insert tab, 537
    line, 543–544
    moving, 548–549
    100% stacked column, 542
    pie, 544–545
    printing, 550–551
    and Quick Analysis Tools, 536
    radar, 548
    recommended *vs.* List of All, 538
    sizing, 549–550
    sparklines, 574–579
    stacked column, 540–541
    stock, 546–547
    surface, 548
    types, 536–548
    X Y (scatter), 546
chart styles
    and colors, 574–575
    defined, 574
    selecting, 575
chart title, 558
    editing, 559–560
    formatting, 559–560
    linking to cell, 560
    positioning, 559–560
checking spelling and grammar, 94–96
Chicago Manual of Style, 335
citations
    defined, 335
    editing, 337
    research papers, 335–337
    versus footnotes, 341
Clipboard, 92–94
closed shape
    creating, 1048
cloud storage, 67
clustered column chart, 539–540
codec (coder/decoder) software, 1145
collaborating documents, 374–376

collapsed outline, 1004
colors
    changing in pictures, 1125–1127
    and chart style, 574–575
    dialog box, 1054
    fill color, worksheets, 447
    font, 559
    matching, fonts, 206
    SmartArt, 1070
    worksheet tabs, 455
color scales, 642
Colors gallery, 1021
column charts, 538–542
    clustered, 539–540
    100% stacked, 542
    stacked, 540–541
column index number, 511
columns, 406
    defined, 225
    deleting, 272–273, 428–429
    formatting text into, 225
    freezing, 599–600
    headings, 405
    hiding, 429–430
    inserting, 272–273, 427–428
    labels, 535
    management, 427–432
    printing column headings, 463
    repeating, 463
    switch data, 576–577
    transposing, 437
    unhiding, 429–430
column widths
    and document table, 274–275
    in forms, 874
    in reports, 900
    worksheets, 431
combo chart, 545
Comma Style,
    number format, 448, 449
commands
    defined, 72
    toggle, 89
comment balloon, 353
comments
    adding, in documents, 355
    confirming user name, 355
    defined, 353
    view and reply, 356–357
compact and repair databases, 684–685
comparison operators, 774
compressed (zipped) folder, 34
    extracting files from, 35
compression
    defined, 1118
    lossy *versus* lossless, 1118
Compress Pictures, 1130–1131
conditional formatting, 638–645
    color scales, 642
    creating, 643–645
    data bars, 641
    and filtering, 643
    formulas in, 644–645

Highlight Cells Rules, 639–640
icon sets, 642
manage rules, 645
Quick Analysis, 638–639
and sorting, 643
top/bottom rules, 640–641
connectors, and lines, 1046–1048
constant
  defined, 812
contextual tabs, 71
contrast
  of pictures, 1124, 1167
controls
  defined, 866
  forms, 876–877
  layout control, 866
  reports, 899
  slide shows, 966
copying
  Excel data, to other programs, 437
  files, 34
  before filtering data, 624
  folders, 34
  formulas, 420
  queries, 776–777
  range, 434
  text, 93
  worksheets, 456–457
copyright
  defined, 1134
  infringement of, 1134
correcting pictures, 1123–1125
Cortana, 16
  Notebook and settings, 16–18
COUNTA functions, 500
COUNTBLANK functions, 500
COUNT functions, 500
cover page, 345
creating
  aggregate functions, 838–844
  background, from pictures, 1131–1133
  closed shape, 1048
  conditional formatting, 643–645
  databases, 707–713
  desktop databases by template, 708–
    710
  document, 135–136
  endnotes, 341–342
  Expression Builder, 826–828
  expressions, 813–816
  family album, 1165
  files, 67
  footnotes, 341–342
  formulas, 417–420
  freeform shape, 1048–1050
  lookup table, 512–513
  mail merge documents, 306–310
  multitable queries, 782–783
  narration notes, 1160
  Photo Albums, 1165
  presentations, 939–947
  reports, 889–896
  shapes, 1044–1050

SmartArt, 1066–1069
source, 335–337
sparklines, 577–579
tables, 271–272
tables, worksheets, 610–612
totals query, 839–840
WordArt, 1074
Criteria row, 768
  Query Design view, 768
crop
  defined, 241
cropping
  pictures, 1129–1130
Ctrl+End (move to end), 407
Ctrl+G (display Go To dialog box), 407
Ctrl+Home (move to beginning), 407
Currency, number format, 448
custom filter, 627–628
customizing
  shapes, 1050–1060
  sparklines, 577–579
Custom, number format, 448
custom web app, 707
cutting text, 93

D

data aggregates, and individual values,
  535
data bars, 641
database management system (DBMS),
  664
database(s)
  adding records, 710–711
  adding records to table, 680–682
  application part, 711–712
  back up, 683–684
  blank desktop database, 708
  compact and repair, 684–685
  creating, 707–713
  creating desktop, by template,
    708–710
  custom web app, 707
  Datasheet view, 673
  as data source, mail merge documents,
    309
  defined, 664
  Design view, 675–676
  enabling content, 665–667
  encrypting, 685
  Filter By Form, 697–698
  filters, 695–698
  multiple-table, 749–754
  navigation bar, 673–675
  object types, 667–680
  opening, 665–667
  printing, 685–686
  saving, 665–667
  selection filters, 695–697
  sorting table data, 699–700
  splitting, 685
  utilities, 683–686
  Web app, 712–713

Database Tools tab, 672
data labels, 558
  adding, 563–564
  formatting, 563–564
  pie chart, 565
  positioning, 563–564
data point, 534
  formatting, 567–568
data series, 534
  formatting, 566
datasheets
  and aggregate functions, 837–838
Datasheet view, 673
  modifying data, 680
data source, 306
data structure
  defined, 609
data table, 558
data types
  criteria for queries, 773–776
  defined, 739
date(s)
  date filters, 627
  date functions, 495, 501–502
  Date, number format, 448
  header and footer option, 462
  updating, 502
decimal places, increase/decrease, 449
deck, defined, 926
decrease decimal places, 449
decrease decimal points
  versus ROUND function, 501
deleting
  cell contents, 273
  cells, 428–429
  columns, 428–429
  endnotes, 343
  field from report, 900
  fields, 612, 874–875
  files, 32–33
  folders, 32–33
  footnotes, 343
  records, 613
  rows, 428–429
  tab stops, 211
  worksheets, 455–456
design
  charts, 574–579
  contextual tab, 461–462
  slide shows, 1017–1020
  tables, 734–737
Design view, 869
  databases, 675–676
desktop, 5
  and components, managing and using,
    11–15
  customizing, 11
  identifying components, 9–10
  virtual, 12–13
desktop database
  adding records, 710–711
  blank, 708
  creating, by template, 708–710

dialog boxes
  colors, 1054
  defined, 72
  Format Cells, 445, 449
  Function Arguments, 497
  Insert Function, 496
  Move or Copy, 456
  Open, 68
  Page Setup, 459, 460, 463
  Paste Special, 436
  Show Table, 768
  Show Table, 768
  SmartArt Graphic, 1068
Dialog Box Launcher, 72
Disk Cleanup, 46
displaying options
  task panes, 563
distribute
  defined, 1093
Document Inspector, 177–178
documents
  adding comments, 355
  adjusting margins, 155–156
  appearance, 222–230
  applying theme, 88
  backup options, 176–177
  beginning and editing, 133–142
  business, fonts for, 202
  changing margins, 107
  changing page layout, 107–109
  changing page orientations, 108,
    156–157
  checking spelling and grammar, 94–96
  collaborating, 374–376
  compatibility, 174–176
  copying text, 93
  creating, 135–136
  customizing application options, 105
  cutting text, 93
  editing text, 89–90
  Format Painter, 91–92
  formatting, 222–225
  header and footer, 110–111, 153–155
  inserting pictures and graphics, 96–97
  inserting symbol, 158–159
  inspecting, 177–178
  mail merge, 306–312
  managing page flow, 162–164
  Markup, 353–355
  navigating, 139–140
  OneDrive, 364–370
  online collaboration, 364–381
  online presentation, 376–380
  opening, 139
  opening template, 86–87
  organization, 153–164
  pasting text, 93
  previewing, 111–112
  printing, 111–112, 178–179
  research papers, 334–345
  resizing and format pictures and
    graphics, 96–97
  reviewing, 353–357

  saving, 138–139
  section breaks, 223–224
  selecting text, 88–89
  settings and properties, 172–179
  sharing, 370–374
  tracking changes, 357–359
  using Backstage view, 104–106
  using Mini toolbar, 90–91
  using Office Clipboard, 93–94
  using Page Setup dialog box, 108–109
  view and edit properties, 105–106
  viewing, 106, 160–161
  watermark, 157–158
  Word Online, 368–370
  working with pictures and graphics,
    96–98
  Zoom setting, 161–162
document theme
  defined, 222
  selecting, 222–223
Draft view, 160
drag worksheet tab, 456
drawing
  tables, 271–272
Drawing group, 1045
duplicate rows, 613–614

E

editing
  chart elements, 559–568
  chart title, 559–560
  document, 133–142
  in Outline View presentation, 1003
  records, 613
  source, 337
editing text, 89–90
Effects gallery, 1021
embedded HTML, 374
embed videos, 1145
enabling content
  databases, 665–667
encrypting databases, 685
endnotes
  creating, 341–342
  defined, 340
  deleting, 343
  modifying, 342
  research papers, 340–343
enforce referential integrity, 755–756
Enhanced ScreenTips, 78–79
enhancing presentations, 953–959
enhancing table data, 291–297
Enter icon, 405
equal sign (=), 418
  logical operator, 509
Error bars, 558
Excel 2016, 66. *See also* chart(s);
  worksheet(s)
  columns, rows, and cells, 406
  exploring, 404–407
  window elements, 404–405
expanded outlines, 1004

Expression Builder
  creating, 826–828
  defined, 826
expressions
  creating, 813–816
  defined, 812
  zooming, 816
External Data tab, 671–672
Eyedropper, 1052–1053

F

F5 (Go To dialog box), 407
family album
  creating, 1165
field property, 676
fields
  adding, 874–875
  deleting, 874–875
  forms, 874–875
  and reports, 899–900
field(s), database
  adding, 612
  Cascade Update Related Fields, 756
  defined, 307, 609, 668
  deleting, 612
  sorting, 622–623
File Explorer
  interface, 28–29
  Navigation Pane, 30–31
  and OneDrive, 365–368
  Quick access, 30
  search box in, 30
  using, 28–33
  View tab on Ribbon, 29
File History, 42
file management, 28–35
file name, header and footer option,
  462
file path, header and footer option, 462
files
  compressed (zipped), 34
  copying, 34
  creating, 67
  deleting, 32–33
  extracting from zipped (compressed)
    folder, 35
  inserting audio from, 1158–1159
  moving, 34
  number, 447–449
  opening, 32–33, 68–69
  previewing, 111–112
  printing, 111–112
  renaming, 32–33
  saving, 69–70
  selecting, 33
  sharing in OneDrive, 371
  working with, 32
fill color, worksheets, 447
fill handle, 409
Filter Arrows, 611
Filter By Form, 697–698
filtering

and conditional formatting, 643
custom filter, 627–628
data tables, worksheets, 624–628
date filters, 627
defined, 624
mail merge documents, 310
numbers, 625–626
text, 624–625
filters
databases, 695–698
defined, 695
selection, 695–697
financial functions, 495, 508–515
and negative values, 515
PMT function, 514–515
first line indent, 209
F4 key, 491
Flash Fill, 411
File Explorer
adding images by, 1120
flipping
objects, 1082–1083
flow chart
defined, 1047
folders
compressed (zipped), 34
copying, 34
deleting, 32–33
extracting files from compressed, 35
moving, 34
opening, 32–33
renaming, 32–33
selecting, 33
working with, 32
font color, 559
fonts, 200
for business documents, 202
color matching, 206
defined, 200
options, 200–202
sans serif, 201
serif, 201
Fonts gallery, 1021
footer, inserting, 110–111
footer and header
document, 110–111, 153–155
footnotes
creating, 341–342
defined, 340
deleting, 343
modifying, 342
research papers, 340–343
versus in-text citations, 341
foreground, 1121
Format Cells dialog box, 445, 449
Format Painter, 91–92
Format Painter
styles versus, 228
Format tab
chart tools, 568
formatting, 200
axes, 562–563
axis title, 560–562

chart area, 566
chart elements, 559–568
chart title, 559–560
data labels, 563–564
data point, 567–568
data series, 566
defined, 200
document, 222–225
gridlines, 566
legend, 565
paragraph, 206–215
plot area, 566
queries, 817
speaker notes, 934
tables, 275–278
table text, 277–278
text in text box, 243
text into columns, 225
videos, 1149–1152
worksheets, 408, 444–449
form layout, 877–879
Form Layout Tools tabs, 874
form letter, 306
form(s)
background image, 879
basics, 864–879
column widths in, 874
controls, 876–877
defined, 669, 864
Design view, 869
fields, 874–875
form layout, 877–879
Form tools, 864–873
Form view, 867–869
Layout view, 868
modifying, 873–877
multiple items form, 871–872
properties, 872
record source, 865
sorting records, 879
split form, 870–871
styling, 877
subform, 869–870
themes, 875–876
Form tools, 864–873
record source, 865
usability testing, 865
using, 866
Formula AutoComplete, 495
Formula Bar, 405
formulas
basics, 488–491
cell references in, 417–418,
488–491
in conditional formatting, 644–645
copying, 420
creating, 417–420
creating structured references in,
621–622
defined, 287, 417
displaying, in cells, 420–421
order of operations, 418–419
parentheses in, 419

semi-selection technique, 419
tables, document, 287–289
text in, 510
updating, 289
values in, 418, 511
Form view, 867–869
defined, 867
to edit data, 873
Fraction, number format, 448
freeform shape
creating, 1048–1050
defined, 1048
modifying, 1048–1050
freezing
defined, 599
rows and columns, 599–600
full page slides
printing, 968–969
fully qualified structured reference,
622
Function Arguments dialog box, 497
functions
aggregate, 837–844
AVERAGE, 499
avoiding for basic formulas, 498
built-in, 828–831
categories, 495
COUNT, 500
COUNTA, 500
COUNTBLANK, 500
date, 495, 501–502
defined, 287, 495, 828
financial, 495, 508–515
Function Arguments dialog box,
497
HLOOKUP, 514
IF, 508–510
Insert Function dialog box, 496
inserting, 495–497
logical, 495, 508–515
lookup, 495, 508–515
Math & Trig, 495, 497–501
MAX, 500
MEDIAN, 500
MIN, 500
#NAME?, 497
nest, as arguments, 499, 510
nonadjacent ranges, 500
NOW, 501
PMT, 514–515, 830–831
and Quick Analysis Tools, 501
reference, 495
ROUND, 501
ScreenTip, 496
statistical, 495, 497–501
status bar statistics, 501
SUM, 498–499
tables, document, 289–290
time, 495
TODAY, 501
Trig & Math, 495, 497–501
VLOOKUP, 511–512
function syntax, 498

G

gallery, 73
  Background Styles, 1021
  Colors, 1021
  Effects, 1021
  Fonts, 1021
General, number format, 448
Get External Data—Excel Spreadsheet
    feature, 749–750
GIF. *See* Graphics Interchange File (GIF)
gradient fill, 1055
graphics
  vector, 1118
Graphics Interchange File (GIF), 1118
grid
  defined, 1091
gridlines, 558
  adding, 566
  formatting, 566
  printing, 463
group, 72
grouping
  multiple levels, 842
  totals query, 840–841
group objects, 1084–1087
guides
  defined, 1092

H

handouts
  printing, 969–970
hanging indent, 209
headers and footers
  document, 110–111, 153–155
  Header & Footer Tools Design contextual
    tab, 461–462
  in presentations, 957–959
  worksheets, 460–462
heading rows, 291
heading(s), rows and columns, 405
hierarchy, outlines and, 1002
Highlight Cells Rules, 639–640
histogram chart, 548
HLOOKUP function, 514
horizontal cell alignment, 446
100% stacked column chart, 542

I

icons, 9
icon sets, 642
IF functions, 508–510
images/textures
  adding by File Explorer, 1120
  bitmap, 1118
  chart elements, 567
importing outlines, 1011
importing worksheets, multiple-table
    databases, 749–754
increase decimal places, 449
indents

cell contents, 446–447
  defined, 209
  first line, 209
  hanging, 209
  left, 209
  right, 209
  values, 447
index creation, 344–345
infographics
  defined, 1044
infringement of copyright, 1134
input area
  absolute cell references and, 489
insert control, 272
Insert Function dialog box, 496
Insert Function icon, 405
inserting
  audio, from file, 1158–1159
  functions, 495–497
  logo in reports, 899
  media objects in, 954
  merge fields, 311
  Photo Album captions, 1167
  picture, 238–239
  pictures, 1118–1120
  screenshot, 239
  sparklines, 578
  spreadsheet, 271
  tables, 270–275
  text box, 242–243
  WordArt, 244–245
  worksheets in workbooks, 455–456
insertion point, 139
Insert tab
  charts, 537
Insights, 142
Internet
  as resource for pictures, 1133–1135
in-text citations
  versus footnotes, 341

J

JPEG file interchange format, 1119
Jump List, 8
justified alignment, 206

K

kelvin (K) unit, 1126
keyboard shortcuts, 74–75
key point slides, 945
keystroke commands, navigation in
    worksheets, 407

L

Label Wizard
  defined, 895
  reports, 895–896
landscape orientation, 108, 156, 458
large datasets, 598–603
  freezing rows and columns, 599–600

page breaks, 600–601
print area, 601–602
printing, 600–603
print order, 603
print titles, 602–603
layout control
  defined, 866
  reports, 901
layouts
  defined, 943
  modifying, 995–996
  Photo Albums, 1167
  reports, 898–899
  SmartArt, 1071–1072
Layout view, 868
  to modify form design, 873–874
  reports altering in, 898
left alignment, 206
left indent, 209
legend, 535, 558
  formatting, 565
  positioning, 565
line chart, 543–544
lines, and connectors, 1046–1048
line spacing, 207–209
line weight (thickness), 1057
linking videos, 1145
lists
  bulleted, 213–215
  numbered, 213–215
  renumbering, 214
Live Layout, 241
Live Preview, 74, 200
Lock Drawing Mode, 1045
Lock screen, 4
logical functions, 495, 508–515
logical operator, 508
logical test arguments, 509
logo
  in reports, 899
lookup functions, 495, 508–515
lookup table
  creating, 512–513
lookup value, 511

M

macro object
  defined, 671
mail merge documents, 306–312
  completing, 310–312
  creating, 306–310
  databases as data source, 309
  Excel worksheet as data source,
    308–309
  filtering, 310
  inserting merge fields, 311
  selecting recipient list, 307–308
  sorting records, 310
  and tables, 310
main document, 306
managing table data, 286–291
many-to-many relationship, 756

margins
   adjusting in document, 155–156
   changing, 107
   reports, 900–901
   worksheet data, 459–460
Markup
   defined, 353
   show, 358
   Simple, 353
marquee/selection net, 1051
masters slide, 1022–1023
Math & Trig functions, 495, 497–501
MAX function, 500
media elements, 1134
MEDIAN function, 500
media objects, in presentations, 954
Merge & Center command, 445
merge fields, 306
merge options, cells, 445–446
Merge Shapes, 1083–1084
merging
   cells, 273–274
Microsoft account
   changing, 67
   OneDrive, 365
   sign in to, 4
Microsoft Office (Office 2016), 66
   getting help, 77–79
   installing add-ins, 79–80
   opening, 66–67
   overview, 66
   starting, 66–67
   using common interface components,
      70–76
   working with files, 67–70
Microsoft Word, 132
MIN function, 500
Mini toolbar, 90–91
mixed cell references, 490
MLA (Modern Language Association), 335
modifying
   Datasheet view data, 680
   endnotes, 342
   footnotes, 342
   form layout, 877–879
   forms, 873–877
   freeform shape, 1048–1050
   layout, 995–996
   multitable queries, 784–787
   objects, 1081–1089
   picture, 241
   placeholder, 995–996
   reports, 898–901
   SmartArt, 1070–1073
   styles, 226–228
   table styles, 276
   text box, 243–244
   WordArt, 1074–1075
module object, 671
move down one cell, 407
move left one cell, 407
Move or Copy dialog box, 456
move right one cell, 407

move up one cell, 407
Movie File, 1145
moving
   charts, 548–549
   files, 34
   folders, 34
   picture, 239–241
   range, 433
   text box, 243–244
   windows, 14–15
   worksheets, 456–457
MP4 Video, 1145
multimedia
   defined, 1118
multiple column widths and row heights,
   432
multiple grouping levels, 842
multiple items form, 871–872
multiple-table databases, 749–754
multiple worksheets, printing, 464
Multitable queries, 782–787
   creating, 782–783
   defined, 782
   modifying, 784–787
   and relationships, 784

N

#NAME?, 497
Name Box, 405, 433
name sorts, 623
narration (spoken commentary), 1159
   creating notes, 1160
navigating
   slide shows, 965–967
   in worksheets, 406–407
navigation bar
   databases, 673–675
Navigation Pane, 30–31
   defined, 667
   display of, 668
negative values
   and financial functions, 515
nest functions, 510
   as arguments, 499
   inside VLOOKUP function, 513
New sheet icon, 405
nonadjacent ranges, 432, 500
Normal view
   defined, 926
   presentation, 926–927
NOT condition, 774–775
notes pages
   printing, 970
Notes Page view
   presentations, 931
Notification area, 8, 41
NOW function, 501
nper
   defined, 515
null values, 774
numbered lists, 213–215
number filters, 625–626

number formats, 288, 447–449
number of pages, header and footer option,
   462
Number, number format, 448

O

objects, 237–245
   alignment, 1091–1094
   arranging, 1089–1094
   defined, 237, 667
   details, 678
   flipping, 1082–1083
   formatting, 237–245
   group, 1084–1087
   inserting, 237–245
   inserting picture, 238–239
   macro, 671
   Merge Shapes, 1083–1084
   modifying, 1081–1089
   module, 671
   order, 1090–1091
   recoloring, 1087–1089
   resizing, 1081–1082
   rotating, 1082–1083
   ungroup, 1084–1087
Office Clipboard, 93–94
Office Online, 4
OneDrive, 4, 67
   documents, 364–370
   and File Explorer, 365–368
   file sharing in, 371
   Microsoft account, 365
   for mobile phones, 365
one-to-many relationship, 756–758
one-to-one relationship, 756
online document presentation, 376–380
opaque
   defined, 1053
Open dialog box, 68
opening
   databases, 665–667
   document, 139
   presentation, 926–933
OR condition, 774
ordering shortcuts, 1091
order objects, 1090–1091
order of operations, 288, 418–419, 812
organization, document, 153–164
   features that improve readability,
      153–159
   viewing a document in different ways,
      159–164
orientation
   reports, 900
orientation, page
   landscape, 458
   portrait, 458
outlines
   changing list levels in, 1003
   collapsed, 1004
   defined, 1002
   expanded, 1004

outlines (*continued*)
    importing, 1011
    printing, 1005–1006
    shapes, 1057–1059
Outline view presentations, 160,
        229–230, 929–930, 1002–1004
    editing in, 1003

P

page breaks
    defined, 600
    large datasets, 600–601
    pointer to move, 601
page flow, managing, 162–164
page layout, changing, 107–109
page number, header and footer option,
        462
page orientation
    landscape, 458
page orientations, changing, 108,
        156–157
Page Setup dialog box, 108–109, 459,
        460, 463
Page Setup option, 458–459
    portrait, 458
    worksheets, 457–463
paragraph
    alignment, 206–207
    borders and shading, 212–213
    bulleted and numbered lists, 213–215
    formatting, 206–215
    indents, 209
    spacing, 207–209
    tab stops, 210–211
parallel construction, 941–942
parentheses
    in formulas, 419
passive voice, 941
Paste Options, 435–437
Paste Special, 435–437
Paste Special dialog box, 436
pasting
    range, 434
    text, 93
PDF Reflow, 358–359
Percent Style, number format, 448, 449
Photo Albums
    creating, 1165
    defined, 1165
    inserting captions, 1167
    layout, 1167
    picture contrast and brightness, 1167
    picture order, 1166
    PowerPoint 2016, 1165–1167
    selecting pictures, 1166
    setting options, 1166–1167
PICT file, 1119
picture fill
    defined, 1054
pictures and graphics
    adding, 996
    alignment, 239–241

artistic effects, 1128
background creation from, 1131–1133
brightness of, 1124, 1167
color changing in, 1125–1127
Compress Pictures, 1130–1131
contrast of, 1124, 1167
copyright, 1134
correcting, 1123–1125
cropping, 1129–1130
defined, 238
inserting, 96–97, 238–239, 1118–
    1120
Internet as resource for, 1133–1135
media elements, 1134
modifying, 241
moving, 239–241
presentations, 996
recolored objects, 1127
removing background, 1121–1123
resizing, 239–241,1129–1130
resizing and format, 96–97
saturation, 1125
selecting for Photo Albums, 1166
sharpening, 1123
softening, 1123
tone or temperature of, 1126
transforming, 1121–1133
worksheet header and footer option,
    462
Picture Styles, 1128–1129
pie chart, 544–545
    data labels, 565
pie slice, 568
pin/add, 7
placeholders
    defined, 943
    modifying, 995–996
    unused, 945
plagiarism, 334
plain text format (.txt), 1011
planning
    presentations, 939–943
playback options, videos, 1152–1154
plot area, 535
    formatting, 566
PMT function, 514–515
Pmt function, 830–831
PNG file, 1119
pointing, 419
points
    defined, 1058
Portable Document Format (PDF), 175,
    897
portrait orientation, 108, 156, 458
positioning
    axis title, 560–562
    chart title, 559–560
    data labels, 563–564
    legend, 565
Poster Frame option, 1150
pound signs (######), 431
PowerPoint 2016, 66
    delivery tips, 971

Photo Albums, 1165–1167
printing in, 968–971
specialty views, 929–932
status bar, 928–929
PowerPoint show, 934–935
power settings, 5
presentations
    active voice, 941
    adding content, 943–945
    animations in, 955–957
    captions, 996
    check slide show elements, 946
    check spelling, 946
    creating, 939–947
    defined, 926
    delivery tips, 971
    enhancing, 953–959
    headers and footers in, 957–959
    hiding sound icon, 1159
    media objects in, 954
    Normal view, 926–927
    Notes Page view, 931
    opening, 926–933
    outlines imported into, 1011
    Outline view, 929–930, 1002–1004
    parallel construction, 941–942
    passive voice, 941
    pictures, 996
    planning, 939–943
    preparing, 939–943
    Presenter view, 933
    proofing options, 946
    Reading View, 931–932
    reorder slides, 947
    reviewing, 946–947
    saving as PowerPoint show, 934–935
    slide layouts, 943–945
    Slide Show view, 932–933
    Slide Sorter view, 930
    speaker notes, 933–934
    storyboards, 939–943
    tables in, 953
    templates, 992–996
    theme, 942–943
    transitions in, 955–957
    using thesaurus, 946
    viewing, 926–933
Presenter view
    presentations, 933
previewing
    document, 111–112
    worksheets, 463–464
primary key
    defined, 668
print area
    large datasets, 601–602
    Page Setup option, 458
printing
    charts, 550–551
    databases, 685–686
    document, 111–112, 178–179
    full page slides, 968–969
    gridlines, 463

handouts, 969–970
landscape orientation, 458
large datasets, 600–603
multiple worksheets, 464
notes pages, 970
outlines, 970, 1005–1006
portrait orientation, 458
in PowerPoint 2016, 968–971
row/column headings, 463
worksheets, 463–464
Print Layout view, 160
print order, 603
Print Preview, 897
print titles, 602–603
Print Titles, Page Setup option, 458
proofing options
presentations, 946
Property Sheet
defined, 816
public domain, 1134
PV (present value)
defined, 515

Q

queries
aggregate functions, 837–844
calculated field, 812–816
changing data, 777
common errors, 817–818
comparison operators, 774
AND condition, 774
copying, 776–777
criteria for different data types,
773–776
defined, 669, 767
expressions, 813–816
formatting, 817
modifying, 776–777
NOT condition, 774–775
null values, 774
OR condition, 774
order of operations, 812–813
Query Wizard, 770–772
running, 776
Show Table dialog box, 768
Simple Query Wizard, 767
single-table, 767–777
wildcards, 773
Query Design view, 767–770
Query Wizard, 770–772
Quick access, 30
Quick Access Toolbar, 76
customizing, 76, 144–145
Quick actions button, 41
Quick Analysis
and charts, 536
conditional formatting, 638–639
and functions, 501
table creation, 610
Quick Layout, 565
Quick Style
defined, 1050

and shapes, 1050–1060
and SmartArt, 1071
Quick Tables, 271

R

radar chart, 548
random access memory (RAM), 13
range_lookup, 512
ranges
converting tables to, 612
copying, 434
defined, 289, 432
moving, 433
nonadjacent, 432, 500
pasting, 434
selecting, 432–433
rate
defined, 515
Reading View
presentations, 931–932
Read Mode, 160
real-time co-authoring, 374
Real Time Typing, 374
recolored pictures, 1127
recoloring
fill color, worksheets, 447
objects, 1087–1089
worksheet tabs, 455
recording audio, 1159–1160
records
adding, 613
defined, 307, 609, 668
deleting, 613
editing, 613
examining, 770
sorting in forms, 879
tables, worksheets, 613
records, database
adding to desktop database, 710–711
adding to table, 680–682
Cascade Delete Related Records, 756
record source
defined, 865
Recycle Bin, 9
reference functions, 495
referential integrity, 755–756
reject Track Changes, 357–358
relationships
defined, 678
establishing, 754–758
many-to-many, 756
and multitable queries, 784
one-to-many, 756–758
one-to-one, 756
and tables, 678–680
Relationships window, 758
relative cell references, 488
Remote Assistance, 47
removing
background, 242
chart element, 562
picture background, 1121–1123

renaming
tables, 676–678
tables, worksheets, 612
worksheets, 457
renumbering
lists, 214
reorder slides, 947
repair and compact databases,
684–685
report(s)
altering in Layout view, 898
basics, 889–902
column widths in, 900
controls, 899
creating, 889–896
defined, 670, 889
and fields, 899–900
inserting logo in, 899
Label Wizard, 895–896
layout, 898–899
layout control, 901
margins, 900–901
modifying, 898–901
orientation, 900–901
Print Preview, 897
report tool, 890–891
report view, 897–898
Report Wizard, 891–895
sorting records, 901–902
themes, 901
report tool, 890–891
report view, 897–898
Report Wizard
defined, 891
reports, 891–895
Report Wizard tool, 889
research papers, 334–345
bibliography, 338–340
citations, 335–337
cover page, 345
creating source, 335–337
endnotes, 340–343
footnotes, 340–343
index creation, 344–345
selecting writing style, 334–335
share and search for source,
337–338
special features, 343–345
table of contents, 343–344
resetting videos, 1152
resizing
objects, 1081–1082
Page Setup option, 458
picture, 239–241
pictures, 1129–1130
text box, 243–244
Resource Monitor, 45
retrieving data, with indexing, 755
reusing slides, 1011–1012
reusing text, 136–137
reviewing
documents, 353–357
presentations, 946–947

revision marks
  defined, 357
Ribbon, 29, 70
  customizing, 75–76, 143–144
  using, 71–74
Ribbon Display Options, 13
Rich Text Format (.rtf), 175, 1011
right alignment, 206
right indent, 209
rotate cell data, 446
rotating
  objects, 1082–1083
ROUND function, 501
  versus decrease decimal points, 501
row height
  and document table, 274–275
  worksheets, 432
rows, 406
  deleting, 272–273, 428–429
  duplicate, removing, 613–614
  freezing, 599–600
  headings, 291, 405
  hiding, 429–430
  inserting, 272–273, 427–428
  labels, 535
  management, 427–432
  printing row headings, 463
  repeating, 463
  switch data, 576–577
  transposing, 437
  unhiding, 429–430
.rtf (Rich Text Format), 175, 1011
rule of thirds, 1093
running queries, 776

S

sans serif font, 201
saturation
  defined, 1125
saving
  databases, 665–667
  document, 138–139
  files, 69–70
  presentations as PowerPoint show,
    934–935
Scientific, number format, 448
screenshot
  inserting, 239
ScreenTip functions, 496
search box, 8, 15–16
  in File Explorer, 30
search features, Windows 10, 15–18
searching
  by template dimensions, 994
  templates, 993
section breaks, 223–224
section header, 1016
sections, slides and, 1016–1017
Select All icon, 405
selecting
  chart styles, 575
  column and row labels, 535
  data source for charts, 534–535

range, 432–433
recipient list, in mail merge documents,
    307–308
research paper writing style, 334–335
  styles, 226–228
selecting text, 88–89
selection filters, 695–697
selection net/marquee, 1051
Selection Pane, 1089
semi-selection technique, 419
serif font, 201
7 × 7 Guideline, 942
shading
  defined, 212, 293
  paragraph, 212–213
  tables, document, 291–294
shapes
  constraining, 1046
  creating, 1044–1050
  customizing, 1050–1060
  defined, 1044
  effects, 1059–1060
  fills, 1051–1057
  freeform, 1048–1050
  lines and connectors, 1046–1048
  outlines, 1057–1059
  and Quick Style, 1050–1060
sharing
  documents, 370–374
  with embedded HTML, 374
  file in OneDrive, 371
  multiple-table databases, 749–754
sharpening pictures, 1123
Sheet Options, 462–463
sheet tabs (worksheet tabs)
  colors, 455
  defined, 405
  dragging, 456
  navigation buttons, 405
shortcut menu, 74
shortcuts, 10
  keyboard, 74–75
short phrases, 941
Show Table dialog box, 768
Simple Markup
  defined, 353
Simple Query Wizard, 767
single-table query
  creating, 767–770
  Query Design view, 767–770
sizing
  charts, 549–550
  Page Setup option, 458
sizing handle, 241
sleep settings, 5
slide layouts, 943–945
slide masters, 1022–1023
slides
  animations in, 955–957
  defined, 926
  delivery tips, 971
  key point, 945
  playing sound over multiple,
    1161–1162

printing, 968–969
  reorder, 947
  reusing, 1011–1012
  and sections, 1016–1017
  summary or conclusion, 945
  title, 945
  transitions in, 955–957
Slide pane, 927
slide shows
  annotating, 967
  checking elements, 946
  controls, 966
  defined, 926
  design, 1017–1020
  navigating, 965–967
  themes, 1020–1021
Slide Show view
  presentations, 932–933
Slide Sorter view
  presentations, 930
  and transitions, 956
Slides pane, 927
SmartArt
  converting text to, 1073
  creating, 1066–1069
  defined, 1066
  diagram type, 1072–1073
  layout, 1071–1072
  modifying, 1070–1073
  and Quick Style, 1071
  text pane, 1069
  theme colors, 1070
SmartArt Graphic dialog box, 1068
Smart Guides
  defined, 1091
Smart Lookup, 77
snapping, 14
Snipping Tool, 11
softening pictures, 1123
sorting
  and conditional formatting,
    643
  mail merge documents, 310
  records in forms, 879
  reports, 901–902
  table data, 699–700
  tables, document, 290–291
  tables, worksheets, 622–624
sources
  creating, 335–337
  defined, 334
  editing, 337
  share and search for, 337–338
spacing
  paragraph, 207–209
sparklines
  charts, 574–579
  creating, 577–579
  customizing, 577–579
  inserting, 578
Sparklines Tools Design tab, 578
speaker notes
  formating, 934
  presentations, 933–934

Special, number format, 448
spelling and grammar
    presentations, 946
    reviewing, 140–142
split databases, 685
split form
    adding, 870–871
    defined, 870
splitting
    cells, 273–274
spreadsheets
    defined, 404
    Get External Data - Excel Spreadsheet
        feature, 749–750
    import, multiple-table databases,
        749–754
    inserting, 271
    worksheets as, 404
stacked column chart, 540–541
stacking order, 1090
Start menu, 5
    configuring, 7–8
    exploring, 5–7
statistical functions, 495, 497–501
status bar, 106
    PowerPoint, 928–929
    worksheet, 405
status bar statistics, 501
stock chart, 546–547
    arrange data for, 547
storyboards, 939–943
    active voice, 941
    parallel construction, 941–942
    passive voice, 941
    short phrases, 941
structured reference
    defined, 621
    in formulas, 621–622
    fully qualified, 622
style manual, 334
styles, 226
    creating from text, 228
    defined, 226
    forms, 877
    modifying, 226–228
    Outline view, 229–230
    selecting, 226–228
    table, 275–276
    versus Format Painter, 228
style sets, 222, 228
    defined, 222
    using, 222
subform, 869–870
    adding, 870
Subtract Shapes, 1084
Sum arrow, 499
SUM function, 498–499
surface chart, 548
switch data
    rows and columns,
        576–577
symbol, 158–159
    inserting in document, 158–159

syntax
    defined, 495
    function, 498
system software, 4

T

tab, 71
    contextual, 71
tab color, changing, 457
table array, 511
table of contents, 343–344
table(s)
    adding records to, 680–682
    Datasheet view, 673
    defined, 668, 953
    designing, 734–737
    Design view, 675–676
    lookup, 512–513
    and mail merge documents, 310
    movement within, 954
    necessary data, 735
    in presentations, 953
    and relationships, 678–680,
        754–758
    renaming, 676–678
    Show Table dialog box, 768
    single-table queries, 767–777
tables, document
    advanced features, 286–297
    alignment, 276–277
    borders, 291–294
    captions, 295–296
    column width, 274–275
    convert text to, 294–295
    convert to text, 294–295
    creating, 271–272
    defined, 270
    drawing, 271–272
    enhancing data, 291–297
    formatting, 275–278
    functions, 289–290
    heading rows, 291
    inserting, 270–275
    and mail merge, 310
    managing data, 286–291
    merge and split cells, 273–274
    position, 276–277
    Quick Tables, 271
    row height, 274–275
    rows and columns, 272–273
    shading, 291–294
    sorting data, 290–291
    table styles, 275–276
    text, 277–278
    using formulas, 287–289
tables, worksheets
    benefits of, 609
    conditional formatting, 638–645
    converting to range, 612
    creating, 610–612
    custom filter, 627–628
    date filters, 627

defined, 609
duplicate rows, 613–614
fields, 612
filter arrows, 611
filtering data, 624–628
manipulation, 621–628
number filters, 625–626
Quick Analysis, 610
records, 613
renaming, 612
sorting data, 622–624
structured references in, 621–622
styles, 614–615
text filtering, 624–625
table styles, 275–276
    modifying, 276
    worksheets, 614–615
tab stops, 210–211
    deleting, 211
    managing, 211
taskbar, 8
    exploring, 8–9
Task Manager, 44–45
task panes
    alternative for opening format, 566
    displaying options, 563
task view, 11–12
Tell me what you want to do box,
    77–78
templates
    creating desktop databases by,
        708–710
    defined, 707, 992
    opening, 86–87
    presentations, 992–996
    searching, 993
    searching by dimensions, 994
    using in word processing, 137–138
text
    appearance, 202–205
    checking spelling and grammar,
        94–96
    convert tables to, 294–295
    convert to tables, 294–295
    copying, 93
    cutting, 93
    editing, 89–90
    filters, 624–625
    Format Painter, 91–92
    formatting into columns, 225
    in formulas, 510
    inserting, 139–140
    pasting, 93
    relocating, 92–94
    reusing, 136–137
    selecting, 88–89
    in SmartArt, 1069
    style, creating from, 228
    tables, document, 277–278
    using Mini toolbar, 90–91
    using Office Clipboard, 93–94
    worksheets, 408–409
    wrap text feature, cells, 446

text box, 1047
  formatting text in, 243
  inserting, 242–243
  modifying, 243–244
  moving, 243–244
  resizing, 243–244
Text pane
  defined, 1069
Text, number format, 448
texture fills, 1056–1057
text wrap options, 240
text wrapping
  cells, 446
  Word, 135
themes
  applying, 88
  defined, 875, 942
  forms, 875–876
  presentation, 942–943
  reports, 901
  slide shows, 1020–1021
  SmartArt, 1070
thesaurus, 141
  presentations, 946
thumbnails, 927
TIFF file, 1119
tiles, 6
time
  header and footer option, 462
  updating, 502
time functions, 495
Time, number format, 448
title bar, 13, 70
title slide, 945
TODAY function, 501
toggle between relative, absolute, mixed
    cell references (F4), 491
toggle commands, 89
Toggle Filter, 697
tone or temperature
  defined, 1126
Total row
  defined, 837
totals query
  calculated field, 842–843
  conditions to, 841–842
  creating, 839–840
  defined, 838
  grouping, 840–841
Track Changes
  accept and reject, 357–358
  defined, 357
transforming
  pictures, 1121–1133
transitions
  adding, 957
  in presentations, 955–957
  and slide sorter view, 956
transparency
  defined, 1053
transposing
  columns, 437
  rows, 437

Trendline, 558
Trig & Math functions, 495, 497–501
.txt (plain text format), 1011

U
ungroup objects, 1084–1087
unmerge cells, 445
updating
  date, 502
  time, 502
usability testing, 865

V
value axis, 535
value_if_false arguments, 509–510
value_if_true arguments, 509–510
values
  in date range, 776
  in formulas, 418, 511
  indents, 447
  worksheets, 411
variant, defined, 942
vector graphics, 1084, 1118
vertex, defined, 1048
vertical cell alignment, 446
videos
  adding, 1145–1149
  bookmarks, 1152
  codec (coder/decoder) software, 1145
  embed, 1145
  formatting, 1149–1152
  linking, 1145
  playback options, 1152–1154
  Poster Frame option, 1150
  resetting, 1152
  tools, 1149–1154
view controls, worksheets, 405
viewing
  document, 160–161
  presentation, 926–933
View tab, 29, 462
virtual desktop, 12–13
VLOOKUP function, 511–512
  and nest functions, 513

W
watermark, 157–158
Web app databases, 712–713
Web Layout view, 160
wildcards, 773
windows
  components, 13–14
  Excel window elements, 404–405
  moving, 14–15
  resizing, 14–15
  snapping, 14–15
Windows 10
  Action Center, 40–42
  configuring Start menu, 7–8
  Cortana, 16

Cortana Notebook and settings, 16–18
customizing desktop, 11
Disk Cleanup, 46
exploring Start menu, 5–7
exploring taskbar, 8–9
File History, 42
fundamentals, 4–18
getting help, 16
identifying desktop components, 9–10
managing and using desktop and
    components, 11–15
Remote Assistance, 47
Resource Monitor, 45
search box, 15–16
sign in to Microsoft account, 4
sleep and power settings, 5
snap, move, and resize windows, 14–15
Task Manager, 44–45
task view, 11–12
understanding interface, 4–11
using search features, 15–18
virtual desktop, 12–13
window components, 13–14
Windows Defender, 43
Windows Firewall, 43–44
Windows Update, 43
Windows apps, 11
Windows Defender, 43
Windows Enhanced Metafile, 1119
Windows Firewall, 43–44
Windows Media File, 1145
Windows Media Video File, 1145
Windows Metafile, 1119
Windows Update, 43
Windows Video File, 1145
Word 2016, 66
  customizing Quick Access Toolbar,
    144–145
  customizing Ribbon, 143–144
WordArt
  creating, 1074
  defined, 244, 1073
  inserting, 244–245
  modifying, 1074–1075
Word Online, 368–370
word processing software, 132
  beginning and editing document,
    133–142
  creating document, 135–136
  customizing Word, 142–145
  inserting text and navigating document,
    139–140
  opening document, 139
  overview, 132–133
  reusing text, 136–137
  reviewing spelling and grammar,
    140–142
  saving document, 138–139
  using template, 137–138
word wrap, 135
workbooks
  completing, 404
  defined, 404

deleting worksheets, 455–456
management, 455–457
worksheets inserting in, 455–456
works cited. *See* bibliography
worksheet(s)
alignment and, 444–445
Auto Fill, 409–411
backgrounds in, 458
column widths, 431
Copy as Picture, 434
copying, 456–457
data, in other programs, 437
as data source, mail merge documents,
308–309
dates and times, 411–412
defined, 404
deleting, 455–456
design, 407
elements, 404–405
entering data, 408
fill color, 447
formatting, 444–449
formatting data, 408
freezing, 599–600
headers and footers, 460–462
inserting in workbooks, 455–456

large datasets, 598–603
management, 455–457
margins, 459–460
move down one cell, 407
move left one cell, 407
move right one cell, 407
move up one cell, 407
moving, 456–457
name, header and footer option, 462
navigating in, 406–407
Page Setup options, 457–463
previewing, 463–464
printing, 463–464
renaming, 457
row height, 432
Sheet Options, 462–463
status bar, 405
tables, 609–615
table styles, 614–615
text, 408–409
values, 411
view controls, 405
worksheet tabs (sheet tabs)
colors, 455
defined, 405
dragging, 456

navigation buttons, 405
wrapping
text feature, cells, 446
word wrap feature, 135
writing style
defined, 334
research paper, 334–335

X-axis, 535
X Y (scatter) chart, 546

Y-axis, 535

zipped (compressed) folder, 34
extracting files from, 35
Zoom control, 405
zoom settings, 161–162
Zoom slider, 106

Go Beyond the Point & Click

The *Exploring* Series charts your learning beyond the "point and click," helping you understand WHY you use Microsoft Office skills along with HOW you perform them. The latest edition provides an easy-to-follow map to achieve the outcomes identified in each chapter, based on how you already use your materials, to help you learn, study, and review efficiently to be successful in this class and beyond.

Student Textbook

Exploring is a tool built to match the way you use your materials: Your first stop is what you are required to do, your second stop is referencing important background information to help you better understand what you need to do. This edition has been set up to help you easily navigate between the two.

- Outcomes, Objectives, and Skills are laid out for you at the beginning of each chapter so you know exactly what you will learn.
- Hands-On Exercises (yellow pages) appear throughout each chapter, allowing you to apply Microsoft skills in an active, hands-on way.
- Enhanced Objective Mapping enables you to efficiently navigate the theory (white pages) to get the answers you need to move forward.
- Step icons help you navigate back to the concepts in the white pages.
- Quick Concept Checks are included at the end of every white page section to help you confirm your understanding of key objectives.
- End of Chapter Exercises allow you to test your knowledge of Key Terms, create projects From Scratch, learn how to Collaborate with others, and be both Analytical and Creative when approaching your data.

Student Data Files

Access your student data files needed to complete the exercises in this textbook at www.pearsonhighered.com/exploring.

MyITLab and Premium Media
www.myitlab.com

MyITLab is your one-stop-shop for interactive simulated and auto-graded homework featuring immediate feedback as well as self-study tools to help you succeed in this course.

- **Hands-On Exercise Videos** allow you to review and study the concepts taught in the Hands-On Exercises.
- **Multiple Choice quizzes** enable you to test concepts you have learned by answering auto-graded questions.
- **MOS Certification Map** provides a clear guide for you to get everything you can out of the series resources to prepare to pass the MOS Certification tests of your choice.
- **Audio PowerPoints** turn the chapter PowerPoints into lectures with narration that students can pause, rewind, and view as much as they like.

Looking for a way to distinguish yourself in the workplace and prove your skills in IT?

Add Microsoft® Office Specialist certification to your résumé!

Prepare for the MOS Exam of your choice by using the resources for *Exploring Microsoft Office 2016, Volume 1!*

Word 2016 Core

Excel® 2016 Core

Access® 2016

PowerPoint® 2016

Find resources in your student text, in MyITLab for *Exploring*, and at *www.pearsonhighered.com/exploring.*